# BAPTISM OF FIRE

**HarperCollins**Publishers Ltd

# NATHAN M. GREENFIELD

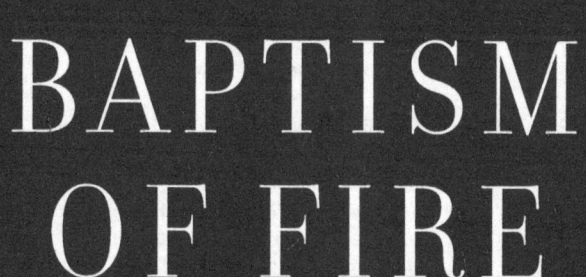

# BAPTISM OF FIRE

———※———

The Second Battle of
# YPRES
and the Forging of Canada,
April 1915

*Baptism of Fire*
© 2007 by Nathan M. Greenfield. All rights reserved.

Published by HarperCollins Publishers Ltd.

Originally published by HarperCollins Publishers Ltd: 2007.
This trade paperback edition: 2008

No part of this book may be used or reproduced in any manner whatsoever without the prior written permission of the publisher, except in the case of brief quotations embodied in reviews.

"Ypres: 1915" copyright 1969 Alden Nowlan.
Quotation reprinted with the permission of House of Anansi Press.

HarperCollins books may be purchased for educational, business, or sales promotional use through our Special Markets Department.

HarperCollins Publishers Ltd
2 Bloor Street East, 20th Floor
Toronto, Ontario, Canada
M4W 1A8

www.harpercollins.ca

Library and Archives Canada Cataloguing in Publication

Greenfield, Nathan M., 1958–
Baptism of fire : the second battle of Ypres and the forging of Canada, April 1915 / Nathan Greenfield.

ISBN 978-0-00-639576-8

1. Ypres, 2nd Battle of, Ieper, Belgium, 1915.
2. Canada. Canadian Army—History—World War, 1914–1918. I. Title.

D542.Y7G74 2008   940.4'24   C2008-901900-8

RRD 9 8 7 6 5 4 3 2 1

Printed and bound in the United States
Set in Caslon
Text design by Sharon Kish

*To my wife, Micheline, the reader for whom I write; and to my parents, Irving A. and Anita G. Greenfield of Brooklyn, New York, who ensured that I grew up to love the word and the music of history.*

*When the people of the little villages through which we passed saw the name "Canadian" on our car they nudged each other and repeated the word "Canadian." It was the name in everybody's mouth those days, for it was now general knowledge that the Canadian division had thrown itself into the gap and stemmed the German rush to Calais.*
—Lieutenant-Colonel George Nasmith

*In spite of the danger to which they were exposed the Canadians held their ground with a magnificent display of tenacity and courage; and it is not too much to say that the bearing and conduct of these splendid troops averted a disaster.*
—Field Marshal Sir John French

# Contents

*Author's Note*   xvii
*Preface*   xix
*Introduction*   1

PART 1: Marching as to War
14 April to 21 April 1915

CHAPTER 1: "It Is a Higher Form of Killing"   29
*The Canadians Man the Trenches around Ypres, and the Germans Install the Gas Cylinders*

PART 2: Operation *Desinfektion*
5:00 p.m. to midnight, 22 April 1915

CHAPTER 2: "The Carnival of Death Sings Loudly"   47
*The First Gas Attack*

CHAPTER 3: "With a Coolness and Discipline That Seems Almost Incredible"   66
*The Canadians Fill the Gap*

PART 3: "We Came to Fight"
12:01 a.m. to 8:30 a.m., 23 April 1915

CHAPTER 4: "In the Nature of a Sacrificial Charge"   95
*The 10th and 16th Battalions Attack Kitcheners Wood*

CHAPTER 5: "I Didn't Know of a Better 'Ole to Go To"   109
*The 2nd and 3rd Battalions Fill In on the Right*

CHAPTER 6: "And Trust to Providence"   124
*The 1st and 4th Battalions Attack Mauser Ridge*

PART 4: Holding the Line
8:31 a.m. to 11:45 p.m., 23 April 1915

CHAPTER 7: "We Sampled Every Kind of Shell Made in Germany"   143
*Lance-Corporal Fred Fisher Earns a Victoria Cross,
and William Doxsee Protects His House*

CHAPTER 8: "It Is Considered Very Unlucky to Be Killed on a Friday"   158
*The Second Attack on Mauser Ridge*


PART 5: Baptism of Fire
12:00 midnight to 8:10 a.m., 24 April 1915

CHAPTER 9: "As Under a Green Sea, I Saw Him Drowning"   179
*The Second Gas Attack and the Destruction of the
13th and 15th Battalions at the Apex*

CHAPTER 10: "No, Alexander Is Not Gone"   199
*The Feldgrauen Storm Towards St. Julien*


PART 6: The Centre Cannot Hold
8:15 a.m. to 12 noon, 24 April 1915

CHAPTER 11: "His Insides Were Hanging between His Fingers"   221
*The Collapse of the 7th Battalion*

CHAPTER 12: "Supplying Bullets, by Relieving the Dead of Theirs"   233
*The Fall of St. Julien*

## Part 7: The Fog of War
12:01 p.m., 24 April to 4:00 a.m., 25 April 1915

Chapter 13: "The Retirement Was *Not Compulsory*"     253
*The Isolation of the 2nd Canadian Infantry Brigade*

Chapter 14: "Do You Expect Me to Wet-Nurse Your Brigade?"     267
*Major-General Snow Refuses to Aid the 2nd Brigade*

Chapter 15: "Can You Tell Me Where the Enemy Is?"     278
*The Fog of War Lifts*

## Part 8: After One Hundred Hours of Battle
4:00 a.m., 25 April to 4:00 a.m., 26 April 1915

Chapter 16: "Why Do They Stop?"     295
*The 10th British Brigade's Attack on St. Julien and the Fall of Mouse Trap Farm*

Chapter 17: "Do Not Shoot! Ve Vas French"     310
*The Canadians Retire from Gravenstafel Ridge*

## Part 9: Standing on Guard
26 April to 10 May 1915

Chapter 18: "The Heaviest [Shelling] Yet Experienced by the Brigade"     331
*The Withdrawal of the 1st Canadian Division from the Ypres Salient*

Chapter 19: "A Perpetual Inspiration to Their Successors"     345
*Prayers for the Dead and Wounded*

| | |
|---|---|
| *Coda* | 350 |
| *Acknowledgments* | 357 |
| *Appendix A: "The Reckoning"* | 361 |
| *Appendix B: Casualties for the 2nd Battle of Ypres (22 to 30 April)* | 367 |
| *Appendix C: The Canadian Order of Battle* | 370 |
| *Appendix D: In Memoriam* | 372 |
| *Notes* | 437 |
| *Bibliography* | 450 |
| *Index* | 463 |

# List of Maps

These maps are based on the maps prepared for the *Official History of the Canadian Forces in the Great War, 1914–1919*, Vol. I, written by Colonel A. Fortesque Duguid and published in 1938. They have been checked against both the maps contained in British Official History, *History of the Great War Based on Official Documents: Military Operations in France and Belgium, 1915*, Vol. I, written by Brigadier-General James E. Edmunds (1927) and G.W.L. Nicholson's *Canadian Expeditionary Force, 1914–1919* (1964). The absence of detailed trench maps for the period of 2nd Ypres means that positions of both guns and trenches cannot be other than approximations.

For ease of reading, I have made the following editorial decisions:
- At the risk of being anachronistic, I have placed maple leaves along the lines that indicate the Canadian sector.
- British guns and units not immediately involved in the action to the north of Ypres are not represented.
- I have not indicated the Princess Patricia's Canadian Light Infantry on the southwest side of the Salient.

## Maps

| | |
|---|---|
| Europe 1915 | xvi |
| Before Gas Attack, 22 April 1915 | 27 |
| 5 p.m. to midnight, 22 April | 45 |
| 12:01 a.m. to 8:30 a.m., 23 April | 93 |
| 8:31 a.m. to 11:45 p.m., 23 April | 141 |
| 12:00 midnight to 8:10 a.m., 24 April | 177 |
| 8:15 a.m. to 12:00 noon, 24 April | 219 |
| 12:01 p.m., 24 April to 4 a.m., 25 April | 251 |
| 4 a.m., 25 April to 4 a.m., 26 April | 293 |

# Europe 1915

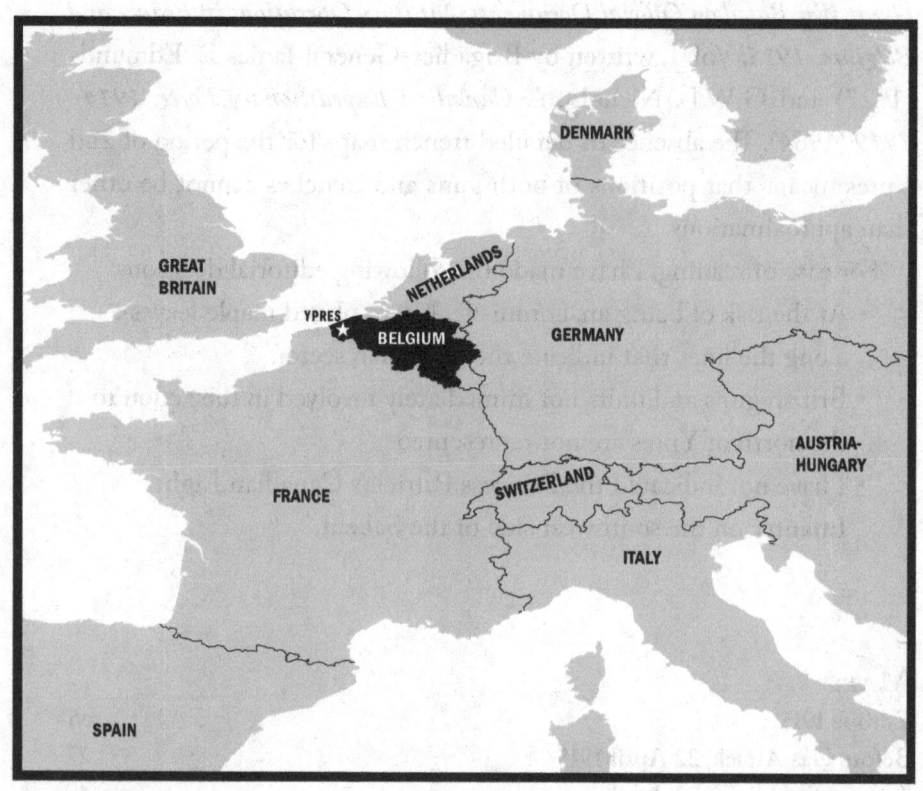

## Author's Note

The armies that faced each other across no man's land at 2nd Ypres reckoned time differently. The Canadians (following the British) ignored the established time zones and used Greenwich Mean Time (GMT) in Flanders. The Germans used Berlin time. Hence, when it was noon on German watches, Canadian watches read 11:00 a.m. Although the French army had already adopted the twenty-four-hour clock, I have, for the sake of consistency, rendered French orders and reports in GMT.

The Canadians used the Imperial system for both distance and weight, and size of shot and shell. Their eighteen-pound artillery pieces fired eighteen-pound shells. Their four-and-a-half-inch pieces fired shells that measured four and a half inches across. The .303 round of ammunition was .303 of an inch. Similarly, their reports use miles and yards.

The Germans used the metric system to measure shot and shell. Their famed "Jack Johnson" shell was fifteen centimetres across. Depending on who is writing, distances are recorded in either metric or Imperial; trusting the reader to understand both, I have not standardized these measures.

To avoid a multitude of *sic*s, I have silently corrected the grammar and punctuation of orders, reports, and interviews—without, of course, changing the substance of the original document. To give the reader a sense of how orders were actually written, I have reproduced several in their entirety: "aaa" is the equivalent of "stop" in a telegram. In a few cases, I have left the underlining, rather than replace it with italics. To help distinguish between German soldiers and officers and the Canadians, British, and French, I have kept the German ranks (*Hauptmann* equals "captain"). To keep from littering the text with footnotes, I have not cited the scores of orders and messages quoted; instead, I have given enough information in the text for the interested reader to find them in the appendix of the first volume of the *Official History of the Canadian Forces in the Great War, 1914–1919*, which lists all orders and messages chronologically. Nor have I formally cited most of the archival documents that can be located via textual references or through bibliographies in the books and articles listed in this book's bibliography. I have also not cited quotations from the German regimental histories; the bibliography, however, provides both the publication information and, where possible, the page references that deal with the 2nd Battle of Ypres.

Finally, readers familiar with the storied history of the Princess Patricia's Canadian Light Infantry (PPCLI) will notice that, save for a quote or two from Agar Adamson, this book makes no mention of that regiment. While the 1st Canadian Division was fighting for its life to the north of Ypres, the PPCLI held trenches directly east of the city and was attacked on 8 May in what is known as the Battle of Frezenberg Ridge. I mean no disrespect to the memory of the men who served in the only privately raised regiment in the Great War. Rather, the reality of what publishers call "real estate," and what the rest of us call book length, means that I cannot present a full rendering of the PPCLI in battle, and so I can do no better than to direct my readers to Stephen K. Newman's *With the Patricias: Holding the Line, Frezenberg, 8–13 May 1915* and David Bercuson's *The Patricias: The Proud History of a Fighting Regiment*. I have, however, listed those men of the PPCLI who were killed during the period of the 2nd Battle of Ypres in the *In Memoriam* section at the back of this book.

## Preface

A few hundred paces from the picture-postcard village of St. Julien, near the intersection of Brugsweg and Zonnebekestraat, at a place called Vancouver Corner, stands *The Brooding Soldier*. His torso rises out of a thirty-five-foot granite column. His massive hands clasp the butt of an upturned rifle that slides up from the column that forms his body. His eyes are not focused on the base of the monument, around which visitors place bouquets and wreaths. Rather, he gazes just beyond, to the ground—a mixture of soils from across Canada. Since 1923, this soldier has stood sentinel on the plain that soaked up so much Canadian blood eight years earlier.

He is so different from the soaring monument at Vimy, which takes the form of the grieving female figure of Canada but nonetheless symbolizes the triumph of that April 1917 battle. He embodies stoic resistance. He stares in mute witness, a signal of a memory that today is almost forgotten—but as late as the 1960s was commemorated with a parade in Verdun, Quebec, on the south shore of Montreal island.

He broods.

Apart from the few hours when they held a small wood called Bois de Cuisiniers, his comrades took no new ground. Indeed, by late on 26 April, the Germans held every position the Canadians had held at dusk on the twenty-second—Mouse Trap Farm, the line running north from St. Julien towards Langemarck, Gravenstafel Ridge, Pond Farm, and St. Julien itself. In just over one hundred hours of fighting, beginning at 5:00 p.m. on 22 April, more than six thousand Canadians became casualties: a third of the 1st Division's complement, or one-half of its fighting strength. Some units suffered their greatest losses of the war.

*The Brooding Soldier* mourns. But he does not admit defeat.

Over those same one hundred hours, the Canadians, who had been in the trenches for barely a week, filled in after the French lines were broken by the first poison gas attack in history, and then they withstood the second. Had the Canadians not stymied the attack, Kaiser Wilhelm's spike-helmeted soldiers would have poured through, taken the Ypres Salient (bagging some fifty thousand Canadian and British troops in the process) and then likely the Channel ports beyond, expelling England, France's main ally, from the continent. The last week of April 1915 offered Dunkirk, twenty-five years early.

An army that had not even existed eight months earlier—an army manned by thousands of farmers, miners, accountants, lawyers, teachers, chemists, students, labourers, trainmen, and real estate agents—stood against German soldiers who had under their belts at least two years of the finest military training in the world and a year of active service, including, for many, action at 1st Ypres in November 1914. An army equipped with, perhaps, the worst field rifle ever issued, the Ross rifle, nevertheless generated enough fire to break up onrushing German troops whose artillery pummelled the Canadian lines. As the battle wore on, an army commanded more and more by junior officers and non-commissioned officers—men who less than a year earlier had been mere cadets—and even by force of personality, moved machine guns into position, advanced in good and at times innovative order, and staged fighting retreats.

The thousands of Canadians who lived through those hundred terrible hours on Flanders fields did not just happen to end up thousands of miles from Canada's eastern shores. Every one of them was a volunteer. Since the late 1920s, the standard story has been that soldiers were dupes whose only real belief was "We're here because we're here, because we're here."* Men like John N. Beaton, a soldier from Brookfield, Prince

---

*The standard story has been well supported by a quirk of technological history. Until recently, the only photographs available from the First World War were in black-and-white, and thus painted the world in shades of drab grey. The story is less well supported by colour photographs that have recently been published. Trenches were not always grey and muddy. For

Edward Island, we've been told, were in the grip of "false consciousness" when they wrote about joining up because of their belief in "liberty and righteousness" and their worries about what Prussian militarism might mean were it to triumph in Europe.[1] While it would be foolish to forget that men joined up for a myriad of reasons—including good pay, adventure, manly pride, and even family tradition—it is equally foolish to think that at almost a century's distance, we are better positioned to see that what they referred to as "duty" to "King and Country" was really an Imperial Lie made manifest; their letters and diaries—and most important, interviews they gave decades later—indicate that they knew exactly what they believed.

That is not to say that there were no men among the thirty thousand who made up the 1st Canadian Division who were critical of the power game of European politics as it played itself out in the years prior to the war. But once Germany invaded Belgium and Prussian militarism threatened not just Europe but the Empire to which they proudly belonged, the Canadians knew which side they were on. No doubt some of the six hundred thousand who signed attestation papers revelled in the sheer bloody-mindedness of the war. But the vast majority did not. They saw Germany as a threat to their way of life and their Empire. They saw fighting Germany as both a personal challenge (a test of survival) and a job that had to be done to preserve what they believed in.

• • •

My chief concern in this book is to describe the battle as objectively as possible. To do this, I use official histories, war diaries, letters, memoirs, and both Canadian and German regimental histories; many of these last have not been used in English before. Where appropriate, I point out military errors and how the collapse of the command-and-control system shaped the battle. Germany's violation of the Hague Convention,

---

months at a time and for hundreds of miles, the grass grew green and the sky was, indeed, filled with singing larks.

which prohibited the use of "deleterious gases," is, of course, central to the story of 2nd Ypres. Indeed, it is the reason for the battle. But equally important to the Canadians' experience were other violations of the rules of war, including *ruses de guerre* (such as Germans dressing up as French or British soldiers), flying planes with British markings, shelling buildings being used as medical stations, bayoneting soldiers trying to surrender, and mistreating prisoners of war.

Part of the historian's job is to help dispel the fog of war. By their very nature, battles are confusing. The historian's need to clarify, however, can sometimes blanch the lived experience of battle from history. Little is gained by reading that "Company No. 1 of the Nth Battalion moved into position behind Bridge No. 4." As much as is possible within the bounds of space, I have gone in the opposite direction and drawn attention to the iron smell of blood, the cutting scent of cordite, the deafening sound of guns and exploding shells, the horrendous sights of men being turned into pink mist, of entrails spilling out over hands, of hallucinations caused by sleep deprivation. I do this not to revel in the gore but to remind my readers of the conditions the Canadian citizen-soldiers lived through and triumphed over.

While it would be foolish to claim that the Canadians were well schooled in the arts of war, they were better trained than has been recognized. Indeed, they were fortuitously fitted for the kind of battle that was handed to them on 22 April 1915. As was shown by the disaster at Festubert in May 1915, which cost 2,204 casualties for no real gain of territory, the Canadians were nowhere near ready to undertake a major assault. But that is not what 2nd Ypres was about.

# Introduction

*The naked earth is warm with Spring,*
*And with green grass and bursting trees*
*Leans to the sun's gaze glorying,*
*And quivers in the sunny breeze;*
*And Life is Colour and Warmth and Light,*
*And a striving evermore for these;*
*And he is dead who will not fight;*
*And who dies fighting has increase.*
—Julien Grenfell, "Into Battle"

As the warm sun of 22 April 1915 burned off the morning mist, George Eyles, Frederick B. Bagshaw, and Robert L. Christopherson were in trenches five miles north by northeast of Ypres, Belgium, some three thousand miles from Canada's easternmost point, then the eastern end of Quebec, in what is now Labrador. The chain of events that brought the thirty-one-year-old Toronto clerk (of the 15th Battalion), the thirty-six-year-old Toronto barrister, and the thirty-nine-year-old Saskatchewan lumberman (both of the 5th Battalion), as well as about eighteen thousand other Canadian men, to Flanders could scarcely have been imagined a year earlier. On 28 June 1914, Gavrilo Princip, a Serbian nationalist, assassinated the heir to the Austro-Hungarian throne, Franz Ferdinand, while the archduke and his wife visited Sarajevo, the capital of Bosnia-Herzegovina, which had been incorporated into Austria-Hungary six years earlier. Over the next few weeks, as thousands visited the "Peace Year" exhibit at the Canadian

National Exhibition in Toronto, politicians in Austria-Hungary, Germany, Serbia, Russia, France, and Great Britain postured, while their generals and admirals dusted off mobilization plans.

The war began on 28 August 1914, when Austria-Hungary attacked Serbia, but it spread almost immediately to include Russia, which saw itself as the defender of the South Slavs.* Germany, Austria's only ally, then mobilized against Russia. Kaiser Wilhelm's order triggered one in Paris, which since 1892 had been bound to St. Petersburg in a defensive alliance against Germany.

For a few days, in public at least, it looked as if the British Empire (and hence Canada) would be able to remain neutral. Soon, however, as Vienna, Berlin, and St. Petersburg called up men in the millions, war preparations got under way in both British Empire capitals. On 27 August, while secret plans for ferrying a British Expeditionary Force to France were set in motion, Sir Winston Churchill, First Lord of the Admiralty, ordered the fleet to ready itself to shadow hostile men-of-war. On 31 August, Canada's minister of militia, Sam Hughes, who, along with Prime Minister Robert Borden, had long expected war with Germany, ordered the country's 226 militia units to ready procedures to recruit troops for overseas service.

A telegram pledging that the Canadian people would "make every sacrifice necessary to ensure the integrity and maintain the honour of our Empire" arrived in London the next day. It was authored by the Privy Council in Ottawa, but it spoke for thousands. In a telegram to his parents, then vacationing on Prince Edward Island, twenty-one-year-old Alan B. Beddoe explained his decision to enlist by quoting Admiral Horatio Nelson's famous words before the Battle of Trafalgar: "England expects that every man will do his duty." A few weeks later, a Prince Edward Island newspaper published a letter from a militiaman to his

---

*The assassination of Franz Ferdinand was not itself the reason Austria-Hungary declared war on Serbia. The *causis belli* was, rather, Serbia's refusal to allow Austrian representatives to investigate Ferdinand's assassination and to serve on the court that would try Princip and anyone else connected to the killing.

mother explaining his reasons for volunteering: "You have three sons and three daughters. Surely you can at least spare one for the sake of our Mother Country, in the defence of honour and righteousness. . . . England wants men, and men she shall get. . . . I know you don't want me to go. Nobody ever wanted their sons to walk straight into apparent death, but how was the cause to Freedom won?"[1]

On 3 August, neutral Belgium rejected an ultimatum from Germany and refused to allow its troops to cross Belgian territory to attack France from the northeast.* That same day, Borden's Cabinet finished two days of meetings that rank among the most momentous in Canadian history, not least of all because everything the Cabinet did—establishing censorship, authorizing the detention of enemy ships, prohibiting the export of items needed by the military, declaring bank notes legal tender, and authorizing a national debt—"was wholly without legal validity until they were afterwards ratified by Parliament."[2] To get around section 69 of the Militia Act, which forbade the deployment of militiamen outside Canada, Borden himself suggested that the regiments "enlist as Imperial troops for a stated period," with the Canadian government covering the cost of their pay, equipment, and transportation.[3] As the sun set in Vancouver on 3 August, the British Empire was officially at peace, but the King's subjects were nervously awaiting Germany's response to a British note protesting the violation of Belgium's neutrality.

The fourth of August was one of those beautiful mid-summer days that can make Canadians forget the long months of winter. Beneath

---

*The ultimatum to Belgium was necessitated by the famed Schlieffen Plan. Although the Franco-Russian treaty was secret, German strategists had long assumed that a war with either France or Russia would involve the other, and thus present them with the strategic problem of fighting a two-front war. War Minister Alfred von Schlieffen's famous plan was designed to get around the tactical problem posed by the belt of forts France had built on its eastern border after the Franco-Prussian War by, quite literally, going around them in a scythe-shaped assault of forty-seven divisions and driving west through Belgium and then southwest to Paris. With France knocked out of the war, Germany would use its railroad network to move troops east to fight Russia, which, it was (wrongly) assumed, would take at least six weeks to mobilize.

the warm sun, a certain Ottawa-born man named Reid worked as a telegraphist on the Yukon Trail, and Larry Nelson canoed in Algonquin Park. In Winnipeg, Bagshaw prepared for the ceremony that would elevate him to a second-degree Mason, while in a small town near Quebec City, twenty-five-year-old Michael Holland L'Abbé watched boys with paste-thickened brushes post the latest war news outside a newspaper office. William S. M. Mactier waited for his news outside a wireless office on a ship steaming for Canada; on a ship steaming for England, where he was to oversee the publication of a medical textbook he had co-authored, forty-two-year-old John McCrae, a Boer War veteran and future author of "In Flanders Fields," also waited for news. None of these men could have imagined that as the British government stood in the House of Commons in London and reiterated its guarantee of Belgium's neutrality, the Militia Service Headquarters in Ottawa threatened to descend into farce.

Moments after Brigadier-General Charles F. Winter arrived at 28–30 Slater Street, a nondescript seven-storey office building that housed the Militia Service Headquarters, Sam Hughes slammed down his newspaper and exclaimed, "England is going to skunk it"—meaning that, he believed, England was going to betray Belgium and France. "By G-d, I don't want to be a Britisher," barked the minister, before demanding that Winter take down the Union Jack flying above the headquarters. Only the timely intervention of the quartermaster general, who was able to quiet the excitable Hughes, avoided the "talk and gossip" that would have followed the removal of the Empire's flag just as it went to war. [4]

Later that day, not long before Christopherson entered a Winnipeg picture show, and while David Moffat of the 8th Ontario Battery Militia enjoyed the warm afternoon on his parents' veranda in Gananoque, Ontario, Sir Edward Grey, who, as British foreign minister, was responsible for the foreign policies of both the United Kingdom and Canada, looked out from the Cabinet room on Downing Street. With German troops still advancing through Belgium, the lamp-lighter's simple act of turning off the lamps became, suddenly, a mixture of poetry and politics.

"The lamps are going out all over Europe," Grey said to his Cabinet colleagues. "We shall not see them lit again in our lifetime."⁵

Less than an hour after Britain's 11:00 p.m. (GMT) ultimatum to Germany to withdraw from Belgium expired, Canadians across the country learned that their country was at war. Shouts and cheers from the street interrupted Bagshaw's Mason ceremony. Projectionists across Canada flashed up the words "Germany has declared war on England." A car drove up to the Moffat place, and the driver handed David a note calling him up. Presumably the telegraphist Reid was among the first in the far-flung northern reaches of Canada to know that the country was at war. Nelson learned the news a few days later, courtesy of some American canoeists, and decided to "hotfoot" it out of Algonquin Park to a recruiting station. Christopherson and his friend waited till the end of the moving picture they were watching and then, having been fortified by a Tom Collins, walked to the drill hall of the 16th Light Horse and told Major Pollet "that the war was on and we wanted to enlist."\* By the time they did so, the ship carrying McCrae to England had passed its first hours sailing without lights, and McCrae had no doubt told others what he recorded in his diary a day later: "It will be a terrible war, and the finish of one or the other."

At first glance, every enlistment centre looked much the same. Pictures of young men flocking to their colours, anxious to prove themselves before "the leaves turn," as the Kaiser put it, crowd our memory. Canadians feared that it would all be over, over there, before they could even get across the pond. Distinctions can, however, be drawn between Germany and Austria-Hungary's rush to embrace war and the Canadian attitude. German and Austro-Hungarian leaders spoke of exterminating the Slavs. Indeed, to forestall the creation of a Greater Serbia—and over-awe the empire's other restive minorities—the chief of the Austrian

---

\*The premier of British Columbia, Sir Richard McBride, was among the first to ready Canada for war. Without seeking authorization from Ottawa or informing the Royal Canadian Navy, McBride arranged for the province to purchase (and transport out of the neutral United States) two submarines being built in Seattle, Washington, for Chile.

general staff had urged war against Serbia no less than twenty-five times since 1913. The leader of the German homosexual movement, Magnus Hirshfeld, supported Teutonic "honesty and sincerity" over Slavdom.[6] The novelists Hermann Hesse and Thomas Mann waxed poetic about the coming struggle. Sigmund Freud wrote that "all my libido goes to Austria-Hungary."[7] The composer Arnold Schönberg hurried to Vienna to enlist; the poet Gerhart Hauptmann rejoiced when German troops were called "Huns." Canadians would have been baffled by the relief felt by Germans and Austrians at the end of the "foul peace" that had prevailed since 1870 (i.e., since the end of the Franco-Prussian War), and by the millions of young men who thanked the war for releasing them from "the 'bondage' of class and status and the 'unnatural' constraints of the market place."[8]

Canada's political leaders and, more important, her volunteer soldiers struck a different note. Borden stated baldly, "We have absolutely no quarrel with the German people," nearly half a million of whom lived in Canada. Rather, Canada's foe was Germany's "military autocracy." Canada did not fight "for the love of battle, not for the love of conquest, not for greed of possessions," Borden declared, but to "withstand forces that would convert the world into an armed camp."[9] French-Canadian politicians supported the war, as did Archbishop Bruchési Paul of Montreal. Perhaps the most surprising supporter of the war effort was Henri Bourassa, who had opposed the creation of the Royal Canadian Navy and, in 1912, had written that the cadet corps taught children "the art of shooting human game at a convenient distance."[10] Bourassa's support, which did not last the war, may have been influenced by the fact that he was in Alsace when the Germans invaded France, and as a British subject, "he only narrowly escaped internment in Germany."[11]

In a letter written in December 1914, while the Canadians were still training in England, John W. MacDonald, who had left law school to enlist, explained the *realpolitik* at play:

> [T]he majority in Canada ... feel the present war is merely for the British a small affair and mainly to help the Brave Belgians. They do not realize

that it is a life and death struggle for the existence of the Empire and that if Germany is victorious ... Britain will be compelled to increase her great navy and in addition support an overwhelming army in preparation for the final struggle which would be issued as soon as Germany [incorporated into itself the industrial might of conquered Europe].[12]

According to Private Harold Peat, the German soldiers who gassed the French and Canadians at Ypres knew, without realizing it, why he and, by 1918, some six hundred thousand others joined up. Just after his 1st Battalion took its place in the line, a German shouted: "What have you come over here to fight us for? What business of it is yours?. . . If you had stayed home in your own country, when we came over and took Canada, we would have treated you all right."[13] Peat was unconvinced by the promise and took the Germans at their word. "Yes; *when they came over and took Canada*. That was the reason we were fighting. We wanted to keep our part of our empire for ourselves. It is ours absolutely, and we had no intention that Germany should own it. . . . If France were subdued, if England were beaten on her own ground, then Canada would be a prize of war. We preferred to fight overseas." In 1937, long after postwar disillusionment (exemplified in Canada by the 1928 novel *Generals Die in Bed*) had set in, a Canadian wartime artillery officer wrote, in his novel about the Great War: "The thousands went into battle not ignobly, not driven sheep or hired murderers—in many moods doubtless—but as free men with a corporate if vague feeling of brotherhood because of a [political or social] tradition they shared and an honest belief that they were doing their duty in a necessary task. He who says otherwise lies, or has forgotten."[14]

Something else all too easily forgotten today is these men's complex patriotism. From Sam Hughes down, the army was imbued with what one historian calls "imperial nationalism."[15] The tens of thousands of Canadians who put down their pitchforks, hammers, and pens in the late summer of 1914 attested to King George not as king of Great Britain but as king of Canada. True, the Canadian Expeditionary Force was part of the British army, but the men who gathered at Valcartier joined an army raised and commanded by Canadians (or approved by Canada's militia minister, who sat in Parliament in Ottawa, not London).* Robert Borden's government did not involve itself in purely military matters. But it raised and paid for the troops—and pointedly retained ultimate control over the tens of thousands of bankers, lawyers, clerks, labourers, milkmen, and farmers who had taken up arms at its behest.

. . .

The 1st Canadian Contingent (later Division) was in many respects a one-man band. The commanders had expected to send the more than thirty-two thousand volunteers to Petawawa, a base about two hundred kilometres up the Ottawa River from the nation's capital.** But instead, Hughes ordered the men to Valcartier, north of Quebec City—a base that had not been built when the war broke out but was completed in weeks, thanks to Hughes's dynamism and $180,000. Where the War Book, which was completed a few months earlier, was silent, Hughes was voluble, especially in determining priority for enlistment: "Equal applicants will be selected in the following order: Unmarried men. Married men without families. Married men with families." These last two groups required letters from their wives as proof they had agreed that their husbands could join up. "In regard to musketry," Hughes commanded, "a high standard will be required."[16]

Whatever Hughes meant when, in the Commons on 26 January 1916, he likened the men of the 1st Division to a "fiery cross [carried] through

---

*Alone among British generals, Lieutenant-General Edwin Alderson answered to two masters: his commander, Lieutenant-General Sir Herbert Plumer (and through him, up the chain of command to Lord Kitchener), and the Canadian government.

**The speed with which thousands rallied to the colours must have been a surprise. For years, many people, including Sam Hughes and his brother, James L. Hughes, chief inspector of Ontario's schools, worried that the preponderance of female teachers undercut the "manliness" of the province's boys. As a counterpoint to the feminine influence in the classroom, both men supported cadet training, physical education, and other "manly pursuits," including the reading of G. A. Hentry's novels, which glorified the British army.

the Highlands of Scotland or the mountains of Ireland in former days," the men of the division were not a demographic cross-section of the country.[17] Some 70 percent had been born in the United Kingdom, though most had either grown up or spent years in Canada. Despite a recession in Western Canada, most left good jobs when they answered the call.[18] Largely because of the need for young men's labour, support for the war was somewhat lower in farming areas; yet nine of the thousand-man battalions came from Western Canada, and only six originated in Ontario. Quebec francophones made up only 3.5 percent of the division; Hughes prevented the formation of a French-speaking battalion, even though there were more than a thousand francophones at Valcartier.\*

More volunteers came from the cities than from the country. Most had some high school or university education; their knowledge of basic chemistry saved countless lives at Ypres. Most had some militia training, which, though it may have amounted to little more than a few days a year, meant that they were familiar with military ways. In some battalions, almost 40 percent had served in the British army during the Boer War. The field artillery, in particular, was well trained. During his 1910 visit to Canada, General Sir John French, who during 2nd Ypres commanded all British forces on the Western Front, was particularly impressed with the artillery's ability to move their guns.

Training at Valcartier was nothing like what we see on television documentaries about boot camps. Hughes's decision to send most of the country's permanent force, whom he called "bar-room loafers," to garrison duty in Bermuda meant that there were only some eighty regular soldiers at Valcartier to train the volunteers.[19] Training—which involved everything from marching, bayonet and squad drills, and musketry to battalion and brigade field manoeuvres—was directed mostly by the more experienced recruits. Despite Hughes's claim that he wanted men

---

\*On 20 October 1914, Hughes relented and authorized the creation of the French-speaking 22nd Regiment, better known as the Van Doos, from the French "*vingt-deuxième*"; the regiment formed part of the 5th Canadian Division.

"who could pink the enemy every time," most volunteers fired fewer than one hundred rounds from their Ross rifles during training.[20] The fifteen rounds the men expended in each of rapid-fire and attack practice—not to mention the clean conditions in which they performed these training manoeuvres—did little to prepare them for the conditions they would encounter just seven months later, when their rifles seized in the heat and dirt of battle. A shortage of shells prevented the artillery from doing much more than firing a few rounds at sheets hoisted on the south shore of the St. Lawrence River. Five times in September, the troops practised brigade-level manoeuvres, some under the critical eye of the governor general, His Royal Highness, Prince Arthur, the Duke of Connaught.* On 15 September, after fighting a night-time retreat from Red Land's invasion, Blue Land had to re-establish its line and organize a daylight attack designed to drive Red Land back.

The most significant difference between today's boot camps and Valcartier, however, was Hughes himself. "Uniformed as a staff colonel; mounted; and accompanied by a cloud of aids, petitioners, and admirers, Hughes was everywhere at once, welcoming arrivals, correcting errors in drill, scolding officers in front of their men, and enthusiastically extracting order out of the chaos he had created."[21] He liked nothing better than scheduling reviews for dignitaries such as the governor-general and the prime minister.

No detail was too small for the militia minister. In addition to claiming that, despite its troubled history, the Ross rifle was "the most perfect military rifle in every sense in the World today," he championed the MacAdam shield-shovel, which was too small and thin to be much of a shield, and because of its loophole (through which a soldier was supposed to be able to aim his rifle), was equally useless as a shovel.[22] In a scene unimaginable today, Hughes would get off his horse or step away from

---

*Prior to becoming governor-general, Prince Arthur had had a long and distinguished military career serving in Canada, as well as in Egypt, South Africa, and India. On 16 June 1902, he was created field marshal; between 1904 and 1907, he served as inspector-general of the British army.

his retinue, pick up a rifle, and show "his boys," as he called them, how to shoot. Other times, he rolled up his sleeves and showed them the proper way to use a bayonet, which every expert considered indispensable to developing the proper lust for blood. Recruits had to be taught to resist the "tendency of 'haymaking'.... It is very difficult and quite unnecessary to cast your opponent over your shoulder like a sheaf of corn on a fork"[23]

The formation of the officer corps also lay in Hughes's hands, which infuriated his Conservative parliamentary colleagues, who sought to pay political debts or bank future IOUs by arranging for appointments for their favourites. Hughes promoted and demoted not only at will but often in front of the men. He summarily dismissed Lieutenant-Colonel John G. Ratteray, who had organized and commanded the 10th Battalion and was active in the Liberal Party in Manitoba, because he harboured a grudge against him.*

The confusion wrought by Hughes worked against the business of boot camp. For days at a time, units were unable to train together because Hughes "placed men into provisional battalions holus-bolus, organized them into brigades, and then reorganized them again."[24] As the minister melded militia units into battalions, the number of supernumerary officers grew. Some battalions had more than one commanding officer (one day the 2nd Battalion had five), and some officers commanded battalions that didn't exist.

Hughes's methods may have been eccentric, not to mention unfair, but according to the historian Desmond Morton, "It is not obvious that better officers were available."[25] Though Brigadier-General Richard Turner was to err grievously at 2nd Ypres, no militia minister would

---

*Ratteray's replacement as commanding officer of the 10th Battalion, the Alberta rancher Russell Boyle, surely made a splash his first day on the job when he threw off his coat with its officer's stripes and said to his assembled men: "Now, I'm the same as you fellows. I'm just an ordinary private, as far as you are concerned, as far as I'm concerned. There were four men on that boat [who] said they'd like to punch the hell out of me. Now I invite you four men, if you have the guts enough to come up, and we'll have it out right here." There were, reportedly, no takers. (Boyle, quoted in Dancocks, *Flanders*, 65.)

have failed to appoint him, for Turner had earned a Victoria Cross during the Boer War. Malcolm Mercer, who commanded the 1st Brigade, was a long-time commander of the Queen's Own Rifles, which formed the nucleus of the 3rd Battalion. Hughes did not let Arthur Currie's Liberal connections in British Columbia prevent him from appointing the commander of a coastal artillery regiment and organizer of the 50th Gordon Highlanders (which became the 8th Battalion) general of the 2nd Brigade. The minister also set aside his distaste for the professional forces and placed Colonel Harry Burstall, who commanded the army's artillery, in charge of the 1st Canadian Contingent's artillery and promoted him to brigadier-general.

• • •

It rained on 23 October, nine days after the Canadians arrived in England, the day the British Expeditionary Force began a battle that secured the ancient Flemish town they called Wipers, the Flemish Ipere, and the French Ypres.\* It rained again on 24 October, and once more the day after that. On 30 October, Lieutenant-Colonel David Watson (2nd Battalion) wrote in his diary, "Such rain & mud, I never saw the like."[26] During the winter of 1914/15, it rained on 89 of 123 days, turning Bustard Camp on the Salisbury Plain into a quagmire.

Letters home and diaries are filled with complaints about the weather and stories about ways of coping. After being drenched during a parade, Major Arthur E. Kirkpatrick (3rd Battalion), who before the war had been a Saskatchewan farmer and thus was no stranger to harsh weather,

---

\*Fought at the end of October 1914, the 1st Battle of Ypres was part of the so-called Race to the Sea, during which the Allies and the Germans tried to outflank each other on the northeast end of one another's line. At the end of the "race" (which began after the end of the Battle of Aisne in late September) lay not the hoped-for breakthrough, but a line of trenches that extended from the North Sea to Switzerland. The British victory at 1st Ypres, which all but destroyed Britain's pre-war army, prevented not just the loss of Ypres, an important symbol because it was the only large town left in Belgian hands, but the loss of the Channel ports. The victory also left the British with a salient that bulged five miles into the German lines and could be shelled from three directions.

thought it best to change out of his wet clothes. Winnipegger R. D. Haig (6th Battalion) disagreed: "The only way to be reasonably comfortable ... was never [to] take your clothes off, because it was much easier to get up in the morning damp-wet than get up in the morning and try putting on cold, damp clothes."[27]

Worse yet, the paint mixture used to camouflage the Canadians' Bell tents "caused the cotton threads to tighten so the weave opened," turning them into sieves.[28] Canon Frederick Scott recalled several tent-destroying gales. One occurred during a concert when a tenor hit a high note. "Like the walls of Jericho at the sound of Joshua's trumpets," he remembered, "a mighty gale struck the building, and with a ripping sound the whole thing collapsed." Another blew down the paymaster's tent. "Five schilling notes flew over the plain like birds over the sea. The men quickly chased them up, and on finding them stained with mud thought it unnecessary to return them."[29]

The mud and water also took its toll on more than thirty thousand pairs of boots, nicknamed "Sham Shoes," which had been designed for use on the South African veldt.[30] The British dipped into their stores to supply the Canadians with waterproof boots sturdy enough to stand up to route-marching on cobblestoned *pavé* roads. Equally despised was the Oliver webbing, which, instead of fitting snugly but comfortably around a soldier's body, was too tight under the arms, especially when it got wet. Worse, the webbing had no place to affix an entrenching tool, and its pouches held only eighty rounds instead of the standard issue of 150. Most seriously, the pouch for extra ammunition sat on the stomach, making it impossible for wearers to fully go to ground. Before leaving for France, seven of the twelve battalions had had their webbing replaced with the British pattern; the British also replaced all the trucks, wagons, and bicycles stowed in the steamers in Quebec City.

• • •

Through the rains and organizational changes—changes that saw each infantry battalion go from four companies to eight and then back to four; artillery batteries go from three six-gun formations to four four-gun formations; and the integration of the Colt machine gun into each battalion—morale held, helped, no doubt, by generous rations and the fact that Bustard was not a dry camp, despite Hughes's wishes. The contingent's health held up too, until the men moved from their soggy tents to the heated huts, at which time hundreds of recruits came down with flu-like symptoms; an outbreak of spinal meningitis killed twenty-eight men.

Though the rain disrupted schedules, training at Bustard Camp was a more serious endeavour than it had been at Valcartier, and it was also more serious than observers at the time and some present-day historians have allowed. Route marches were combined with musketry training, and the men, in addition to firing 155 rounds at targets, took daily rapid-fire practice using blank cartridges; the rate of fire the Canadians aimed for was that of the British army at Mons, which convinced the Germans they were facing a machine-gun regiment. Lectures on night operations, the duties of pickets and guards, the construction of entrenchments, and methods of keeping in touch by day and by night were augmented by practice in the field, including practice digging trenches. Through December and January, Lieutenant-Colonel G. Gillson, a Royal Horse Artillery officer with experience at the front, gave up-to-date artillery instruction. During the week of 5 December, Lieutenant Edward Bellew and his (2nd Brigade) machine-gun crews studied scouting, choosing a firing position, the functioning and repair of the Colt machine gun, semaphore, and occupying and entrenching at a new position. And every soldier had more bayonet training.

By design, war diarists write in unemotional language. Still, one cannot help feeling the excitement when they report of battalions and entire brigades on manoeuvres, for those are the ones watched by the general officer commanding, and thus are the ones where early reputations are made. At Kitcheners Wood and at Mauser Ridge two battalions attacked at once, but 2nd Ypres was in essence a small unit battle, fought by companies, platoons, and even smaller units.* Thus the time spent training groups of about two hundred men for the "intricacies of attacking woods or villages . . . [and] occupying defensive positions" paid off.³¹ Lieutenant-Colonel Arthur P. Birchall, a fourteen-year veteran of the 7th Royal Fusiliers on loan to the Canadians, schooled the 1st Brigade in the lessons of small unit fighting with his book *Rapid Training of Company for War*.

The 1st Brigade was not the only one to have such training. According to Bill Bagnall (14th Battalion), the Canadians were able to "check, battle back and to gain contact with flanks for hours unprotected" because Captain George Massey Williamson of the 9th Lancers had trained many "in taking cover, in taking advance, enflanking positions to advance attacking with infantry."³² The Canadian contingent's training had been rushed and often confusion reigned, but whomever Private Alex Sinclair (5th Battalion) overheard calling it "the Comedian Contingent" overstated the case.³³

. . .

By 15 February 1915, the Canadians had landed in France, where they were warmly welcomed. Just how warm the brass thought the welcome might be is clear from the message pasted into the men's pay books. The message reminded His Majesty's troops to be "courteous, considerate and kind . . . and always look upon looting as a disgraceful act." The colonials were warned that in "this new experience you may find temptations both in wine and women. You must entirely resist both temptations, and while treating all women with perfect courtesy, you should avoid

---

*Canadian battalions counted one thousand men. This number includes, however, officers, transport riders, farriers, cooks, engineers, and men on sick leave—men not normally included in an attack, in other words. By the Somme in mid-1916, approximately 10 percent of the battle strength of a battalion was held back from an attack—these men were the armature around which the battalion would be rebuilt if, as was so often the case, it was decimated in the attack. It is unclear exactly how many men of each battalion actually attacked Kitcheners Wood and Mauser Ridge, but a good guess is between 750 and 850. Accordingly, between 1,500 and 1,700 troops attacked Kitcheners Wood and Mauser Ridge, respectively.

any intimacy."³³ Kitchener's admonition against wine did not survive the train trip to Hazebrouck, in French Flanders. Whether the admonition against "intimacy" survived any longer is unknown. However, given the 1,249 cases of venereal disease treated at Bustard Camp, and the fact that by the end of the war the Canadians had the highest rate of venereal disease (150 per 1,000 men, as compared to 30 per 1,000 for the rest of the BEF) of any army on the Western Front, one might doubt it.

• • •

During the last week of February and first week of March, the Canadians were sent into the trenches with British units for instruction in the mysteries of trench warfare, including, of course, how to deal with lice, rats, and the Flemish mud. Twenty-seven-year-old Captain Harry Crerar (Artillery) found this last especially striking. "I never saw anything like the way it sticks. After I've been walking ten minutes, I have at least five pounds of it on either foot," he wrote in his private (and illegal) diary.* Over the next ten days, the Canadians learned *in situ* about the use of hand grenades and Verey lights (flares that lit no man's land at night), safe ways of strengthening trenches and parados, the strange art of manning a listening post, how to navigate over duck boards through the zigzagging trenches, the ten-minute "morning hate" (bombardment), and the habits of the enemy.

Habits varied. Somehow the Saxon regiment in front of Sergeant Harold Baldwin learned that his 5th Battalion had originally been a mounted unit and greeted him and his comrades with shouts of "Hello, you Fifth! What have you done with your horses?" The following morning, war turned, at least momentarily, to mirth as the Canadians espied upon the German parapet a little wooden horse. After the Canadians fired on the toy, it vanished for a moment—only to reappear "swathed in bandages."³⁵ A German in the trench opposite the one held by Edmonton-

---

*Between mid-1944 and the end of the Second World War, Crerar commanded the 1st Canadian Army, which liberated northwestern Europe.

born S. W. Metcalf (10th Battalion) "hollered across about him living in Edmonton. He mentioned some of the names of the streets and buildings ... and he said he was going back to Edmonton after the war." The Germans in front of the trench where the 2nd Battalion spent 17 to 23 February were less friendly, and had set up a number of fixed rifles that could be fired automatically when a head mistakenly appeared. By the end of the ten days, the Canadians could no doubt sing about a certain "Mademoiselle from Armentières," a song not contained in *Regimental Songs: Canadian Expeditionary Force, 1914–1915*, a book supplied by the newspaper baron William Southam, Esq.

The trenches the Canadians trained in may have been considered quiet, but "wastage" was an almost daily occurrence. W. Stevens of the 14th Battalion saw his buddy Pat Rattigan die an instant after he climbed to the top of the trench to pound sandbags into place. The 2nd Battalion's first casualty was Private R. T. Cardew, General Mercer's batman, who died when a shell hit a trench shelter where he had taken cover.

During the week of 26 February, Brigadier-General Arthur Currie wrote at least nine condolence letters; the most painful was the one to Mr. and Mrs. Beaumont Boggs, the parents of Herbert Boggs, who was assigned to the 7th Battalion after signing up on 24 September 1914. Currie did not have to look up Boggs's address, for Herbie grew up at 620 Fort Street, in Victoria, one door down from the home of Mr. and Mrs. Arthur Currie. In the 7th Battalion alone, twenty men were wounded while learning their new trade.

Canadian artillery fired back. Sharpshooters, including one from the 8th Battalion who scored three kills, took more personal revenge. In an article published in the *Daily Telegraph*, one described taking thirty minutes to crawl the thirty yards to the edge of the German trench. "I peered through a loophole, saw nobody in the trench, then the German behind raised up his head again. He was laughing and talking. I saw his teeth glisten against my foresight, and I pulled the trigger. He just gave a grunt and crumpled up."[36] The next day, he shot one in the heart and another squarely in the back.

・・・

The Canadians were fast learners, and the British, who were planning an assault at Neuve-Chapelle, wanted their 7th Division out of the trenches to take part in the attack—so on 3 March, the Canadians took over sixty-four hundred yards of trench at Fleurbaix. The next day, General Mercer wrote his wife: "My brigade is holding a bit of the line—about 2,300–3,000 yards. The lines at one point are only some 65 yards apart, at another 85 yards, average distance from 200–350 yards." He closed his letter with words that scarcely would have occurred to him on a Sunday in Toronto: "We attended service this morning for the men not in the trenches. It was in a barnyard. A son of Fighting Dan Gordon was the preacher—a capital fellow."[37]

On 10 March, the Canadians played a supporting role in the disaster at Neuve-Chapelle. Positioned on the British left, they made a demonstration in the form of rifle and artillery fire aimed some distance to the left of the actual attack, with the hope that the Germans would mistake the Canadians' fire for a second attack and divide their forces.

The battle should have ended in victory. The 535-gun artillery barrage, which began at 7:30 a.m., completely surprised the Germans. It cut their wire and destroyed their first trenches, opening the way for sixty thousand British troops whom the Germans had failed to detect. But the battle turned sour when the British, as per their orders, paused some two hundred yards beyond the German lines while their artillery bombarded Neuve-Chapelle itself.

The delay allowed those Germans who were not overrun to retreat to pre-set defensible positions, and it also allowed reserves to be rushed forward. The following day, the Germans counterattacked with the 6th Bavarian Reserve; one of the runners was an Austrian-born private named Hitler. By the end of the battle on 13 March, the British had lost 11,652 men for an advance of less than a mile; the Germans had lost 8,600 men.

On 12 March, next to the names of soldiers killed by wastage over the past week, the Toronto *Globe* carried a report from a British officer on the Canadian headquarters staff praising Lieutenant-General Edwin Alderson's troops: "The Canadians are rapidly learning the tricks of the war, besides introducing new ones. The Canadian artillery gave the Germans a frightful tying up." Kitchener too praised the colonials: "Although they were not actually engaged in the main attack, they rendered valuable help by keeping the enemy actively employed in front of their trenches."

No paper reported that the Canadians were unable to keep up their expected rate of fire because their Ross rifles jammed, owing to incompatibility between the rifle and the British-made ammunition. No action was taken on General Currie's 15 March request for a "most rigid investigation," even though he urged it with the strongest words: "[A] serious interference with rapid fire may prove fatal on occasions." Loss of faith in the Ross rifle was especially acute in the 10th Battalion. On 1 April, for the second time in less than a week, Colonel Robert Boyle ordered that "all Lee-Enfield rifles *must* be handed into Q.M. Stores by 9:00 a.m. tomorrow morning. Same will be replaced by Ross rifles."[38]

Ten days later the Canadians arrived in Ypres—driven there in double-decker buses still sporting their London advertisements—where they were to relieve the French along 4,250 yards of trench on the British left. The Canadian lines faced north by northeast. On their left (east) were three French formations belonging to the 45 Algerian Division: the Tirailleurs, the African Light Infantry, and the Territorials.

• • •

In October 1914, Captain J. F. C. Fuller, a British officer who had watched as the Canadians refused to unload their ships at Plymouth, wrote to his mother that they "would make fine soldiers if only all their officers were shot."[39] Without realizing it, Fuller had laid the foundation for that most tired of Canadian clichés. Days after the Canadians were withdrawn from the line—having endured four days of combat and part of the first and the entire second gas attacks—the New Brunswick–born Sir Max Aitken (the future Lord Beaverbrook) wrote in the *London Times* of the heroic stand made by soldiers whose pluck overcame the fact that they were "neither disciplined nor trained." Before the year was out, *The Times History of the War* had rhapsodized that stand at 2nd Ypres and attributed it to the fact that the Canadians were a "race of sportsmen."[40] A few months later, in *Canada in Flanders*, which had been through twelve printings by March 1916, Aitken attributed the Canadians' success not to discipline or training—but to the innate resourcefulness of "amateur soldiers."[41]

German regimental histories, by contrast, credit the Canadians' success to something more than luck or pluck. Indeed, a little over a year later, during the Battle of the Somme (September 1916), the Germans rated the 1st Canadian Division as one of the best in the British army. On 6 August, the Germans mistook the 2nd Australian Division, which beat back a German counterattack at Windmill Hill in Pozières, for the Canadians, whom Franz Kaiser, the regimental historian of the Preuss. Infanterie-Regiment Nr. 63 (4. Oberschlesisches), praised as "Americans from the Wild West." The historian of Reserve-Infanterie-Regiment 211, which had fought at 2nd Ypres, quotes an officer named Wienart as saying, of the soldiers who took Courcelette, "They told us they were Canadians, old friends from the fighting in Flanders. That made sense!"[42]

Almost all of the officers named by Hughes came from significantly different backgrounds than the officers Captain Fuller knew. Almost none attended military academies like Sandhurst; one who did, Lieutenant Bellew (7th Battalion), earned a Victoria Cross. The majority, however, were weekend and summer militiamen who were full-time labourers, businessmen, professionals, and farmers. Brigadier-General Currie was a Victoria real estate agent with a deep financial secret.[43] Lieutenant-Colonels E. W. B. Morrison (who served in the Boer War) and David Watson were, respectively, the editor of the *Ottawa Citizen* and the managing director of the Quebec City *Chronicle*. Major Victor Odlum had just purchased the Vancouver *Daily Star;* after the death of Lieutenant-Colonel William Hart-McHarg on 23 April 1915, Odlum became commander of the 10th Battalion. Lieutenant-Colonel Robert G. Edwards Leckie, a mining engineer, commanded the 16th Battalion. Lieutenant-Colonel John Creelman, commander of the 2nd Brigade's artillery, was a successful Montreal lawyer. Lieutenant-Colonel Frederick Loomis (13th Battalion) was a building contractor, and Lieutenant-Colonel George Tuxford (5th Battalion) was a beef farmer. Captain Thomas C. Irving, who commanded the 2nd Field Company, Canadian Engineers, was an auto mechanic and a driver. And below them came not just loggers, hunters, fishermen, and sportsmen—as post-war myth would have had it—but thousands of city-dwelling clerks, manual workers, and, especially from Montreal, accountants.

Patriotic bluster aside, few military experts would have given the Canadians decent odds for a clash with the Kaiser's army. Even though the Canadians were more familiar with up-to-date tactics than has traditionally been assumed, most of the German units were incomparably better trained and armed. Between the ages of seventeen and twenty, all German males served a two-year term in the army. For the five years after that, they belonged to a reserve unit that trained fourteen days a year. For the next five years, they were part of the Landwehr, which trained for a week or two every other year. And of course, by April 1915, when the Canadians arrived in Ypres, the soldiers on the other side of no man's land had already been on active duty for eight months. Most had fought at 1st Ypres the previous October.

No general would have considered the Canadians' various backgrounds to be a plus in the terrible logic of battle, but the fact that they were fighting a largely defensive battle *was* a plus. Defending is easier than attacking—if for no other reason than the defender gets to choose the ground on which to make his stand. (The corollary of this, of course, is that the attacker gets to choose where to attack.) Another plus was the fact that the Canadians were volunteers. This speaks to that most intangible of military assets: morale. But how could the fact that their officers and NCOs (non-commissioned officers) were not professional soldiers improve their chances in a battle where the enemy was shooting bullets, firing shells, and releasing poison gas? The answer is that 2nd Ypres was not a set piece choreographed from on high as, for example, Vimy was. That creeping barrage, which covered thousands as they advanced towards the ridge in April 1917, was timed to the second; at 2nd Ypres, counterattacks were undone by a collapse in communications, which among other things prevented Canadian and British gunners from learning that the counterattacks had been delayed.

No battle should really be spoken of in the singular. Every one is really a kaleidoscope of thousands of different actions across a larger or smaller expanse. This is especially true of 2nd Ypres for two reasons. First, the primitive state of communications—and the fact that dozens of runners were shot down—meant that for much of the battle, senior commanders had little, if any, idea of what was happening on the firing line. And even when they knew what was going on, they had no effective means of exerting coherent command and control.

Second, although generals, their staffs, and the men on the ground—and, of course, historians—speak of a front or firing line (represented by a line on a map), these terms are often little more than metaphors. At 2nd Ypres, much of the "line" was, in fact, a field of fire between gun pits and isolated trenches, with each subsidiary section commanded by a major, a captain, or as casualties mounted, NCOs and even privates. In 1938, A. Fortesque Duguid, who served as an artillery officer at 2nd Ypres and wrote the *Official History of the Canadian Forces in the Great War 1914–1919*, observed that "when discreetly disciplined, carefully trained, vigorously led and above all when imbued with resolute and unflinching determination to make their cause triumphant, [civilian soldiers] could compete with and vanquish the product of Military Autocracy."[44]

The junior officers whose grasp of command so appalled Fuller were able to lead not because of military tradition but because, as professionals, small businessmen, or farmers, they were used to taking the initiative and making reasoned decisions, either on their own or in consultation with others.* By contrast, on 27 April 1915, when the better-trained Lahore Division lost its lead officers, its coherence fell apart.

• • •

*Baptism of Fire* tells the story of how this untried Canadian army withstood not just a determined German attack but also the first and second poison gas attacks in history. It tells the story of how the Canadians filled an almost five-mile gap—how they were bloodied, blown up, gassed. Bent but not broken. It tells the story of how over the course of one hundred hours, volunteer citizen-soldiers—some fighting thousands of miles from home—held off many times their number of *Feldgrauen*, who, had they taken Ypres, would have captured some fifty thousand British and Canadian troops and likely advanced to the English Channel. Even if Borden's government in Ottawa and Prime Minister Sir Herbert Asquith's in London had survived that shock, the disaster would have been almost incalculable. Every Canadian soldier in Europe—including at least ten of the fifteen general officers and scores of colonels, lieutenant-colonels, majors, sergeants, and corporals who would command at

---

*In a sense, these men were heirs to a tradition that stretched from Lord Horatio Nelson through to the Antarctic explorer Robert F. Scott, who died just two years before the Great War began. Nelson's genius, a recent historian has argued, lay not so much "in his total mastery of the battleground" but in his ability to "promote individuals of the same independent stamp as himself." Scott's men took on the Nelsonian ethos of "brotherhood, mutual confidence, experience, aggression, courage, flare and independence." Reared on stories of Nelson and familiar with Scott's saga (and his tragic death in Antarctica), the Canadians—who, it must be remembered, thought of Canadianness as a species of Britishness—displayed what a Spanish observer of Nelson's 1797 victory at Cape St. Vincent saw as the distinguishing features of the Englishman at war: "He rests in certain that his comrades, actuated by the same principles as himself, will be bound by the sacred priceless law of mutual support. Accordingly, both he and all his fellows fix their minds on acting with zeal and judgment on the spur of the moment, and with the certainty that they will not be deserted. Experience shows, on the contrary that a Frenchman or a Spaniard, working under a system which leans to formality and strict order being maintained in battle, has no feeling for mutual support, and goes into action with hesitation, preoccupied with the anxiety of seeing the commander-in-chief's signals, for such and such manoeuvres" (quoted in Crane, *Scott of the Antarctic*, 25).

Vimy Ridge, fought almost exactly two years later—would have been a prisoner of war, a status they would have retained for more than three and a half years.*

It takes nothing away from the great victory at Vimy to say that the Canadian stand at Ypres was itself the crucible of nationhood. The thousands of Canadians who began to mourn when they spotted a father's, brother's, son's, or friend's name among the long columns of dead did not concern themselves with the niceties of the Dominion's constitutional status; the dead had died for "King and Country," and as the editorialists made clear, the "country" that bled was Canada. Canada as part of the British Empire, yes. But the country named on the dead soldiers' brassards was Canada, and its maple leaf would be forever engraved on the tombstones of those few who had a proper grave. The hands that Major John McCrae imagined catching the torch passed by those who but days earlier had "lived, felt dawn, saw sunset glow" lived in hundreds of towns, villages, and cities not in England, Scotland, Wales, or Ireland, but across the sea, in Canada.

---

*The list of general officers would have included Arthur Currie, Frederick Loomis, George Tuxford, Harry Burstall, Robert Rennie, Louis Lipsett, David Watson, Edward Hilliam, and Victor Odlum.

Part 1

# Marching as to War
14 April to 21 April 1915

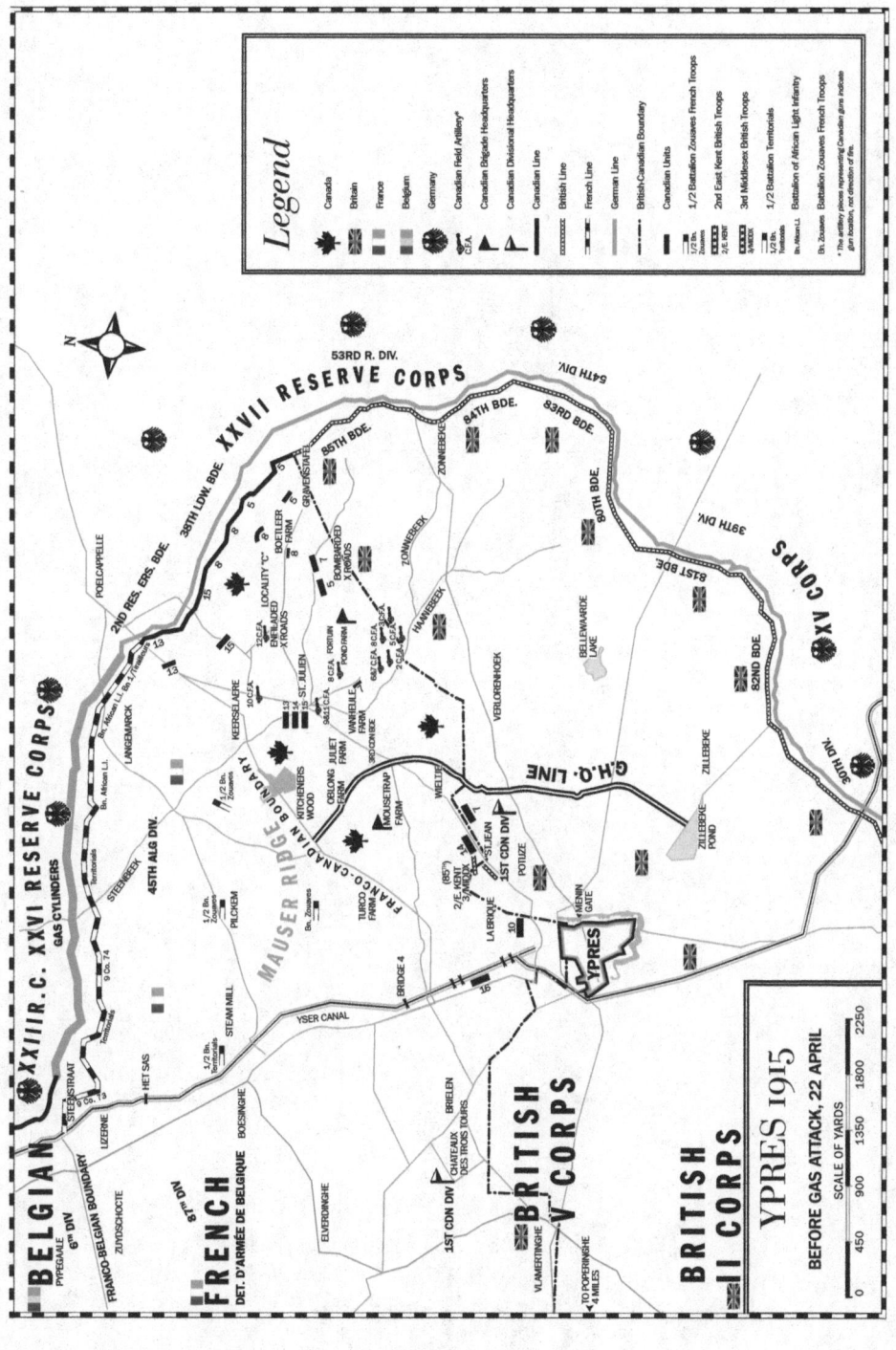

Chapter 1

## "It Is a Higher Form of Killing"
The Canadians Man the Trenches around Ypres,
and the Germans Install the Gas Cylinders

> *In no future war will the military be able to ignore poison gas. It is a higher form of killing.* —Fritz Haber

Between 14 and 17 April 1915, the 2nd and 3rd Canadian Infantry Brigades relieved the French 11th Division, then holding four thousand yards of the Allied line immediately to the left of the British, on the northeast side of the Ypres Salient. Had the Canadians marched out from Ypres, the last significant Belgian town in Allied hands, during the day, they would have seen a landscape quite removed from the war they had come so far to fight. Just outside Ypres, within sight of the ruined belfry of the medieval Lakenhalle (Cloth Hall), which one Canadian described as the "Houses of Parliament without a roof or windows or doors or ceiling,"[1] stood dozens of farms that grew the asparagus sold in the town's market square.

The verge between the city and the Allied lines that arced around the town caught the eye of the historian of Reserve-Infanterie-Regiment 239. "Green shoots of the spring crop draw green lines that are cut by the rows of poplars along the road and interrupted by orchard," he wrote. "In between are red and black dots—they are the rooftops of farmhouses and pools and ponds.... There are small copses with bushes and trees with the white stroke of the birch rising slenderly from them." He made it sound idyllic, but had the 2nd and 3rd Brigades of Brigadier-Generals Arthur Currie and Richard Turner marched out from Ypres's ramparts under a warm sun and fleecy clouds born of the waters of the North Sea, some fifty miles away, German gunners aided by spotter planes would have rained shells down upon them.

To protect the Canadians he took command of shortly after the SS *Franconia* tied up in Plymouth on 14 October 1914, Lieutenant-General Edwin Alderson ordered that they move forward only at night. To men used to the Rockies, the Laurentians, and Canada's vast prairies, the undulating fields north and east of Ypres must have looked like small beer indeed.* To the great surprise of men like Sergeant J. Raymond MacIlree, however, the 7th Battalion, even with guides, had, after passing the farms that grew the asparagus, become "gloriously lost" among the water courses, shell holes, ditches, fallen trees, dikes, muddy communication trenches, and destroyed farm buildings (which the historian of RIR 239 either did not see or took for quaint ruins). Soldiers made awkward by the weight of their heavy greatcoats, their sixty-pound packs, their fourteen-pound Ross rifles, and the ammunition crates or machine-gun parts they carried stumbled at the lip of shell holes, and some pitched "headlong into the filthy mire."[2] Though they marched and crawled at night, they still faced a hail of German bullets; to avoid one burst, James Lockerby flopped down and found himself lying beside a bloated dead cow.

The closer the Canadians got to the trenches, the more the excitement built. They knew that soon they would be just a few hundred yards away from the very same German regiments that had been stopped by the British Expeditionary Force—known as the "Old Contemptibles"—at 1st Ypres. But before the Canadians reached their destination, the stench wafting downwind from the French line shoved aside their dreams of glory. Part of the unpleasant smell was easily identified; for six months,

---

*The slope that leads from St. Jean to Gravenstafel Ridge, the destination of the 8th and 5th Battalions, rises at a gradient of 1 percent to a height of 128 feet.

the French had used their trenches as latrines. But in the darkness of the night, only the most macabre could have guessed what else contributed to the stink: half-decomposed bodies—of both those who fought under the *Tricolore* or the *Reichskriegflagge*—that had been left where they fell. (In an attempt to mask the sickening odours, in the days to come Canadian field engineers rushed large quantities of disinfectant to the front.)

Dawn revealed the haphazard nature of these burials and the different ways the green Canadians coped with the grisly scenes. Here and there, said MacIlree, "arms stuck out of the parapet"; one particular arm became a favourite of men of the 10th Battalion, who liked to pause a moment when passing to shake the dead man's hand. MacIlree's description of the trench as "eerie" seems almost too ordinary for a place where decomposing bodies oozed out of the ground at the bottom of the trenches. Sergeant Harold Baldwin of the 5th Battalion was sick with horror when, while deepening his stretch of trench, he brought up his shovel with a boot that still contained a foot. Another man's shovel brought up "the other foot, with the leg bone still sticking." After rolling the "ghastly thing" into a sack, Baldwin risked becoming a sharpshooter's trophy when he lay himself across the parados* to vomit his guts out.[3]

The officers' quarters, though a bit back from the line, were not much better. Within two days of taking over a French billet, Lieutenant-Colonel John Creelman and the other men of the 2nd Brigade's field artillery were itching and scratching from the lice-infested bedding straw they slept in. Lieutenant-Colonel John A. Currie, who commanded the 15th Battalion (and was no relation to Brigadier-General Arthur Currie, commander of the 2nd Infantry Brigade), slept next to a "blood-bespattered wall which told of a desperate struggle in [the] room during the great battles of the previous November."[4]

---

*A parados is the rear side of a trench, while a parapet is the side facing the enemy; sandbags are normally piled a foot or so higher on the parapet so the men in the trench are not silhouetted against the parados.

The maps the French handed over to the Canadians showed a continuous four-and-a-half-mile line running on a slightly northwest–southeast axis from the Ypres–Poelcappelle road to the Ypres–Passchendaele road. The facts on the ground could not have been more different. The first 1,650 yards, for example, "consisted of 15 isolated portions of trench"; some sections were so small that they amounted to little more than firing pits.[5] Few, if any, of the subsections had adequate parados or parapets. The parapet of one section was barely waist-high. In another, the parapet was so badly constructed that those manning it had to lie exposed on top of it. Instead of running east to west, to face the Germans to the north, some sections ran north to south, which allowed the Germans to enfilade them. In front of Baldwin's trench, there was no wire at all; elsewhere, one or two rotten and rusted strands ran in front of the trench for a short distance, often for less than ten feet. Even the French machine-gun emplacements and artillery positions were improperly situated and unprotected.

What Captain Thomas C. Irving, who commanded the 2nd Field Company, Canadian Engineers, characterized as the "deplorable state" of the French trenches can be partially explained by the difference between French and British defensive doctrine. French doctrine was a variant of the republic's attack philosophy: *attaquer à outrance* (attack to excess). Instead of holding a trench at all costs, the French soldiers would fall back and then use their seventy-five-millimetre guns, the quickest-firing guns then available, to isolate the Germans, confident that their fighting spirit (*élan*) and swift bayonet work would carry the day. For the British, and thus for the Canadians, "*the cardinal principle of the defensive scheme . . . is a determination to hold the front trenches at all costs.*" The Principles of Defence states, "The front trenches must be kept in good repair and be constantly improved. It is only by hard and constant work that this can be accomplished."[6]

Working mostly at night, and using only spade and muscle power, the Canadians connected as many trenches as they could. Where the notoriously high water table of Flanders permitted, they dug the trenches deeper, using the excavated earth to fill thousands of sandbags to reinforce the parapets and parados. (Sharp-ended Maxim machine-gun bullets travelled so fast they could cut through a foot and a half of sandbags.) The Canadians who had refused to do the "coolie work" of unloading their ships at Plymouth now built machine-gun emplacements, shovelled out new dugouts, and strung miles of telephone and telegraph wire.[7] Despite incessant machine-gun, sniper, and shellfire, they dug saps (thin trenches with listening posts at the end) into no man's land. Soldiers manhandled hundreds of crates, each containing thousands of cartridges, through the narrow trenches, and stored away thousands of "iron rations" of biscuits (the famed hard tack that for centuries had filled the stomachs of the Royal Navy), preserved meat, tea, and sugar. As soon as their daily rations arrived, near 9:00 p.m., groups of about fifteen men divided what on a typical night was two and a half loaves of bread, hot stew or bully beef, biscuits, tins of jam, cheese, and some bacon.

During daylight, some work continued, though mostly the men grabbed what sleep they could, wrote letters home, and as men at war have done for millennia, found ways to entertain themselves. One of the men in Lockerby's unit made a tin biscuit box into a banjo, which he played whenever the shells started coming close, to show the Germans not one hundred yards away that the Canadians were "quite unconcerned and enjoying life as usual."[8] On 16 April, the day after his 10th Battalion took its place in the line, Lieutenant-Colonel Russell Boyle wrote his wife: "The German artillery is playing merry hell at this very moment, and the shells are shrieking and howling around, but not doing any particular damage. When they get too nasty, I phone back to our own artillery, and get them to plaster the German trenches in front of my section a bit. This usually brings them to a reasonable state of mind."[9]

• • •

The Germans too were busy. In early April, while the Canadians prepared to relieve the French, a specially trained and equipped German engineering unit, Pionier regiment 35, installed a top-secret weapon in the trenches just north of Langemarck, a short distance northeast of where the Canadian line joined the French Tirailleurs. At first, the men of Reserve-Infanterie-Regiment 234, including one Leutnant Speyer, thought that the "strange figures moving through the trenches ... dragging mysterious steel cylinders" were bringing up their much-loved beer. Nervousness replaced anticipation when the sappers, their faces covered by modified Dräger* breathing apparti, dug the fifty-seven hundred cylinders into the parapet, instead of connecting them to spigots.

Speyer's men were not the first *Feldgrauen* to worry about these mysterious cylinders. A month earlier, the same cylinders had been dug into the parapets protecting General Berthold von Diemling's corps on the southeastern side of the Ypres Salient, near the British at Hill 60; gas killed two men when a stray British shell damaged a cylinder. After almost two weeks of the winds blowing towards Diemling's troops, Generaloberst Duke Albrecht of Württemberg, commander of the German 4th Army, ordered the cylinders moved to the northern side of the salient, directly in front of the French trenches held by units belonging to 87 Territorial and the 45 (Algerian) Division, often called the Turcos or Zouaves.[10]

Although what today are called weapons of mass destruction were banned by the Hague Conventions of 1899 and 1907, the idea of developing such weapons was still in the air. In 1914, the French had used rifle-launched *cartouches suffocants* filled with an eye, throat, and nose irritant. Secretary of State for War Lord Kitchener opposed the use of gas on the battlefield, but in late 1914 or early 1915, Sir Winston Churchill's Admiralty carried out tests to see if gas could be used in battle at sea. (The results were negative.) Between September 1914 and February 1915, at least five civilians wrote to the Department of Militia and Defence in Ottawa proposing schemes for delivering poison gas. The response to one read partly, "I am to thank you for your offer but to state that the use of asphyxiating or deleterious gases is not allowed by the International Declarations signed at the Hague, 29 July 1899."[11]

---

*The Dräger breathing apparatus was designed to help sailors escape sunken U-boats.

Oberste Heeresleitung (OHL, the German high command) had fewer scruples. In late September 1914, even before the Western Front had solidified into trench warfare, the chief of the German general staff, Erich von Falkenhayn, approved a plan to develop incendiary, smoke, irritant, or stink shells. Gestation time for this first generation of German gas weapons was short: by 27 October, three thousand Ni-shells filled with sternutatory dust (similar to sneezing powder) were on their way to the front. (The effect of these shells was negligible, however; indeed, the Allies were unaware of their use until after the war.) A few weeks later, the chemist Hans Tappen, whose brother worked for OHL, proposed adding the irritant xylyl bromide to the shells. By the end of January 1915, eighteen thousand T-shells (T for Tappen) had been used against Russian troops. The air of the Russian winter was too cold for the xylyl bromide to vaporize, however, and these shells too were ineffective. Neither a change in the chemical mixture nor the more favourable temperatures of Flanders in March led to more successful outcomes.

The German gas program was saved by the chemist Fritz Haber, who was already famous for having synthesized ammonia, an accomplishment for which he was awarded a Nobel Prize in 1918. In late 1914, Haber worked for the War Raw Materials Office developing a process to make artificial nitrates.* Though he was aware of the Hague Convention's limitation on the development of poison gas, Haber cleared his conscience (and later that of Otto Hahn, another future Nobel laureate recruited by Haber to the gas program) by arguing that the French had already voided the convention, and that gas "was a way of saving countless lives."[12]

Haber made two vital changes to the German gas program. First, he replaced the mixture of xylyl bromide and bromoacetone with chlorine, a significantly more irritating and deadly chemical. Second, he decided to deliver the gas not by exploding shells but by cylinders fitted with hoses

---

*The Royal Navy's blockade had cut Germany off from its traditional source of nitrates, Chilean guano, the key ingredient in both the fertilizer needed to produce food and the gunpowder needed for shells and bullets.

that extended over the parapet. Haber's calculations showed that a wind of five miles an hour would move the gas safely away from the German lines but still allow for the formation of a lethal gas cloud. In recognition of Haber's work, Kaiser Wilhelm put aside his anti-Semitism and commissioned him a captain in the militia; after the first gas attack, on 22 April, the Kaiser embraced Haber and awarded him the Iron Cross First Class.

Some officers in OHL opposed the use of deadly gas. Generaloberst Karl von Einem wrote to his wife, "I fear it will produce a tremendous scandal in the world.... War has nothing to do with chivalry any more. The higher civilization rises, the viler man becomes."[13] Crown Prince Ruprecht was also discomforted, albeit partially because he realized that, in time, the Allies would be able to use gas "against us ten times more often than we could."[14] (The fact that the prevailing winds at Ypres blew towards the German lines didn't ease his mind.) General von Diemling was "disgusted" by what OHL dubbed Operation *Desinfektion*.[15] OHL's lawyers assured Falkenhayn, however, that because the gas was released from cylinders, it did not violate the Hague Convention, which obligated Germany (as well as Britain, France, Austria-Hungary, and Russia) to "abstain from the use of projectiles the object of which is the diffusion of asphyxiating or deleterious gases."[16]

Given the failure of earlier attempts to attack using gas and the fact that there had been no large-scale tests of this top-secret weapon, OHL remained sceptical about its prospects for success. Still, the Germans believed that such an attack would augment the assault on the Western Front, which was designed to cover the withdrawal of sixteen regiments stationed around Ypres. (Falkenhayn had ordered these regiments sent east to Galacia, in Poland, where they attacked Russian troops in the Carpathian Mountains.) Although Duke Albrecht believed that if everything went perfectly, his men would take Ypres—and thus either capture tens of thousands of British, French, Belgian, and Canadian troops or force the Allies to abandon the symbolic salient—his orders conformed to Falkenhayn's wishes to "not set any too distant objectives for the attack."[17] On the German right, units of the XXIII Reserve Corps were assigned the task of jumping the Yser Canal at Het Sas, about seven miles northwest of Ypres. The main thrust, however, was directed at seizing the "ridge along the road Boezinge-Pilckem-Langemarck-Poelcappele," and then "[digging] in immediately and [establishing] mutually covering strong points."[18] Just days before the attack, OHL had vetoed the Navy Infantry Corps' offer of two regiments to bolster Duke Albrecht's force.

. . .

The poisoned cloud that Haber toasted at a party a few days after the gas attack on 22 April was perhaps the worst-kept secret in modern warfare.* The first hard evidence of it came on 13 April, when Private August Jäger (RIR 234) crawled over the German parapet, through no man's land, and surrendered to French troops belonging to the 11th Division.[19] In addition to telling Général Edmond Ferry about the gas cylinders and revealing that the signal for launching the attack was three red flares dropped from an airplane, Jäger gave Ferry his *Riechpäckchen*. Made of either cotton or jute tow (short fibres woven into matting), the protective gas mask resembled a surgical mask; to neutralize the chlorine, it was soaked in a solution of sodium hyposulphite.

Ferry's superior, Général Henri Gabriel Putz, was sceptical. Putz thought that Jäger "had exhibited such great knowledge of the German position and defence arrangements, that he [Putz] had come to the conclusion that the man had been primed and sent over with the intention to deceive."[20] Putz later upbraided Ferry for sending the information garnered from Jäger to the British and the Canadians.**

Over the next thirty-six hours, evidence piled up. At 7:00 a.m. on 15 April, Private Julius Rapsahl surrendered to the French near Langemarck. Rapsahl too carried a gas mask and told a story similar to Jäger's. Six and

---

*Not all of Haber's friends and relations were pleased by his role in initiating gas warfare. Haber returned home to find that his wife, a chemist in her own right, had committed suicide using his service revolver. Before the year was out, Haber had married one of his assistants.

**A German court sentenced Jäger to ten years in prison for treason after Ferry's article "*Ce qui s'est passé sur l'Yser*" was published in 1932.

a half hours later, General Alderson was notified that the Germans had moved up reserves, and that they "intend[ed] on making use of tubes with asphyxiating gas."[21] Before the morning was out, Allied intelligence officers had still more evidence, in the form of a German communiqué claiming that on 14 April, "the French employed mines emitting yellow asphyxiating gases." (Germany's practice was to blame the Allies for tactics its own army would soon be using.) Another communiqué—this one accusing the British of using—was published on 16 April. During the night of 15 April, Currie wrote in his private diary, "Attack expected at night to be preceded by sending of poisonous gases to our lines and the sending of three red lights."[22]

After the war, Major Andrew McNaughton said that since no one could imagine what a gas attack would look like, little was done to prepare for one.* Hindsight can, however, obscure as much as it reveals. Actions *were* taken. At least one British plane stayed out until 7:00 p.m. and may have seen some of the cylinders at Broodseinde. McNaughton was issued ninety extra shells with which to probe for the gas cylinders. And after hearing that "this evening the enemy will attack our lines using asphyxiating gas to overcome our men in the trenches," the Canadian Medical Corps readied for one thousand wounded.[23]

The night of 15 April passed without a gas attack, but it was not quiet. Just before 6:00 p.m., movement in front of his 5th Battalion alarmed Lieutenant-Colonel George Tuxford, who, though Welsh-born, was something of a legend for having led the largest cattle drive in Canadian history, from his farm in Saskatchewan, north across the Rockies, to the boom town of Dawson City, so its citizens would not go meatless. His men stood to, arms at the ready, until midnight. Sometime during the night, Lieutenant-Colonel Robert Leckie's 16th Battalion received "orders to stand ready to move at a moment's notice" from the village of

---

*Lieutenant-General McNaughton commanded the Canadian army between the outbreak of the Second World War in 1939 until mid-1943; he was minister of defence from mid-1944 through the end of the war.

Cassel to Brigadier-General Richard Turner's headquarters at what was officially called the Château du Nord but soon acquired the nickname Shell Trap Farm (a name, Canada's official historian wrote puckishly, that was "so fitting that it was soon changed again to 'Mouse Trap Farm'").[24]

Leckie's men were not called out, though they were not untouched by German guns. At 8:30 p.m., Major Ross was "shot through arm and on the head"; of this latter wound, the war diary adds hopefully, "Seems light." At least four members of the 7th Battalion stationed near Locality "C," a strategic position on the southern side of Gravenstafel Ridge, were not as lucky. The battalion's war diary records, "Very heavily shelled 4 killed 10 wounded. Trenches in poor condition. Position enfiladed by enemy artillery fire."

The next morning, the Belgian army, which occupied the extreme left (west) of the Allied lines at the Yser Canal, issued an information bulletin titled "*Usage de gaz asphyxiants.*" The bulletin's title testifies to the speed at which the Allies, who did not have the technology to launch a gas attack themselves, accepted that such attacks were imminent. The bulletin said:

> The Germans have had made in Ghent, on a rush order, 20,000 mouth protectors of Tulle, which the soldiers will carry in a waterproof bag 10 cm. by 17.5 cm.
>
> The mouth protectors, soaked with a suitable liquid, will serve to protect the men against the heavy asphyxiating gas which the Germans intend to discharge towards the enemy lines, notably in front of the XXVI Reserve Corps.
>
> The men of that corps have recently received at Roulers special instruction to learn the handling of gas cylinders; these last will be placed on the ground, to the extend of one battery of 20 cylinders every 40 meters.[25]

• • •

Thirty-six hours later, it was the British, not the Germans, who attacked. At 7:00 p.m. on 17 April, sappers detonated thousands of pounds of gunpowder and gun cotton they had secreted in tunnels beneath Hill 60, about six and a half miles to the right rear of the Canadian lines on Gravenstafel Ridge. Named for its height in metres, Hill 60 provided the Germans with a panoramic view of the salient. British troops followed fast on the explosion, which tore apart the hill, sending debris from German trenches (and much of the hill itself, which was little more than a waste heap) as much as three hundred feet in the air. The Tommies quickly gained the lip of the craters and some territory beyond.

The Germans counterattacked in force. Amid the rubble of the hill, unit cohesion quickly gave way to hand-to-hand combat. Even more devastating for the British were the thousands of shells fired by the forty-four German batteries that arced around what amounted to a small salient of its own. Some of those batteries fired T-shells. The gas from those shells combined with the fumes of the high-explosive shells to create a torturous mixture that burned eyes and throats. The flash of the explosions, and the resulting smoke and dust, cut visibility to ten yards or less. What trenches the British were able to dig soon became "choked with dead, wounded, debris and mud as to be well nigh impassable." Worse, the German shells cut the telephone lines that connected the British to the artillery behind them, "so that support offered by the British guns was necessarily less effective."[26]

Armies almost never willingly give up ground—even such militarily unnecessary ground as the Ypres Salient. But if the Allies held on to Ypres for symbolic reasons, the Germans fought to regain what they called Höhe 60 (or at least stop the British on the remains of the hill) for an important tactical reason. Had the British advanced into the German lines to the left and right of the hill, they would have found hundreds of gas-filled cylinders that had not been moved to the north side of the salient. Although the Germans did not retake the remnants of Höhe 60, they achieved the key objective of preventing the British from discovering the gas cylinders.

By 21 April, the battle had so drained the British forces in the area that Brigadier-General Malcolm Mercer was ordered to have his 1st

Canadian Infantry Brigade (then acting as the division's reserve) ready to march within an hour's time. While Mercer's men prepared themselves for an order that never came, German officers ordered the men of Reserve-Infanterie-Regiments 233, 234, 235, 236, 238, and 239 to hoist their packs and march out of their bivouacs in the Houthoulst Forest. They were headed for collection points a short distance behind the German lines, above the village of Langemarck.

PART 2

# Operation *Desinfektion*
5:00 p.m., 22 April to 12:00 a.m., 23 April 1915

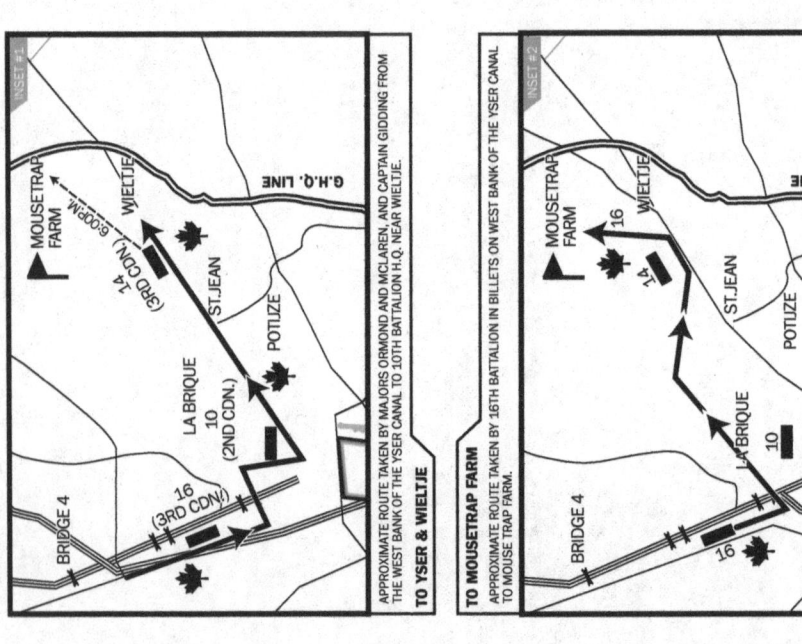

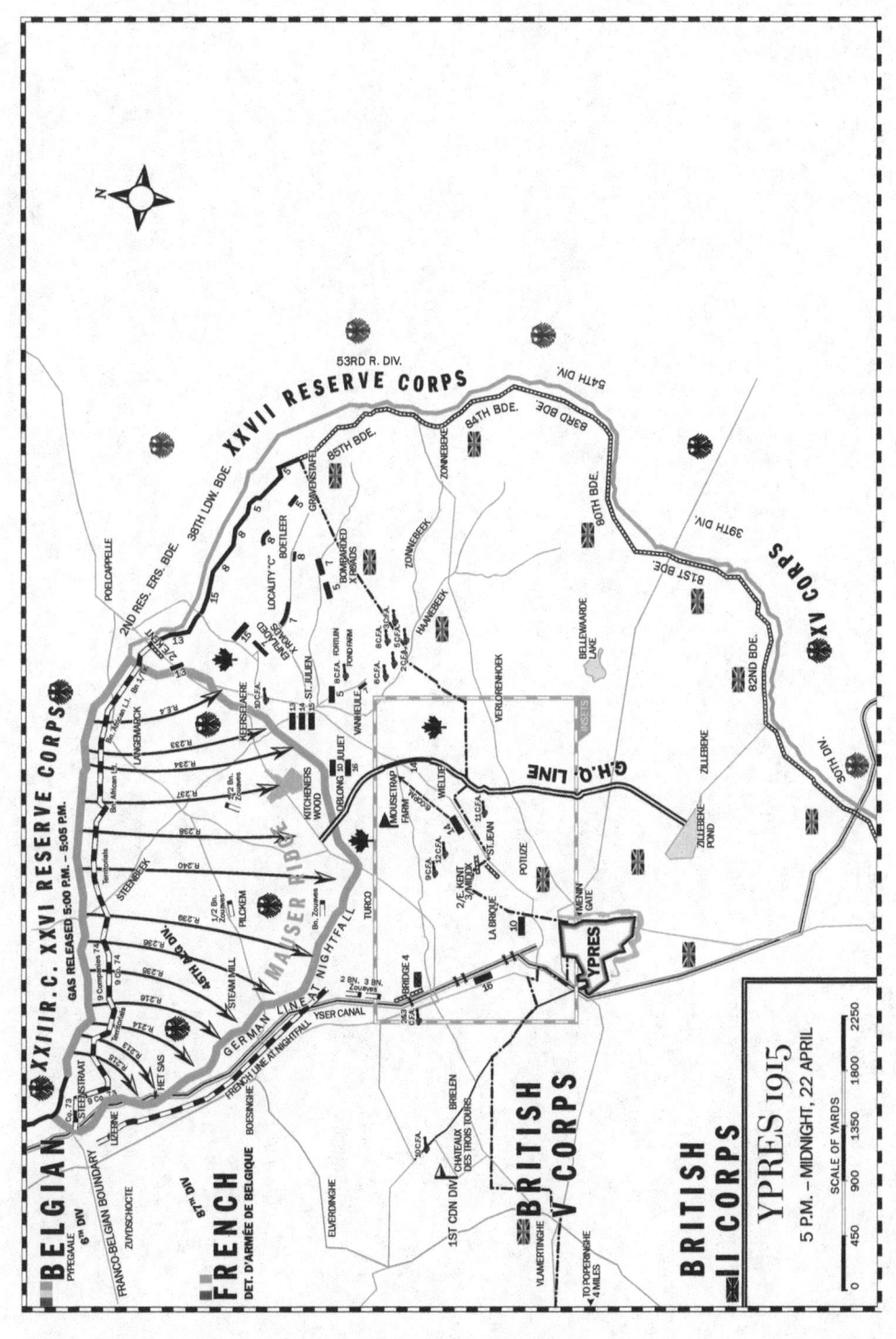

CHAPTER 2

# "The Carnival of Death Sings Loudly"
## The First Gas Attack

*Le carnaval de mort se chante à grands éclats*
*Le carnaval lugubre à l'haleine empestée*
*Le carnaval de haine et de rage entêtées*
*Serpente au long des champs dans la Flandres, là-bas...*
—Maurice Gauchez, "Les gaz"

On 20 April 1915, as their comrades on the southeastern side of the salient poured thousands of shells onto Höhe 60, German artillerists on the northern side stepped up their shelling of Ypres and the villages to its north, east, and west. During the first hours of the bombardment, shells struck the dead as well as the living. In the little village of Elverdinghe, three and a half miles northeast of Ypres, Major Arthur E. Kirkpatrick of the 3rd Battalion watched as shells fell in the "cemetery, smashing tombstones to atoms and disinterring the dead, throwing bodies to the surface and exposing them in a disgusting manner."

Jack Johnsons, fifteen-centimetre heavy shells named for the first African-American heavyweight champion, fell on the city that the Kaiser's gunners sought to destroy. Demolishing the city was part of a larger plan that included turning her population into refugees who would clog the roads and make it difficult to bring up reinforcements. With a roar like a railroad train, these shells gouged forty-foot-wide holes into the ground as they threw up huge plumes of black smoke. Canon Frederick Scott of the 16th Battalion, who joined the 1st Canadian Division against the wishes of his Montreal presbytery, saw one crush a large house, and in the rubble he later saw his first mangled body. By nightfall, he had counted more than a hundred dead and wounded soldiers and civilians.

Through 21 April, the bombardment built. (Germany suffered nothing like the Shell Crisis then gripping the British and the Canadians.) Some shells landed in St. Julien, a short distance east of Ypres, near the headquarters of the 13th Battalion. Shrapnel exploded in a blue haze over the trenches of the 8th and 5th Battalions on Gravenstafel Ridge. High-explosive shells, nicknamed "whizz-bangs," also pummelled the 8th Battalion, leaving in their wake blasted trenches and "a disagreeable poisonous-smelling gas, which particularly affects the eyes." At 6:00 a.m., high-explosive shells destroyed part of the 5th Battalion's parapet and damaged a machine-gun emplacement. A very heavy fusillade began in the early afternoon, destroying trenches and a dugout.

The words "Casualties 4. Killed 2. Wounded 2," written by Captain Edward Hilliam, the 5th Battalion's war diarist, capture neither the humour with which the Canadians faced the shells nor the horror of instant death. In a letter home, Private Victor Swanston described how at one point his buddy H. P. used his rifle as a baseball bat and swung at the incoming whizz-bangs, yelling, "Come on, Fritz, put one over the plate!" A second later, a shell ripped through the roof of the shelter where Swanston stood, killing "two of the men at our feet and [tearing] all the flesh from the inside of the other man's leg." H. P. was one of those hit. When a medic saw H. P.'s wound, he told Swanston that his friend would not last the night and gave the farmer from outside Ottawa a handful of morphine tablets, saying, "Give him a few of these every time he yells."

• • •

At 10:00 p.m., not long after Canon Scott paced off the ground for the first Canadian cemetery in Flanders, Leutnant Richard Drach, who commanded the 4th Company of Reserve-Infanterie-Regiment 238 received the order for his men to stand to. And soon, for the second time in three days, spike-headed Germans were marching out of the Houthoulst Forest towards their assembly point near Mangelarre, a village about a mile behind the German front line.* A few hours later, thousands of other *Feldgrauen* moved into their positions, all, recalled Leutnant Becker, "brim[ming] with confidence." Near 2:00 a.m., Oberst Otto Peterson ordered his Pioniers to remove the sandbags protecting the chlorine-laden cylinders. Then they screwed thin lead tubes into the valves. Somehow, despite the bright light of the moon, French scouts didn't see the Dräger-wearing Pioniers slip over the parapet and cut breaks in their wire, nor did they see Peterson's men bend the long lead tubes in their direction. The scouts missed their one chance; within moments, the tubes were hidden by sandbags.

. . .

The shelling grew heavier on 22 April. An awful smoking hole that Canon Scott found had moments earlier been a hospital. The hole gave him the same "eerie feeling [he] had experienced when looking down the crater of Vesuvius." A short time later, another of the "uncanny" explosions blew out the stained glass of a chapel where Scott was helping to tend the wounded.[1]

Throughout the abnormally warm afternoon, shells ignited fires that burned all the more fiercely because of the moderate northerly breeze. Across the city, houses collapsed—sometimes trapping people inside, and sometimes raining dust and brick on the thousands of "poor creatures, mostly women and children, with a sprinkling of old men, wearily march[ing] along carrying the small worldly possessions that they could not force themselves to leave behind." The lucky mothers had only "misery stamped on their faces." The unlucky carried bloodied infants through the devastated streets. Sergeant-Major George W. Gorman of

---

*The Germans had also assembled for the attack on the night of 4/5 April.

the 8th Battalion, a thirty-six-year-old who had been a journalist before the war, watched the exodus from Ypres. "Old people and sick people," he wrote, "many of whom had been bedridden for years, or who had remained near the family stove, brought up the rear of this big army of refugees.... One old man, evidently past eighty, trundl[ed] a wheelbarrow in which was an old lady of equal age, with her feet bound up.... He would stop to rest every ten feet."[2]

Shrapnel drove some into the ditches beside the road and others onto the fields beyond them. At a place called Dead Man's Corner, the terror became too much for one young mother, who stopped in her tracks, her children gathered helplessly around her. Amid the tumult, a Canadian major stopped his horse, reached down, and took her hand before placing her family in the care of a corporal, who took them to a nearby farmhouse. Sergeant Harry Leacock of the 7th Battalion saw "one woman [who] had her breast torn open by a piece of shell."[3] Half a century later, the image of a "woman carrying a baby and the baby's head gone" still haunted Nathaniel Nicholson (16th Battalion), who also had gone to see the Lakenhalle on what all agreed was, except for the shelling, a fine spring day on which the larks did indeed sing.

The bursting shells also fell on Canadian positions, though not all positions and not all at once. The men of the 1st Battalion, billeted in Vlamertinghe, stopped their football game every few minutes so they could watch the shells bursting over the city two miles away. The 4th Battalion, also in billets on the west side of the Yser Canal, spent the afternoon in company training.

On Gravenstafel Ridge, things were different. At 4:00 a.m. on 22 April, Lieutenant-Colonel Tuxford noticed numerous German planes flying undisturbed over his trenches on the right of the ridge. An hour later, likely using the coordinates provided by those aircraft, German gunners let loose a fusillade. One that began at noon destroyed the parapets that Tuxford's men had built up during the night. Eighty high-explosive shells hit nearby unused trenches.

The bombardment raised tensions at Lieutenant-Colonel William

Hart-McHarg's 7th Battalion headquarters in the village of Wieltje, three miles behind the Canadian line. In the morning, Hart-McHarg had given thirty-five-year-old Victor Odlum, nicknamed "Pea Soup" Odlum because he would not allow his men their rum ration, permission to go to Ypres to see the effects of the bombardment. By the time Major Odlum returned, the shelling had taken its toll on everyone's nerves. Talk centred on a possible gas attack. "We could not visualize an attack with gas," remembered Odlum. "We could not guess where the gas would come from or how we would recognize it when it did come." The Canadians had been ordered to take all necessary precautions, but "we did not know what were the necessary precautions, and no one could tell us. So, in the end, like all the others, we simply did nothing except prepare for [an ordinary] attack."

Despite the shells racing overhead and the explosions to their rear and far right, the men of the 13th Battalion, who held the far left of the Canadian line, were significantly less tense than their comrades on Gravenstafel Ridge. At 4:00 p.m., Lieutenant Ian Sinclair, two captains, and an infantryman, Todd Bath, "enjoyed a glorious tea of Scottish shortbread and chocolate biscuits outside Bath's dugout."[4] An hour later, as Pionierregiment 35 waited for the order to open the valves atop the gas-filled cylinders, Lieutenant-Colonel Edward Morrissey lay on the parados, sunning himself and talking to the tall, handsome Captain Guy M. Drummond, the scion of a wealthy, bilingual French Montreal family (and considered by many to be a future prime minister), who was writing a letter to his mother. Farther back, near where the Yser Canal meets Ypres, Private Bernard C. Lunn (16th Battalion) and his buddies were in their skivvies, having stripped off their uniforms to delouse them. Majors Joseph MacLaren and Daniel Ormond and Captain George Gidding, all of the 10th Battalion, were on horseback, riding along the west side of the canal. And near Vlamertinghe, Colonel Mason and a couple of other officers of the 3rd Battalion eagerly opened a recently delivered parcel from Fortnum and Mason, the purveyor of fine foods on Piccadilly Square.

• • •

Throughout most of 22 April, the atmosphere of the German and the Canadian headquarters differed greatly. Shortly after 1:00 a.m., Peterson's communication officer picked up the telephone that connected to the trenches north of Langemarck and said, "*Sieben, sieben, sieben, sieben*" ("Seven, seven, seven, seven"). Within minutes, more than four thousand men belonging to the 46th, 52nd, 51st, and 53rd reserve divisions readied themselves to go over the top. At 1:45 a.m., the wind that was needed to push the deadly gas forward abated, and soon there came an order delaying the attack to sometime between 4:00 a.m. and 7:00 a.m. At 5:20 a.m., the order came to launch the gas in twenty-five minutes. But ten minutes before the valves were to be opened, the wind changed direction and the attack was again put off. "At 8.30 a.m. (GMT) the battalion received the message that the attack would not take place before 4.00 p.m. (GMT). Everyone and everything was to stay where it was in the densely packed trenches."[5]

Despite the heavy shelling and the growing column of refugees from Ypres, General Alderson and his staff at the rather grandiosely named Château des Trois Tours, a two-storey house with three small towers on the west side of the Yser Canal, considered the situation to be normal. Even word near noon that a Royal Air Corps pilot flying behind German lines had seen "signs of activities about Forêt d'Houthulst" and a column of troops moving south towards the village of Poelcappelle* did not trigger alarm.[6] Such movements were normal, for both the Germans and the Allies tried not to keep their troops in the trenches for longer than four or five days. After that, they were rotated to their battalion reserve (close to, but not at, the line) and then to the divisional reserve, where they could bathe, rekit, and rest a little. At 2:45 p.m., the most important message Alderson's staff had to send to Mouse Trap Farm was the following:

---

*Poelcappelle was about a thousand yards north of the juncture of the Canadian and French lines.

To 3rd Can. Inf. Bde..
A.A. 645. 22nd April 1915.

There are one hundred mouth organs at divin'l HQ. for you aaa Please call for them aaa No cards available just now but will send you some out of next consignment

From 1st Canadian Div. 2.45 p.m.<br>
*By wire received before 3.05 p.m.*

At 5:00 p.m., a German spotter plane dropped three red flares. A moment later, Big Bertha, the huge howitzer that fired two-ton shells, began firing on Ypres.

• • •

The flares signalled Peterson's Pionier regiment to open the valves on the thousands of steel cylinders, which together contained 160 tons of chlorine. The men "leapt from cylinder to cylinder so that the gas cloud was released evenly. A hissing sound began, as though a hundred pipes were letting off steam," recalled Leutnant Becker of RIR 238. "As the cloud rolled forward it was yellowish-green, a hellish, sulphurous haze." As brigadier-generals and their staffs climbed to the roofs of the trenches to watch the cloud move towards the Allied lines at almost five miles an hour, regimental officers ordered their men to put on their gear, including their *Riechpäckchen*. Regiments divided into columns, companies into platoons. Leutnant Drach (RIR 238) recalled that "behind the cloud as if through a thin veil, one can see the landscape bathed in glorious sunshine. It was an enchanting sight."

• • •

The Canadians' commander, General Alderson, and General Harry Burstall were among the first to see the gas cloud form and blow over the French lines. At 5:00 p.m., they had just finished visiting the 12th Battery, Canadian Field Artillery, near Gravenstafel Ridge. Immediately after hearing heavy rifle fire from the French lines to his left, Alderson saw two clouds of yellowish-green smoke. As the clouds rose, they spread out and soon merged into one gigantic cloud. Two or so miles to Alderson's left rear, Captain John W. Warden, a veteran of both the Spanish-American and Boer wars, was also watching the wall of gas and wondering what it was.

Alderson's fortuitous visit to the 12th Battery had put him in a position to see the gas attack begin, and he soon realized that behind the furious bombardment unleashed with it, the Germans were advancing rapidly; unfortunately, this would be the last time the general was so well informed. His presence on Gravenstafel Ridge meant that he risked being cut off from the Château des Trois Tours. By the time he and Burstall reached the hamlet of Fortuin, about a third of the way back to Wieltje, the units billeted there had already stood to. By the time the generals reached Wieltje, where they had left their horses, the French "on the Sector from the POELCAPPELLE road to the canal," Alderson wrote in his report, "were retreating before the gas."

• • •

The effect of the chlorine on the soldiers was almost instantaneous. Exposure to as little as thirty parts per million causes vomiting, coughing, and difficulty breathing. Exposure to one thousand parts per million is fatal. The German gas cloud was made up of hundreds of times this amount. Chlorine's outer shell of electrons is incomplete (it has seven electrons in a ring that can contain eighteen), and thus the element is a powerful oxidizing agent, which is why it is used as a bleach and is added to water to kill bacteria.

Inhaled chlorine combines with water vapour and other bodily fluids to form hydrochloric acid—which, because of its reactivity, burns lungs and other tissues. The body's immediate response, the secretion of more fluids, is deadly. Some of the fluids meant to defend the body are turned into more hydrochloric acid, and those fluids not so affected fill the lungs, causing drowning. Wilfred Owen, in his famous poem "*Dulce et Decorum Est,*" captures the new type of death unleashed that afternoon:

> But someone still was yelling and stumbling,
> And flound'ring like a man in fire or lime . . .
> Dim, through the misty panes and thick green light,
> As under a green sea, I saw him drowning.

It did not take long for British and Canadian medical officers to realize that the French had been poisoned by chlorine gas. Their shock, however, is clear from the words of one medical officer, who exclaimed, when he saw the blue faces of the North African troops, "Cyanosis,* but how the Hades?"[7] Over the next few days, in field stations and in hospitals behind the line, men lay dying. Some were in a state of stupor, too weak even to swat away the flies that were attracted by the smell of rotting flesh; others were sitting and gasping for breath, their faces a deep blue, until "they passed into the undiscovered country."[8]

• • •

"As the sun broke from behind a cloud," recalled Leutnant Becker of RIR 238, "this new and monstrously beautiful image was lit up before us." The regimental historian who recorded Becker's words also noted that from a "chemical point of view," it was greatly advantageous for the gas attack to have been delayed to 5:00 p.m. "The ground had been warmed by the spring sun," he wrote. "And, therefore, the chlorine cloud did not stick to the ground as much as would have been the case in the early hours of the morning." In other words, because the ground was warm, the gas stayed high, where men could not help breathing in more of it.

For a short time, the Germans heard the sound of the French firing their rifles into the cloud. More than one German officer wrote of an

---

*Caused by oxygen-deficient blood, cyanosis is a bluish discoloration of the skin.

artillery barrage so heavy that it seemed as though "all hell had broken loose." Before Becker's men, exploding shells "threw up pillars of earth and wood and stone." Amid the earth and wood and stone were pieces of the bodies of French territorial and North African troops.

Sergeant Leisterer, whose Reserve-Infanterie-Regiment 233 attacked near the spot where the French lines joined the Canadian, recalled the first moments of 2nd Ypres:

> At the beginning a whitish gas drifted from the long tubes over the parapet. Soon it took on a yellowish green colour, rolling in an interminable cloud, sneaking across the earth towards the enemy trench.
>
> One had a sensation as if some beautifully horrible natural event was taking place. The impression was tremendous. But now was not the time for dreaming. The rattling and bursting on the other side—as if all Hell had broken loose.
>
> Just let them fire. Our cover is good.
>
> Without stopping the gas flowed toward the enemy. Soon, it had covered 150 metres and had reached the enemy trench. It must have had an effect by now.
>
> And in fact, the firing soon became less and less, so that we put our heads above the cover without exposing ourselves to danger.

• • •

When he saw the greenish-yellow cloud form, the Royal Air Force's Louis A. Strange (6 Squadron), who was on a gun-spotting mission, dropped down two thousand feet to investigate. He quickly realized that he was witnessing the beginning of the first successful poison gas attack in history. As he raced back towards the aerodrome at Abeele, just outside the village of Poperinghe, to brief Lieutenant-General Sir Herbert Plumer, commander of V Corps (to which the 1st Canadian Division belonged), French and Canadian troops began breathing poisoned air and dying.*

---

*Strange's report may not have been Plumer's first word of the attack. Within minutes, British

Among the first French troops to feel the effects of gas was Jean-Marie Bonhommie, a forty-nine-year-old lieutenant with the 73e Régiment d'Infanterie Territoriale. Somehow, he remained conscious. "Many of us had fallen exhausted while others were so incapacitated that they were unable to hold [their positions] under the poisoned cloud."[9]

Part of the gas cloud rolled over the extreme left of the 13th Battalion. Concerned about the reliability of Algerian troops on his left, Lieutenant-Colonel Frederick Loomis had placed his strongest company (commanded by Reggie McQualigan) and a machine-gun company (commanded by Jimmie Ross) on the battalion's left. As McQualigan's and Ross's men watched the greenish-yellow haze engulf the Algerian lines, their eyes watered, then burned; their throats tingled, then burned. According to Lieutenant Sinclair, bleeding Zouaves, some of whom had arrived just in time to die, poured into the trenches at the same time as the gas. As the Zouaves yelled "*Gaz, gaz!*" someone near Sinclair realized what the gas was and told his comrades to "pee on [their] handkerchiefs and keep them across [their] faces."

Though disgusting to breathe through, urine-soaked handkerchiefs were more effective than the water-soaked socks used by reserve companies stationed behind the line. Chlorine dissolves in water, but the water quickly turns to a bleach-like liquid, which would have burned the men's faces; worse yet, breathing through chlorine-soaked cloths quickly exposed the men to lethal quantities of chlorine gas. Urea, one of the main components of urine, is caustic, and thus neutralizes the hydrochloric acid.

Likely the first Canadians to die at 2nd Ypres were nine men from Colonel Lawrence V. Moore Cosgrave's Divisional Artillery. When the gas was released, they were behind the Algerian lines, moving up three batteries to support Turner's 3rd Infantry Brigade. As the concussions

---

soldiers at a V Corps reporting centre five miles southwest of Langemarck started smelling a strange odour and felt a tingling in their noses and throats. It is not known, however, when their report reached V Corps headquarters.

from exploding shells pummelled the ears of Allied and German soldiers, the gas cloud rolled towards Cosgrave's men. They were soon passed by fleeing Turcos, who must have looked like those who, a short time later, would stream past Lieutenant-Colonel E. W. B. "Dinky" Morrison's ammunition column, then heading towards Ypres. "Many of them were Turcos who were apparently mad with fear, and the fact that they were foaming at the mouth as the result of the gases added weight to this supposition," wrote Morrison. Cosgrave grabbed one passing soldier, only to find that the panicked North African did not speak English.

Then came the smell. One of Cosgrave's men, a former chemist in a drugstore, immediately identified the cloud as chlorine. As the poisonous vapour thickened around him, Cosgrave reached for his field telephone to warn the nine men moving the guns. But to his horror, he discovered that the phone no longer worked. "I had three or four men with me and they didn't get it," he later recalled, "but the lads out in the lines got it."

• • •

Fortunately, the phone lines between the front-line French commanders and Colonel Jacques Mordacq's headquarters continued to work. As the cloud engulfed his men, Major Villevaleix, who commanded the Tirailleurs, called with a message that made Mordacq wonder if the major had "*perdu sa tête*" (lost his mind). In a halting, painful, and broken voice, Villevaleix said, "We are being violently attacked by an immense column of yellow smoke coming from the German lines all along the front; the Tirailleurs have begun to evacuate their trenches, beaten in retreat, many are falling asphyxiated." Moments later, Villevaleix called again, and before the line went dead, he managed to tell his stunned commander, "*Tout le monde tombe autour de moi, je quitte mon P.C.*" ("Everyone around me has fallen, I must flee my H.Q.").[10] Many of those who survived the gas attack lived only long enough for men like Sergeant Leisterer (RIR 233) to pick them out through the thinning gas cloud and start shooting: "There, they are running.... They are taking to the hills.... Really, there another one was running back. There two. They are blacks. Go ahead! Just level them.... It's just like shooting at hares. We're firing at them standing without any cover. Here and there one somersaulted and fell on the ground."

While Leisterer's men shot down the French, Mordacq rode out to investigate, accompanied by several Saphi troops. Soon he too saw the yellow cloud, and he and his North African cavalry, whose uniforms included a trademark white cape, felt first the tell-tale tingling in their noses and throats, and then a violent buzzing in their ears as breathing became more difficult in the poisoned air. If anything, though, the scene before them was even more difficult to take in. Men who just moments earlier had proudly worn their distinctive *képis* were now just fugitives "without weapons, haggard, greatcoats thrown away ... running like madmen, begging for water in loud cries, spitting blood, some even rolling on the ground making desperate efforts to breathe."[11]

• • •

With Alderson still en route to his headquarters, the first word that the Canadian command had of the attack was a message that the 3rd Brigade sent at 5:13 p.m. It begins, incongruously enough, with the words "Situation quiet," before going on to say, "Left section reports observing at 5:00 p.m. a cloud of green vapour several hundred yards in length between the French trenches to our left and those of the Enemy." A message sent by the 2nd Brigade at 5:25 p.m. also calls the situation normal before going on to draw attention to the strange lighting effect of what were thought to be "melinite shells."

• • •

In the two minutes that followed the 3rd Brigade's 5:13 message, German officers counted down to when soldiers from about a dozen Reserve-Infanterie-Regiments—their *Riechpäckchen* tied around their faces, their sixty-pound packs on their backs, and their Mauser rifles slung over their shoulders—would go over the top.* Whatever differences separated the Germans from the Allies, little divided the millions of soldiers in the moments before they charged into no man's land:

> Enervated by the effort of screwing themselves up in the minutes before zero hour, their senses numbed by the deafening racket around them, caught up unthinkingly in the corporate rush forwards, the troops were more like zombies devoid of their everyday feelings of fear, squeamishness or compassion. No abstract concepts *persuaded* them to go forwards; nor did rational calculations make them deem it wise to turn back. They were caught up in the sheer momentum of the forward rush; an unthinking mass pushing forward.[12]

Preceded by sappers with assault boards and wire-cutting tools, the *Feldgrauen* for the most part faced little opposition. For Leutnant Sackure (RIR 238), the attack felt like "a training exercise." The resistance that survived in isolated pockets was "quickly dealt with in short exchanges of fire or bayonet." The Germans, recalled Lieutenant Bonhommie, "crossed our front lines with unseen speed, fell on our forward batteries and took and reversed our second lines, the majority of the defenders of which were captured."[13]

As the cloud rolled farther into the salient, Leutnant Mattenklott's 8th Company seized a French battery of seven heavy guns. Other units quickly and easily reached their objective, Pilckem (Mauser) Ridge, and then continued past (surprisingly, given the German army's reputation for discipline) "without waiting for orders." By dusk, Mattenklott's men had torn a hole almost three miles deep in the Allied lines; all together, the *Feldgrauen* had opened up an almost five-mile gap in lines that had been static since 1st Ypres.

After overrunning the French in their sector, Leutnant Drach's men

---

*From the Allied point of view, ranging from left to right, the units were the 215, 213, 214, 216, 237, R Jg 24, 239, 240, 238, 235, 236, 234, and 233.

used the Algerians' own trench to shoot at the fleeing troops. Later they would learn that one of the few surviving French artillery units had shelled the Dreikellerhaus, killing three senior regimental officers. But at the moment, all they knew was that French shells were falling *behind* them, and they were free to execute their attack as planned, "turn[ing] half to the right" immediately in front of Langemarck. Drach's men seized one of the bridges spanning the Steenbeek (*beek* means "creek" in Flemish), but they found it too narrow to march across in fours. A number of men broke ranks, and soon their hobnailed boots were splashing through the creek. Just as their comrades broke into the French trenches two miles to their right, Drach's men arrived at the railroad line that bisected the salient. A quick investigation revealed that the railroad cars spotted earlier by German aviators "were simple wagons and not the suspected armoured train." Drach's men "reached the road from Langemarck to Pilckem with unexpected quickness."

. . .

During one of the nights before the attack, a major belonging to Reserve-Infanterie-Regiment 239 made a fool of himself when he told his men they could orient themselves at night by using the star above Ypres, only to realize a moment later that the star would be in a different position at 9:00 p.m. than it was at 4:00 a.m. He then pointed to the turret of a house that he believed housed an *estaminet* (a bar that served hot food) and named it the Star of Pilckem. The regiment's historian does not record what the divisional priest thought of the (blasphemous) fact that the Star of Pilckem became "almost as well known as the Star of Bethlehem is in the Bible." He does record, however, that shortly before gas billowed over the ground, the priest raised his right hand and made the sign of the cross over the kneeling German soldiers.

When these soldiers stood up and looked over their parapet, "where before there was just emptiness, gutted houses and dark basement halls and open terrain," they saw "hundreds of people as holes, trenches, dugouts spewed forth their inhabitants into the daylight." Then what the regimental historian referred to as the "pent-up desire to fight, the primordial German desire to combat (that can only actualize itself in times of peace during festivities when students draw their rapiers)" erupted. Even in translation, the awful horror of the event comes through:

> It is a unique picture. The setting sun like a fireball. The spring green landscape.
>
> The sky a flaming red with puff balls of pink and whitish clouds and everywhere the grey shadows racing ahead.
>
> The light mirroring from the bayonets. Here and there glittering sparks.
>
> In front of the assault line and assault columns, the yellow greenish gas cloud; it is rolling forward in big condensed layers like an aerial wall carrying disaster into the enemy lines. It crawls over green fields, descends into the trenches and flows through the batteries high. High in the air like birds of prey, shrapnel bursts near them.

By the time the French artillery on the west side of the Yser Canal began firing on the German trenches, RIR 239's 2nd Company was already on the road that connects Horteeter and Pilckem, its flank covered by its 1st Company. Amid "shouts of hooray" and the sound of French shells exploding to the right and left of them, the Germans heard a house blow up, then the clatter of bricks, now just so much debris, falling among trees. Everywhere, bullets "raced through the air, knocked into walls and hit the ground." Within fifteen minutes, the 4th, 3rd, 9th, and 10th Companies had reached the 2nd French line, where they found gassed French soldiers on top of the trenches, "vomiting their guts out."

The 2nd Company's orders were to dig in at the railway embankment, three thousand yards from its jumping-off point. Again, the officers could not reel in their men. A mine blew up and showered the 2nd Company with smoke and dust. Then the men came under shellfire from French guns on the other side of the canal and gunfire from isolated pockets of French soldiers who had survived in the farms around Pilckem. Small units soon silenced these last; a house with a machine gun was taken in an attack preceded by smoke grenades. The hamlet itself soon fell, and the victors found "half-finished letters . . . books and reports," and food still on the tables.

. . .

Among the French soldiers taken prisoner was Captain Tremsal of the 1st Battalion of the Light African Infantry, which had been stationed at the northern end of Langemarck. Within moments of the release of the chlorine, a runner from a trench almost two hundred yards away from Tremsal's had arrived. "Captain, there's no way of holding out," he told him. "They're sending poison at us." As the cloud changed the light over Tremsal's trench, he ordered Lieutenant Chevalier to move his reserve section behind the ruined houses near Langemarck. Before the move was complete, however, Tremsal's men began to flee. Tremsal tried to rally them, calling out, "*Les Joyeux n'ont jamais perdu de tranchées, ralliement à moi!*"* But it was too late. Soon,

> [an] atrocious sensation of burning caught in our throats and our lungs refused to breathe the same poisoned air, bloody froth came from our noses and mouths in such large quantities that the pastron of my hood was covered. The asphyxiating started to be felt. Remaining there was impossible. I yelled the order to retreat. . . . Whoever fell, and because they could not breathe could not get back up, died there. Finally, after superhuman efforts, suffocating, we arrived at the exit to the park [of Langemarck] but not without having left many of our own behind.

Tremsal's path of retreat took him, Lieutenant Chevalier, and some thirty other men through the railroad yard and behind some train cars. For those few moments, they must have believed they would escape,

---

*"The Joyeux have never lost a trench, rally to me!" The Joyeux is a nickname used for French soldiers, much like the British "Tommy."

especially after they found Captain Renaud and another soldier taking cover in the same spot. But before Tremsal could finish saying, "*Les misérables! C'est ça leur guerre!*" a shell exploded, throwing him and five or six other men onto the railroad tracks, where the Germans swarmed over them.[14]

• • •

Closer to the Canadian line, about a thousand yards to RIR 238's left, RIR 234 attacked Langemarck itself. (The same men had failed to take it at 1st Ypres.) Hauptmann (Captain) Hattendorf divided his force in three, sending his 1st Company to the left of the village, his 2nd to the right, and his 3rd directly into the village, a little less than a thousand yards in front of the German trenches. At first, the units encountered little resistance. Indeed, the regimental historian almost mocks the asphyxiated Moroccans: "With laughing eyes and a happy hooray, Leutnant Ohl passes the 4th Company and is the first to jump into an enemy trench."

Leutnant Grotrian's 3rd Company raced through the empty trenches and then into Langemarck. On the way, they passed the "decomposing bodies of Germans, English, women, dogs and fowl" that Private Harold Baldwin and a buddy had seen a day earlier, when they slipped over their parapet to make an unofficial visit to the deserted village.[15] The boom of guns and the echo of exploding shells erased the silence that Baldwin had found brooding over the scene of utter desolation. Half a stone wall with wooden beams that once held a roof still stood; except for the wooden frame, broken like so much kindling, all that remained of a house was a heap of stones. At the centre of the village stood a doorway that for centuries had led into a stone church. More than a few of Grotrian's men must have shuddered when they glanced at the door and realized, "All that remains of the church is a doorway with the date 1620."[16] Grotrian probably did not shudder, for as his report triumphantly puts it, "Now we were inside and took possession of the rubble into which our artillery had turned the village in the course of the winter."

Grotrian's commander, Hattendorf, was among the first to take prisoners. About two hundred yards beyond Langemarck, Hattendorf's men saw forty Frenchmen fleeing. Hattendorf did not, however, shoot them in the back, as Leisterer had done. Instead—inspired, perhaps, by the dream that one decisive cavalry attack could end the war—he pulled out his sabre and charged, followed by Grotrian and the rest of his company. After catching up with the fleeing French, Hattendorf took the surrender of the French commander. Before they were escorted back to the German lines, Grotrian exercised the prerogative of the battlefield and took a French soldier's four-edged bayonet.

Battle soon wiped the smile from Leutnant Ohl's face. The vagaries of the winds meant that the gas was "not effective in every place." An isolated machine gun from either the 1st or 2nd Tirailleurs (the units on the extreme right of the French line, abutting the Canadians) cut up Ohl's men. More worrisome, RIR 234 had lost contact with RIR 233—part of which had taken a wrong turn and got mixed up with the 234. As Canadian and British commanders would be doing for days, German officers ordered reserves forward to plug a gap.

When Ohl's unit passed through the French lines, he and his men laughed at the trenches, which were a far cry from the rumours they'd heard of concrete dugouts lit by electricity and protected by landmines. "We had been kept at bay ... for half a year," he wrote, by men whose shelter consisted of a "few lousy lean-tos that barely kept out the rain." As if to underline the difference between the French and the Germans, with their "love of order," Ohl reported, "I'd never seen the men dig as diligently as they did this night. We even built a parapet, [and] installed wire obstacles supplied from the sappers' depot." Ohl was especially proud of the "goodies," including chocolate and jam, his men ate during the night.

## Chapter 3

# "With a Coolness and Discipline That Seems Almost Incredible"
### The Canadians Fill the Gap

> *In our heart of hearts believing*
> *Victory crowns the just,*
> *And that braggarts must*
> *Surely bite the dust,*
> *Press we to the field ungrieving,*
> *In our heart of hearts believing*
> *Victory crowns the just.*
> —Thomas Hardy, "Men Who March Away"

Reaction by the Canadians in the field was almost immediate. By 5:30 p.m., while the staff at the Château des Trois Tours read outdated messages saying that the situation was "normal," Major D. Rykert McCuaig had already committed elements of his 13th Battalion to battle. As soon as the gas cloud cleared, the major led Captain Walker's 1st Platoon across the Franco-British line. The few Algerians left had retreated behind a rise about one hundred yards from the Poelcappelle road; by the time McCuaig's men reached them, the Algerians were already exchanging fire with the advancing Germans, likely members of Reserve-Infanterie-Regiment 234.

With the French line to his left ruptured, McCuaig first thought his men should work behind the Algerians to try to extend their line to their left (west). But there was no time to do so. Instead, McCuaig ordered some of his men to join the Algerians, which quelled their rising panic. And in a move that may seem odd to civilians but dates back to Roman times, McCuaig ordered most of his men into positions on the Poelcappelle–St Julien road at a *right angle* (running south) to the Algerian line. In doing this, McCuaig "refused his flank"—that is, he set up another front line to protect his own flank, which otherwise would have been "in the air," inviting the Germans to roll up his battalion from its own left. At least one of McCuaig's men, William F. Chambers, a nineteen-year-old trainman from Cobourg, Ontario, was captured before the line was stabilized.

Moments after seeing the gas cloud, which he mistook for a new French or German gunpowder, Lieutenant-Colonel Currie ordered his 15th Battalion's No. 2 Company to occupy positions at the back of the St. Julien churchyard, which was strewn with bodies and caskets blown out of the ground. These ghastly sights no doubt contributed to Currie's decision to ignore his men's suggestion that he take shelter in "a bomb-proof cellar." Whatever compelled Currie to stay out of the shelter saved his life, for "inside of ten minutes it was destroyed by a couple of 'coal boxes.'"

Currie's headquarters, meanwhile, were engulfed by the maelstrom created by the German shells. "The air was thick with spent particles of steel and lead that rattled on the pavement and the tiles" of the building, located in the ruins of a windmill, and on the roof of a nearby blacksmith's shop, where the member of Parliament had found tools forged in a factory not far from the 15th Battalion's drill hall on King Street in Toronto. At times, the "rain of heavy shells made it impossible for any living being to move around the streets." Currie saw a shell obliterate three of his men. Before long, the retreating Turcos reached St. Julien, where Currie and his French-speaking adjutant, Lieutenant Joseph Dansereau, a twenty-five-year-old Montreal engineer, tried to rally them. Expecting the Germans to be quick on the heels of the French, Currie ordered his staff to pack up their papers and be ready to evacuate. His brigadier, General Turner, responded to Currie's message that his position was threatened and his men falling by telling him to "hang on."[1]

Just over a thousand yards south of St. Julien, Major Andrew McNaughton and the gunners of his 7th Field Artillery Battery also saw the gas cloud. Soon, they too were enveloped by fumes strong enough to knock a man out. All at once, "Turcos came running back as if the devil was after them, their eyeballs showing white, and coughing their lungs out—they literally were coughing their lungs out; glue was coming out of their mouths." Amid the swirling gas fumes, McNaughton's men continued firing. "Somehow we felt it was the normal course of war," he recalled. "It was unpleasant, it's true, but nobody got very excited about it."[2]

Farther back, both officers and privates acted without waiting for orders. Seeing the gas cloud, the men playing football with Private Sid Cox near the 10th Battalion's billets in Ypres formed up on their own and started "to hike towards this trouble." As soon as they realized "something was up," Privates Baron Richardson Racey and Whitley Symonds cut short the good lunch a pretty Belgian girl had just served them in an *estaminet*. They ran, likely through the Menin Gate,* towards the farm where their unit was billeted. Before long, they encountered the retreating French, who croaked out, "*Les Allemands viennent avec le gaz asphiziant.*" ("The Germans are attacking with asphyxiating gas.") In the confusion of bursting shells, stunned and choking French soldiers, "batteries of artillery going hell for leather towards St. Julien," hysterical civilians, and burning farms, Racey and Symonds had trouble finding their unit's command post. When they did, they were ordered to help extend a nearby trench filled by Turcos and British troops.

Just as Racey and Symonds reached St. Jean from the west, Captain Irving's 2nd Field Company engineers passed through the village going

---

*Dedicated in 1927, the rebuilt Menin Gate has inscribed on it the names of 54,896 officers and men, including more than 7,000 Canadians—some 1,500 from 2nd Ypres alone—who died in the Ypres Salient but have no known graves. These names are gathered together in Appendix D, an *In Memoriam* section at the back of the book.

in the other direction. When he first saw the strange cloud drift from the French lines, Irving had ordered his men to stand to. About a half hour later (shortly after 5:30 p.m.), as large "numbers of French troops came straggling down the road in great disorder, their artillery galloping their horses," Irving's men paraded in full battle kit and hitched their horses to their transport wagons. By 6:00 p.m., Irving knew the situation had deteriorated, though not because he'd received any official information. More wounded French infantry continued to retreat, and shells were landing along the road near his billet.

At first glance, Irving's order to take the wagons across the Yser Canal—that is, away from the direction of battle—looks defeatist. It wasn't. An engineering battalion is only as good as the tools of its trade: spades, barbed wire, corrugated iron, wood for bracing, sandbags, and explosives. And the decision to transport the materials out of immediate danger was not without risk. His drivers had whatever protection their speed offered. But Lieutenant Robertson's men manhandled their tool cart over the fields, then down the road and across a bridge—all the while under heavy shellfire. By the time they returned for the pontoon wagon, exploding shells had killed a corporal and a sapper, and wounded a sergeant.

Later in the war, Irving would not have had the authority to issue the order to mine the bridges, which he did once he arrived at the canal. Were there to be a general retreat, tens of thousands of Canadian and British troops would have headed to these bridges. According to the historian Bill Rawling, himself a former field engineer, "Bridges are very important. You never destroy them unless you have to because you never know when you are going to need them. It's often better to lose a bridge to the enemy with the hopes of retaking it later than it is to destroy it."

Irving, however, was not taking any chances. Around 6:30 p.m., as shells fell into the canal, Irving's men crawled onto four bridges to affix them with explosives and electric firing charges. Pausing only to take cover from the exploding shells, another group of sappers dug three fougasses (improvised landmines) into the ground immediately in front of Bridge No. 4, the same bridge that Generals Alderson and Burstall crossed to return to the Château des Trois Tours.

After noticing the gas cloud, Majors MacLaren and Ormond and Captain Gidding dug their spurs into their horses' flanks and turned west towards their 10th Battalion headquarters. Fifteen minutes of hard riding brought them to their battalion headquarters at Wieltje. Just moments after they began a meeting with their commander, Lieutenant-Colonel Boyle, a Jack Johnson exploded, blowing out all the windows in the room. Boyle realized that the orders he had received just half an hour earlier—orders telling him that that night his battalion was to be a working battalion—were badly outdated. Without waiting for a request from Brigadier-General Turner or orders from his own commander, Brigadier-General Currie, Boyle ordered his 10th Battalion, which was Currie's reserve, to stand to.

Having seen the gas cloud and the beginnings of the French retreat, Captain John Warden, commander of No. 1 Company of General Currie's 7th Battalion (in reserve near Wieltje), ordered his men to fall in and hasten to the regimental headquarters. There, the battalion's commander, Colonel Hart-McHarg, ordered them into the field with orders to "stop every soldier [we] met retiring and compel them to advance again with us." On the way, Sergeant Raymond MacIlree smelled the cause of the "weird light" in the western sky and remembered from his high school chemistry class both the refractive qualities and the smell of chlorine. Despite the shellfire exploding all around them, the Canadians' discipline and morale held. MacIlree heard one fellow soldier shout out, "Shut up, you bastard," after an artillery transport driver galloping his limber yelled, "They've broken through! They've broken through!" Around 7:00 p.m., Currie ordered Warden's men to Locality "C," the most important strategic point on Gravenstafel Ridge, then scarcely visible in the gathering night.

• • •

On both the far right and the far left of the attack, the Germans encountered unexpected resistance. While German units pushed the

French out of the way and crossed the Yser Canal at Steenstraat and Het Sas, occupying about a thousand yards of a line on the west side of the canal, they had more trouble closer to the junction between the French and the Belgians.

When Willie Breton, who was stationed with a few men in a listening post on the extreme right of the Belgian force that adjoined the French left, first saw the strange smoke rise from the German lines, he thought their trenches had caught fire. As the cloud came closer and he felt his throat seize, he heard the cry "The Boche are there!" Fortunately, no one fired, for the men streaming towards the Steenstraat Bridge were in fact French; many fell gasping for breath as they tried to run to safety.

A few moments later, Breton and his men were ordered back to the main Belgian line, where they found their surprisingly calm comrades ready to fire at the Germans. Though they had no official information, Breton's commandant and his lieutenant grasped the seriousness of the situation. Years later, Breton could still hear his commandant's voice: "Let's go, my braves. This is the moment to show the Boche that the Belgians won't back down. I'm counting on you that each of you will defend [this position] till death."

Two of the first five *Feldgrauen* to reach the bridge over the Steenstraat were shot down. "Hellish fire came from our trenches," recalled Breton. "We were firing as fast as we could. The barrel of my gun burned my fingers. But those damned Boche kept on advancing."[3] Still, the Belgians held on.

• • •

A couple of hundred yards from where McCuaig's men began sketching a new defensive line, Sanitätssoldat George Müller, a medical orderly belonging to RIR 233, violated the spirit, if not the letter, of the 1907 Hague Convention. After patching up a wounded comrade and racing through shellfire to catch up with his unit, he saw a trench filled with almost twenty stunned Zouaves. Jumping in with them, he quickly realized that the snarls and threatening hand gestures of "those black fellows" were meant to hide something. The fact that not one had aimed his rifle at him, however, gave Müller their measure, and he pulled his pistol. As he took aim at one and then another, they understood that he was not joking. Despite their numbers, they surrendered. Müller then thrust himself between two men and pulled out a thick canvas-covered roll that the Algerians had tried to cover with earth. Along with about twenty prisoners, Müller, to his great joy, brought back the Zouaves' battle flag.

• • •

At about the same time, near Mouse Trap Farm, engineers belonging to one of the companies that was now manning the GHQ Line* (which formed Turner's right flank) found themselves racing *towards* the Germans to retrieve their pack mules. Had the mules been unloaded, they would have been sacrificed. But they were loaded, and with an extremely important cargo: bridging equipment that the Germans could have used to jump the Yser Canal. The company's war diary does not say what caused the animals to stampede, but it is reasonable to assume that they were spooked by the exploding shells and the sound of bullets cutting through the air—one of which shot Major Fell's horse out from under him. Nor does the war diary tell how many men fled to pursue the stampeding mules. It says only that when the animals were recovered, the Germans were about eight hundred yards away on a "ridge N.W. of the farm."

While the engineers of the 3rd Field Company saved their equipment in a field just northeast of Ypres, the commander of the 16th Battalion,

---

*The GHQ (General Headquarters) Line, which figures prominently in the story of 2nd Ypres, was a defensive line running more or less north to south from a position two thousand yards east of Ypres; at Mouse Trap Farm, the line curved northwest for about twelve hundred yards. Because French maps and orders refer to it as the GHQ 2nd Line, some Canadian orders do so as well. There was no GHQ 1st Line, however. Except when quoting, I refer to it as the GHQ Line.

Lieutenant-Colonel Robert Leckie, a forty-five-year-old consulting engineer, Boer War veteran, and pre-war regimental militia commander, took matters into his own hands. At 5:30 p.m., he had received orders to stand to. As the French fell back, Leckie barked out two important orders. The first was to provide each man with a hundred extra rounds of ammunition, thus giving every soldier 150 rounds. The second was for his men to dig in on the western side of the Yser Canal, to be in position to repel the Germans were they to try to cross the canal near Ypres.

. . .

While Müller was capturing the Zouaves' flag and other men of his regiment were working their way behind the Canadian lines, RIRs 238 and 234 bagged an even bigger prize in the woods south of the Hannebeek. The English and the Canadians called these woods Kitcheners Wood, not for Lord Kitchener but because they furnished the wood for the kitchens of the farms that dotted the land north and east of the Bois des Cuisiniers, or Cooks' Wood. In the southwest corner of the woods stood four heavy guns belonging to the London Territorial Field Artillery.

Today, it is difficult to grasp the importance of these guns. Tactically, of course, they were critical. The numbers had improved since the war broke out, when British forces had only six heavy batteries, but in April 1915, they still had only 150 heavies. Symbolically, these guns were as important as a Roman legion's standard. The British attitude towards their guns was exemplified by Alfred Lord Tennyson's "Ode on the Death of the Duke of Wellington."

> For this is England's greatest son,
> He that gain'd a hundred fights,
> Nor ever lost an English gun.

But as General Turner noted in a letter to his wife, written just over a week after 2nd Ypres, "The guns of which you hear so much are a side issue. They were British guns in the rear of the French lines and were found by our men when they charged the wood in the night attack."*

Had they been able to, the Germans would have moved the guns. Instead, the company's tool maker disabled them. Then the *Feldgrauen* pushed the one gun not dug in ignominiously into a nearby swamp. At the same time, men of RIR 238 found that the "woods were crammed with ammunition, dugouts and huts." Patrols sent beyond the woods, to Hof Soetaert and Hof de Roode Karriere (Oblong and Juliet farms) netted "40 horses including the Faithful Lady—a half blood that became known to all members of the regiment's adjutant." As dusk settled, both regiments dug in on the southern side of what regimental histories, no doubt to tweak British noses, refer to as Das Gewehrholz—the Gun Woods.

• • •

As the Germans advanced through Kitcheners Wood, two trucks filled with gassed French soldiers stopped next to the Vansteene Farm, just outside Poperinghe. Young Jeanne Battheu, who had seen and smelled the strangely coloured cloud, watched as orderlies set down rows of men whose eyes bulged and tongues hung out. She and other children watched as these men's clothes were stripped off. Then the children were told to carry pails of milk and repeat the words "Here, *du lait, du lait.* A cup of milk." As the evening turned into night, the eight- or nine-year-old Jeanne watched *les gazés*, "with their tongues hanging out, crying, 'Mother, Mummy. *Ma tante, Maman.*"[4]

• • •

At 6:00 p.m., artillery fire from his left rear told McCuaig that the Germans had seized not just the guns but also their ammunition. Because of the heavy shelling earlier in the day, McCuaig had moved men to

---

*This last point, perhaps, explains why Sir James Edmonds, in the official British history of the Great War, says nothing about how the guns were lost. He does note, however, that after they were "found," a message "was sent to bring up teams to remove them."

positions a few hundred yards to his left rear, an area then protected by the French line. As dusk fell, he learned that both Major Edward Norsworthy and Captain Guy Drummond had fallen, with all but six of their hundred-man platoons.

. . .

The collapse of the French lines and the capture of their heavy guns meant that the only artillery remaining on the western side of the salient belonged to the Canadians. At Neuve-Chapelle six weeks earlier, the Canadian gunners had been part of a 535-gun group responsible for 1,450 yards, or just over 2.7 yards per gun. In the hours after 5:59 p.m., when Colonel Cecil Romer at the Château des Trois Tours directed the 1st Division's artillery to support the French, the Canadians had forty guns, mostly eighteen-pounders, to cover some twelve thousand yards of front, or three hundred yards per gun. Fortunately for the tens of thousands of Allied soldiers in the Salient, both gunnery and artillery transport were Canadian specialties.

The commanders of the Canadian guns were among Canada's most experienced—and most decorated—officers. At the Battle of Leliefontein, during the Boer War, three Canadians earned Victoria Crosses for saving their guns, and one earned a Distinguished Service Order. Richard E. W. Turner, who was awarded the VC for rescuing two artillery pieces that had been surrounded by the Boers, was now Brigadier-General Turner, the field commander most responsible for the disposition of Canadian troops. In that same Boer War battle, Lieutenant Edward "Dinky" Morrison, who now commanded the 1st Brigade, Canadian Field Artillery, earned a DSO for saving guns belonging to his "D" battery. Lieutenant-Colonel Creelman, who commanded the 2nd Brigade, Canadian Field Artillery, and thirty-seven-year-old William B. M. King had also served as gunners in the Boer War.

Another brigadier, Arthur Currie, had commanded the 5th B.C. Regiment, Canadian Garrison Artillery, since 1895. One of Creelman's young officers, Major McNaughton, was already working on how temperature and weather affected shells in flight; while en route to England, he lectured on how infantry and artillery could be better coordinated. A year before the war broke out, Sir Ian Hamilton, the British inspector-general of overseas forces, had reported that the militia's batteries were ready for active service.

Unsure of the exact position of the troops on his left, Lieutenant-Colonel J. H. Mitchell kept his three batteries, positioned near St. Julien, firing at the German front lines. The 2nd Canadian Field Artillery Brigade, stationed about two thousand yards southeast of St. Julien, was in a better position to follow General Alderson's order to relay its guns and fire on the advancing Germans. By 8:30 p.m., the 5th Battery had fired more than 260 shells at various parts of the German trench.

Twice before dusk, Dominion gun crews shifted from firing from a thousand or more yards away and began firing "open sights" at Germans who were but a few hundred yards away. Shortly after the battle began, Major King, whose guns were about seven hundred yards north of St. Julien, saw German soldiers occupying a house from which riflemen could have picked off his men. King could have moved his guns from the orchard where they were hidden. But doing so would have taken time, something the Canadians did not have. Worse, it would have risked opening St. Julien, five hundred or so yards to King's south, to a direct attack. King wasted little time defending his position. With uncharacteristic bravado for a Canadian, he called out, "That house is full of Boche. Watch me blow them out at point blank."[5] Seconds later, the advance guard of a force (likely belonging to RIR 233) ran from the ruined building.

At 7:00 p.m., an Algerian who had stayed with King's guns yelled, "*Allemands!*" and pointed to some spike-helmeted troops just a few hundred yards away. King's men then reversed their guns, one of the most difficult manoeuvres in warfare. To do this, the men nearest the trail (the long steel rod that hitches to the limber) picked it up and, quickly but smoothly, walked 180 degrees to the left or right, until the gun's maw faced the onrushing Germans.

As soon as the men put the trail down, the gun-layer looked over the barrel, and if the muzzle was not pointing directly at the Germans, he called for the gun to be moved again. As soon as the gun-layer was satisfied, the range-setter turned a brass wheel counter-clockwise, stopping when the clinometer reached five hundred yards. At the same time, the two fuse-setters turned the brass nose cones on the shells to the mark next to "1" (for one second). The fuse-setter closest to the gun then handed his shell, with the base of the cartridge leading, to the gun-loader, who had opened the breech by taking hold of the lever with his left hand, depressed a spring, and drawing the lever "smartly towards him." Once the gun-loader took hold of the shell, he turned and rammed it into the breech. A second later, he took hold of the lever again and swung "the breech screw smartly round into its position in the gun."[6]

As soon as the gun-loader let go of the lever and stepped back, he yelled, "Ready!" and then, "Set!" Only then did the gun-layer pull a lanyard or a lever. Milliseconds later, the shell would shoot out of the gun's muzzle at over 1,615 feet per second. As it travelled through the air, the timer ticked off. When it hit one second, a bursting charge exploded, pushing an iron plate into a resin mixture full of shrapnel balls. The force of the explosion broke the nose off the shell. Hundreds of one-ounce, half-inch balls moving at more than a thousand miles an hour then formed a cone in front of the advancing German troops.

Before the last of the balls hit the ground, the gun-loader was again pulling on the lever and preparing to ram another shell into the breech. Each of King's guns was capable of firing between fifteen and twenty shells per minute. As the German dead piled up, leaves cut from the willow trees rained down on the Canadian gunners.\*

Shortly after his guns forced the Germans to ground, King sent a message to Lieutenant-Colonel Loomis, the commandant of St. Julien. In a few more hours, the headquarters would be a shambles. Shells would

---

\*The other guns that had to be reversed belonged to the 9th Battery commanded by Major Macdougall.

destroy his telephone lines, and bullets would cut down his runners. But at 7:00 p.m., he still had the reserves to respond to King's call for infantry support. Sixty riflemen from the 14th and 15th Battalions, and even more important, a machine-gun crew belonging to the 13th Battalion, led by nineteen-year-old Frederick Fisher, answered King's call for help.

We don't know exactly how Lance-Corporal Fisher, who had left McGill University to enlist, worked his machine gun forward from the St. Julien graveyard to the ruins of a house near King's guns.[7] One thing is certain, however: he could not have run with it like a Hollywood action hero.* Fisher's machine gun weighed thirty-five pounds, and the tripod on which it sat, which included a stool for the gun's operator, weighed another sixty-one pounds. And then there were the heavy boxes containing belts of bullets. All this, plus each man's own rifle and pack, had to be carried forward under fire.

Flanders, popularly thought of as flat, actually undulates and is crisscrossed with ditches and folds. Fisher made use of these natural features. He would have set up his Colt machine gun and fired a short burst, perhaps eighty rounds, intended not so much to hit the Germans as to force them to go to ground. That would give some of Fisher's men time to advance to the next ditch, fold, or patch of tall grass. Then they would shoulder their rifles and start firing again, trying to force the Germans to take cover once more, while Fisher and the rest of his crew advanced a little farther. They must have been very good, for they made it to the ruined house without casualties.

As daylight faded and King's guns kept firing, ammunition ran low.

---

*Hollywood also does not accurately depict how machine guns were used. Though both the water-cooled German Maxim and the gas-cooled Canadian Colt could fire about four hundred rounds per minute, they rarely did so. Gunners did not pull on the trigger and fire away, sweeping wildly from side to side. Firing without stopping would have soon worn out the gun's barrel. Instead, a gunner squeezed the trigger for as few as five seconds and then waited a moment or two for the barrel to cool before firing again. Properly situated guns would not have to move far to the left or right; instead, a group of guns established an interlocking field of fire.

Twice, drivers braved incoming shells and rifle fire, and lost their horses, to try to bring in more shells. Finally, a non-commissioned officer (NCO) asked for volunteers, and fifty-five men offered to carry shells six hundred yards across the German line of fire to King's guns. Each step these men took was proof that, as H. R. Gordon, a *Toronto Star* reporter who set aside his pen to join the 1st Division, put it, "Every yard of ground . . . has great consequences, both material and moral." Gordon also wrote of the kind of fatalism necessary to be a soldier:

> Our six months' training . . . has strengthened and trained our minds and spirits even more than our bodies. Certainly we're very different in outlook and behaviour from the gang that were at Valcartier. I've been reading through the Gospel of Mark and the latter half of Isaiah lately. Certainly out here one realizes the feebleness and frailty of the thread of our individual lives. Heaven is very near, and hell, too. But I think we're all quite tranquil. I know I may get killed the next minute, but I don't worry in the least about it. It's a great relief to be able to be like that.[8]

The battlefield version of this was the belief that unless a shell or a bullet had your name on it, you were safe. Over the four hours that Fisher protected King's guns, four German bullets came bearing the names of his men; Fisher himself, who would die the next day while protecting another gun, was awarded the Victoria Cross for his actions, the first of four earned by Canadians at 2nd Ypres.

In a letter to his wife, written on 3 May, General Turner recalled that ninety minutes after the gas attack, "I really thought all was lost. The enemy came sweeping down round our rear, and all that I had left were our servants, the engineer company, and about 50 of my grenade company. All the rest had been sent forward to fill the gap."*

In the field, things were in chaos with hundreds of shocked and

---

*The letter is in the possession of the Canadian War Museum.

dying French troops streaming back and huge gaps opening up in the line. Turner's headquarters at Mouse Trap Farm were about a thousand yards southwest of the village of Morteldje, the deepest point of the German's bowl-shaped advance. Immediately to his north were the engineers Turner had written to his wife about, as well as three companies of the 14th Battalion and a smattering of Zouaves who had joined the Canadians after the French lines retreated.

Between the GHQ Line and the canal yawned a three-thousand-yard gap, in the middle of which was a single surviving French machine gun. To the right of the troops immediately ahead of Mouse Trap Farm, running towards the village of St. Julien, was a smaller, though not insignificant, gap of a thousand yards. St. Julien was home to Loomis's headquarters and the battalion reserve. King's 10th Canadian Field Battery was a bit north of the village. To Loomis's right, running generally northwest, was a gap of some seventeen hundred yards.

• • •

As bad as the situation was, Turner and his staff thought it was even worse. Garnet Hughes, Turner's brigade-major (and the son of Militia Minister Sam Hughes), sent a series of panicky messages to both the Château des Trois Tours and General Currie, whose 8th and 5th Battalions held the trenches on the far right of the Canadian line on Gravenstafel Ridge. At 6:25 p.m., Hughes sent Alderson a runner with the message "Left of our sub-section is retiring." Seven minutes later, he sent a runner to Currie with even worse news: "The left of our left section is retiring having been driven in." At 6:45 p.m., Hughes sent still another message to Alderson:

To 1st Canadian Div.
B.M. 741. 22nd April, 1915.

Your wire to us is down aaa Our left driven back and apparently whole line forced back towards ST. JULIEN Two and a half reserve companies have been brought up and are occupying G.H.Q. line. aaa Have no more troops available

From 3rd Canadian Inf. Bde.. 6.45 p.m.

G.B.H.

Twenty-five minutes later Hughes sent his most alarming message: "We are forced back on G.H.Q. line. Attack coming from west. No troops left. Need ammunition badly. Have asked 2nd Brigade to support."

Historians have criticized Turner and Hughes for these messages. They see in them the first signs of the incompetence that would mar the Canadian attack on Kitcheners Wood and underlie Turner's disastrous decisions later in the battle. Hughes's 7:10 p.m. message implied that something like a general retreat was about to occur. Because he had no message from Loomis saying that his line had collapsed, Hughes had no reason to think that his men were not engaged in battle—as indeed they were.

Exactly why Turner, who had readied his own revolver when bullets started hitting Mouse Trap Farm, did not take a stronger hand with Hughes has never been satisfactorily explained. The two most likely possibilities are that Turner suffered something of a breakdown at the beginning of the battle, or that he was too inexperienced to grasp fully what was going on and how Hughes's messages confused things. Fortunately, other Canadian commanders, artillery officers, majors, captains, sergeants, and even privates were better. Indeed, Alan Clark, whose book *The Donkeys* is a blistering account of the British General Staff's performance throughout 1915, wrote that the Canadians rose to the defence "with a coolness and discipline that seems almost incredible as we look back upon it."[9]

• • •

As confusion emanated from Mouse Trap Farm, a couple of hundred yards away Private Racey's war ended. After joining his battalion near the farm, Racey was sent on a listening patrol with three other men.

Somehow, he ended up about forty yards behind the others. When he tried to catch up, the small party halted him and asked in French who he was. "I like a damned fool thinking they were a stray party of French told them in broken French and English who I was." Racey got the shock of his life a moment later, "when about a dozen spiked helmets jumped at me before I could say Jack Robinson; one grabbed my rifle, another my bayonet and the rest tugged off my equipment and there I was." With shells screaming overhead, Racey was marched back to a farmhouse and searched. "After about an hour the door was opened and a lieutenant entered and I had a long chat with him; [he] spoke English very well," Racey remembered. "He asked me how many Canadians there were and I told him 100,000, shades of Ananias,* and quite a lot more truthful and useful information. He seemed very pleased with the progress they had made and expected to be in Ypres the next day."

• • •

At 7:00 p.m.—ten minutes after Alderson ordered the 16th Battalion to be ready to march to Turner's 3rd Brigade headquarters—Major von Drigalski ordered the men of Reserve-Infanterie-Regiment 239 to "stop and dig in." Drigalski's concern for what a later psychologist called "cognitive orientation and a commitment to task-completion" paled when set against the raw emotions of men caught up in the drama of their own advance.[10] His troops paid no heed to his order, a fact the regimental historian dismissed by observing, "But who can stop the troops marching ahead?" Before they raced forward, one soldier put the artillery banner on his bayonet so the artillery would be able to see where RIR 239 was.

Soon, however, the advance became uneven, as fire from the few surviving Zouave units began to play behind the Germans. Some units dug in. Others, like the section of the 1st Battalion led by Leutnants Adam and Rettig, turned away from the fire and linked up with the

---

*Ananias was an early Christian who "gave up the ghost" (Acts 5:5) after lying about how much money he had to give to the church.

3rd Battalion to secure Pilckem Heights. Sergeant Eizenbart and Soldat Zweig led an assault by parts of the 11th Company on one of the last French batteries dug in near a steam mill, five hundred metres northeast of the road from Pilckem to Boesinghe; other units crossed the canal at Het Sas. These last took twenty prisoners and "kill[ed] the resisting artillery crew with their carbines" before writing "11–239" (for 11th Company, RIR 239) on the gun barrels. Eizenbart and Zweig's comrade, Leutnant Kemp, duplicated their feat several hundred yards away. The regimental historian wrote, triumphantly:

> The 2/239 took 11 heavy guns abandoned by the enemy near the Stroyer Farm and Leutnant Müller ... advanced toward the Blaminghe Farm to the south.... They found two heavy guns that were defended by about 20 Frenchmen who were dispersed suffering losses but were not able to take the guns with them; though they did get away with the guns' chucks.

Shortly after counting their booty—twenty-two heavy guns and seven machine guns—the *Feldgrauen* received orders to withdraw to more defensible positions farther east of the canal. As night gathered around them, the Germans dug deeper into the soft earth, secure in the knowledge that their new trenches were more than two miles from where they had gone over the top.

When Müller's men looked up from their digging, they would have seen a strange light in the sky. This light, however, came not from the sun's rays refracting through the remnants of the chlorine gas, but from the fires of the incendiary shells that rained down upon Ypres. "As darkness came on fires broke out ... and the periodic explosions of 17-inch shells threw clouds of embers and burning debris into the air, as if volcanoes had suddenly opened up," wrote Dinky Morrison in his report. "The constant rain of shells into the city, the roar of the flames, and the detonations of ammunition wagons, together with the shrieks of the terror-stricken fugitives and the howling of the gassed Turcos, constituted a fair imitation of the infernal regions."

• • •

Amid all this confusion, accurate information was at a premium. At 7:00 p.m., Canon Scott watched in horror as the driver of a passing artillery battery yelled, "It is a general retreat. The Germans are at our heels." Moments later, Scott stopped a staff car and asked, "Is this a general retreat?"[11] The officer quickly told the padré never to utter the word "retreat" at the front.

Things were no clearer up the chain of command. At 7:45 p.m., about the same time the 16th and 10th Battalions received orders to march to Turner's headquarters, two messages arrived at Major-General Sir Horace Smith-Dorrien's headquarters at Hazebrouck, in French Flanders. One incorrectly informed him that the 3rd Brigade's front had been broken as far as Wieltje. A month after 2nd Ypres, Smith-Dorrien told Currie that when he "heard of the gas attack and the retirement of the French Colonial troops, he threw up his hands and foresaw the greatest disaster that ever overtook the British Army." He imagined tens of thousands of men, their guns and transports, rushing for the few crossings over the canal, "with a victorious army thundering at their heels." Then came the message that the Canadians were holding on. "At first he refused to believe it and sent his own staff officer to verify the report."[12]

• • •

Fighting flared again near the canal as Smith-Dorrien waited nervously for word of the state of the Canadian line. At 7:30 p.m., Reserve-Infanterie-Regiment 215 attacked the Belgian trenches north of the Steenstraat creek. The Belgian Grenadiers held their fire until the Germans were less than forty metres away. Then, as the Germans approached cover, King Albert's men opened up with both rifles and a mortar. Even though the Germans managed to set up machine guns and rake the Belgians' positions, the screams of pain told King Albert's riflemen that their fire was taking its toll, and soon the Kaiser's men withdrew.

The Belgians did not, however, have long to savour their small victory. Shortly after the Germans withdrew, red and green flares lit the sky above the Belgian positions. Moments later, shells began falling on their trenches. As soon as the Germans were sure they had the range, the shelling increased, and then a machine-gun crew moved up, trapping the Belgians between the Scylla of shellfire (including T-shells) and the Charybdis of machine-gun fire. But despite mounting casualties, the Belgians held on, their faces covered by cloth masks that had been dipped in the waters of the canal.

. . .

As the Belgians threw back the German attack, Smith-Dorrien's army was on the move. At 8:00 p.m., Lieutenant-General Plumer released to Alderson the 2nd and 3rd Canadian Battalions; the men of the latter unit were sharpening their bayonets when they got the order to stand to. Plumer also assigned two British battalions, the 2nd East Yorks (the Buffs) and the 3rd Middlesex (the Die Hards), to Alderson, who in turn assigned them to Turner. These two battalions became the nucleus of a provisional brigade named for the British colonel Augustus D. Geddes; they were the first of thirty-three British battalions that over the next few days would fight under Canadian command. At around the same time, Turner learned that the 10th and 16th Battalions had been placed under his command, and that he was to use them to organize a counter-attack at C.10.d, the coordinates for Kitcheners Wood. (The Canadian attack, which was more or less straight north, was to be coordinated with one by the French coming from the west.) Shortly afterwards, Turner learned that the 2nd and 3rd Battalions were also on the way to him; the 2nd Battalion were to support the attack on Kitcheners Wood, and the 3rd Battalion were to fill the gap between the woods and St. Julien.

During the Napoleonic Wars a hundred years earlier, artillery had two functions: to batter down walls and to crush advancing soldiers. The development of rifled canon capable of firing shrapnel or high-explosive shells from five or more miles away meant that artillery could take on a third function, isolating the battlefield from reinforcements. German artillerists sought to accomplish this in two ways. First, they bombarded

Ypres, causing a flood of humanity to surge onto and block the roads that Canadian and British troops needed to reach to the front. In an effort to relieve congestion on the roadways, Morrison moved his artillery into a field, still covering some of the retreating French troops; all around his unit, "women and children, completely exhausted, had fallen asleep in the ditches beside the road." Still, as the moon rose, "the main road from Ypres was completely choked with fugitives, making forward progress impossible," recalled Major Kirkpatrick.

German artillery also sought to make the roads too dangerous for the Canadians to use. Immediately after crossing the canal, Kirkpatrick's 3rd Battalion came under rifle fire from German units that had advanced some distance beyond Mauser Ridge. Kirkpatrick was dividing his battalion into two ranks so that his men could use whatever cover ditches on the side of the road offered, when suddenly they heard the *swish, swish* of German shells. The first struck the No. 11 Platoon of "C" Company, killing and wounding several men. Another hit one of the battalion's machine-gun sections, killing four men, including Lieutenant Ross Brinkley, a popular rugby player. "Not one of us wavered; not one of us swerved to right or left, to front or back," claimed Private Harold Peat.[13] The Canadians did close up the ranks, but Peat's words are too redolent of wartime poetry to be completely believed. More plausible is his description of his comrades jumping over the bodies of the newly fallen Canadians in response to their commanders' whispered order to close up ranks.

Other Canadians, like the 1st Battalion's Sidney H. Radford, who caught pneumonia at Valcartier but still managed to slip himself into a draft leaving a British convalescent hospital for France, were luckier. A mile or so behind the line, a bullet flew right by Radford's eyes and into a tree. A 16th Battalion private, Nathaniel Nicholson, recalled that at one point on their way forward from Ypres, Captain Merritt ordered his unit to break step:

> He suddenly said right in line which we went over in this direction for quite a distance and then left in line and then we went in that direction

and then he said left in line and then went in that direction again and then right in line and we were in the same direction we were [originally] heading. But [in] that space created by him giving that command a shell burst. Why he gave it I don't know. But if we had gone straight along there would have been quite a number of fellows hit.

As long lines of Dominion troops made their way towards Mouse Trap Farm, they saw horrific sights, including a young teen carrying his grandmother on his back and groups of children standing in doorways crying. Amid the roar of guns and bathed in the strange half-light of the burning city behind them, Peat's battalion marched in "dogged and resolute silence," each man alone with his thoughts.[14] As the 2nd Battalion moved through the blasted landscape, passing the now homeless men and women, the men sang "It's a Long Way to Tipperary." Though word had filtered back that the Canadian line had indeed held, those two thousand men marching to battle knew nothing about the front to which they were heading.

. . .

At around 9:00 p.m., McCuaig's 13th Battalion faced some anxious moments when the Germans forced the Turcos off the breastworks they had been holding since shortly after the gas attack. Had the Turcos not rallied a second time and joined the Montrealers in their trenches along the Poelcappelle road, McCuaig's left flank would have been "in the air." The battalion machine-gun officer wasted little time in ordering Sergeant Trainor and Lance-Corporal Stanley J. Parks to set up their Colt machine guns on the road. As the night deepened, Trainor and Parks—protected by only a few paving blocks pried from the road—held off several attacks. They could, of course, do nothing about the constant shelling, which, because the Germans had captured guns to McCuaig's rear, came from three directions, causing terrible casualties.

At midnight, Loomis responded to McCuaig's messages that his men were short of ammunition by telling him to use his own judgment when deciding how long he could hold on. As the battle for Kitcheners Wood raged through the night, Captains Jamieson and William H. Clark-Kennedy readied a new line three hundred yards behind the Poelcappelle road that the 13th Battalion would repair to if reinforcements did not arrive by dawn.

At about the same time, a thousand yards behind McCuaig's line, Major King, who for four hours had been the only organized resistance in front of St. Julien, was ordered to evacuate his position. This was no easy task. Twice during the daylight hours, ammunition wagons had been destroyed on their way to the 10th Battery. King held out little hope for the survival of a transport team. Displaying the kind of initiative Sir John French had praised when he toured the Dominion in 1910, King ordered two of the guns to be hitched to teams of horses. While these teams pulled the guns back towards St. Julien, the two remaining guns were mounted on their limbers, which were then attached with drag ropes. At 11:00 p.m., just as they were about to begin manhandling the guns across the rutted and shell-pocked field back to St. Julien, two new teams of horses arrived to do the job.*

Some distance from where McCuaig's men readied a new line, George W. Frost, a forty-two-year-old lance-corporal belonging to the 10th Battalion, found himself an army of one. When the gas attack began, the former master mariner from Leslieville, Alberta, was swimming in the Yser Canal. A short time later, as he made his way towards Mouse Trap Farm, where his unit was, Frost passed by the western edge of Kitcheners Wood. There he saw the four heavy guns abandoned by the British. He also saw a group of coughing Algerian soldiers, who told him, "*Allemands cum*," before they continued their retreat.

Frost hid in a ditch, and just a few moments later, he saw a dozen men three hundred yards away. He thought they were German, but in the fading light of dusk, he wasn't sure until he saw them enter a house and then leave—with a French soldier as their prisoner. Frost waited

---

*Later, Creelman's guns moved back into position.

and then crept back towards a small hut topped by a crucifix that he had earlier used for shelter. On his way to it, he saw more Germans digging a trench just south of the woods. Though alone, he put his rifle to his shoulder and took careful aim. Soon German soldiers, including one carrying machine-gun parts, started falling.

With each passing minute, Frost expected to see waves of khaki-clad Canadian troops come up behind him. Once darkness fell, he resumed his trek towards his crucifix shelter. As he neared it, he was astonished to hear the guttural tones of German. "What had become of my company? Where was my battalion? I was surrounded," he thought as he reloaded his magazine and vowed not to be taken alive. After a few quiet moments "that seemed more like years," Frost realized he had not been noticed and began to crawl south towards the burning city of Ypres. When he neared it, he found a French officer who was able to direct him towards Mouse Trap Farm, where he rejoined the 10th Battalion.

Around 10:30 p.m., Lieutenant-Colonels Boyle and Leckie, commanders of the 10th and 16th Battalions, respectively, met with Turner and Hughes at Mouse Trap Farm. In almost every way, the meeting was the antithesis of those that would precede both the famous attack at Vimy Ridge and the successful 1918 attacks that earned the Canadian corps the sobriquet "Shock Army of the British Empire."[15] At those later meetings, information from trench raids and aerial surveillance was shared with senior officers and company and platoon leaders. After rehearsals, the officers adjusted their attack plans. The most up-to-date maps, indicating each unit's path and objective, were distributed. Artillery officers told infantry officers about their progress in counter-battery attack-planning and about the shape and speed of the creeping barrage that would protect the first wave of infantry. Platoon and company leaders were told which rifle pits they should leave for the second wave of attackers to deal with. Senior officers ensured that unit commanders knew which units were on their flanks, an innovation that greatly improved communications.

In the cramped, chaotic headquarters at Mouse Trap Farm, less than a mile from the Germans' hastily dug trenches, none of this took place.

Neither Turner nor Hughes, nor anyone else, had reconnoitred the ground that the 10th and 16th Battalions would soon be crossing. Turner and Hughes had also not coordinated the attack with the few artillery batteries capable of hitting Kitcheners Wood. More astonishing still is the fact that no one in Turner's command even tried to coordinate the Canadian attack with one that was to be carried out by French units on Turner's left. Indeed, Turner should have known since 10:50 p.m., when Hughes himself sent a runner to Alderson telling him that the "French on our left have asked for help and we are sending what men of theirs have stayed in the area," that the French were in no position to attack.

As their commanders gleaned whatever information they could from Turner's staff, the men of the 10th and 16th Battalions waited in the fields around Mouse Trap Farm. As the minutes ticked towards midnight and the moon rose higher in the sky, Major Markham thought to himself, "Damn this staff, we are only two days out of the trenches, and now they are messing us around on night manoeuvres."[16]

He could not have been more wrong.

Part 3

# "We Came to Fight"
### 12:01 a.m. to 8:30 a.m., 23 April 1915

## Legend

- Canada
- Britain
- France
- Belgium
- Germany
- Canadian Field Artillery*
- Canadian Brigade Headquarters
- Canadian Divisional Headquarters
- Canadian Line
- British Line
- French Line
- German Line
- British-Canadian Boundary
- Gas Attack Perimeter
- Canadian Units
- 1/2 Battalion Zouaves French Troops
- Zouaves French Troops
- 2nd East Kent British Troops
- 3rd Middlesex British Troops
- 5th King's Own Scottish Borderers
- Reserve-Infanterie-Regiment

* The artillery pieces representing Canadian guns indicate gun location, not direction of fire.

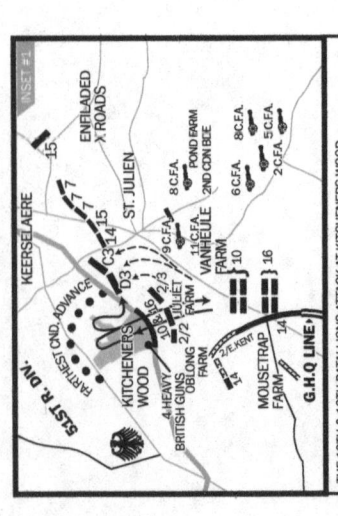

**ATTACK AT KITCHENERS WOOD**
THE 10TH & 16TH BATALLIONS ATTACK AT KITCHENERS WOOD.

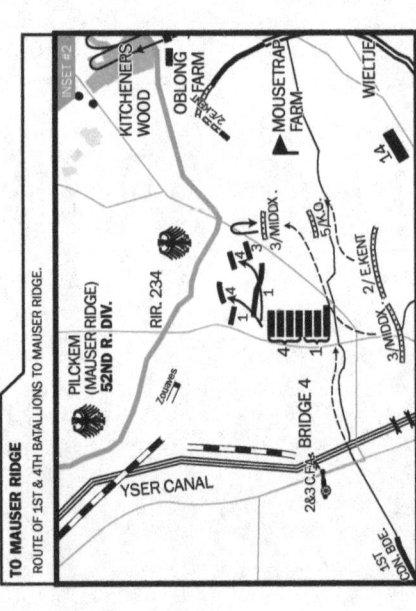

**TO MAUSER RIDGE**
ROUTE OF 1ST & 4TH BATALLIONS TO MAUSER RIDGE.

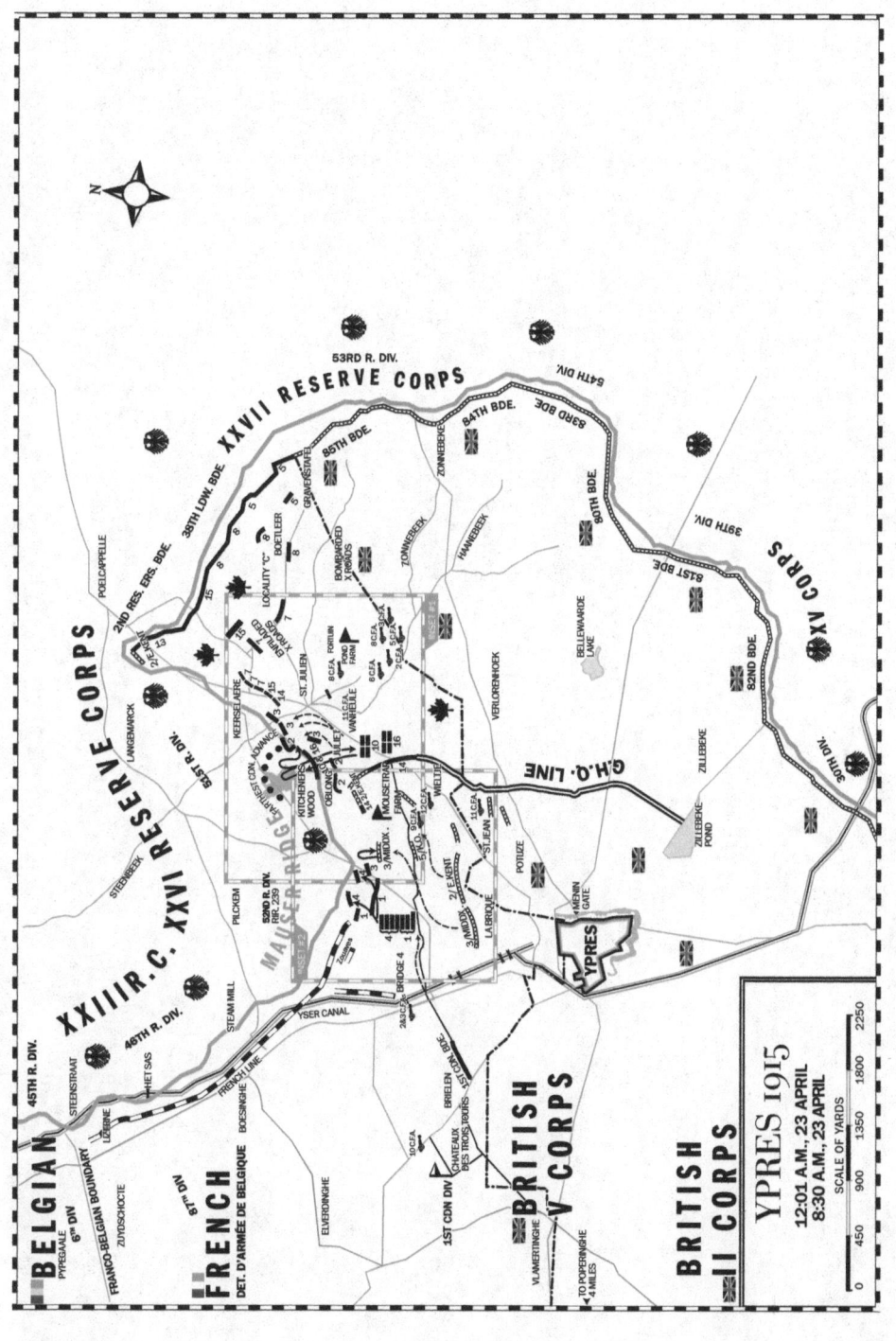

CHAPTER 4

# "In the Nature of a Sacrificial Charge"
## The 10th and 16th Battalions Attack Kitcheners Wood

> *For the word "Canada," theirs to fight*
> *And keep on fighting still;—*
> *Britain said fight, and fight they would,*
> *Though the Devil himself in sulphurous mood*
> *Came over that hideous hill.*
> —WILFRED CAMPBELL, "LANGEMARCK AT YPRES"

The fifty-seven-word message issued at 10:47 p.m. on 22 April 1915 was unique in Canadian history.* With it, Lieutenant-Colonel Hughes conveyed General Turner's order for the 10th and 16th Battalions, then assembling in the fields near Mouse Trap

---

*22/5/15
To: 10th)
16th) Bns.
3rd Bde. C.F.A.

10th and 16th Bns. in that order will counter attack at 11–30 p.m. Bns will assemble in C.23.a. north of G.H.Q. line. AAA. Clear wood C.10.d. AAA. Direction N.W. to U.27 AAA. Attack on frontage of two Companies. AAA Remaining 6 Companies in close support at 30 yards distance on same frontage. AAA Artillery shell C.5.c. and N.W. of that square.

3rd Cn. Inf. Bde.
Time. 10-47 p.m.
(sgd) G.B. Hughes, Lt-Col.

Farm, to undertake the first attack by a Canadian army on foreign soil.

Perhaps because the 16th Battalion belonged to his 3rd Brigade, and its commander, Lieutenant-Colonel Robert Leckie, was a fellow Boer War veteran, Turner would have preferred to have it lead the attack. But the 10th Battalion, which belonged to Brigadier-General Currie's 2nd Brigade and was commanded by Lieutenant-Colonel Russell Boyle, arrived first. Indeed, as it neared 10:00 p.m., Turner feared that he might have to send Boyle's men in alone, for "time was urgent" and the 16th Battalion had not yet arrived.

As Boyle's and Leckie's men, including stragglers like Lance-Corporal Hugh M. Wallis (13th Battalion), who joined the 16th Battalion on its march out of Ypres, strained to hear their officers over the roar of exploding shells, Turner waited nervously for the 2nd Battalion to arrive. Its task was not to attack but to link up with the French on Turner's left, who, Turner had been told at 8:00 p.m., would be attacking the Germans' right flank at the same time the Canadians attacked their front.

The 10th and 16th Battalions had encountered light fire on their march to Mouse Trap Farm. But under the eerie glow of the burning city behind them, the men of Lieutenant-Colonel Watson's 2nd Battalion soon found themselves in something of a shooting gallery. Even before they'd crossed the canal, one of Watson's men had been crushed to death by bricks and mortar blasted off a building. According to Private Michael Holland L'Abbé, a twenty-four-year-old Montreal accountant, the road that led to the canal received "its quota from German iron foundries." Set against the splash of shells falling into the dark waters of the canal, the order to double march seemed unnecessary. "We were velvet-toed," L'Abbé remembered, "and simply floated across" a pontoon bridge that spanned the Yser Canal a short distance northeast of Ypres.

The *swish-swish* of bullets above heads clad only in woollen caps* told the men as they clambered onto the other side of the canal that this

---

*Steel helmets were not issued to Canadian troops until 1916.

machine-gunner had aimed too high. The next did not. When a shell exploded amid the platoon ahead of him, L'Abbé dove into the mud, the *ta-ta-tatatatatat* of spent machine-gun bullets falling around him. The groans filling the air told him that some of the men had waited too long before diving.

Watson's junior officers understood why their men went to ground, but those officers also had a job to do, and that job was getting their men to the front. An officer shouted, "Get up and double into the field on the right." On cue, two men rose, making it almost to their knees before they were cut down by a machine gun. Then, to his surprise, L'Abbé found that he too was up and running, dodging "'iron rations' swishing through the air." His march forward would be repeated by thousands of men over those terrible April days:

"Advance!"

Good Lord: Was he crazy! Wait till this damned machine gun stopped firing anyway. We were all right here. Another minute or two wouldn't matter.

It flashed through my brain in a second, but in about the same time I was on my feet advancing with the rest. Head well down, and walking as low as possible, like a man facing a blizzard....

Our boys were up there. We were going to help them and stick it [out] we would. March? My God, how we did march. Heads down, rifles slung over the shoulder, and thumb under the pack-strap. Never had we marched like this. Never would we again. We had not met a soul since crossing the canal. Except the dead. Dead men had to be avoided as much as possible. Sometimes in the darkness it couldn't be helped.

A man's leg was lying on the roadside. From just below the hip. I don't know where the rest was, and it didn't interest me. It was our first taste of War as it is, and it sickened us for the moment.

Just a leg!

• • •

Historians have long faulted Turner for his plan of attack. According to the historian Daniel Dancocks, the formation used by the Canadians—two ten-deep columns of four men marching shoulder to shoulder—fit a battle where neither magazine rifles nor machine guns existed. As the historians James R. McWilliams and R. James Steel so graphically put it, "[A] bullet missing its intended target in the front rank could hardly fail to claim a victim in one of the . . . succeeding waves."[1]

L'Abbé's memoir, *Over There*, however, provides some evidence for the historian Tim Travers's claim that officers who used closed-formation advances were not just hide-bound traditionalists. Officers on both sides of the line used this formation because it moves men forward faster. And according to Travers, troops under intense fire gain "comfort from close proximity to each other."[2] But for Private Sid Cox of the 10th Battalion, the proximity got a little too close; he told the soldier on his left to get his canteen "the hell out of my ribs."

• • •

The attack began at 11:45 p.m. on 22 April. The final command—"Follow the North Star"—was, according to Lance-Corporal Wallis, only slightly clearer than the blizzard of orders that preceded it, which had the men taking off and putting on their packs and overcoats, and fixing, unfixing, and again fixing their seventeen-inch bayonets. In the end, they left their packs and overcoats behind and advanced with their bayonets attached to their Ross rifles.

Regimental records disagree on how quiet were the first moments of the Canadians' first attack in the Great War. According to the 10th Battalion's war diary, "Not a sound was audible down the long lines but the soft pat of feet and the knock of bayonet scabbards against thighs." By contrast, the 16th Battalion's regimental historian concludes that the first part of the attack must have been quite noisy as troops turned "into file to get through openings in hedges, jump ditches, and regain touch with flanking platoons."[3] The Germans apparently heard none of this.

Nor did they hear Canon Scott, who went through the ranks calling, "It's a great day for Canada, boys."[4]

Between 11:45 p.m. and 12:01 a.m., with only a stray shell causing two or three casualties, Leckie and Boyle managed to get almost eighteen hundred green soldiers halfway across a field directly in front of the battle-hardened Germans, who, although tired and hungry, were still flush with victory from the gas attack. Then the Canadians' luck began to run out. Or, to be more precise, Turner and Hughes's decision to forgo reconnoitring began to tell. The lead platoons of the 10th Battalion encountered a hedge interlaced by a wire fence.

Even before the Germans heard the Canadians' scabbards scraping against the fence, they had been expecting an attack. All the signs were there. At 10:00 p.m., scouts belonging to RIR 238 "picked up a British [Canadian] patrol and concluded the enemy was approaching."* For almost two hours, they had been under ineffective shellfire. (Unsure of where the German trenches were, the Canadians had been firing over them into the woods.) The regimental historian's claim that one of these shells hit an ammunition hut, which then burned through the night, can be doubted; every Canadian report describes Kitcheners Wood as a dark patch on the skyline.

It had been days since the Germans had a good sleep, a hot meal, or a drink of cold water. Each soldier in his mind's eye would have replayed what he'd seen over the six hours since the gas attack: the "Indian soldier" (likely a Turco) found floating in a shell hole with only his head above water, the firefights, or the moment when a favoured comrade fell. Many

---

*The regimental historian of RIR 238 may be linking two different events here. There are no Canadian records of a patrol being sent out and failing to return, though given the fact that a number of records were destroyed when Mouse Trap Farm fell later in the battle, the absence is hardly surprising. If RIR 238 did capture a Canadian patrol, it likely had little to do with the attack on Kitcheners Wood, for, as noted, Turner had not ordered the ground to be reconnoitred. However, the Germans would probably have viewed the presence of a patrol in their vicinity as an indication of a coming attack.

stiffened their own resolve by mocking the French, whose trenches they had overrun so easily. More than a few would have thought back to 1st Ypres, when they attacked "with no overview of the strategic situation, no clear knowledge of the terrain, the strength and positions of the enemy, or of the appropriate fighting tactics," and were repulsed by a thin British line.[5]

In the waning minutes of 22 April, their senses heightened. Squinting into the darkness, listening first to the Canadian scabbards scrape across the wire fence and then to the steady tramp of feet as the Canadians formed up again, men from Prussia, Saxony, Essen, and Wiesbaden waited. Up and down the line, they clutched their Mauser 98 rifles—some at the ready, others almost at the ready. The difference was only a hand that—almost of it own accord—snuck a pat on a coat pocket to make sure that spare ammunition clips were where they should be. A few men could not stand the tension and fired; at least one found a mark, hitting Major James Lightfoot in the leg. A German in front of Private Sid Cox called out, "Hey, Canada. Hey, Canada. Come here."

He did not have long to wait. Within moments, the patrols sent out by Leutnant Bunnermann had returned to the German lines, calling, like Teutonic Paul Reveres, "*Die Briten kommen!*" Across the length of the German lines, officers fired Verey lights, which made the onrushing Canadians visible under a harsh glow.

• • •

Fighting night-blindness, German riflemen and machine-gunners belonging to both RIR 234 and RIR 238 (on the Canadian left) opened up. "Everyone took up their arms and we fired at the shortest distance as much as our guns could bear," recalled Leutnant Drach of the 238. For a moment or two, he thought the Canadians were heading for his trench. Then, under the still brightly lit sky, they turned towards their own right.

Drach mistakenly believed the Canadians had either seen the gap between his and the next regiment's trench or "noticed that the trenches there were not as heavily manned." In fact, the Canadians were supposed to bear *towards* Drach's trench. Most, however, veered towards their right—that is, away from the trench—to avoid fire from a machine gun placed near Oblong Farm. It is a mark of the Canadians' inexperience that Boyle felt his orders to attack Kitcheners Wood did not permit him to detach a unit to deal with the menace the Germans had set up on what they called Hof Soetaert.

• • •

The first German fusillade left the Canadians staggering. "Bullets were ripping past. Fellows were dropping everywhere. I held up my hand in front of my face to ward off bullets," recalled a 16th Battalion NCO.[6] They had attacked without bombs or effective artillery support, confirming in the mind of Private W. J. McKenna the rumour that the 16th Battalion's officers considered "the attack to be in the nature of a sacrificial charge." Down the line in the middle of the 10th Battalion, Major Lightfoot, who was still on his feet despite taking a bullet in one leg, yelled, "Come on, boys, remember that you're Canadians!" Stirred by his call to arms, the Canadians advanced into the maelstrom.

In an instant, the 16th Battalion lost Captain John Geddes, a popular officer who had been a football player before the war; he died echoing Lightfoot's call. Other men screamed and fell. Others ran on, simple geometry dictating who survived and who did not. German machine guns fired so fast that many who fell were hit five times before their bodies came to rest on the soft earth of Flanders. As he ran forward, Private Gerald Hartman wondered how anyone could survive fire "so intense it seemed nothing could live in it."[7]

"Men on each side of me were crying out in pain," recalled a member of the 16th Battalion. "I personally felt I must surely be hit, the hail of bullets was so thick. The cracking of bullets close to the ears made them sting, and it was impossible to make oneself heard even to one's nearest neighbour."[8] Over the course of the three-hundred-yard charge, men beside him dropped, opening a gap that others filled, until they fell away in turn. Several times, "the whole front line seemed to melt away, only to be instantly closed up again."⁹ As they moved forward, the Canadians saw dead and wounded comrades lying in heaps.

• • •

The German patrols reached their trenches just ahead of the Canadians. Each side reported bitter hand-to-hand and bayonet fighting. According to its war diary, the 10th Battalion "struck the ENEMY trench, where fast work with bayonets and butt earned them the trench in less than a minute." In that minute, Leutnants Damm and Bunnermann of RIR 234 died, and Leutnant Kohlmann and Signaltrompeter Shafer were taken prisoner. Ahead of the advancing Canadians, Leutnant Kiel and his 11th Company retreated into the woods. It is a measure of the ferocity with which the Canadians fought that the 234's regimental historian wrote, "During the night several British battalions preceded by Black Ghurkhas attempted to break through near our 2nd Battalion. They broke out of the Hof de Roode Karriere [Juliet Farm] at surprising speed and staggered several lines deep." Both the "British" and the "Black Ghurkhas" were Canadians; the 16th Battalion, the Canadian Scottish, was a kilted regiment. The 16th Battalion's war diarist estimated German losses at 100 dead, 250 wounded, and 30 captured. The 234th's historian says only, "Many Canadians died in bayonet combat. But finally we lost the trench."

• • •

German and Canadian records differ on how far the Canadians penetrated into Kitcheners Wood. The 234's historian hedges his bets twice in two sentences: "At any rate, they did not succeed in advancing farther than the edge of the woods. Some small detachments probably did enter the woods but the woods remained substantially in our possession. So there can be no question of an all-out break through."

Canadian records show that with the exception of the southwest corner, held by RIR 238, the Canadians did seize the woods, and a few detachments even went a mile or so beyond. "The ENEMY were completely taken by surprise," wrote the 10th Battalion's war diarist, "and hundreds desired to surrender, but owing to the fierceness of the attackers and the large number of the ENEMY and the fact that some of the ENEMY continued to shoot, very few prisoners were taken and many lives were lost by ENEMY forces."

• • •

Within the pell-mell of battle, during which "clashing bayonets flashed like quicksilver," luck determined who would live and who would die.[10] One Canadian lunged his bayonet at a German, but it glanced off the *Feldgraue*'s equipment. A Dominion soldier running right beside him bayoneted the German in short order.

One German who had gone to ground almost did not survive. When Bernard C. Lunn saw him, the 16th Battalion private thought only of putting into practice what he had learned in hours of drills, including twisting the bayonet to let air into the wound so it would bleed more freely. For some reason, however, Lunn paused just long enough that the "heat of the proposition" cooled. Although he knew that just yards away Canadian blood soaked into the Belgian earth, he pulled back his bayonet and, after disabling the Prussian with a kick to his stomach, pushed him into a hole.

That hole was filled with *Feldgrauen* who promptly surrendered to Lunn. Bayonet at the ready, he climbed into the hole and was going through their weapons when he found that they were trying to hide their officers beneath their greatcoats. Lunn does not say why he chose one particular man for closer inspection. But he chose well. "I got down to this fellow and I tugged at his belt. It came off with a little trench knife with it." In a hidden pocket, he found a miniature Luger.

• • •

Although the units within the woods became hopelessly intermixed, a certain amount of cohesion persisted at the old German trench. Boyle's men gathered on the left and Leckie's leaned towards the right. After giving his men a moment to catch their breath and savour the "surprise and elation to find oneself over the parapet, and into the enemy's trench," Leckie had them reverse the trench's firing step so they could shoot north into the woods.

Not far away, part of the 10th Battalion had a more difficult time. Fire, likely from RIR 238, forced Boyle to abandon a trench closer to the woods. Worse, as Major Daniel Ormond, the battalion's adjutant, saw when he went to the southwest corner of the woods, on the extreme left of the 10th Battalion's line, a scant fifteen yards from the Canadian trench, a German redoubt had survived. Shortly after the major arrived, at 12:15 a.m., a German shouted, in excellent English, "We have you surrounded: surrender."[11] Over the next few hours, this small patch of ground in the southwest corner of Kitcheners Wood saw move and countermove.

Ormond was soon joined by a thirty-six-year-old lieutenant, William A. Lowry, and thirty-four other men who had orders to destroy the redoubt. For an attack hastily thrown together in the darkness of the night, it was surprisingly well organized, and thus is one more indication that the Canadians at Ypres were more than just lucky. Ormond led a diversionary frontal assault, while Lowry led about ten men in a flanking manoeuvre. Risking whatever fear would be stirred by the sound of the "levers of the machine guns being worked backwards and forwards, testing their action," Lowry had his men (who at this point had about a half an hour's worth of battle experience) familiarize themselves with the ground.

Lowry later wrote, "Then we opened fire, and the bomb [grenade] throwers commenced throwing their bombs," which, unfortunately, fell short. The rifle fire was also not what Lowry had hoped, for the bolts on their Ross rifles jammed after a few rounds of rapid fire. German machine-gunners and riflemen faced no such problems, and their fire was murderous.

As Lowry yelled, "At 'em Canadians," he and his men charged.[12] Before they were halfway to the redoubt, however, German gunners had killed all but Lowry and another soldier. Lowry made his way back to the Canadian trench by the light of German flares and tracer fire. Ormond's unsuccessful feint cost eighteen lives. To contain the Germans, Ormond ordered his men to dig a two-hundred-yard cross-trench; this new trench, to borrow a nautical expression, crossed the "T," allowing the Canadians to enfilade the Germans.

Entrenching was something the Canadians had practised at Valcartier and, when weather permitted, on the Salisbury Plain. But unlike the well-wrought trench then on display in Hyde Park, the one Ormond's men dug was a hasty affair, more notable for the speed of its construction than for its perfect zigzags, parados, barricades, and cut-outs. Those not detailed to provide covering fire unhooked their grubbers (small entrenching tools with a hoe on one end and a pick on the other) from their waist belts. After lining up on their knees facing the German trench, the men moved a yard apart and made a half turn to the right, so they were one behind the other. Each man began digging a hole about two feet wide, six feet long, and eighteen inches deep, placing the earth in a pile in front of him. Even from such a prone position, Ormond's men would have had a serviceable trench in less than fifteen minutes.

• • •

As Ormond made his way to the southwest edge of the woods, Leckie led a mixed group into it. Just before striking out, Leckie had learned that he now commanded the 10th Battalion; Boyle, the unit's commander, had been mortally wounded moments after switching on his flashlight to read a map.* Shortly after leaving their trench, Leckie's party came upon the four 4.7-inch British guns amid signs that they had not been won cheaply: "They were piled high with dead—British, Turcos and Germans."[13] Moments later, the 10th Battalion almost lost its new commander when a German being taken prisoner lunged at him

---

*Leckie already knew that the battalion's second-in-command, Major Joseph MacLaren, had been wounded and evacuated; later in Ypres, MacLaren was killed by shellfire.

with his bayonet. Leckie did not see him, but his men did—and wasted no time in filling the *Feldgraue* with cold steel.

. . .

By the time Leckie reached the northern edge of the woods, several groups of Canadians were a mile or more beyond them. Germans challenged the group led by Lance-Corporal Wallis. Rifle at the ready, he tried to warn them off. But when the leader of the German group rushed towards them, Wallis and his four men shouldered their rifles and fired, wounding him and causing the others to break and run. Leaving the wounded man under guard, Wallis and others ran after the fleeing Germans.

This chase took Wallis and his men a mile or so down a road that ran across the northern edge of Kitcheners Wood. As flares lit the sky, *Feldgrauen* alternately surrendered or fired. Concerns about being cut off from the other Canadians led Wallis to return to the woods. Somewhere just south of the northern edge, he ran into an officer (either Lieutenant-Colonel Leckie or Lieutenant-Colonel Boyle) and gave him important news: "I was looking for troops to my left . . . and found none." The officer was surprised, recalled Wallis. He "thought he was being supported on the left" by the French. This was the first a senior Canadian officer had heard that Général Henri Putz had not undertaken his promised attack.*

Some two miles beyond the woods, Private Cox's party came upon a beautiful horse, which he surmised belonged to a German colonel. For a moment, the horse lifted Cox out of the maelstrom of battle. "Poor devil was tied up," he remembered, "and when we let him go, we didn't know what we were going to do with him. We said, 'Jeez, it would be nice to have this to ride, lovely animal.' I don't know what happened to him." Cox's reverie did not last long. A moment after setting the horse free, he saw a German step out of a nearby hut. Maybe the German wanted to

---

*A short while later, Wallis's men dug a trench not far from where Major Ormond's men had dug theirs. This stretch of Flanders was uncommonly hard. "Sparks would fly when you hit the hard soil," Wallis later recalled.

surrender. Maybe not. Cox did not wait to find out. He pulled his trigger and "got out of there in a hurry."

Corporal Jack Wennevold of the 10th Battalion, a former U.S. Marine, almost did not make it back to the woods from the small copse where he and Sergeant Christopher Scriven had secreted themselves. When Wennevold was hit, Scriven lugged the 165-pound corporal back to a hut guarded by another soldier. When he laid the injured American down, Scriven saw that Wennevold's hip bone had deflected the bullet, which had then ripped open his stomach "from stem to stern." Scriven and the other soldier stuffed first-aid bandages into the gaping hole, but they did not think Wennevold would recover. He did—only to be killed a few weeks before the Armistice in 1918.

• • •

As the battle ebbed and flowed around them, some *Feldgrauen* escaped their captors. The Germans, many of whom had perfected their English working in such places as Vancouver and Swansea, shouted out what purported to be orders that sent the soldiers guarding them scurrying. When the opportunity presented itself, many simply walked to freedom in the darkness of the woods.

• • •

Somewhere in all this confusion, the war ended for both Lance-Corporal Frost and Captain Cecil Mack Merritt. Frost lived. "In my anxiety to do something, I went with others too far, and found later that I was surrounded for a second time, and early on Friday morning, I was made a prisoner while nursing an injured ankle," he wrote to his wife from a prisoner-of-war camp. Merritt died. The thirty-eight-year-old Ontario businessman, who commanded a company of the 16th Battalion, was hit in the leg during the charge but refused to be carried back to a dressing station. When a party of Germans counterattacked, "he got up to shoot over the parapet with his revolver."[14] A moment later, a bullet cut through his brain.

• • •

After Leckie returned to the southern edge of the woods, he scribbled a message to Turner that outlined what they had won, albeit at a terrific cost; the two battalions, which six hours earlier had counted some 1,800 officers and men, now had only 10 officers and 449 men between them.* With both of his flanks "in the air," Leckie told his brigadier, he could not hope to hold the woods without reinforcements.

Leckie's messenger, who arrived near 2:00 a.m., must have seemed like an apparition summoned up from the Book of Revelation. A blood-soaked dressing covered Major Gilbert Godson-Godson's throat, which had been torn open by a bullet shortly after the Canadians' first attack of the Great War.

---

*Each battalion counted five officers; the 10th Battalion had 186 men and the 16th Battalion 263 men.

CHAPTER 5

# "I Didn't Know of a Better 'Ole to Go To"
### The 2nd and 3rd Battalions Fill In on the Right

> *In a great mess of things unclean,*
> *Sat a dead Boche; he scowled and stunk*
> *With clothes and face a sodden green,*
> *Big-bellied, spectacles, crop-haired,*
> *Dribbling black blood from nose and beard.*
> —ROBERT GRAVES, "A DEAD BOCHE"

As the 10th and 16th Battalions formed up to attack Kitcheners Wood, the French three miles to their left, near a bridge that spanned the canal at Boesinghe, still held some territory. At 10:00 p.m., the French army chaplain, Abbé Albert Gaillot, disobeyed his Zouave captain, who had refused him permission to cross the bridge with stretcher-bearers to retrieve wounded men. "It would be folly, padré," the captain said. "You certainly would not return. It would be getting you killed uselessly with the men who would be accompanying you."[1]

The forty-five-year-old Dominican, who was in Canada evangelizing when the war broke out, did not argue, but he was soon struggling across the bridge. He returned about an hour later with some wounded men. Before trying to recross the bridge, Gaillot signalled the officer commanding the barricade that the Zouaves had erected in the meantime. Shaken by the horrific scenes of the day, the officer took Gaillot for a

German in disguise and fired a single shot from his revolver. The early morning light of 23 April revealed the padré's cold corpse.

About an hour before Gaillot met his end at Boesinghe, Lieutenant Jacques Hardelay, an engineering officer, prepared to destroy the railroad bridge that crossed the Yser Canal near Ypres. Hardelay's task was more difficult than that of the Canadian engineers, who mined wooden bridges with powerful melinite. Hardelay had only the less powerful chedite to use on the steel pylons of the railroad bridge, which meant that he had to place twice as many charges as the Canadians did. Twice he fell into the inky cold waters of the canal, only to climb back up and continue placing the mines.

At daybreak, German machine-gunners who had snuck into a house near the canal saw Hardelay as he climbed the embankment of the road next to the bridge. Their bullets cut him down just as he was about to jump over the rail at the top of the bank. "The machine gun continued firing all the day and fired at his body. One of my sappers," recalled Colonel Mordacq, "tried to bring back the body, but he was killed also. . . . It was only at night that two other sappers . . . succeeded in bringing back the bullet-ridden cadaver."[2]

• • •

While their comrades attacked Kitcheners Wood, the 2nd and 3rd Battalions continued their march towards Mouse Trap Farm. Lieutenant-Colonel Robert Rennie's 3rd Battalion, which had been placed under Brigadier-General Turner's command at 8:00 p.m., received its baptism of fire while marching parallel to the German trenches west of Turner's headquarters. Major Peter Anderson, who commanded the battalion's snipers, saved more than a few lives when he rushed into the road and parted the men, who had been marching in fours, into twos and directed them towards ditches on either side of the road. "The hailstorm broke loose all its fury and bullets hissed and spat on the gravel road. It lasted for fifteen minutes, then ceased."[3] Moments later, Anderson watched helplessly as a shell destroyed a machine-gun section.

After his battalion reached its destination, Anderson was ordered to see who was on its left flank. Not far into the darkness, he entered a house and found two Algerian soldiers, one of whom was badly wounded. He also found bread still warm from the oven and plenty of cheese; a family had been forced from their home by gas and fighting. About six hundred yards from the 3rd Battalion's left flank, Anderson heard men speaking English on the skyline. He stole up to them and asked who they were. The soldier told Anderson his name and what unit he belonged to:

*Anderson:* Why have you told me this?
*Soldier:* Because you are a senior officer, sir.
*Anderson:* Do you know where I come from?
*Soldier:* No.
*Anderson:* Do you mean to tell me that anyone can come here without being seen, who is a stranger to you, and you will tell him anything he wants to know? Never tell a stranger anything. I came from your rear, but I got into your lines without being challenged.[4]

As Lieutenant-Colonel Watson's 2nd Battalion passed a crossroads about five hundred yards south of Mouse Trap Farm, the men experienced a moment of relative quiet, during which the pungent smell of cordite abated. Then came "a wild rattle of musketry, increasing with the moments, and a machine gun chiming in to complete the chorus." Looking back on those moments, Private Michael L'Abbé wrote: "The hardest thing to do is stand still under fire, waiting for orders. No order had come to get down, and we were in fours. A couple of men were hit. One pretty badly." The thunder of exploding shells and the stab of light from star shells mocked the night as L'Abbé and his comrades groped their way forward:

On our left, star shells were steadily ascending. On our right, star shells were ascending. In front of us, and almost behind us. On our right rear. Where on earth were we, and where was the front?

Nobody knew. The officers didn't know. All they knew was that we were here to scrap to the finish. That much they told us.

Watson's men arrived at Mouse Trap Farm near 1:30 a.m., about fifteen minutes after the 3rd Battalion. Lieutenant-Colonel Leckie's 2:00 a.m. message from Kitcheners Wood led Turner to set aside his instructions to use the 2nd Battalion to extend his left. Instead, the brigadier divided the 2nd Battalion, tasking Captain Geoffrey Chrysler (No. 3 Company) with taking up a position behind Oblong Farm (three hundred yards southwest of Kitcheners Wood), where advanced German patrols had set up a machine gun. Turner then ordered the 2nd Battalion's No 1. Company to a position behind a rise to the left rear of the 10th Battalion, on the southwest side of Kitcheners Wood. Major George W. Bennett's men were to attack on the 10th Battalion's left; their most important goal was to destroy the heavily defended redoubt. Companies 2 and 4 waited in the fields west of Mouse Trap Farm. Their primary duty was to find shelter from German shells.

• • •

While Watson and Rennie led their men to Mouse Trap Farm, the Germans moved their own reinforcements to the front. When he heard that the English had broken the German lines, RIR 234's commander ordered Hauptmann Hattendorf "to redress the situation." Hattendorf led a mixed force from the regiment's 6th and 9th Companies; his primary goal was to recapture the four heavy British guns. Since time was of the essence, recalled Leutnant Grotrian, Hattendorf ordered his men to cross a road peppered with Canadian shrapnel. Once they were safely on the other side, Hattendorf and his officers noticed that some soldiers had not followed them.

No doubt deeply embarrassed at the lack of steel shown by his men, Leutnant Gerberger returned to those who had failed to cross the road and barked out another command. A few minutes later, it was the

German's turn to be lost. "No one knew whether to go left or right," he recalled. Soon, however, the force found Hauptmann Von Germar's dugout. Von Germar led Hattendorf's men "along the eastern edge of the wood before turning left to walk [west] along the northern edge," and then finally turning south.

Once they reached the southwestern edge of the woods, heavy fire forced the Germans to seek cover. Almost certainly this was also the engagement Ormond was referring to, although he overestimated the number of Germans when he wrote that "at least eight hundred of the enemy came up to this point." One bullet tore into Hattendorf's right jaw, exiting from the left side of his nose. As the rest of the men made their way to a trench held by RIR 238, Grotrian brought the heavily bleeding Hattendorf to the rear. He returned to the trench just in time to face a frontal assault from the 2nd Battalion's No. 1. Company, commanded by Major Bennett.

· · ·

In the hour or so before 3:50 a.m., as his men prepared to attack the machine gun that played on the 10th Battalion's left, Bennett sent out three reconnaissance patrols. When the first did not return, Leslie Gordon, the company's second-in-command, volunteered; he too was never seen again. Then Bennett himself walked off alone into the half-light.

· · ·

In the fields east of Mouse Trap Farm, L'Abbé and several hundred other men from the 2nd Battalion had more prosaic concerns. As a steady stream of walking wounded and stretcher-bearers came back, L'Abbé heard the order to dig in for the third time that night. His well-practised hand must have swept by his waist twice before the horror fully registered: his grubber was missing. As if on cue, the shelling then began "getting almost personal."

L'Abbé tried digging with his bayonet, but the ground was too hard. He checked nearby corpses, but none had his grubber. Then he remembered the infantryman's dictum—"Dirt is your friend"—and he climbed into the nearest hole. As the shells dropped ever closer, L'Abbé used his hands to dig deeper.

As he pulled his hands out from under the straw at the bottom of the hole, he saw they were covered with the remains of bloated, decayed corpses. The hole was "an open grave" that was just about his size. However much it reeked of death, it provided some safety. L'Abbé recalled the famous Bruce Bairnsfather cartoon of two men huddled in a hole surrounded by exploding shells. One says to the other, "I didn't know of a better 'ole to go to."[5]

Watson had in the meantime concluded that Bennett would never come back from reconnoitring. But just before he ordered L'Abbé and the other men out of their holes to attack, the captain returned with information about the German positions.

. . .

Just before the sun peaked over the horizon, Major Bennett's men crested a rise and charged the redoubt held by RIR 234. "Woe to us," thought Grotrian, "if they succeeded. Everyone knew what would happen to us was the same fate as the 5th Company," which was destroyed when the Canadians retook the British guns. For a moment, Grotrian's men fired wildly and he feared their discipline would break. Despite being barely able to hear their own voices, he and his officers ran up and down the trench steadying their men, and "made them aim more deliberately and . . . use their ammunition more economically." It took another minute or so, but then "it became clear that the Canadian attack had been thwarted. The figures in front were no longer advancing. They had lain down and soon we discovered that some of them were trying to crawl back. Now our men became calmer. They were firing more deliberately in front of us."

Unlike Grotrian, the Canadians never had any doubt about the Germans' musketry. Before they could break into a double march down the slope towards the German trench, Bennett and two lieutenants were dead, and another two lieutenants fell wounded. When the sun rose, the ground in front of Grotrian's trench was "sown with corpses." A hundred Canadians charged; fewer than fifteen managed to make it to the far left of the Canadian lines, where they joined the 10th Battalion.

• • •

Shortly after the 2nd Battalion's failed attack on the German redoubt, Lieutenant Reginald Tupper (16th Battalion)—who had eight years of militia experience, although he was only twenty-two—and his machine-gun crew arrived near the Canadian cross-trench. He must have set his gun up on the northwestern side of the redoubt, however, for he soon found himself almost surrounded by Germans. Whichever unit engaged Tupper's, it soon got the better of the grandson of Canada's seventh prime minister, Sir Charles Tupper. Bullets smashed the hands of one of the machine-gunners, who later counted fourteen bullet holes in his kilt. The badly wounded Tupper crawled a mile or so to a dressing-station behind the line.

The regimental historian of RIR 234 praised the Canadians for their marksmanship, their use of hand grenades, and their bravery at digging trenches directed towards the German guns. The Germans responded by sending a detachment under Leutnant Winkler into the woods. They intended to "break out of the cover of the woods" and take the Canadian trench. The plan almost worked. But at 5:30 a.m., as Winkler and his men advanced along the edge of the woods, "the enemy blew up the ammunition from the heavy guns," causing a tremendous explosion that killed some of the German attackers and wounded several others.

RIR 234's commanders did not organize another attack. Nor did they withdraw from their redoubt. Defending it, however, was complicated by two problems: the men were extremely tired, and they had not had a hot meal or much to drink for almost two days. Here, fate—in the form of British huts full of both food and tea—intervened.

• • •

While Bennett's 2nd Company attacked the Germans who held on in Kitcheners Wood, elements of Chrysler's 3rd Company flushed them out of Oblong Farm, southwest of the woods. While digging a trench in the sandy soil, Private Alan Beddoe took a moment to enjoy ripping through the German telephone wires he unearthed. Before dawn, the Canadians had established a machine gun on the farm. At dawn, the gunners saw "troops moving on the other side [and] opened fire." Because these soldiers were wearing kilts, "the word came back, 'These are Canadians. Don't fire.'" But the bullets had found their marks, putting an end to this *ruse de guerre*.

. . .

At dawn on 23 April, Lieutenant Louis Strange and his observer, Captain Harold Wyllie, climbed into their biplane to over fly the Ypres Salient. No matter what rumours had swirled during the night, neither was prepared for what he saw—or, to be more precise, did not see. "To our amazement we could find no signs of troops in their usual trenches, but soon discovered a new front line of trenches about four or five miles closer to Ypres." To determine who held these trenches, Strange dropped his plane down until he "obtained ample evidence that this new line, extending from Boesinghe [on the canal] to St. Julien, was held by the enemy." Oddly, neither saw evidence of the thousands of troops that were "confronting the Germans in their new positions."[6]

. . .

Twelve hours earlier, the Germans had torn a four-mile gap in the Allied lines. At 5:30 a.m., the gap that began at the extreme left of the 13th Battalion remained. But despite having lost comrades to shelling, Major Rykert McCuaig's men beat off several attacks during the night. Indeed, late on 22 April, McCuaig was more concerned by the Germans who "had penetrated for a considerable distance and were working round in rear of us" than he was by those in front.[7] By midnight, the Germans' chances of breaking McCuaig's line lessened when a detachment from 2/East Kents, commanded by Captain Tomlinson, arrived.

The Buffs allowed McCuaig to reoccupy forward positions he had abandoned just after the gas attack. Then the half-light of dawn illuminated another *ruse de guerre*. This time, the Germans took the part of the French. They called out in English, "We are the French," but when they failed to reply to a French officer who shouted to them in French, the British and Canadians fired on them.

On the other side of the gap that yawned to McCuaig's left, running generally along a north–south axis behind the village of Keerselaere, were three companies belonging to the 7th Battalion, commanded by Lieutenant-Colonel Hart-McHarg, and parts of two other battalions, covering almost five hundred yards to St. Julien itself. The situation in and around St. Julien had hardly improved from the previous night, when Major Odlum had visited Lieutenant-Colonel Loomis. But the sixteen-hundred-yard gap between McCuaig and Hart-McHarg was not undefended. Though unable to provide interlocking fire, both McCuaig's and Hart-McHarg's men were able to shoot into the gap. Canadian field guns southwest of St. Julien augmented this rifle and machine-gun fire. Even though German regimental histories almost always claim that the Germans had to fight uphill, in this case Captain John Warden's company (7th Battalion), stationed at Locality "C" in the middle of the gap, did indeed hold the high ground. Units belonging to the 15th and 8th Battalions were a couple of hundred yards to Warden's left and right, some immediately in front of Boetleer Farm, which housed Lieutenant-Colonel Louis Lipsett's (8th Battalion) headquarters. Together, these scattered units formed the semblance of a defensive line.

• • •

About the time Strange and Wyllie took off from the aerodrome at Abelee, L'Abbé and his comrades readied for a German attack. Suddenly, a "German loomed up about ten yards away, coming towards us on the double." It looked as though the counterattack had begun. But just as L'Abbé was about to fire, he "noticed a brawny Highlander close behind coaxing him along with his bayonet." L'Abbé then saw that blood streamed down the Highlander's leg, and he directed him towards a nearby dressing station that also served as a holding point for POWs.

The barn to which L'Abbé had directed the Highlander was filled with wounded and prisoners, some in need of water. L'Abbé ran to one of the streams that cut across the farm to get water for the wounded. He returned to a nightmarish scene. "Then the old Hun began to shell the farmhouse systematically, knowing quite well that it was being used as a dressing station," he remembered. "Two wounded, a German and a Canadian, were stepping through the door of the barn when a 'five point nine' burst at their feet, blowing them to smithereens. Part of the German's body could be seen lying a few yards away."

What happened next appears to have been another violation of the Hague Convention, which requires combatants to wear uniforms with national markings. As the barn was being evacuated, L'Abbé saw a plane with what looked like British markings fly up and down the Canadian lines. A moment later, when a terrible—and well-aimed—fusillade began, he realized that the plane had been giving the Kaiser's gunners the range. The plane soon returned "to watch the concert." Its pilot, one of the Kaiser's "Knights of the Air," circled, "doing stunts for the edification of his own artillery, which was using shrapnel among the fleeing wounded. It was brutal. We determined it would be a fight to the finish."

Shortly afterward, L'Abbé and hundreds of other men from the 2nd Battalion fell in and, with elements of the 3rd Battalion, advanced to their right, bringing them to the northwest corner of a mustard field, slightly to the right of 16th Battalion's trench and just south of Kitcheners Wood. When told to "advance individually and try to make the trench in front of the woods," L'Abbé, and no doubt others around him, thought, "What wood? We had never seen the wood, and had not the vaguest idea of what was on the other side of the mustard."

Years later, L'Abbé could afford wry humour when he wrote that joining "a front line in broad daylight, across a perfectly flat stretch of ground, is not what I would choose for a morning's exercise." Given the Canadians' lack of field experience, the advance could have been a disaster. It was not, however, because Major Arthur Kirkpatrick did not order his men to advance in close formation. Rather, as bullets whizzed overhead and plunked down beside them, they "emulate[d] the lowly worm gliding through the ungarnered harvest." The few who had not had their Canadian-made Oliver webbing replaced with British webbing no doubt cursed the designer for putting the extra ammunition pouch on their stomachs.

The distance between the mustard patch and the Canadian lines varied from a bit more than a hundred yards for L'Abbé to as many as eight hundred yards on the right wing. Kirkpatrick's description of the advance of "C" and "D" Companies underlines the difference between this action and the attack on Kitcheners Wood: "Each section would dash forward a few yards and fall flat, then another and another, and while many a man fell in a khaki heap in silent death, the thinning lines kept steadily on."

The hundred or so yards that L'Abbé crossed to get to the Canadian lines were gruesome. "Kilted and khaki figures . . . in strange attitudes" marked his way. Still, these dead bodies offered a measure of protection because they prompted each machine-gunner to lift his gun just a little bit higher or move across that small vector without firing. Soldiers ran from behind one corpse to another, further complicating the gunner's and riflemen's task. Even weighed down by a pack, a greatcoat, and a Ross rifle, a man in good shape can dash across a hundred yards in about thirty seconds. According to the historian Bill Rawling,

> When firing at a figure running across one's front, the rifleman or machine gunner must judge not where the runner is at that moment but where he will be in a half a second. Predicting where a moving object will be is extremely difficult. If the running soldier slows up by even the slightest amount, the bullet will whiz right by him. Runners can improve their odds

by zigzagging, which not only effectively slows them but makes predicting their path even more difficult, for zigzagging is surprisingly hard to pick up from the flank.

L'Abbé survived both the German bullets and a bayonet that had been left on the side of the trench he jumped into.

It's not clear why Kirkpatrick ordered his men to move on their stomachs and in small groups. Perhaps he was aware that Lieutenant-Colonel Arthur Birchall (4th Battalion) taught that in the face of machine-gun fire, advances should be made by small groups hugging the ground; perhaps he knew that in General Currie's 2nd Brigade, similar tactics were being taught by a British captain named Williamson. Or perhaps Kirkpatrick simply ordered his men to do what he had learned during militia training, for, as Rawling has shown, small advances were *de rigueur* in the militia—not because of prescient military theorists but because militia units "were not large enough to do anything else."[8]

• • •

Even from their lowest observation level, neither Strange nor Wyllie would have been able to see that Canadian machine-gun crews held the most important positions—two farmhouses between the extreme right of the 2nd Battalion's line and St. Julien. It is unclear whether Captain W.H.V. Hooper and Lieutenant William J. Doxsee knew of each other's plan to take these two farmhouses. Both operations, which occurred about the time Strange's plane took off, underline the surprisingly good performance of junior officers, who were not shy about taking the initiative even though they lacked battlefield experience.

Captain Hooper moved first, taking his house with a flanking manoeuvre. The enemy garrison at what became Doxsee's House, 150 yards away, fled without firing a shot when Doxsee's 5th Platoon burst out of a shallow ditch seventy-five yards away; Doxsee's men, however, killed at least three *Feldgrauen* and took another prisoner. "Lieutenant Doxsee immediately set to work to get the house which was undoubtedly the key to our position in a state of defence," reported Captain George Richardson, "and at daybreak was ready for the attack which was launched." Behind these words is the hurried work of hungry and tired men whose uniforms, despite the lingering chill in the late dawn air, were wet with sweat and smudged, like their faces and hands, with both dirt and blood. Behind these words are orders coughed out from raspy throats badly in need of a cool drink of water. Behind these words are muscles that pulled doors off hinges, moved whatever furniture could be found, and used bayonets to pry bricks loose—the detritus of war hastily fashioned into life-saving barricades. Behind these words is the moment when a partially naked soldier squatted behind a fence or a tree, beneath a sky stained by smoke from fires that burned all night.

In the clear light of dawn, the Germans massed in a trench to the north side of Doxsee's House. Through holes cut in the walls, Doxsee's infantrymen and machine-gunners poured fire into the trench, while two sharpshooters, Sergeant Harry C. Ablard and Lance-Corporal McGurk, left the relative safety of the house to find perches. Each man accounted for eighteen kills before he was shot dead by German marksmen. Some of the emotion their comrades felt at their deaths can be heard in Captain Richardson's after-action report: "They lay exposed where they fell and could be readily counted."

A hundred or so yards to the 2nd Battalion's left ran the trenches held by the 10th and 16th Battalions. At 2:00 a.m., the Canadians held most of Kitcheners Wood. But as dawn approached and reinforcements failed to arrive, Leckie ordered the 10th and 16th Battalions to withdraw to the old German line and one 150 yards farther south. The retirement was carried out without losses, but daylight brought misery to the wounded lying before the woods. German machine-gunners and riflemen, who still held the redoubt in the corner of the woods, shot at anybody who moved—including stretcher-bearers, one of whom was killed. Private Lunn, one of the last to leave the woods, ran a gauntlet of German fire. "I remember staying beside a tree and just every time I moved—pit, pit, pit—and I started to crawl and I crawled back to the trench." Soon after reaching his trench, Lunn heard a soldier call from no man's land, about 150 yards away. Lunn immediately volunteered to go get him, but his captain ordered him not to.

Risking both a court martial and German bullets, Lunn ignored his captain and went back over the top, crawling to the injured soldier, who immediately grabbed for Lunn's water bottle. Realizing that he had forgotten it, and that the wounded soldier did not have one, Lunn threaded his way back to his trench. A fellow soldier tried to stop him from risking his neck again, but Lunn protested that the man wanted water. And he went over the top once more, an act he repeated several times.

• • •

At 5:30 a.m., a German plane flew over the 16th Battalion's trench, south of Kitcheners Wood. Soon shells started falling, blowing both earthworks and men apart. The blasts created "over-pressures or vacuums in the body's organs, rupturing the lungs and producing haemorrhages in the brain and spinal cord," killing men without leaving a mark on their bodies.[9] Shells that fell on the battalion headquarters were aimed in accordance with the Hague Conventions. Those that fell on first-aid stations—whether or not they were crowded with casualties (they were) and, more to the point, could be seen by German spotter planes—violated the rules of war.

• • •

Had Strange and Wyllie seen the Canadians at Oblong Farm, they would have been alarmed by what appeared to be a one-and-a-half-mile gap between them and the Zouaves, the last real remnant of the French lines. In reality, the gap was much smaller.

The first 750 yards was protected by two forces, the GHQ Line and the Die Hards (3rd Middlesex). Though the GHQ Line was hardly a well-wrought trench, it still provided reasonably good protection for small bodies of troops. It was not, however, well situated to defend against a German advance from the north. Still, the troops at its northern end (three companies of the Buffs) were able to provide reasonable fire towards both Oblong Farm on their right and the French units on their left. Colonel Augustus Geddes, a career officer, placed his 3rd Middlesex men in a trench facing north, a little over a thousand yards to the east. On their way to taking up this position, the Die Hards lost two officers and eighty men to machine-gun fire from Mauser Ridge, where hundreds of Canadian and British troops would soon suffer and die.

## Chapter 6

# "And Trust to Providence"

### The 1st and 4th Battalions Attack Mauser Ridge

> *"Forward, the Light Brigade!"*
> *Was there a man dismay'd?*
> *Not tho' the soldier knew*
> *Someone had blunder'd:*
> *Theirs not to make reply,*
> *Theirs not to reason why,*
> *Theirs but to do and die.*
> *Into the valley of Death*
> *Rode the six hundred.*
> —Alfred, Lord Tennyson,
> "The Charge of the Light Brigade"

As the sun burned off a morning mist that cloaked hundreds of Canadian, British, French, and German bodies, all frozen in grotesque positions, German newspapers reported that the Kaiser's army in Flanders had advanced five and a half miles, crossed the Yser Canal, taken sixteen hundred French and English prisoners, and captured thirty guns, including four heavy English guns. By the time Berliners had finished their breakfast, the Canadians had learned, *avant la lettre*, the truth of Churchill's dictum that "the only thing worse than fighting a war with allies is fighting a war without them."*

Of the three major counterattacks in the opening part of 2nd Ypres, the first one on Mauser Ridge received the most attention from senior officers. Indeed, the orders for that attack came from the commander of the French army, Général Ferdinand Foch, and the commander of the British Expeditionary Force, Field Marshall Sir John French. Shortly after midnight on 23 April, Foch ordered Général Henri Putz to ensure that the Belgian army and the remaining Zouave units on the eastern side of the canal retained their positions, and he asked him to organize and deliver a counterattack that would recapture the lost ground. At about the same time, after a meeting with his commander, General Plumer, General Alderson ordered Brigadier-General Mercer to have Lieutenant-Colonels Frederick Hill and Arthur Birchall prepare their 1st and 4th Battalions, respectively, then in reserve at Vlamertinghe, to cross the Yser Canal. At 1:45 a.m., Mercer received the order to cross the canal on a pontoon bridge and then establish a fifteen-hundred-yard firing line running east from the bridge.** At 3:15 a.m., after briefing his officers, Mercer ordered his men to move north towards the line held by the 3rd Middlesex Battalion. At 3:45 a.m., Mercer was told to coordinate his attack with one by the French on his left: "At 5 o'clock [a.m.] two French battalions are to make a counter-attack against Pilckem, with their right resting on the Pilckem–Ypres road. You will cooperate with this attack by attacking at the same time with your left on this road."

The historian's ability to reconstruct, to the minute, the time of these messages and the exactitude of the coordinates belies the quality of the information available to these generals and the logic of their orders. Neither Foch, who was almost twenty miles away in French Flanders,

---

*Churchill is reported to have said this about fighting with the French in 1940 and with the Americans in 1941.

**The order read: "Take your battalions across the pontoon bridge in C.19.c and take up a position facing north along track running from C.19 and 20. Keep your right west of Cross roads in C.20.c."

nor Putz, who was some miles closer but nowhere near the fighting, had a clear grasp of what was happening on the battlefield. Says the historian Tim Cook:

> Despite some undulations, the territory in front of Mauser Ridge is very flat. And this gave the advantage to the defenders, even if they were only on a small rise, which Mauser Ridge is. More importantly, the Germans had had time to dig in and prepare fields of fire. That said, it is the cruel fate of the infantrymen in battle to be called upon to sacrifice themselves for tactical and strategic objectives—which in this case was stopping the Germans.

The order to cooperate with the Canadians may testify to the French generals' belief in *élan*, but they failed to take account of the reality that the gas attack had shattered their soldiers. Worse, they ignored the fact that any attack undertaken without artillery preparation was likely to fail.

At Vlamertinghe, Alderson and Plumer could see the hundreds of refugees and wounded soldiers, as well as the glow from fires then consuming Ypres. Though Alderson saw the gas cloud rise from the German trenches and Plumer heard of it shortly thereafter, their grasp of what was going on the battlefield was as poor as Foch's. True, they knew that a counterattack was under way at Kitcheners Wood, but at 1:45 a.m., when he ordered Mercer to cross the canal, Alderson knew nothing about its status. According to Canada's official historian, A. Fortesque Duguid, when Alderson issued this order, he had doubts about the French positions. Two hours later, when he ordered the brigadier to coordinate with the French attack, which was planned for 5 a.m., his doubts could only have been stronger. For in those two hours, little, if any, official information about the French had reached Alderson's headquarters.

Whatever doubts he had hardly mattered. Alderson was under Plumer's command, and Plumer was under General Smith-Dorrien's command, and General Smith-Dorrien was under Field Marshal French's command. And Sir John did not entertain any doubts. "I fully concurred in the wisdom of the General's [Foch] wish to re-establish our old line and agreed to co-operate in the way he desired," he wrote a few days later.*

At 4:15 a.m., Mercer received the message ordering the 5:00 a.m. attack. Colonel Geddes, who had long since received his copy of the order, had already informed his Die Hards that the 1st and 4th Battalions would soon be passing through their lines. By contrast, the Canadians were quite surprised to discover Geddes's men when they moved up towards their jumping-off point.

• • •

As the Canadians readied to attack—and the British arranged for them to pass through their lines—their guns, some from the 1st Canadian Brigade's artillery section and some from the 10th Canadian Field Battery, were also on the move. Getting these last into position required quick work by men such as John Armstrong. Having withdrawn their guns under fire from a position five hundred yards north of St. Julien, Armstrong's unit had just settled the horses when the bugle sounded "Stand To." Immediately, groups of men sprang into action. The sergeant who commanded each gun (No. 1) checked to see if the bore was clear. At the same time, the gun-layer (No. 2) removed the muzzle and breech covers, and examined the breech, safety catch, firing mechanism, extractor, ranging and other gear. The gun-ranger (No. 3) examined the sights, break, elevating and firing gear, and set the traverse to zero. Behind him, the gun-loader (No. 4) examined the limber box, and six other men harnessed the horses to the limber, which was then moved into position near the gun. According to regulations, guns were to be attached to their limbers only after the section commander gave the order, and only by Nos. 2 and 3, who would lift the trail and place it on the hook.

---

*Sir John's report continued, in prolix prose, "[I] stipulat[ed], however, that if the position was not re-established within a limited time, I could not allow the British troops to remain in so exposed a position as that which the action of the previous twenty-four hours had compelled them to stay." But that is exactly what he did.

It was, Armstrong recalled, a wild ride:

> By the time we left Ypres and got to Hellfire corner, Fritz had spotted us and opened up on us. It was the one and only time we went into action at the gallop. For about three miles down the road we went as fast as we could. Fritz followed us all the way up with 5.9 shells. We got in behind the canal bank and we were ordered to prepare for action.[1]

After the gun crews arrived at the canal, someone gave the drivers directions that required almost superhuman control over the horses. As if galloping along a shell-pocked road under increasing shellfire wasn't difficult enough, now, in the half-light of dawn, they were told that "about 200 yards further up [they'd] go through a gap in the bank and then along the canal to go into action." On the ground these directions meant that six horses at a full gallop, pulling a limber carrying a gun, shells, and men together weighing more than five thousand pounds, had to make not one but two hard right turns on five-foot steel wheels in the space of some twenty yards.

One wonders if Armstrong realized how redolent his description was of the diction of Tennyson's "Charge of the Light Brigade":

> Down through the gap we went, right to the canal bank. We pulled up under some trees, and though the Germans had a direct view, the trees prevented them from finding out just where we were. We got orders to "Action Front." We unloaded the gun limbers and they took them away. There were shells popping all around us and machine gun bullets too.

In the end, eight British howitzers and eight Canadian eighteen-pounders were unequal to the task of supporting an attack on a mile of well-defended trench. But they were able to force the Germans to abandon Turco Farm, an intermediate point about 250 yards before the main German line on Mauser Ridge.

"And Trust to Providence"  129

• • •

When Mercer read the 4:15 a.m. order to attack, he had only forty-five minutes to organize his men. Surprisingly good discipline for such green troops ensured that by 5:00 a.m., the 4th Battalion was arrayed across a two-hundred-yard frontage on Hill Top Ridge. Ahead lay fifteen hundred yards of ground that first sloped gently about thirty feet down to a depression, later nicknamed "Colne Valley" (an ironic reference to the picturesque Essex village), then climbed up about thirty-three feet to the top of Mauser Ridge. Two lines of pollard willow trees ran from east to west across the Canadians' line of march. A third line of trees ran along the left side of the Canadians' attack front, and a hedge ran north to south along the right side of the Canadians before it turned to the right (east) about seventy-five yards in front of the German trenches. The trees and hedge provided little cover from the Germans on top of Mauser Ridge, however; worse, they impeded the Canadians' ability to advance. Seventeen minutes before zero hour, Birchall and Hill received word that the French would be attacking a mile or so to the Canadians' left at exactly 5:00 a.m.

• • •

The *Feldgrauen* who occupied what they called Pilckem Ridge had spent the night running wire, deepening their trenches, sighting machine guns, eating what food they could, and trying to catch a few moments of sleep. On their far right, where their line curved towards the canal, were Allied troops, probably Belgian. Musketeer Uppel of RIR 239 won a commendation for excellence "when, while being fired at from both sides, he approached the enemy sharpshooter holes, crawling towards them armed with hand grenades which allowed him to drive back the approaching enemy."

• • •

As zero hour came and went, the ground between the Hill Top and Mauser ridges remained quiet. Birchall knew why the Canadians had not made much noise; his 4th Battalion was still behind the Die Hards. What confused him was that he was unable to see or hear signs of the French attack. At 6:25 a.m., Alderson sent a message: "French say they started attack at 5 o'clock, but they are in advance of you and further to the west." That would have put them on Birchall's left front.

It's unclear exactly how long it took the Canadians to pass through Geddes's troops and re-form. Most historians state that the attack finally started at 5:25 a.m. More recently, the historian Andrew Iarocci has put the start time between 5:50 and 6:30 a.m., thus suggesting that it took about an hour to sort out and re-form the battalions. RIR 239's history is of little help; the first sentence that refers to the Canadian attack reads, "Soon a thin line of infantry is emerging from the morning mist." Perhaps the best evidence for Iarocci's later start time is the dog that didn't bark, which in this case is Lieutenant Strange's report, which makes no mention of an attack being under way while he was flying over the salient at around 5:00 a.m.

At all events, sometime before 6:30 a.m., Birchall saw trees moving on his left, which he took to be the advancing French, and he ordered his officers to blow their whistles. Mercer's description of "the whole advance being carried out in most perfect order as if on parade" has misled one historian of the battle into thinking that Birchall's men advanced in the same closed formations used by the 10th and 16th Battalions at Kitcheners Wood.[2] In fact, Birchall and Hill's plan of attack resembled that used by the 2nd and 3rd Battalions. Their men moved "forward across the open fields by sections extended to ten yards and leap-frogging."[3] The tactic caught the eye of the regimental historian of RIR 239. "They approach along the Pilckem–Ypres Road and along the canal," he wrote, "adroitly using the terrain" to hide themselves. According to Victor Trowles (4th Battalion), "We crossed two or three fields, you know, little rushes and dropped down and we finally got into a ditch where . . . we were quite protected."

Trowles and the men who advanced safely with him owed their success largely to their commanding officer. As Iarocci has shown, Birchall's training manual, titled *Rapid Training of a Company for War*, de-emphasized closed-formation attacks and advocated instead company or platoon advances that were covered by neighbouring units. He also advised making use of the terrain and argued, according to Iarocci, that "special detachments of infantry [be] posted, if possible, on the flank." Though machine guns would not be organized to trap Germans in boxes of exploding steel until Vimy, almost exactly two years later, Iarocci found that Birchall's machine-gunners did not act on targets of opportunity alone. Dragging their almost hundred-pound guns from the declivity to scrub grass on the right, they "attempted to lay down suppressive fire," and thus create a veil behind which the infantry could move forward.[4]

Private William Bingham (4th Battalion) described the advance in a letter that credited his survival to Birchall's tactics and a benevolent God:

> Scores of my chums fell all around me, some of them never to rise again. Those who reached the trench we started out to take seem to have charmed lives. Bullets and shells were falling all round us like rain, but we still kept going on, making rushes of 75 to 100 yards at a time until we finally reached the trench in front of us, covering over 1,000 yards of open country, with nothing but Providence to protect us from the thousands of German bullets and shells.[5]

Though Mercer's men had practised manoeuvres similar to those they'd used at Mauser Ridge, mistakes occurred. One of the worst took place in a field "dotted with manure piles." Trowles recalled how his buddies sought shelter behind them, but the manure piles did not stop the machine-gun bullets, and in fact acted as "target attractors" for German artillery. At 7:00 a.m., with Birchall's men about halfway to their objective and his own following quickly behind, Hill sent a runner to Mercer to report that the attack was progressing well.

By the time the runner reached his brigadier, however, the information was outdated. By then, Birchall's and Hill's men were in the middle of a killing ground. As soon as the Canadians passed the hedge and trees, and before they could again go to ground, the Germans "opened the gates of hell and pushed [them] in."[6] Less than a year earlier, Corporal Edgar Wackett had concerned himself chiefly with the wonders of double-entry bookkeeping. In the early morning of 23 April 1915, on that Flanders field, he wondered how it was "possible for any human being to live in the rain of shot and shell that began to play on us.... For a time every other man seemed to fall."[7]

Shellfire does different things to the men who survive it. Some it makes mute; others hysterical. Most, however, cope. And as hard as it is for civilians to believe, most men who have been under the storm of steel do not report panicking. Private W. T. Colyer, who served with the British Artists' Rifles, recalled how a green soldier feels during his first exposure to battle:

> Was I panic-stricken? No. Not in the least. It would be hard to analyze my feelings as I gazed at the ugly brown hole in the green field. Astonishment, excitement, realization, relief, foreboding, curiosity and even a morbid kind of satisfaction—these emotions possessed me almost simultaneously and left no room for the sensation of fear. Nothing to be frightened of in fact—provided it did not burst any closer, that is to say.[8]

In the middle of battle, where men live in a grotesque arabesque, the body of a man shot down becomes "nothing except something to avoid stumbling over," said Private George Bell of the 1st Battalion. He recalled:

> Ahead of me I see men running. Suddenly their legs double up and they sink to the ground. Here's a body with the head shot off. I jump over it. Here's a devil with both legs gone, but still alive. A body of a man ... [is simply] another obstacle. There goes little Elliot, one of the boys from the print shop where I worked in Detroit, only ten yards from me. Poor devil.

There's nothing more I can do for him. What's one man, more or less, in this slaughter? . . .

My hand feels as if [it] were hit by a club and there's a burning sensation in my fingers. A bullet has seared them, smashing the grip on my rifle. I drop the useless weapon. There's a dead Tommy. He'll never need his rifle again, so I pick it up without stopping.[9]

Every one of the officers in Bell's battalion was killed or wounded.

. . .

Farther down the line, Private Sidney Radford and a few other men took shelter from the German shells in a shallow ditch while their colonel ran behind a haystack on the other side of the road. Through the din of the explosions, they heard him call for them to fall in behind him. Exhausted by the sprint across the road, Radford dropped down to catch his breath as the rest pushed on into the German fire. As soon as he could, Radford rose into the hail of German gunfire and advanced with the next unit that came over. He mistook a forward German trench for the main trench on Mauser Ridge and recalled getting "pretty close." Before he started to climb up the ridge, a shell exploded, blowing him into the dirt- and bullet-filled air. "As soon as I flopped, I thought that I heard a terrific explosion. . . . And I did a somersault and I screamed."

Somehow, amid the confusion of battle and the searing pain of shrapnel cutting straight through his boot and into his foot, Private Radford had the presence of mind to stop screaming, throw off his equipment, abandon his rifle, and begin crawling back, past other wounded and dead men, towards Hill Top Ridge. Before too long, a soldier he knew cut off Radford's boot and covered the bleeding foot with a field dressing he took from a pocket at the bottom of Radford's greatcoat. After what seemed like ages, a Zouave picked Radford up and carried him on his shoulders to a farmhouse, where he was put on a stretcher in an upstairs room. After "a shell came over and hit the corner of the farmhouse and blew it away," Radford was taken to the cellar.

Radford was luckier than most. Only eleven of the fifty-five men in Private Alfred A. Wakeling's 4th Battalion platoon (on Radford's right) survived:

> We no sooner showed ourselves than a terrible fire was opened up, machine gun and shrapnel. It came from all directions on our front and both flanks; our boys went over in dozens. There was nothing to do but push forward, and we had only just started.
>
> One particular spot I noticed was awful. It was a small piece of ploughed land with just a little ridge to it. Bullets were hitting and whistling everywhere. We could do nothing for our wounded, only leave them on the field, and trust to Providence.[10]

• • •

Canadians may have considered the artillery supporting the attack meagre, but the Germans did not. "Under the protective veil of their own artillery, the enemy infantry is screwing itself closer and closer to the German position," reported the historian of RIR 239. "In spite of heavy losses caused by the well-aimed infantry fire of the 52nd Reserve, they are gaining ground." For a few moments, it even seemed to the men of the 239th that the Canadians had caught a break from the German artillery, which was dropping shells, including tear-gas shells, on their own trench instead of on the Canadian positions. "The troops were getting nervous," wrote the regimental historian, in a comment that hides almost as much as it reveals. The gunners corrected their range only after Private Lettemen ran back through the vicious artillery fire without any cover and told them they were not on target.

At the height of the attack two platoons from the 5th Company were rushed up to bolster the 2nd Company, and the 6th Company was dispatched to support the 3rd Company, but the German defensive line was never in serious danger. After seeing the well-situated machine-gun sites, loopholes, obstacles, and other fortifications that the Germans had constructed during the night to fortify Mauser Ridge, one Allied officer wrote, "Ah! The Germans had not been wasting their time since the day before. What they achieved [on Mauser Ridge] it must be admitted was really superhuman."[11]

• • •

The Canadian attack ground to a halt sometime after 7:20 a.m. Ten minutes later, Birchall asked Hill for reinforcements. When these reserves moved up a few moments later, they filled the gap between Birchall's men and the Middlesex units farther right, near Turco Farm. The farm itself belonged to neither army; earlier Canadian artillery had chased the Germans away, but continuing fire forced other Die Hards to withdraw.

On the left, where the bulk of the 1st Battalion had attacked, the situation was equally confusing. Forced to the ground near a row of trees on the left of the Canadian advance, Major Albert Kimmons was the most senior Canadian officer to see French soldiers on the field. They had, according to the laconic French official history, "carried out two counter-attacks which miscarried."[12] After two runners sent to the French for help were cut down, Kimmons and Lance-Corporal Edward Mockler set out to try to reach them themselves. Kimmons never made it. Mockler told of being shot by a machine gun, and of his agonizing six-hour crawl back to the Canadian lines. A fortnight later, the day U-20 torpedoed the SS *Lusitania* off the coast of Mockler's beloved Erin, the nineteen-year-old died in an English hospital.\*

---

\*Among the 1,195 men, women, and children who died when the famed Cunard liner went down was Mrs. George Ryerson, the wife of Colonel George Ryerson, who founded the Canadian Red Cross; her daughter was one of the few survivors. One of the Ryerson sons, Lieutenant Arthur C., fought at 2nd Ypres and was wounded while heroically carrying shells to his unit, the 9th Canadian Field Artillery Battery. Shortly after being hit, he experienced what was perhaps an almost greater horror when he came across the body of his brother, Captain George (3rd Battalion). Being wounded probably saved Lieutenant Ryerson's life, for shortly thereafter, a large shell hit his unit's dugout, killing five men and wounding seven others.

At 8:30 a.m., Mercer received word from Alderson that "[the] French attack does not seem to be successful.... It is believed that there are still two French Battalions on the East side of the Canal." He was advised to get in contact with them. By 8:30 a.m., Mercer knew that the French attack had indeed not been successful. In fact, he knew that there had been no French attack; as the historian Daniel Dancocks put it, Mercer "was on the warpath... looking for the officer who was supposed to be in command of the French operation."[13] At a meeting held before 7:45 a.m., Colonel Mordacq had assured Mercer that the French had three and a half battalions of Zouaves on the east side of the canal and two more battalions ready to cross; a message sent to the Château des Trois Tours at 7:35 a.m. repeated this information, adding that an attack "by successive battalions with maximum of machine guns [was] trying to throw the enemy back toward the N.W." Ten minutes later, while hundreds of Mercer's men lay dead and wounded, and others huddled behind what little cover they could find while the Germans rained shot and shell on them and swept the field with machine-gun fire, Alderson received word that, far from launching an attack, the French had "no formed units left" on the east bank of the Yser. Additionally, French troops on the other side of the canal were "suffering from the effects of asphyxiating gas and incapable of much resistance."

At 7:55 a.m., Alderson's adjutant, Colonel Cecil Romer, sent a message to Plumer saying that since the French counterattack had not been successful, he was ordering his men on Mauser Ridge to stand fast and dig themselves in. Romer also said that because he was "by no means confident of the French on my left," he was keeping the East Yorks on the west bank of the Yser Canal.*

---

*Amazingly enough, at 8:15 a.m., Alderson received the following message from Colonel Hare in Elverdinghe: "Report from French Commander attacking on East Side of Canal 7:10 a.m. [begins,] 'All goes well. Seventh Zouaves are holding well and making trenches. The 2nd Zouaves have crossed the Canal two Companies of them being already deployed at wide intervals and in touch with Canadians who have commenced to move forward.... The morale of the troops somewhat upset this morning by asphyxiating gases is excellent.'"

There had been no French attack, and the dead Canadians could be counted as lucky, like those who, though pinned down, remained untouched by exploding shells. The unlucky suffered indescribable agony—far beyond anything they could have imagined when they first wondered what "bullets entering various parts of one's anatomy" would feel like.[14] One who so suffered was Private Goldwin Pirie, a twenty-one-year-old who before the war was a Canadian Bank of Commerce clerk in Toronto. For three days, he lay at the bottom of a shell hole, his right arm and pelvis smashed by the impact of Maxim machine-gun bullets moving at almost three times the speed of sound.

At 8:30 a.m., Birchall and Hill received the astounding order that in the absence of the French, their shattered battalions should fill the gap east to the Yser Canal.

PART 4

# Holding the Line
8:31 a.m. to 11:45 p.m., 23 April 1915

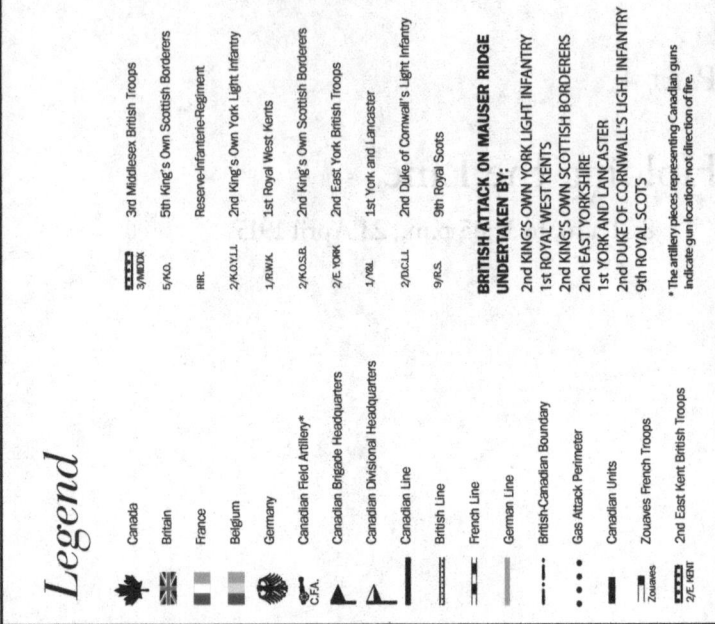
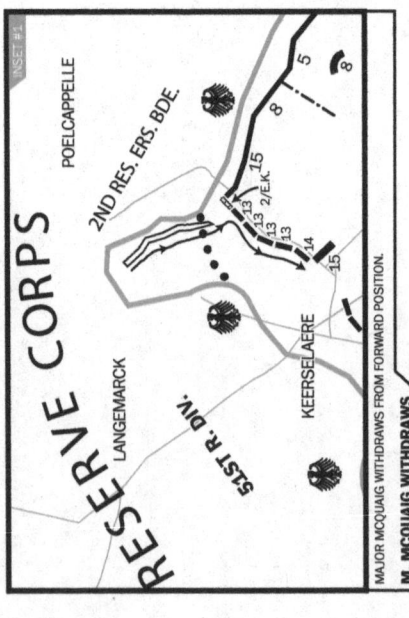
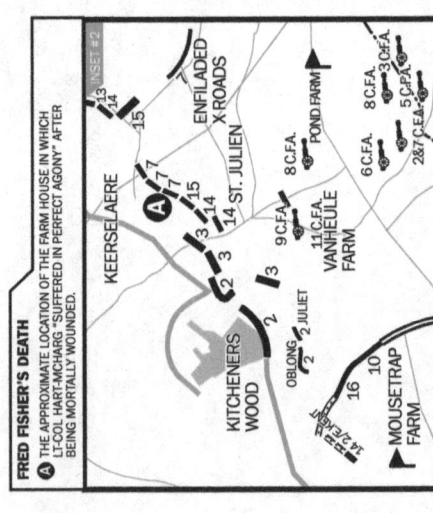

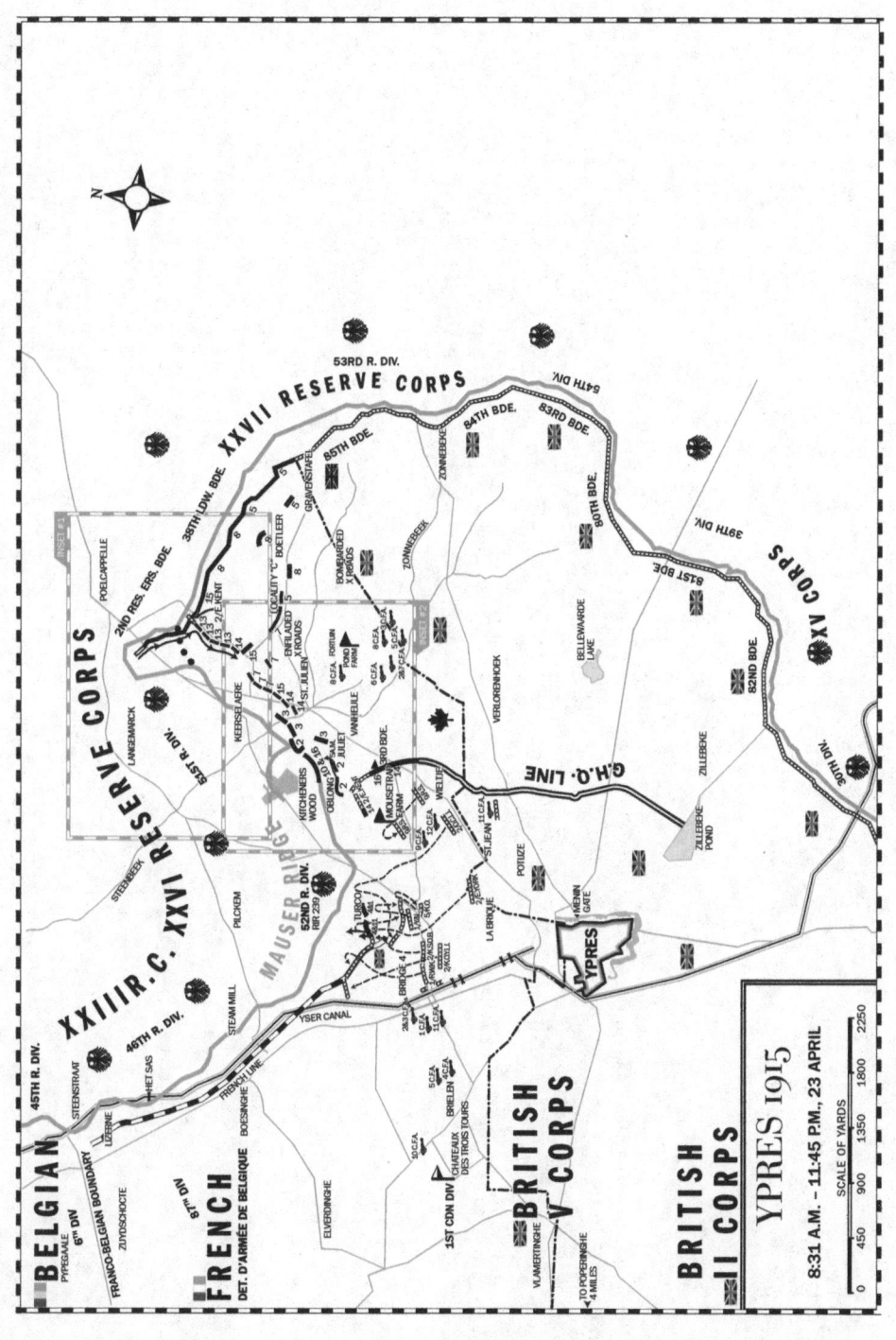

## Chapter 7

# "We Sampled Every Kind of Shell Made in Germany"

### Lance-Corporal Fred Fisher Earns a Victoria Cross, and William Doxsee Protects His House

> *There are tears in things.*
> —Virgil, *Aeneid*

After suffering through a night of intense shelling, Major Rykert McCuaig and the men of the 13th Battalion would no doubt have wondered what Otto Henning, the regimental historian of RIR 233, had in mind when he wrote that after having safely passed through Langemarck, the regiment experienced "not insignificant" losses from artillery. Between 4:00 a.m. and 7:00 a.m., the only guns that fired in the 233's direction belonged to the 2nd Canadian Field Artillery Battery, which discharged fewer than sixty-five shrapnel shells—an average of one every three minutes.

An engagement with what Henning called "the Scottish" likely cost the life of Lance-Corporal Frederick Fisher, the machine-gunner who had protected Major William King's battery the day before. The engagement began when a unit commanded by Oberleutnant Brandt reached a farm on the St. Julien–Poelcappelle road, which ran more or less north from St. Julien for a thousand yards to the village of Keerselaere before turning slightly northeast for a mile and a half to Poelcappelle. Uncharacteristically,

Henning neither names the farm nor indicates its position in relation to other farms near Keerselaere. But the fact that he referred to the enemy as Scottish, and that Brandt's men "dug in . . . without any link to the left or the right," suggests that the farm was one of those just ahead of McCuaig's kilted line.

At first, the Canadian machine-gunners had the advantage, as they fired into the advancing Germans' right flank. The tide turned, however, when Brandt ordered his men to enfilade the Canadian trench. Trapped in the trench, the Canadians raised their hands in surrender. As the Germans entered the trench,

> all of a sudden a machine gun started rattling so that the men had to get down again.* In order to reach the Brits [Canadians], three men crawled out along a hedge to the road trench and fired along the trench, totally surprising the Brits.
> 
> The men of the 1st Platoon seized on the British confusion and stormed ahead capturing the entire trench including 3 officers and 42 men and a machine gun. There were also 15 dead and some wounded enemy.

According to Canadian records, Fisher died in an engagement that began when Lieutenant J. G. Ross, in an effort to disrupt German enfilade fire, ordered the machine guns forward. To gain the best position he could, Fisher crawled into a shallow trench. Just as he was about to squeeze his gun's trigger, a German bullet struck and killed the former McGill University student. As he stepped over Fisher's body to get to the gun, Sergeant McLeod was also cut down. Fisher's Victoria Cross citation cites his actions on both 22 and 23 April; of the latter, it says, "After obtaining four more men, he went forward again to the firing line and was himself killed while bringing his machine gun into action

---

*Canadian records of Fisher's death say nothing about a surrender. If the Canadians had raised their hands in surrender and then started shooting, they would have been in violation of the Hague Convention.

under very heavy fire, in order to cover the advance of supports."[1] The deaths of Fisher and McLeod deaths forced Ross to abandon the gun. Crawling away from the enfilade fire, he ordered another gun crew into action.

. . .

At 8:30 a.m., ten minutes after Lieutenant-Colonels Birchall and Hill learned that their men beneath Mauser Ridge were now expected to extend their line a thousand yards left to the Yser Canal, Major Kirkpatrick's 3rd Battalion detachment linked up with Captain Claude Culling's 2nd Battalion to the east of Kitcheners Wood. Unable to accommodate Kirkpatrick's 160 men in his trenches, Culling asked him to pass through his lines and form up behind Doxsee's House for an attack on a German trench. (Had they been present, British army regulars like Colonel J. F. C. Fuller, who blanched when Canadian officers were unable to get their men to unload their ships at Plymouth, would have viewed what happened next as just one more example of what it's like to have to fight with the colonials.)

Once behind Doxsee's House, the all-too-green Canadians suffered a momentary collapse of discipline when they refused their officers' command to attack. Lieutenant Doxsee wasted little time in trying his own hand, ordering his men to cover him and Kirkpatrick's to follow him. Only two did: one from his own garrison and one of Kirkpatrick's men.

Both Doxsee's man and Kirkpatrick's were shot dead before they had taken twenty strides. The bland words of Captain Richardson's report—"Finding himself alone, [Doxsee] turned and regained the house unhurt"—hide more than they reveal. Did Doxsee run or crawl back? Was he shot at? Or did the German sharpshooters take a moment to savour hitting two men in short order, unintentionally giving him a few life-saving seconds?

After giving the men time to dig their own trench, Kirkpatrick's officers led them in an attempt to outflank the German trench. Eight were killed outright by heavy fire, ending the attack.

Before the sun was completely up, the Germans tried another *ruse de guerre*, sending twenty unarmed *Feldgrauen* over the parapet in front of a trench near the house.* Claiming to be French and apparently so dressed, they invited some men over for coffee. Taken in, a few men went so far as to start shaking hands. Doxsee shouted for his men to return to their trench and ordered his machine-gunners to fire on the hastily retreating Germans. As the light of day strengthened, Doxsee's marksmen, shooting through loopholes cut into the house's second storey, killed forty Germans before the rest abandoned the trench; another eight fell when the Germans fled for safety.

• • •

At 9:00 a.m., Canadians facing the northwest corner of Kitcheners Wood fired on a lone figure, Oberleutnant Grotrian of RIR 234. Just as the firing began, he saw Leutnant Bruckner, who shouted a regimental order to him. Grotrian outranked Bruckner, and although the fire was becoming more "lively," the *Oberleutnant* took a moment to yell back disdainfully, "You cannot give me any regimental order," before jumping into the bed of a brook. The story is interesting because by the time Grotrian told it to the regiment's historian, he had long known that Bruckner did, indeed, have the authority he needed. In the brook, Grotrian found that the regiment's commander, whom he almost spiked with a French bayonet he had taken from a prisoner the previous night, had given Bruckner the order that Grotrian had scornfully dismissed.

Several hours later, while Grotrian organized his unit's relief from the redoubt on the southwest side of Kitcheners Wood, his luck almost

---

*There is some debate about these *ruses de guerre*. German records do not mention them, and a British investigation concluded that the Canadians had misinterpreted the sight of Germans wearing their greatcoats. The number of times the Canadians reported seeing Germans dressed as Canadians leads me to believe, however, that at least some of them must have been *ruses de guerre*. Since it is not possible to determine when the Canadians were correct and when they were in error, I have reported each incident as the Canadians themselves did, so as to indicate the number of times the Canadians stopped these German advances.

ran out. While pausing "to look at the booty of telescopes and distance measuring devices" the British had abandoned, he dropped his guard. "[A] Canadian must have seen me from Hof Soetaert [Oblong Farm] and sent me his greetings. Fortunately, the bullet only chafed my skin. My jaw remained intact."

• • •

At 9:25 a.m., Lieutenant-Colonel Robert Rennie's 3rd Battalion headquarters learned that Kirkpatrick had seen the Germans reinforcing the northern end of Kitcheners Wood (an earlier report had put the number of reinforcements at between five hundred and a thousand), and that German artillery continued to pound ground that was littered with the men who were wounded in the attack on the woods. Over the next several hours, shellfire—some of which, Kirkpatrick claimed, targeted stretcher-bearers—prevented Chaplain Beatty's men from reaching wounded soldiers. Kirkpatrick could not say for sure how many men were killed by German shellfire, but his memoir minces few words: "The field over which we had advanced was shelled all day long, for what other reason except to kill the wounded one cannot imagine."

• • •

The men who carried crates containing almost thirty thousand rounds of ammunition to Kirkpatrick's position endured physical and mental trials unlike anything depicted in the *Boy's Own Annual*. Their world had become a maelstrom unimaginable before the invention, only twenty years earlier, of smokeless powder, shrapnel, and high explosives. "Terror and death coming from far away seemed much more ghastly than a hail of fire from people we could see and with whom we could come to grips," wrote a veteran of the Somme in 1916.[2] No amount of skill or moral standing could protect a man against shrapnel. A single five-millimetre ball could kill almost instantaneously. As Ernst Jünger wrote from the other side of no man's land: "A shrapnel ball had ripped through rifleman Stolter's carotid artery. Three packets of lint were sodden with blood in no time. In a matter of seconds he had bled to death."³ Nor could anything protect a soldier from the explosive wave or splinters that followed the detonation of a high-explosive shell:

> The splinters were irregular in shape, so producing a very rough wound with a great deal of tissue damage and frequently carried fragments of clothing or other foreign matter into the body, which made infection almost inevitable. Very large shell fragments . . . amputate limbs, decapitate, bisect or otherwise grossly mutilate the human frame.⁴

And then there were the bullets that swept the field. "A bullet would flash through the sleeve of a tunic, rip off the brim of a cap, bang against a water-bottle, bury itself in the mass of a knapsack."⁵ Some that passed through flesh left a "neat channel" and caused death only if they hit a vital organ, artery, or vein. Some hit bone, turning the body's armature into "secondary projectiles which produced massive damage" to nearby tissue and organs. "Some bullets also set up hydraulic effects, their passage driving body fluids away from the wound track at pressures which surrounding tissues could not withstand."⁶ The bullets raking the terrain crossed by Kirkpatrick's resupply columns had another way of killing. They could pierce a crate and hit the charge of a round, starting a chain reaction that would wipe out the men carrying the crate.

As they moved to the field of fire, they could see shells bursting all around them. Tired as they were, they could still wonder, Where will the next one hit? If nearby, will the wound kill or maim—or will it be a "Blighty" that shows I have discharged my duty?* For the men resupplying Kirkpatrick, courage was "stoic endurance," the ability to face horror and terror and still trudge onwards.⁷ And as difficult as it is to accept at our distance from the reality of war in general (as opposed to a news clip judged acceptable for family viewing), and the Great War in particular,

---

*A "Blighty" was a wound that was serious enough to warrant evacuation to England but not serious enough to permanently disable or disfigure a soldier.

courage included showing the intestinal fortitude to ignore the cries of broken and bleeding comrades lying on the ground nearby.

. . .

The full light of day revealed the human detritus of battle. From a trench on the far right of Kitcheners Wood, Private L'Abbé could see that a "German Officer with a highly polished pair of new field boots was lying on his back, and appeared to have his glazed eyes on my piece of trench." Behind him "stretched Number One Company, in an irregular extended line, mostly lying on their faces, in the usual grotesque attitudes of the dead." A mere ten yards away lay Major Bennett, still clasping his walking stick in his right hand. At one point, L'Abbé heard a weak voice calling from around a corner; there he found Walter, a schoolmate from Montreal, who had been shot through the left arm:

> "'Water,' he whispered, and I crawled back to my equipment to get it. On my return he was just 'going out.' Then he slept. I opened his eye-lids. He was dead. Another Mother's son.

When L'Abbé returned to his position, Private Ned Langton, a twenty-three-year-old former bank clerk, told him to peer over the parapet. Not more than ten yards away, amid several dead Germans, sat one who was very much alive and motioned for water. L'Abbé urged him towards the trench, "but he shook his head and commenced to drag himself towards the bushes." Langton took aim but held his fire after L'Abbé said, "Have a heart, Ned. He's wounded." When the *Feldgraue* was but a few yards from the woods, he jumped up and dashed for safety.

Langton and L'Abbé were not the only Canadians with their heads above the parapet. Wee George, the unit's shortest soldier, also ignored General Alderson's warning that "if you put your head over the parapet they [German snipers] will hit that head."[8] When he spied a German soldier making a dash for safety, Wee George called out, "Look at the fucking Hun running!" Two shots rang out. One sent the Hun "sprawling against a tree and headlong into the bushes." The other hit Wee George's head. L'Abbé turned towards the eighteen-year-old in time to see "a surprised look [come] into his eyes [as] he fell into Birdie's arms, his blood pumping over Birdie's hands and clothing." They laid Wee George's body in the ditch beside the other dead Canadians.

The men who had pulled out of Kitcheners Wood before dawn expected the Germans to soon come pouring through it. To prepare, the exhausted men of the 16th Battalion extended their trench to the right, towards positions held by the 2nd Battalion, and dug crevices for the wounded to take cover in. The frontal attack never came, largely because the reserves that had a week earlier been stationed in the Houthoulst Forest were now in Galacia.

• • •

German gunnery tactics were designed to demoralize as well as to kill. German artillerists focused their fire—sometimes for a few minutes, sometimes for much longer—on sections of trenches. "It was very trying on the men in the trench as they had practically no cover," remarked Lieutenant-Colonel Leckie, but his words cannot capture the moment when three or four men are blown apart at one time—or the terror of waiting. However, his words do demonstrate both the (necessarily) impersonal tone of operations reports and the way the war changed conceptions of military psychology.

Prior to the Great War, military men wrote of "nerve" as the "inner source of brave actions." Once doctors realized that shell-shocked men did not, literally, suffer from the shock of exploding shells, soldiers began writing that their nerves were under control, by which they meant that they were able to "stand and not tremble."[9] Major John C. Matheson (10th Battalion), who had left behind a job at the Canadian Bank of Commerce, may not have used the word "nerves," but in a letter written less than three weeks after 2nd Ypres, he makes the same point: "All day long [while being shelled] we had to stick to our posts in case of a counter-attack, and believe me it was more nerve-racking than the bayonet charge itself, as all around us were the dead and wounded."[10]

To offset the ever-present fear of being wounded, the men developed a certain sardonic humour. "It's extraordinary how one becomes expert in 'forecasting' shells. We know almost to the yard the line of flight of a shell by the noise it makes and consequently can economize in the practice of ducking to a wonderful extent," wrote Captain Harry Crerar in his illegal diary a few days after 2nd Ypres. "We all have a profound respect for the 'Johnsons'—they are plain brutes. They generally come at us in fours—Their concussion shakes the very earth for a quarter mile around and they send fragments of shell about the same distance."

• • •

The 16th Battalion's regimental historian, Hugh M. Urquhart, wrote that the withdrawal from Kitcheners Wood was complete before dawn; he appears to be in error. Private Sid Cox and a few others did not leave the woods until around noon, by which time a rumour had spread that the *Feldgrauen* had donned kilts and were preparing to come out of the woods shooting. When they left the woods, Cox and his comrades immediately had to take cover behind some logs and trees. Their first calls to fellow Dominion troops were met with gunfire and shouts of "OH, we've heard that. You can't fool us." Unfortunately, Cox does not say what he shouted back to establish that he and his fellow soldiers were, indeed, Canadians.

• • •

Neither of the regimental histories of the two German units facing Oblong Farm, which for them was in front and slightly to the right of Kitcheners Wood, report any significant activity during 23 April. The same is not true of either the 2nd Battalion's regimental history or the men who occupied Hof Soetaert. The Germans kept up regular machine-gun and rifle fire, shooting most of the runners sent out by forty-year-old Lieutenant John E. McLurg. "There wasn't very much sense in trying to do any rifle [firing] ourselves because you put your finger up and you got it shot off," recalled Private Beddoe.

Several times during the day, Germans dressed in kilts appeared before McLurg's position, only to be shot down by a Colt machine gun that had been set up in a nearby farmhouse by Hubert Rogers, a forty-eight-year-old chauffeur and mechanic. To keep the machine gun supplied with bullets as the day wore on and supplies dwindled, Beddoe remembered, Rogers threw "an empty belt to us and we would fill it with our very sparse supply of ammunition and throw it back to [him]." Each time a shell came crashing down, Rogers fired off about four rounds, which was "all they could spare, just as much as to, say, thumb their noses at them—You didn't get me that time."

. . .

Neither the 1st and 4th Battalions' war diarists nor the units' regimental historians record what Lieutenant-Colonels Birchall and Hill thought when, with their men pinned down beneath Mauser Ridge, they learned that they had been ordered to extend their left flank a thousand or so yards west to the Yser Canal. Military messages are by necessity devoid of emotion:

> Whole line is now digging in. Line extends from ypres–pilkem Road to I think about 600 yds. East of road. Casualties are heavy. middlesex are on our right and I do not know exactly how far they extend. We reached a point about 450 yds from German Trenches. As all my companies are up in line and I cannot well move them to a flank in daylight I cannot extend our road (line) towards Canal unless absolutely necessary. I am trying to find out situation between road and canal. Have sent a message to O.C. 1st Battalion giving your message and requesting him to extend his line to the left of the road.

Nevertheless, the message hints at Birchall's exasperation, as, perhaps, does the fact that he did not respond to General Mercer's message for more than two hours. Hill's response to Birchall is equally suggestive. Noting that with only one hundred men in reserve, he does not have enough soldiers to fill the gap, he orders these men to dig in "toward the rear on a higher piece of ground from which he could cover some of the gap and protect the exposed Canadian left flank."[11]

Birchall too soon ordered his men to dig in, however. Alfred Wakeling, a forty-three-year-old who had joined the British army when he was fifteen and had fought in both Egypt and South Africa, recalled that as bad as the assault was, the hours after digging in were far worse.* "We had no artillery behind us and we had to hold the trench at all costs. Their artillery started shelling us right away to drive us out. I think we sampled every kind of shell made in Germany. For 14 hours they kept it up continually—Jack Johnsons, shrapnel, gas shells, coal boxes."[12] In his war memoir, *Goodbye to All That,* the poet Robert Graves, who would later see action on the Somme, wrote of the effect of an exploding high-explosive shell:

> My ears sang as though there were gnats in them, and a bright scarlet light shone over everything. My shoulder got twisted in falling and I thought I had been hit, but I hadn't been. The vibrations made my chest sing, too, in a curious way, and I lost my sense of equilibrium. I was ashamed when the sergeant-major came along the trench and found me on all fours, still unable to stand straight.[13]

For the wounded strewn across the fields beneath Mauser Ridge, Wakeling could only pray.

Private Aylmer Fraser (4th Battalion) was one of the lucky wounded. Hit in the first minutes of the assault, he managed to get his entrenching tool out and dig a little hole; it must have been positioned just right, for bullets and shrapnel peppered the ground around him. Later, he ran to a farmhouse about a thousand yards from the German line. The house,

---

*Wakeling's unit lost forty-four of its fifty-five men.

however, was no haven. "They shelled it all day," he recalled, "and the house was just packed with wounded—some of the poor beggars got hit again. I lay in the cellar till ten at night, then beat it. The shells were still flying, but I got away all right."[14]

Among the dead Fraser ran past was Lieutenant Cameron Brant, a twenty-seven-year-old from Hamilton, Ontario, whose attestation papers list his complexion as "Dark." The former sheet-metal worker's great-grandfather was Joseph Brant, the legendary Mohawk chief who led his braves into battle alongside the British during the American Revolution.

• • •

At 11:07 a.m., as word spread in Paris that the Germans had used chlorine gas against French troops at Ypres on 22 April, Birchall received a message that the French had advanced five battalions between his men, who were pinned down, and the canal. He could see no sign of the French troops, however. A flurry of messages from Birchall to Mercer and Mercer to Alderson resulted in Alderson's asking the French to "advance to join up with the Canadian left flank."[15] No record exists of the French response, but by 12:15 p.m., Birchall's far left was (finally) in contact with them. He found to his dismay, however, that instead of sending him five thousand men to fill the gap to the Yser, the French had sent fifty—one for every two hundred yards, or scarcely enough for a picket line.

Trained military man that he was, Birchall must have been expecting the message he received at 12:50 p.m., telling him that "owing to very exposed approaches big [entrenching] tools cannot be sent up in daylight but will be forwarded as soon as possible." But neither Birchall nor Hall could have expected to read, forty-five minutes later, that "the Enemy was apparently running out of ammunition."[16] General Turner annotated his copy of the message with the comment that this was "an example of the value of information received from the rear."

In three hours of fighting using the most up-to-date tactics, men of the 1st and 4th Battalions had managed to advance only a few hundred yards towards Mauser Ridge. They could not hold Turco Farm, the attack's high-water mark. The same artillery fire that pockmarked the farm also ruined its buildings and littered the ground with dead and wounded, and could not be called off once the farm was in British and Canadian hands. Instead of holding the farm, which could have served as a jumping-off point for a later attack on the ridge, the combined force was forced to withdraw, "and had to make do with digging cover at the base of the ridge, which was far from satisfactory since the ground was very wet, making the trenches shallow, muddy affairs."[17]

• • •

At 10:50 a.m., as Birchall signalled Alderson that he doubted his men could move to the left during daylight, a messenger sent by Lieutenant-Colonel Frederick Loomis arrived at Alderson's headquarters. The message he carried is interesting for what it tells about both the tactical situation then facing the commandant of St. Julien and his frame of mind, which mirrored Birchall's.

The information was extremely worrisome. The Germans had moved a machine gun into a trench a bit more than five hundred yards northwest of St. Julien. Loomis had lost touch with the men in the trenches on his left—trenches that at least in theory were in communication with those that ran to Turner at Mouse Trap Farm. In other words, the entire right wing of the Canadian line*—three battalions and parts of two others, or over four thousand men—was, at least momentarily, cut off from the Canadian command; the Canadians remained in contact, however, with the British on their right. To protect the men on his left, Loomis planned to pull them back to trenches closer to St. Julien—a necessary move that would, however, increase the gap in the Canadian line. Apparently neither Alderson nor his staff picked up the exasperated tone when Loomis wrote, "Enemy in great force convinced something must

---

*The line ran north from Loomis's garrison in St. Julien toward a position just south of Keerselmne (the Apex) before turning east on Gravenstafel Ridge.

be done quick. I should know what to expect if we are not to receive support."

At 11:03 a.m., Lieutenant-Colonel Gordon C. W. Gordon-Hall, a forty-eight-year-old career British army officer born in Allahabad, India, responded to Loomis. The first part of his message, which told of an Allied attack at map square C.15.c, must have given Loomis some comfort, even though that map square corresponded to Mauser Ridge, miles to Loomis's left front. The fact that such an assault was under way offered hope, for it was unlikely that the Germans would attempt another major push while they themselves were under attack. Word that the attack was supported by five and a half French battalions was also welcome because it told Loomis (falsely, as it turns out) that the French had rallied and would soon, perhaps, be able to reinforce his men. Most welcome, no doubt, was the news that parts of Colonel Geddes's detachment were on the way to a nearby farm and would come under Loomis's command.

The second part of the message was more problematical. It read:

> As regards your Z.310 [message] the Divisional Commander quite appreciates difficulty of your position. He suggests your throwing back your line from D.1.b towards C.6.c. If possible some sort of line might be dug by supports and your troops fall back on to it. Report what steps you propose to take.

Loomis would have immediately realized the uselessness of this order. C.6.c was on a forward slope and thus exposed to direct artillery fire, which would have greatly impeded the digging of trenches and lessened his ability to protect the men. He certainly blew off some steam in his 1:10 p.m. message to McCuaig, when he informed him that he was to receive reinforcements—but that he could not use them to counterattack: "In addition to 2 companies of the 14th Battalion, which will reach you at dark, you will get two English Companies during the afternoon. It is not intended to counter [attack] owing to Orders Higher Authority. Left flank of trench is to be thrown back everything else must be held." It is not difficult to imagine Loomis's reaction to the message he received just moments after the two companies of the Royal Scots arrived in St. Julien. That message ordered the Scots to leave and ready themselves for what became the second attack on Mauser Ridge.

Somehow, Loomis's men held on. Those nearest St. Julien fought off four attacks and endured hours of shelling. Those from McCuaig's 13th Battalion—who were still in the old French trenches, which stuck out like a forefinger pointing northwest—held out against shellfire and rifle fire (some of which came from their rear), as well as hunger and thirst, both of which grew worse as the unseasonably warm April day wore on. "Twice during the day the enemy, supposing the defence had been beaten down, came over to occupy the demolished trenches and twice, with rifle and machine gun fire, the Highlanders drove him back."[18]

## Chapter 8

## "It Is Considered Very Unlucky to Be Killed on a Friday"

### The Second Attack on Mauser Ridge

*The first to climb the parapet*
*With the "cricket balls" in either hand;*
*The first to vanish in the smoke*
*Of God-forsaken No Man's Land;*
*First at the wire and soonest through,*
*First at those red-mouthed hounds of hell,*
*The Maxims, and the first to fall,—*
*They do their bit and do it well.*
—James Norman Hall, "The Cricketers of Flanders"

The decision to mount a second attack on Mauser Ridge was made even as the men of the 1st and 4th Battalions were digging in after their attack. Early on the morning of 23 April, Sir John French travelled from his headquarters in French Flanders to Général Foch's headquarters in Belgian Flanders. Sir John told Foch that with the Germans close to pinching off the salient—and thus capturing thirty thousand British and eighteen thousand Canadian troops—prudence demanded that the Allies abandon it and Ypres, and establish their front line on the Yser Canal.

Legally speaking, Foch could not order Sir John, the commander-in-chief of the British Expeditionary Force, to remain in the trenches protecting Ypres. But politically and emotionally, Foch held all the cards. Before the BEF even landed in France in 1914, Lord Kitchener had ordered Sir John to do more than just cooperate fully with the French forces; he was to take his lead from them. We don't know whether the commander of the Groupe Provisoire du Nord recalled for Sir John the moment in 1914 when all seemed lost at the Marne and Foch signalled Général Joseph Joffre, "My centre gives way, my right is retreating, situation excellent, I am attacking." He did, however, promise that "he had ordered up large French reinforcements and that the troops from the North had already arrived to reinforce Général Putz," who was holding a line near the canal. This news disarmed the British field marshal; it turned out to be an out-and-out lie.* Although Sir John warned Foch that if the French line "was not re-established within a limited time [he] could not allow the British troops to remain in so exposed a situation as that which the action of the previous twenty-four hours had compelled them to occupy," he left the meeting at noon, having "agreed to cooperate in the way [Foch] desired" (i.e., to order another attack on Mauser Ridge).¹

At first glance, the orders issued by Général Fernand-Jean-Henri Quiquandon for this attack seem impressive:

(I) The Germans seem for the moment to have exhausted their ammunition.

(II) The hour for the general counter-attack has arrived.

---

*After the war, Foch admitted that his promise of troops was part of an elaborate con. After the first twenty-four hours of the battle, during which his troops had twice failed to materialize, Foch said to Sir John, "You have proved that you can hold on for twenty-four hours. Hold on for another twenty-four and this time I give you my word of honour that reënforcements shall arrive" (Liddell-Hart, 137). Sir John was susceptible to this con because he had known since November 1914 that all that was keeping him from being sacked was the support of the French.

(III) Consequently, the Colonel Commanding the 90th Bde. (Col. Mordacq), with all the troops at his disposal, will attack on the front BOESINGHE-PILCKEM on the East of the Canal, with their right resting on the YPRES-PILCKEM road in close touch with the British Army.

(IV) On our right the English, warned of our attack, will advance on LANGEMARCK.

(V) Artillery-Col. FRACQUE with all the artillery on the Western bank of the Canal at his disposal, and of the British artillery placed to the N.W. of YPRES, will prepare a serious Artillery fire for 5 minutes and will form a wall of fire in front of the infantry to facilitate its advance.

(VI) Hour of attack. The attack will commence at 3 p.m. The artillery will increase its range from that moment.[2]

On closer inspection, however, these orders show just how poorly Quiquandon, and by extension Foch and other senior commanders, understood the situation on the battlefield. As already noted, Brigadier-General Turner thought little of the claim that the Germans had "exhausted their ammunition." Brigadier-General Mercer, whose men were pinned down beneath Mauser Ridge, and Lieutenant-Colonel Loomis in St. Julien, not to mention the war diarist of the 5th Battalion on the Canadian right, would not have disagreed with Turner. On the quietest portion of the Canadian line, the 5th Battalion's trenches across Gravenstafel Ridge, heavy fire killed three and wounded eight.

Because Quiquandon's order refers only to Colonel Mordacq's shattered brigade and not to new troops under Général Putz, it should have raised an eyebrow or two among the British. The proposed attack against Langemarck should have given even more pause. First, there is no mention of such an attack in the orders that Lieutenant-General

Alderson sent to Colonel Augustus Geddes at 1:30 p.m. Second, the 13th Battalion was the closest Canadian unit to Langemarck, and by 1:30 p.m. Major McCuaig's men could barely hold their trenches, let alone launch an attack. The orders issued over Lieutenant-Colonel Gordon Gordon-Hall's name also make no mention of this attack.

The phrase "will prepare a serious Artillery fire of 5 minutes" may sound good. But even from the vantage point of mid-April 1915, five minutes' fire by fewer than thirty guns was hardly "thorough preparation." At Neuve-Chapelle, 535 guns were in action for thirty-five minutes, firing more shells than were fired in the whole of the Boer War. Still, by the standards of the attack on Kitcheners Wood and the first attack on Mauser Ridge, the bombardment should have been better than nothing.

Unfortunately, these last orders, which called for the artillery to begin firing at 2:45 p.m., contributed to the failure of the attack. This was not, however, because the Canadian and British guns failed to fire or missed their targets. Rather, they started to fire on schedule and with some effect, according to the historian of RIR 239. "From the other side of the canal, from the direction of Boesinghe, the shells come rushing toward us," he wrote. "One round after another. Heavier calibers rained down on the terrain behind us into Pilckem on to the battery positions." Behind these words are the agonies of bombardment:

> When one heard the whistle [of a shell] in the distance, one's whole body contracted to resist the too excessively potent vibrations of the explosion, and at each repetition it was a new attack, a new fatigue, a new suffering.... [T]he most solid nerves cannot resist for long; the moment arrives when the blood mounts to the head; when fever burns the body and where the nerves are exhausted, become incapable of reacting. Perhaps the best comparison is that of seasickness.... To die from a bullet seems nothing; parts of our bodies remain intact; but to be dismembered, torn to pieces, reduced to pulp, this is the fear that flesh cannot support and which is fundamentally the great suffering of the bombardment.[3]

Like his Canadian counterparts, this German regimental historian does not mention that under such conditions, at least 6 percent of the men will involuntarily urinate or defecate, humiliating acts that were to some almost as difficult to bear as the shelling itself.

• • •

Though the shellfire killed a few Germans, it did not accomplish its main task—stunning those on Mauser Ridge so that the attackers could gain the trenches before the Germans were able to man their defences fully. When the curtain of fire lifted, there were some disoriented Germans, but there were no French troops on the edge of the German parapet. Indeed, there were no troops advancing at all.

The promised French troops were nowhere to be seen. Nor were the troops under the command of Geddes and Brigadier-General Robert Wanless-O'Gowan in position to begin their attack.\* At 3:00 p.m., Wanless-O'Gowan's 13th Brigade was under fire—but at a pontoon bridge over the Yser Canal, more than a mile from the starting point for the attack. The artillery barrage did two things. It warned the Germans that an attack was imminent. And it exhausted the batteries' supply of shells, ensuring that when the attack did begin, there was no "wall of fire in front of the infantry to facilitate its advance."

Blame for this blunder cannot be laid at the feet of the gun commanders. They simply carried out their orders. Instead, blame attaches first to the French, who failed to advance at the appointed time. Indeed, when the 7th Zouaves finally did advance, they went east, rather than north towards Mauser Ridge. The measured tones of the 1st Royal West Kents' war diary hardly do justice to the confusion that resulted when the Zouaves crossed *in front* of the advancing English. It was, wrote the regimental historian, "apparent that the French Algerian troops on

---

\*Though nominally under Wanless-O'Gowan, Geddes was for all practical purposes in command of the western (or left) side of the attack, with Wanless-O'Gowan's men taking the east (or right) wing.

our left would crowd out our firing line as they were coming across our front. In consequence of this the supporting lines were held back under the cover of the canal bank and low ground and only one platoon at a time pushed up to support the firing line."[4] The regimental historian of RIR 239 was even more dismissive of the French attack: "Now the Frenchmen may approach. There they are. And there they retreat."

Blame also attaches to Alderson and his staff. He allowed only thirty minutes between the French advance and the English attack. Shortly before 3:00 p.m., Alderson, who had not yet received copies of the French orders, increased the time to forty-five minutes. At that point, with no large French formations in sight and no copy of the French orders in hand, he should have contacted the French to find out if their planned attack was on schedule. And he should have at least tried to alert the artillery commanders that the planned assault *might* be in trouble.

Alderson can also be blamed for underestimating how long it would take the British troops to get into position. Neither 3:30 nor 3:45 p.m. was a realistic start time. At 3:45 p.m., Wanless-O'Gowan informed Alderson that his troops, who had been marching since 9:00 a.m., would have to be fed before going into battle, something that Alderson's staff had not realized. Nor did Alderson arrange for the British officers to reconnoitre the ground or meet with Mercer, who had watched the first attack on Mauser Ridge through his binoculars. Moved once again to 4:15 p.m., the attack finally got under way at 4:25 p.m. British forces were not fully engaged for another half hour, when the 2nd Battalion of the Duke of Cornwall's Light Infantry Battalion entered the fray on the far right of the British line.

• • •

In the moments before the attack, tensions ran high on both sides of no man's land. The Germans occupied the higher ground and thus held the natural advantage. Still, their situation was far from ideal. Most men had not slept since they were ordered to their collection points late on 21 April. And there was not enough food or water. Their greatest worry, however, was that after two days of battle, each man had only thirty rounds left. Since a German soldier at rapid fire was expected to get off some fifteen rounds per minute, the Kaiser's riflemen had only enough bullets to keep up fire for slightly more than two minutes.

As the men waited on Hill Top Ridge for the whistle—waiting to charge over ground strewn with dead and wounded pinned down under a hot sun, just as their forefathers had before Waterloo—some prayed, some rubbed amulets, lucky coins, or locks of hair. Almost all thought of their families. Up and down the line, men stole a glance, wondering if this or that shell hole was far enough, and if they could make falling into it look convincing. Almost to a man, however, the Tommies knew that amid the chaos of the assault, they would move, drawn forward by their mysterious ties to their buddies. Men in battle fight on, no matter the odds or the threat to themselves. Once in battle, they fight not for abstractions like liberty or the niceties of international law but for their regiment, its traditions, and—most important—their comrades.

Their legs weak and leaden, their stomachs churning and their bowels feeling loose, the King's soldiers knew that when the show opened, they would mount the step out of the ditch and protect their comrades' flanks. For them, personal honour—defined as standing alongside their buddies—was "valued more than life itself."[5] Some, realizing what day of the week it was, would have recalled the adage "It is considered very unlucky to be killed on a Friday."[6] Others, recalling that that day, 23 April, was St. George's Day, the feast of the patron saint of England, must have steeled themselves by repeating a half-remembered speech from Shakespeare's *Henry V*:

> Once more unto the breach, dear friends, once more;
> Or close the wall up with our English dead.
> . . . . . . . . . . . . . . . . . . . . . . . . . . .
> Follow your spirit, and upon this charge
> Cry "God for Harry, England, and Saint George!"

. . .

The attack quickly turned into a disaster. In the centre, the 2nd King's Own Scottish Borderers lost heavily while advancing to the lines held by the remnants of Birchall's battalion. Captain Charles E. Bland and a few men managed to reach an empty trench one hundred yards from the start line but still four hundred yards from the German lines. Bland, a highly decorated Boer War veteran who had earned a DSO in 1914, died "trying to pull a wounded man into cover."[7] Private Victor Trowles of the Canadian 4th Battalion, who had joined Geddes's Detachment for the attack, was luckier, if no more successful. Forced to ground by rifle and machine-gun fire, Trowles saw an injured soldier from the Yorkshire Light Infantry nearby. "He was only a little fellow and I went over and got his field bandage out and patched [his wound] up. Hadn't more than got it tied and he was hit in the same place again. Made me think, 'Now, what's the use of doing this?'" Private James Fraser, also of the 4th Battalion but not part of the attack, watched in horror as the Germans opened up on the English, who were advancing in close formation; they were "simply bowled over like ninepins."[8]

After the commander of "C" Company was wounded, Lieutenant-Colonel Birchall took over. Private Harold R. Peat's account of the charge Birchall led may be overheated, but it gives a good impression of the emotions, flow, and disorder of the battle. Amid explosions, the crackle of gunfire, and the screams of men,

> Colonel Birchall pulled his revolver from his holster, looked at it a moment and then threw it on the ground. Then he took his small riding switch and hung the loop over the first finger of his right hand.
>
> "Ready, boys!" he cried, and twirling the little cane round and round, he strode ahead.
>
> It was a terrible piece of work. On every side shells and bullets were falling. Men went down like ninepins at a fair. But always ahead was the colonel, always there was the short flash of his cane as it swished through

the air. Then he was hit, a bullet in the upper right arm. He did not stop; he did not drop the cane.

"On, boys, on!" And the men stumbled up and forward.

Seven times Colonel Birchall was a mark for enemy fire. Seven times fresh wounds gushed forth with his life's blood. He was staggering a little now, but never a falter; on and on he went, the little cane feebly waving.

Men say that at times the lines seemed to waver and almost to break; that the whole advancing force, small and scattered as it was, seemed to bend backwards like cornstalks in the wind, but always they saw the colonel ahead and recovered balance.

Colonel Birchall fell dead on the parapet of the German trench, but he got what he had come after.\* His men were with him. There were seven hundred dead and more dead and wounded in the battalion, but the trench was theirs and Fritz was again begging for mercy.[9]

• • •

While they expected an attack, the Germans were taken by surprise by this late-afternoon assault, and their line momentarily wavered. Aware of their small supply of bullets, and of the fact that anxious and surprised riflemen tend to waste them by firing too high, the Kaiser's officers moved behind their men, urging them to fire low and straight. "In such moments," writes the regimental historian of RIR 239, "when one is almost at the point of losing courage, the personality of the commander and a couple of encouraging words mean everything." Again and again, they shouted above the cacophony of battle to "keep a stiff upper lip." No doubt the most welcome words the riflemen heard were that an ammunition column had arrived.

• • •

Up and down the British line, men and officers died quickly. The 1st

---

\*Here Peat's rhetoric overflows reality; neither the Canadians nor the British reached the German parapet.

York and Lancasters lost some four hundred men—including a colonel, his adjutant, and a captain—on their first rush, which got no closer than a thousand yards from Mauser Ridge. The rest of the battalion withdrew and "managed to set up their machine guns in relatively safe positions ... where they were able to bring harassing fire to bear" on the Germans.[10] The Buffs, positioned to the York and Lancaster's right, reached the high-water mark, thirty yards from the German trenches.*

The most vicious fighting occurred at Turco Farm. As the Duke of Cornwall's Light Infantry entered, a German rose—perhaps to shoot, perhaps to surrender. Before he could do either, his head exploded. A British soldier ran towards a house; before he'd taken three steps, he was cut almost in two by a machine gun. A few English got close enough to Germans that neither side could use their rifles. A bayonet at the end of a Lee-Enfield rifle held tightly by a British soldier pierced a German chest; the German's own rifle fell as blood spurted from his mouth. On each side of what can barely be called a line, men stepped forward to protect their buddies and within seconds lay dead or maimed.

In a few cases, Germans tried to surrender. However much they may have hoped that raised hands and shouts of *"Kommerade! Kommerade!"* would stop the onrushing British, though, they knew that "the defending force, after driving their bullets into the attacking one at five paces' distance, must take the consequences. A man cannot change his feelings [about the enemy] again during the last rush with a veil of blood before his eyes. He does not want to take prisoners but to kill."[11] With their ranks depleted, the men of the Duke of Cornwall's Light Infantry could not consolidate their forward position at Turco Farm and were ordered to withdraw, abandoning the strategic prize for the second time in less than twelve hours.

• • •

---

*Corporal Hall did not receive the 8:00 p.m. order to withdraw, so he and his men stayed in their hastily dug trenches for another two days, without food and water but not bothered by the Germans, who were about as far away from them as first base is from home plate.

The Second Battle for Mauser Ridge was over by 7:00 p.m. After dark, when the reliefs ventured out, the butcher's bill became clear. In addition to Birchall, the 4th Battalion lost 404 men and officers. The 1st Battalion lost 440 men. The British lost more than 1,300 men; of the 500 men of the 3rd Middlesex Regiment who went into battle, fewer than twenty had survived.

Most historians have agreed with the conclusions put forward in Sir James Edmonds's British official history: "The price paid had been very heavy, and actually no ground was gained that could not have been secured, probably without any casualties, by a simple advance after dark, to which the openness of the country lent itself."[12] True enough, but perhaps beside the point. Edmonds, it seems, has fallen into the presentist error of using knowledge he has after the war to judge decisions made in the heat of battle. The French failed to launch their attacks. Alderson erred, and his superiors *were* grievously ignorant of the terrain. But they did not know, as Edmonds did, that the Germans were not preparing to storm down from Pilckem Ridge and attack Ypres. Indeed, the fact that they launched another gas attack less than twelve hours later and destroyed much of the Canadian line indicates that the generals' fears were well founded.

The attacks on Mauser Ridge were necessary, however remote their chances of success. They achieved their strategic goal, which was to stop the German advance. Though Colonel Mordacq, the only senior officer to write about the engagements, errs by ignoring the impact of the Canadian attack on Kitcheners Wood on the Germans' tactical position and their generals' strategy going forward, his analysis of the fighting at Mauser Ridge is, nonetheless, sound. "The losses, without doubt, were heavy," he wrote, "but the results were important; this time, not only were the Germans stopped but it was we who had taken the initiative of the attack. From the point of view of morale, this was enormous and it is what I emphasized in my reports to my superiors."[13]

Although it may be that the critics were killed later in the war, I have found not one soldier who disparaged the decision to fight at Mauser

Ridge in any of the scores of memoirs, letters, and interviews I consulted for this book. By attacking, the Canadians and then the British made the Germans think that they had vast reserves of men to call upon. They did not, but the Germans did not know that.

Today, when we watch Canadian soldiers sipping Tim Hortons coffee in Afghanistan, it is difficult to comprehend the exhaustion of battle. That exhaustion, however, is apparent in Trowles's last words about the 2nd Battle of Mauser Ridge. After being called off the line late on the twenty-third, he went back to a farmhouse and then flopped down to sleep. When he awoke the next morning, he had his rifle in one hand and in the other "a piece of fat bacon ... with one bite out."

• • •

As the survivors of the two assaults on Mauser Ridge pulled back to Hill Top Ridge, a two-pronged attack on the Yser Canal bridgeheads that had been seized by the Germans on 22 April came to an ignominious end. Colonel Mordacq's Zouave battalion had been tasked with attacking the Germans at Steenstraat, the northernmost bridgehead, about five miles up the Yser Canal from Ypres. Launched at 4:45 p.m., this attack made little progress, or as the French official historian put it, "At 8 p.m. it had not obtained any appreciable results." In fact, the attack barely got started. At 9:15 p.m., Putz signalled Foch that the Allied forces hardly got past the starting line "because of a barrage laid down by the enemy artillery." Of a simultaneous attack by the 87th Territorial Division on Het Sas, a larger crossing a mile closer to Ypres, the French official history is even more laconic, saying only that it "had miscarried."[14]

• • •

While the French command learned of the failed attack at Steenstraat, Major McCuaig's 13th Battalion began withdrawing from its forward positions, which protruded a couple of hundred yards into the area the Germans had seized from the French in the early hours after the gas attack on 22 April. By moving his men back to the main trench,

McCuaig smoothed out his part of the Canadian line, so it ran on a northeast–southwest axis. The first phase of the evacuation—moving the wounded to the 15th Battalion's trenches—went without a hitch.

As soon as the Germans realized what was happening, they loosed a furious three-sided attack. McCuaig's men had no grenades with which to answer the German bombing parties, who threw "potato masher" grenades into the trenches the Canadians were abandoning. The evacuation was successful because of a rearguard action led by Lieutenant Charles B. Pitblado.

The withdrawal left the right side of the Canadian line looking like a T-square, with the outside right angle, called the Apex, facing northeast; a small detachment of the Buffs occupied the point of the Apex. The right side—that is, the side going east across Gravenstafel Ridge—consisted of part of the 15th Battalion, followed by the 8th and 5th Battalions.* The left side of the T-square, which ran south towards St. Julien, consisted of the 13th Battalion, a unit of the 14th Battalion, parts of the 7th Battalion, a company of the 15th Battalion, and then two more companies of the 14th Battalion (these last standing directly to the east of St. Julien). A few hundred yards in front of the 14th Battalion's positions were the trenches of the 3rd Battalion and Doxsee's and Hooper's houses.

. . .

Groups of men—some wearing spiked helmets, others Canadian khaki or one of the four tartans given to the Highlanders on Salisbury Plain—spent the darkest part of the night on the move. Those belonging to Reserve-Infanterie-Regiment 235 broke their bivouacs in the Houthoulst Forest and marched through Langemarck to a position just north of the woods. Rubble-strewn streets, houses with roofs cracked open to reveal their timber skeletons, blasted stone fences and trees—all led the diarist Rudolph Binding to write, "Langemarck is a heap of rubbish and all rubbish-heaps look alike; there is no sense in describing one."[15]

---

*The British 85th Brigade was adjacent to the 5th Battalion's right.

On both sides of the line, equine and human muscle moved tons of shells and tens of thousands of rounds of ammunition; more than ten tons of shells were brought to the Canadian guns near St. Julien and to those clustered fifteen hundred yards south of the village. Spade-wielding soldiers filled sandbags and dug traverses, reserve trenches, and dugouts, where the lucky grabbed whatever sleep they could. Lieutenant-Colonel Louis Lipsett, whose 8th Battalion faced north, ordered his machine-gunners to cut holes in their own parapet and his listening patrols to inch towards the 77 Landwehr Regiment; fearing another gas attack, Lipsett positioned water-filled Dixies (oval cooking pots) and cotton bandoliers all along his trench.

Across the Canadian lines, which now extended almost five and a half miles, stretcher-bearers, sometimes using blankets, planks, even wickerwork torn from the sides of stretchers, struggled with the wounded. Moving a wounded man was so difficult that even with a proper stretcher, stretcher-bearers had to use slings that went around their shoulders. Strangely, one veteran recalled, it was always the leg end that seemed to weigh more. One injured Canadian who was hidden from the stretcher-bearers was Private Sidney Radford. His leg wrapped in a blood-soaked blanket, he lay alone in the cellar of the farmhouse he had tumbled into during the first attack on Mauser Ridge.

From the north came Rennau, one of RIR 234's supply officers, startling one Dr. Werner and others who were sitting with their backs against the wall of a windmill a mile or so from Keerselare. "All of a sudden out of the dark of the night, huffing and puffing and swearing at the shrapnel exploding all around, a thick set figure appeared followed by a long line of men carrying loads," wrote the 234's historian. Behind him came men "dragging along food in bags." They had hardly appeared when the much-loved Rennau asked, "Where's my regiment, where's my battalion?" After a joyous greeting, during which, no doubt, Werner's men tried to wheedle a little something to eat, the doctor showed Rennau the way to RIR 234's 1st Battalion and reminded him to be careful of shrapnel. Just as quickly as Rennau had arrived, he vanished, slipping into the dark under the willow trees next to the Haanebeek with the words "I don't care [about the shrapnel]. I have to go to my battalion. Those guys haven't had any food for a day and a half."

Some Canadian positions were simply too dangerous to try to supply even with such a basic requirement as water. In such cases, the men had to quench their thirst with water collected from holes they dug in the bottom of their trench.* The 2nd Battalion was supplied with not just food and water "but also with letters and parcels!"[16] Those unfamiliar with military psychology can be forgiven for thinking that the exclamation at the end of that sentence registers the regimental historian's surprise that, in the middle of a battle, effort would be made to bring up letters and parcels from home. Instead, Colonel W. W. Murray's exclamation signals his recognition of the importance of mail (not to mention sweets in parcels) for maintaining morale. Through basic training and regimental rituals, armies convert civilians into soldiers whose primary identification is not with their loved ones at home but with the men who surround them. However, mail momentarily lifts soldiers out of the tension-filled situation in which they find themselves, thus providing a psychological release and restoring them to face the hardships to come. Moreover, timely mail delivery "helps raise morale by illustrating the efficiency of the organization to which [the men] belong," and on which their lives depend.[17]

. . .

Small actions flared up and down the Canadian line. A hundred yards to Lipsett's left, the 15th Battalion spent the night dodging rifle fire that came from every direction save their left. Using a flare pistol taken from a German prisoner, Captain Hooper repeatedly lit up the night just as the Germans were preparing to attack his thin defensive line. Meanwhile, what appeared to be a massed attack forced Major Daniel

---

*Surprisingly, the 15th Battalion, just to the right of the Apex, was not one of these. Near 3:00 a.m., a party brought both food and ammunition.

Ormond's men to abandon the listening posts they had laboriously pushed forward. And patrols sent out by Lieutenant-Colonel Tuxford brought word that the Germans, partially shielded by drizzle, were massing behind their lines.

As the rumble of gunfire and explosions from the battle raging on the east side of the Yser Canal (another German advance was checked by the Belgian army) rolled through the deepest part of the night, Tuxford and Lieutenant-Colonel John Currie grabbed what rest they could.

...

Not long before midnight, an ambulance left a ruined farmhouse near the 7th Battalion headquarters carrying the mortally wounded Lieutenant Colonel Hart-McHarg, the battalion commander. His agony is, of course, no more important than that of any of the thousands of Dominion and British soldiers who were mortally wounded on St. George's Day, 1915. By chance, however, more is known about it.

In the early afternoon, having received orders to move his 7th Battalion to a position between Keerselare and St. Julien, Hart-McHarg decided that, although he trusted Major Odlum's reconnaissance, he wanted to see the area for himself. Together with Odlum and Lieutenant Barry Matheson, he passed through his unit's right flank and walked towards Keerselare, which lay at the bottom of a small hill. Once there, the three men went into one of the houses. From a back window, they saw "a strong party of the enemy peering over a hedge at the back of the lot ... curiously watching our movements." The three Canadians beat a hasty retreat.

Matheson ran to a ditch on his left, and Odlum and Hart-McHarg ran back up the hill. But instead of taking them to safety, their path took them above the rooftops of the village. The Germans opened fire, and Odlum threw himself into a shell hole. A moment later, Hart-McHarg rolled into the hole and fell on top of him.

"They've got me," Hart-McHarg gasped.

"How?" asked Odlum as he rolled out from under his stricken commander.

"Through the left thigh."

Odlum offered to bandage the wound, but Hart-McHarg, who could feel that it was more serious than it appeared, said no and begged the major to go for help. Odlum, who was next in line to command, should have waited for darkness. But Hart-McHarg's suffering became too much. Because of the angle between Hart-McHarg and the German rifleman, the bullet had entered his thigh from the left rear and travelled up towards the right front, penetrating his stomach. Odlum shouted to Matheson that he was going for help, then he climbed out of the hole and ran for the top of the hill. "I made the grade, dodging like a rabbit and frightened stiff."

At the battalion's headquarters, Odlum found Captain Herbert Rae Gibson, the medical officer, and told him what had happened. He stressed that Gibson "was not under any orders to go down until dark intervened but that he could go [earlier] if he wanted to." Gibson waited the short time till dusk and then, with a party of stretcher-bearers, followed Odlum back to Hart-McHarg. After dressing the wound, Gibson and his crew waited until darkness and then carefully carried their commander's broken body to a ruined farmhouse near the 7th Battalion headquarters.

There, in "perfect agony," Hart-McHarg waited for an ambulance that would take him to a field dressing station and ultimately to a hospital, where, three days later, he died. Hart-McHarg's last hours were miserable. Morphine could not dull his pain. But somehow Odlum's presence made a difference. Each time the new commander of the 7th Battalion was called back to headquarters, Hart-McHarg protested. "He wanted me," recalled Odlum, "to hold his hand and wipe the unwilling froth from his mouth."

Part 5

# Baptism of Fire
12:00 midnight to 8:10 a.m., 24 April 1915

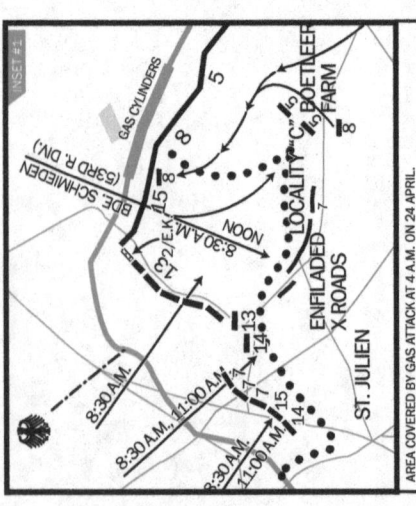

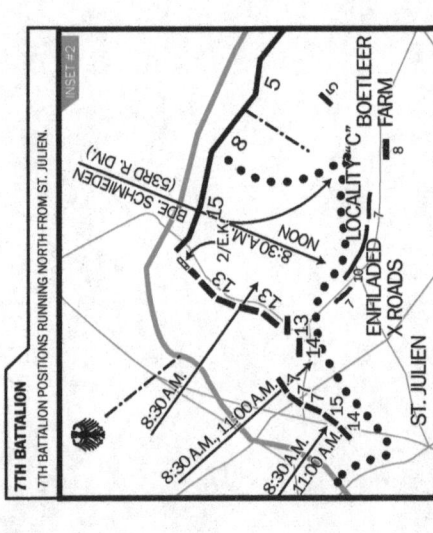

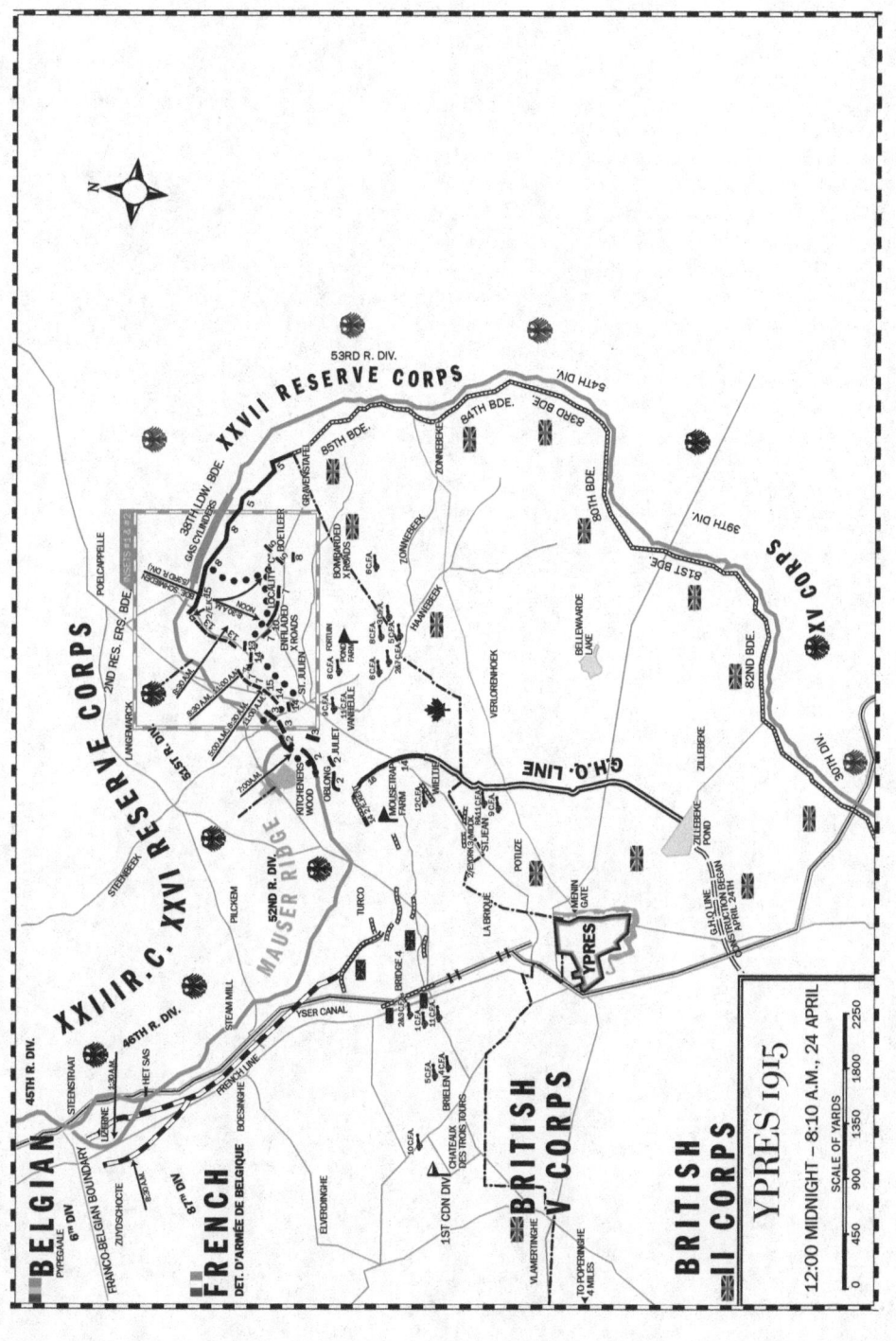

## Chapter 9

# "As Under a Green Sea, I Saw Him Drowning"

### The Second Gas Attack, and the Destruction of the 13th and 15th Battalions at the Apex

*These were the men out there that night,*
*When Hell loomed close ahead;*
*Who saw that pitiful, hideous rout,*
*And breathed those gases dread;*
*While some went under and some went mad;*
*But never a man there fled.*

*For the word was "Canada," theirs to fight,*
*And keep on fighting still;—*
*Britain said, fight, and fight they would,*
*Though the Devil himself in sulphurous mood*
*Came over that hideous hill.*
—Wilfred Campbell, "Langemarck at Ypres"

For Dr. Fritz Bergeder, the regimental historian of RIR 202, the cool of the night, the gentle south-by-southwest breeze, and the absorbent loom of Flanders played the role of wind and wave, which, sailors are wont to say, scrub their fields of battle clean. Scenes of death and destruction; clots of exhausted, dirt-stained men; gurgling shell holes; discarded kit; the iron smell of blood and cutting odours of cordite—all transfigure beneath the shining light of the moon. Even flares and cannon shots take their place in an idyll not expected in a regimental history:

> In spite of the murder and dying, the Flandrian earth meanwhile awakened to new spring life. Fresh green covered her meadows. The low bushes burned with white fire into the land. When the farms with their homely thatched roofs slept under the softly rustling trees, tenderly fondled by the light of the moon, there were flares like trembling stars in the air. Every now and then there was a single cannon blast that made the silence even more tangible.

Bergeder must not have looked to the west, where the battle for the Ypres Salient still raged.

At 1:30 a.m. on 24 April, troops belonging to the 45th and 46th Reserve Divisions moved through the bridgeheads at Het Sas and Steenstraat. According to *Der Weltkrieg, 1915–1916*, "heavy and costly fighting . . . continued late into the night," but finally, the Germans carved out a wedge, the apex of which was the village of Lizerne, a thousand yards west of the canal.[1]

. . .

At 3:00 a.m. on 24 April, something alarmed the Canadian sentries along Gravenstafel Ridge, and along the line men stood to arms. After two days of battle on their left, the men of the 8th Battalion sensed their turn had come. They were, according to Major Harold Mathews, "hoping and almost praying for the Germans to come on and give them a chance to use the cold steel." At 3:30 a.m., while the family of the 10th Battalion's Bruce McLellan readied for bed in Indian River, Prince Edward Island, and the neighbours of the 5th Battalion's Victor Swanston finished their dinner in Lumsden, Saskatchewan, three flares—two red, one green—rose into the air above Pilckem Heights.

At 4:30 a.m., gunners pulled hundreds of lanyards connected to firing pins. Milliseconds after each gun's firing pin hit the primer in the back of the shell, the primer exploded, igniting the propellant, Verkurztes Rohren-Pulver, and producing a tremendous amount of gas (and heat). The breech held the rapidly expanding gas, pushing the shell through rifled grooves that twisted their way up the length of the barrel and then forcing it out its maw at up to one and a third times the speed of sound. Seconds later, these shells rent the night, the sound of their explosions melding together. "It was one roaring, shrieking blast of destruction," recalled Sergeant Harold Baldwin (5th Battalion), who described the "magnified thunderclap of their heavy shrapnel; the moaning of the Black Marias [coal boxes]; the hiss and scream of their medium-sized shells and the hated whiz bangs, bursting over every section of the trench." Like so many others, Baldwin found that the only way to encompass what he had lived through was to reach for the Sunday school language of his youth: "Hell's gaping craters were open everywhere; now and again a shriek of an oath told that some lad had been stricken down; our parapets were crumbling like matchwood; but all we could do was wait."[2] Major Odlum too stood in awe:

> If it had not been for the tragedy of it all, their work would have been beautiful in its precision. The Jack Johnsons came methodically—one, two, three, four, five, six—out about 300 yards in front of the Battalion HQ, where our front line was. Then they shifted about 50 yards and repeated. Then another 50 yards and the same thing over again.

Another hundred or so yards and Odlum himself would have been blown apart. He was saved by the German firing plan. At just the right moment, a German gunner, a K2, on the gun's port (left) side turned the brass crank clockwise, elevating the gun's barrel so the shells started falling over already blasted ground.

A few hundred yards away, shells fell near Major Kirkpatrick's 3rd Battalion. Here, though, the Germans erred, directing their guns on an abandoned trench. The ferocious bombardment fell also on the 13th

Battalion's trenches to Kirkpatrick's right. One buried four men, including William S. M. Mactier, who clawed his way out from under the dirt. At Locality "C," about twelve hundred yards behind Mactier's line, Bruce McLellan and several other men took cover in a ditch as six two-hundred-pound shells fell a mere twelve feet away.

As the German gunners counted down the seconds until they fired, the 15th Battalion's officers counted out the last of the much-loved rum ration. "We had no sooner got it down, than the enemy started an attack. ... You could hardly breathe for the concussion! They also had the range and the loss of life was awful, and oh, the horrors, the sights were dreadful," recalled thirty-four-year-old Lance-Corporal J. D. Keddie. He was right about the Germans having the range; according to Lieutenant-Colonel John Currie, they laid down a coal box every twenty feet. One turned Sergeant-Major Vernon into pink mist. When another exploded, two men "standing under cover of the broken wall of the windmill crumpled up like green leaves in a forest fire."[3] A splinter from that shell cut into Lieutenant William H. Shoenberger's leg, breaking his ankle. Under the hail of fire—and the gas that soon followed—the battalion's signals officer crawled a quarter mile back to a dressing-station.

Somehow, through the dust, debris, and flashes, men belonging to the 15th Battalion's No. 3 Company, which faced almost directly north, noticed two or three men go over the German parapet. "They appeared to have helmets on much like those worn by divers, with [a] hose in their hands from which came a heavy green gas." The Canadians opened fire, "but the gas soon rose to about 10 feet and we could not see through it."

...

The 8th Battalion, on Currie's right, suffered somewhat less than did his 15th Battalion from shelling, but when it came to gas, Lieutenant-Colonel Lipsett's men bore the full measure. "It rolled almost like a heavy Scotch mist, swallowing up the landscape as it came," recalled Lieutenant-Colonel Tuxford, whose 5th Battalion was on the 8th Battalion's right. Tuxford had been woken by his adjutant, Captain Edward Hilliam, immediately after the alarm went up. By the time Tuxford said, "I wonder if it has anything to do with the gas we have heard about," almost two thousand Dominion soldiers had been immersed in the unimaginable horror of a wall of green vapour at least fifteen feet high.

The "filthy loathsome pestilence" caused the lucky to "cough, spit, curse and grovel on the ground trying to be sick," wrote Major Mathews in his report. The unlucky, including two men next to J. Lester Stevens, died almost immediately; Stevens survived because he was able to hold his breath long enough to wet a handkerchief with water or urine and tie it around his face. Another Canadian fell next to a Private Fisher, who recalled his high school chemistry quickly enough to wet his handkerchief and put it over his face. Stretcher-bearer George T. Boyd fell unconscious but lived because he landed face down and "breathed through the damp Flanders earth."

Mathews underscores the point that once in battle, men fight for their comrades. The terror and horror that engulfed them did not stem from "the fear of death or anything supernatural." Rather, the greater "dread [was] that we could not stand the fearful suffocation sufficiently to be each in our proper places and able to resist to the uttermost the attack which we felt sure must follow."

Tuxford called Lipsett, whose 8th Battalion headquarters at Boetleer Farm was itself surrounded by the advancing green death.* "He replied himself, at once, his voice choking, and gasping for breath. 'It's gas—very bad—can't talk,' was all that I could make out."[4] By then, some of the gas had drifted over Tuxford's own lines, where it claimed the lives of those not fast enough to wrap wet bandoliers around their faces.

The scenes unfolding in the 15th Battalion's trenches (on Tuxford's left) were even more horrifying. Neither water- nor urine-soaked handkerchiefs were enough. It "was impossible to breathe in it [the gas cloud], giving the effect of having cotton batting in one's lungs." Soon, however, Currie's men found that neither prayer nor their thin, wet membranes

---

*Boetleer Farm was a thousand yards to Tuxford's left rear.

could protect against the Kaiser's poison. Men died, but not necessarily those who seemed most likely to. According to Mathews, "Many of the physically strongest men were more affected than their apparently weaker comrades." One, Lieutenant Herbert Maxwell Scott of Abbotsford, British Columbia, fell where he stood.* "We just lay in bundles at the bottom of the trench, choking and gasping for breath," recalled Lieutenant Ian Sinclair, whose trench was near Scott's.[5] But the bottom of the trench turned out to be the worst possible place to seek shelter:

> The men who gave way to the gas most easily suffered more in proportion, as unlike smoke or ordinary vapour this beastly gas seemed to be heavier than air and settled to the ground all the time, leaving a fine sediment on everything in its wake. Consequently, anyone lying on the ground would be much more seriously affected than others standing up or manning the parapet. It was owing to my having to be continually on the move exhorting the men to stick to it that I got off as lightly as I did.

Nor did fleeing necessarily improve a man's chances of surviving; many who fled in search of clearer air died before they had run very far.

Gas also drifted over the trenches held by the 13th Battalion. Major McLaren ordered his men to wet their handkerchiefs with water or urine and tie them around their faces. Mercifully for Lieutenant Sinclair, who did not have a handkerchief, the gas dissipated as it rolled over the few hundred yards between his trench and those belonging to the 15th Battalion and the part of the 13th Battalion that, because of the shape of the Apex, was *behind* the 15th. With others, he retired behind a hill, choking, coughing, and sputtering—but alive.

The gas was released several hundred yards to the right front of the trenches held by the 3rd Battalion, but the wind carried it that far any-

---

*Scott was a descendent of the nineteenth-century novelist Sir Walter Scott, author of *Rob Roy* (1818) and *Ivanhoe* (1819), both of which depicted war and battle in the most romantic terms.

way. As they had when the German Albatross flew over them after they'd evacuated their forward trenches, the men of the 3rd Battalion played possum, recalled Private Frank V. Ashbourne, a pre-war optician whose brother Bertram was captured during the battle. He remembered:

> At the back of those [2nd line] trenches we lay down flat and covered our mouths with wet clothes, waiting for the Germans to come up. They came slowly, thinking we were all dead from their gas, but not so. It drifted slowly over us and showed the Germans about seventy-five yards away. We were suddenly ordered to rapid fire and I don't think that more than a dozen Germans got away alive. We advanced again and regained our front trench with minimal losses.[6]

And through it all, German gunners kept firing hundreds of 4.1s, 4.5s, and Jack Johnsons, killing, maiming, and disorienting thousands of men with a two-inch signet on their shoulders that read CANADA.

• • •

Even before the gas was released, German troops, their noses and mouths again covered by *Reichpäckchen* soaked in a hydrosulphite solution, moved towards the Canadian lines. Under the cover of darkness, units of RIR 233 moved to within 150 metres of the Canadian line. Using cover provided by many streams and creases in the ground, they closed to within fifty metres of the Canadians just before the gas was released. No doubt, the *Feldgrauen* assumed their advance would be as easy as it had been after the first gas attack.

They were soon disabused of this notion. The regimental historian of RIR 233 errs when he identifies the troops, but he makes clear that the regiment was stymied: "The Brits [on the left side of the attack line] put up tough resistance from their positions on the top of the flat ridge 25." Canadian records tell us more. Even as he gasped for breath in St. Julien, Lipsett managed to get an SOS to Lieutenant-Colonel John Creelman's 2nd Field Artillery guns, positioned a little over two miles behind the lines of the 8th and 5th Battalions. Creelman's guns responded almost immediately; the half ton of shrapnel they fired every minute in front of the Germans slowed them significantly. Equally surprising to the Germans was the rifle fire that came from both their left and the 8th Battalion in front of them. (The fire from their left came from Tuxford's battalion, which fired to its left, into the left flank of the advancing army.)

The 5th Battalion's fire would have been even greater had it not been for their Ross rifles. As the guns overheated and jammed, men who had endured their own gassing and watched as their comrades to their left endured an even greater amount of torment cursed their rifles. "We instructed the men to lay the handles on their entrenching tool alongside them on the trench, so when the jam occurred, by sharply hitting the bolt, it might be released," Tuxford remembered. If this failed, they were to place the rifle on the ground and stamp hard on the bolt with their heels. Those who could not free their bolt—perhaps as many as half—could only "weep in anguish," betrayed by a rifle that, under less harried conditions, Canadian marksmen had used to win four international competitions between 1909 and 1913.[7] Tuxford's measured words mask the moment when, in the heat of battle, commanders—their faces covered with water- or urine-soaked handkerchiefs, their voices hoarse from gas—yelled instructions over the sound of explosions, moans, screams, and rifle fire.

Though badly gassed, the 8th Battalion held on, helped by three of Tuxford's platoons. Like their comrades who stormed Kitcheners Wood or attacked Mauser Ridge, Lipsett's men, the "Little Black Devils," displayed a *sang froid* that can be partially attributed to the strange alchemy by which a regiment takes on the character of its commander. The former British regular Lipsett could no doubt have named more than a few British officers who would have wagered long odds against Corporal J. E. Simpson's men, who were engulfed in gas so quickly that they did not have time even to don the makeshift gas masks. Nor would they have expected mere youths like eighteen-year-old J. Carey to maintain the presence of mind to aim his rifle carefully.

By the time Simpson yelled "Fumes!" he and his men were "coughing and spitting, and gasping for breath, and blind as well." Simpson—who had never before seen battle—guessed that the Germans would be coming fast behind the gas. Somehow, he pulled himself onto the parapet and saw the Germans climbing over theirs. "I called to all who could to get up 'fire rapid.' We killed all who got over, and no more attempted."[8] After pulling himself high enough to peer over the parapet, Carey too saw hundreds of Germans. One in particular caught his attention. Fighting the urge to fire wildly—and with his hands and feet beginning to turn cold—Carey took careful aim and squeezed his trigger. In an instant, the "big fat fellow ... limp[ed] like a big pack rabbit performing in a pantomime." While still laughing at the sight of the German falling "down on his shoulder with his heels sticking up and wiggling funny," Carey fired again. The wiggling stopped. A few minutes later, Carey turned towards a swishing sound and saw that it had been caused not by someone striking a match but by a bullet cutting through his neighbour's head.[9]

As soon as the fumes cleared, the German wave approached the left side of Mathews's trenches. It was "met by so rapid a machine-gun and rifle fire that fifty or sixty Germans were killed and the attack absolutely collapsed," wrote Mathews in a report that passed silently over the fact that here too the rifle Sir Sam Hughes had called "the most perfect military rifle in every sense in the World today" failed as often as it fired. It hardly mattered whether the rifle failed because of overheating or dirt in the firing mechanism, or because it was too precise to accept ammunition even a few millimetres wider than its design specifications.* What mattered to the 8th Battalion men in the long minutes after 4:00 a.m. was that their rifles jammed. They too used their boots and entrenching tools to bully open the bolts. One Canadian must have damaged his, however, for when he pulled the trigger, the breech could not hold the exploding charge, and he was killed by blowback.

---

*For reasons that are unclear, .303 ammunition manufactured in England was slightly larger than .303 ammunition manufactured in Canada.

Surviving the horror of the gas and driving the Germans off sparked something new in those who had been civilians just three-quarters of a year earlier. "The men wanted to kill and go on killing," wrote Mathews, "and it was hard to prevent them climbing out of the trench and making an attack on the enemy." But for the Canadians, unlike the Germans who'd advanced on Mauser Ridge thirty-six hours earlier, discipline held, *pace* Fuller.

• • •

The far left of the 15th Battalion remained relatively untouched by the gas cloud; however, its position prevented it from firing at the Germans attacking the battalion's right. Even worse, at 4:01 a.m. the artillery unit tasked with supporting the 15th Battalion responded to its SOS not with shells but with the message that it could not help because its guns had been pulled back. At the time, Sergeant William Miller probably had a few colourful words to say, but in a letter to the inspector of artillery, he wrote simply, "Our own Artillery for some reason or other seemed to be standing cold.[10]

The outcome of RIR 233's attack on the right side of the 15th Battalion is clear. The Germans punched a large hole in the Canadian line, and hundreds of *Feldgrauen* rushed through it. Exactly what happened after the gas attack is more difficult to pin down. The 233's history reports only that the Canadians put up a brave fight, and that "the enemy was thrown out of their position with little losses on our side."

Scores were overcome by the gas, but when the Germans entered the Canadian trench, which they later called "a grave," they found more than just dead and dying men.[11] According to Lieutenant-Colonel John Currie, they found men with guns and bayonets:

> The fighting was very strenuous while it lasted. It was a case of butt or point whichever came handiest.... Captain McGregor went down with a wound in the head, but he still kept on using his rifle till a second bullet laid him low. Lieutenant Langmuir, revolver in hand, fell after he had

killed eight of the foe.... Smith and McDonald ... charged the Germans with the bayonet.... Captain McKessock was operating his machine guns like mad.... With a wound in his shoulder McKessock took one gun out of the forward line, mounted it in the rear of a ruin about two hundred feet behind its original position and began ripping holes in the German ranks that were appalling. He was finally overcome from loss of blood.[12]

Written towards the end of 1915—and designed to rally the home front (and to rehabilitate Currie's reputation, which was damaged when he went missing after appearing somewhat disoriented at General Currie's reporting centre in Fortuin on 24 April)—the stylized account does not jibe well with Captain George MacLaren's after-action report.* For one thing, McKessock was a lieutenant, not a captain. For another, MacLaren makes no mention of McKessock's moving the machine guns. And Currie makes no mention of a Lieutenant Smith's decision to send men to a reserve trench behind his position because his right flank was open. Further, Currie overstates things when he writes, "The line held against the first attack. Although the Germans broke through in several places they were driven back and paid a fearful price for their daring." His line did not hold, and his men did not exact a "fearful price." By the time the Germans came within range, too many men wearing the C/15 on the collars of their greatcoats had been killed, wounded, or incapacitated by the gas.

Historians have ignored Currie's claim that the Germans "were in the habit of dipping their rifle bullets in red phosphorus solution because where they struck the men's clothing they invariably started even wool clothing burning."[13] The Germans had no such practice. What they did have, which Currie could easily have mistaken for incendiary bullets,

---

*A week or so after 2nd Ypres, Lieutenant-Colonel Currie surfaced in Boulogne, France, and was ordered by Brigadier-General Turner to return at once or face arrest. He was soon sent back to Canada. Today, the lieutenant-colonel would likely be diagnosed with post-traumatic stress disorder.

were grenade incendiary bombs, some of which were fired by the 8th Battery of the 51st Reserve Infantry Brigade. Fragments from these bombs likely caused the burns and started the fires to which Currie refers; Major Daniel Ormond also noted that "some sort of projectile that set fire to their clothing" exploded over the wounded who lay in front of Kitcheners Wood. Despite these flaws, however, Currie's account gives an idea of the pell-mell of the battle that occurred in a small stretch of Flanders.*

*More historically important (because of the controversy it has engendered) is Currie's claim that one of the burned uniforms was worn by a sergeant found "foully crucified ... on a barn door." Shortly after the story appeared in the press, Kaiser Wilhelm's government demanded a retraction. After the war, the Weimar government demanded proof that German soldiers had crucified a Canadian. Several soldiers came forward with eyewitness accounts, including Private George Barrie:

> On the 24th of April at St. Julien, I saw a small party of Germans about 50 yards away. I lay still and in about an hour they left. I saw what appeared to be a man in a British uniform. I was horrified to see that the man was literally crucified, being fastened to the post by eight bayonets. He was suspended about 18 inches from the ground, the bayonets being driven through his legs, shoulders, throat and testicles. At his feet lay an English rifle, broken and covered in blood.

A British army investigation ruled, however, that it could not find proof of the incident. Nevertheless, the story continued to circulate, providing the basis for a bronze sculpture called *Canada's Golgotha* (1919). The three-foot-high sculpture was withdrawn from exhibition in 1920 because two soldiers who claimed to be witnesses to the crucifixion could not agree on the location of the barn. In the ensuing years, the story came to be seen as either an example of war-time propaganda or the equivalent of an urban legend.

In 2000, the Canadian Museum of Civilization included *Canada's Golgotha* in an exhibition on religious art. The *Anglican Journal of Canada* wrote at that time that the "statue is a piece of wartime propaganda. There is no evidence to substantiate its story of the crucifixion of a Canadian soldier. On an aesthetic level, a soldier crucified in his great coat and boots lacks the vulnerability of a naked figure. German soldiers jeer but it all seems contrived."

In 2002, Iain Overton, a British documentary maker whose Ph.D. dissertation focused on First World War myths, reported that they had found evidence from a British army nurse that corroborated Barrie's testimony. The nurse named the Canadian as Sergeant Harry Band. A year after Band disappeared—on 24 April 1915—Band's sister, Elizabeth, received a letter from one of Band's comrades: "I am sorry to say that it is perfectly true. Harry was crucified, but whether he was alive at the time, I don't think anyone can say for sure."

More authoritative is the report made by Private Tom B. Drummond, a twenty-four-year-old who barely made the height requirement set by Militia Minister Sam Hughes. Even as Lipsett fought off the effects of the gas that rolled over his headquarters, he ordered Drummond to plug the gap on the 8th Battalion's left. As Drummond's men left their reserve position near Boetleer Farm, they felt the "thrill which comes with the idea of meeting the enemy face to face." Then they moved into the fire zone that German gunners had established to prevent relief parties such as Drummond's from reaching their destination.

High explosives, shrapnel, coal boxes, whizz-bangs, and machine-gun fire cut down Drummond's men until only he and one member of his platoon were left standing. To escape the hail of fire, they jumped into a shell hole where the chlorine gas had settled. Drummond saved himself by wrapping a wet scarf around his face. A few moments later, having advanced several shell holes closer to the gap, Drummond found two other men. "Both of them were choking and spitting. It seemed impossible to get air into their lungs; or, having got it there, to get it out again. Strings of sticky saliva drooled from their mouths." Had he been able to pause a moment, Drummond might have thought it was another man in another lifetime who was thrilled by the idea of meeting the enemy face to face—and not himself just a few minutes earlier.

Drummond never made it to the broken line, but he did see the death throes of the 15th Battalion's No. 1 Company:

> Quick peeks over the edge of our shell holes discovered a line of men on our left leaving the line, casting away equipment, rifles and clothing as they ran. Some managed to get halfway to where they were going only to fall writhing on the ground, clutching at their throats, tearing open their shirts in their last struggle for air, and after a while ceasing to struggle and lying still while a greenish foam formed on their mouths and lips.[14]

Of the two hundred men who had stood on the far right of the 15th's line at 3:00 a.m., only six survived to answer the roll call later on 24 April.

The collapse of this company (and part of the company on its left) opened a gap of several hundred yards, and through it poured hundreds of fresh German troops from Regiment-Erzats-4. Their first objective was the 15th Battalion's trench. As soon as that was in German hands, some soldiers reversed its firing-step, creating a new German front line. Their main goal, however, was to break into the open country south of the trench, advancing on Gravenstafel Ridge and, ultimately, St. Julien itself. However valiantly Currie's doomed men fought, the hard tactical truth is that they could only slow the German advance.

• • •

As hand-to-hand combat raged in the 15 Battalion's trenches, scores of wounded and gassed men, their faces smeared with blood, dirt, and sweat, streamed back through the roar of shells exploding all across the Canadian front. Some struggled into an orchard some distance behind the junction of the 8th and the 5th Battalions. In the gathering light of dawn, Private Jack H. Bowyer of the 5th Battalion's "C" Company, which General Currie had ordered to support Lipsett, did what he could to make these grievously wounded men comfortable. To protect them, he took them by the side of a barn. He gave one man his own coat, then covered others with coats he found on the ground. During the night, Bowyer got cold and went back to see if he could find another coat. He found instead that "they were all dead, great bunch[es] of bubbles at their mouth and nostrils; they drowned."

• • •

Shortly before Bowyer succoured the wounded, Lipsett ordered the last of his reserves, two platoons commanded by Lieutenant N.G.M. McLeod and Captain Arthur Morley, respectively, to march five hundred yards northwest of Boetleer Farm in an effort to extend the 8th Battalion's line. Once Morley got there, the thirty-four-year-old lawyer, who eight months earlier had been battling in Winnipeg courtrooms, saw that the "men of the 15th were all gone. Their former trench was full of Germans." Above them flew the *Reichskriegsflagge,* with the black Hohenzollern eagle in the centre.

. . .

At 4:30 a.m., Lieutenant-Colonel Hughes sent word to Colonel Augustus Geddes, part of whose detachment was holding the line east of Kitcheners Wood, that General Turner had ordered the 10th and 16th Battalions out of their positions in front of the woods, "owing to our right in D.3 [the Apex] being driven in"; a separate message ordered the 2nd Battalion to take up these positions.[15] Once again, Hughes was wrong. D.3 referred to the line held by the 8th and 5th Battalions, and though battered, they were holding on. Indeed, twenty minutes later, Lipsett signalled his brigadier, General Currie, that he had the situation in hand. He might have overstated his confidence, however, for after noting that a thirteen-hundred-yard gap existed between his lines at Boetleer Farm and the garrison at Locality "C," he wrote in his after-action report that with the forces available to him, he doubted he could have stopped a determined attack. In any case, the force that had been "driven in" (the 15th Battalion) belonged not to Currie's brigade but to Turner's, as did the 13th Battalion, which, though tattered and worn, was still holding its line facing west.

At 4:40 a.m., Hughes signalled General Currie that the 10th Battalion was being returned to him. The withdrawal of the two battalions in broad daylight could have been a disaster, but it succeeded because the two worked together. The 16th Battalion provided covering fire to divert a German machine-gunner a hundred yards away from shooting at the 10th Battalion men before they crested a low ridge and made it safely to the communication trenches and ditches that had been dug during the night. The last part of the escape route ran through the same ploughed field they had marched through to attack Kitcheners Wood the night before. And once again, German guns commanded the yards that led to safety. According to 10th Battalion Private Sid Cox, the escape became a Hobson's choice of how you wanted to get hit:

We had to run about fifty feet, jump into a cabbage patch or a wheat field, or something over there, and you would see three or four [men] run and they would get one—and then you'd think, "Well, I'll crawl," and then you would see three or four crawl, and they would get one. "No, I'm going to run."

Private Charles Bloxham escaped from Kitcheners Wood carrying a wounded man on his back. Once safely away from the woods, Bloxham helped round up stragglers, which earned him a Distinguished Conduct Medal and, probably far more important to him at the time, the rescission of a ninety-day sentence of field punishment meted out for looting a liquor store in France.

Then it was the 16th Battalion's turn. The plan was similar. With the 10th Battalion gone, however, the 16th Battalion effectively divided into two, with those who had not yet left their trenches providing covering fire for those trying to escape. Instead of having to crest a ridge to get to the relative safety of the communication trenches and ditches, Leckie's men had to run across a road to get to a wide depression, which was still subject to rifle and machine-gun fire. Man by man, the depression grew deeper, worn down by the knees of soldiers who crawled on their stomachs to avoid being shot. Just beyond the furrow, a hedge provided some cover from German fire. And just beyond the hedge, past the same fields they had marched through to attack Kitcheners Wood, the "spring's green fields and blossoming hedges lay basking in the warmth of the April sun."[16]

. . .

Even Currie, whose fondness for profanity was well known, must have searched for a new expletive when he met the remnants of his 10th Battalion at Fortuin a half-hour after they withdrew from Kitcheners Wood. He had sent Turner a battalion of almost eight hundred men and officers commanded by Lieutenant-Colonel Russell Boyle. At Fortuin, he met a unit barely 25 percent as strong: 171 men and three officers commanded by Major Daniel Ormond. Currie sent Turner a battalion and received back less than two companies. Currie's ability to give, as Ormond recalled, "a cheery word" to the men before ordering them off to reinforce Captain John Warden at Locality "C" is all the more notable because it is likely that the general first learned of Boyle's death when he saw Ormond in command. The fortitude of the 174 men Currie ordered to Locality "C" is also noteworthy, for they had been in the field—most of the time under fire—for almost two days with no sleep, little food, and no time to wash or replace damaged equipment.

• • •

At first glance, Turner's decision to order the 16th Battalion to the GHQ Line makes a certain amount of sense. The battalion belonged to his brigade, and the GHQ Line, a hundred or so yards east of his headquarters at Mouse Trap Farm, was, according to the book, one of the last lines of defence of Ypres. But the GHQ Line ran northeast-southwest—which is to say, in the wrong direction. If the Germans broke through the Canadian lines to the east or west, they would have had little trouble flanking the line and reaching Ypres. If they broke through from the north, they would have been able to roll up the troops in the GHQ Line. Turner's decision to send the 16th Battalion to the GHQ Line was the first sign of what became an obsession that undermined the Allies' position in the salient. As we will see, by mid-afternoon the Canadians, forced to withdraw from Locality "C," had had to abandon St. Julien, were being pressed hard on Gravenstafel Ridge, and had seen the 13th Battalion and parts of the 15th and 14th Battalions destroyed on the western side of the Apex. Yet Turner would hold thousands of British and Canadian troops in the GHQ Line—even though he had been ordered to use them to fight.

• • •

The confusion emanating from Mouse Trap Farm engulfed the Château des Trois Tours and stretched as far as General Sir Herbert Plumer's headquarters at Poperinghe, which did not learn of the 4:00 a.m. gas attack for more than three hours. At 4:55 a.m., Hughes telegraphed General Alderson and repeated the erroneous report that the 2nd Brigade had been "driven in." A little over half an hour later, Alderson's staff telegraphed Turner asking for more information and reminding him of the "necessity of keeping St. Julien." At 6:30 a.m., Alderson received a report from General Currie informing him that while the 8th and 5th Battalions were still in their trenches, the "Germans have broken through Highlanders [15th Battalion's] trenches about 1,000 yds. Left of Section II of 8th Battalion"; Currie's message is notable for what it did not say—that less than three hours earlier his men had been gassed.

Sixteen minutes later, Alderson's adjutant, Colonel Cecil Romer, telegraphed the headquarters of the 13th British Brigade that "so far as is known the situation is that our right Brigade [i.e., Currie's 2nd Brigade] is attacked early this morning lost a trench but counter attacked with success." At 6:50 a.m., Hughes signalled Alderson to tell him two things: 1) "Firing quieter," and 2) "We do not feel uneasy."

Exactly how, with German shelling unabated, Hughes could say "firing quieter" has never been explained. Neither has the fact that Hughes and Turner felt no unease, even though they had not heard from their 15th Battalion in almost four hours.

The first inkling that their units were in danger came to the officers at Mouse Trap Farm at 7:00 a.m., when a message from Colonel Loomis reported that the "number of stragglers coming back" towards St. Julien clearly indicated that the Canadian line had been broken. This was, however, not the first message to be sent with this news.

At 5:15 a.m., Major Odlum, whose men were holding different positions on the Canadian line, received a most unwelcome order transferring his 7th Battalion from Currie's 2nd Brigade to Turner's 3rd Brigade. Odlum was not, of course, aware of the confusion at Mouse Trap Farm; indeed, he did not even know where Turner's headquarters was, and he was not in telephone communication with it. Worse, his men—in three separate sections of trench, running south from the Apex, east from near

Keerselare, and two near Locality "C"—were in precarious positions since the collapse of the 15th Battalion. (Turner seemed not to be aware of the 15th's collapse, although Odlum could not have known that.) Fearing that he and his men "were orphans," Odlum immediately sent a runner to find Turner and inform him of the 7th Battalion's situation.

Records do not indicate if or when Odlum's runner reached Mouse Trap Farm. At 6:45 a.m., he sent another runner to ask for new orders and reinforcements, and to tell Turner that "the situation on [his] right, which owing to the nature of the salient, was also [his] rear, was serious and that [he] was in danger of being cut off." It would appear that this runner also never reached Turner's headquarters. For, after Turner received Loomis's 7:00 a.m. message telling him the troops to Loomis's left (which included Odlum's) were being cut apart, Turner apparently made no effort to contact Odlum.*

Even accounting for the disorder of battle, the messages Hughes and Turner sent to Loomis are nothing short of absurd. Loomis wrote: "Quite a number of stragglers coming back evidently line broken and just received message from Burland saying breakthrough on our right. I will endeavour to collect stragglers and delay retirement quick. If any supports will be available please let me know."** At 7:05 a.m., Hughes responded with the message that "our right section has given way," which of course Loomis already knew. Hughes then ordered Loomis to counterattack using two companies that were, in fact, already engaged. Loomis scraped together fifteen signallers, orderlies, and runners and led them up the slope of Gravenstafel Ridge. From there, he could see

---

*In desperation, just before 7:00 a.m. Odlum signalled General Currie: "Shelling continues heavily and attack on right is apparently being pressed. Many men of 15th Batt., mostly wounded, are streaming through. Col. Currie, OC 15th Batt., is here collecting stragglers. Unless reinforcements are received the situation on the right may become worse. If the line here gives way my battalion will be cut off." But since Odlum's battalion had been transferred to Turner's command, Currie could do nothing to help.

**Lieutenant-Colonel Burland commanded the three platoons of the 14th Battalion that on the twenty-second had been rushed to the area between Kitcheners Wood and the southern flank of the 13th Battalion.

the remnants of his 13th Battalion, aided by the 2/E Kents on its right and parts of the 14th and 15th Battalions on its left, fighting off a frontal attack. Even more worrisome, hundreds of German soldiers had flooded through the broken line and were positioning themselves for an attack on the Canadian rear. Seeing that fifteen men would not turn the battle, Loomis risked his command by leaving the area near St. Julien so he could explain the situation to Turner and convince him to withdraw the order to attack.

Loomis's three-and-a-half-mile dash must have started near 7:25 a.m., for twenty-five minutes later, Hughes signalled the Château des Trois Tours that "our line is broken C.6.c. to right. Organizing at St. Julien and occupying GHQ line. No troops in rear. Support needed. Please give situation on our left." At 7:15 a.m., Hughes was still sending messages to Currie's 15th Battalion, which had been all but annihilated three hours earlier. Among them was one that said that the "impression exists in your regiment that they are to retire on GHQ line." The message underscores how poorly Hughes and Turner grasped the situation on the west side of the Apex: "This [impression] must be corrected at once. You are to hold your front line. If driven out collect your men organize a counter attack and regain it. You are <u>on no account</u> to retire on GHQ line."

A glimpse of the disarray that gripped the Château des Trois Tours and Mouse Trap Farm—charitably called "the fog of war" by Canada's official historian—can be seen in a 6:10 a.m. message from Major-General Thomas D'Oyly Snow, who commanded the British 27th Division, on the Canadian right:

> If my guns assist you today as I hope they will please arrange more definite target than yesterday aaa Yesterday we were asked to fire at our extreme range on certain areas aaa After sighting I found out target was about 2500 yards behind enemy's position aaa Possibly that was what you wanted but I doubt it aaa SNOW.

## Chapter Ten

# "No, Alexander Is Not Gone"
### The *Feldgrauen* Storm Towards St. Julien

> *A sleeping army lies in front of one of our brigades; they rest in good order, man by man and will never wake again—Canadian divisions. The enemy's losses are enormous.*
> —Leutnant Rudolf Binding

While Hughes issued nonsensical orders over Turner's name and the communication system broke down, 2nd Ypres turned into a battle of battalion commanders, like Lieutenant-Colonel Lipsett and Majors Odlum and Ormond, and platoon and company commanders, none of whom had a grasp of what was going on elsewhere on the battlefield.

They performed better than could have been predicted. Lipsett's first priority was dealing with both the catastrophic break in the Canadian line and further German attacks. Near 5:00 a.m., he ordered his last reserve unit, a half company commanded by Lieutenant Gerald O'Grady, to reinforce Captain Morley's position on the far left of the 8th Battalion's line (where it had joined the 15th). O'Grady never made it. He was shot dead shortly after leading his 125 men into what had been firmly held Canadian ground at 2:30 a.m. At 4:00 a.m. it had become a field of green gas, and an hour later it had become a no man's land where German troops roamed almost at will.

* * *

As O'Grady's command passed to Sergeant-Major Frederick Hall, RIR 236 moved into its forward position in a brick factory south of Langemarck, and part of RIR 234 prepared to launch an attack on the section of the Canadian line that ran north to the Apex (where the 13th Battalion's line had joined the part of the 15th Battalion that held trenches running to the east). These two regiments clashed with elements of 7th, 14th, and 15th Battalions, which held the trenches running north from St. Julien.

Captain George Alexander, whose company stood in the middle of the 15th Battalion's position, reported simply, "Germans stopped at 5:00 a.m. by crossfire." German records tell us more. The men of RIR 234 divided. Those on the extreme right moved west towards Kitcheners Wood. The rest advanced until they crossed the Poelcappelle–St. Julien road, which ran less than a hundred yards in front of the trenches of the 15th and 7th Battalions. "There they ran into such heavy machine gun and infantry fire . . . that they had to immediately take cover in the road ditch and entrench." The unexpectedly heavy fire caused the battalion staff to take cover in an empty farmhouse. While German bullets "poured through doors and windows" at Odlum's headquarters, some fifteen hundred yards to the northwest, here Canadian bullets streamed into the farmhouse. A Leutnant Kneiling was hit bringing up orders.

According to the regimental historian of RIR 236, the 234's right also found it heavy going once it came within range of Canadian gunners:

> When the lead companies clashed with the enemy at about 5 o'clock in the morning, they received heavy machine gun and shrapnel fire from the Gun Woods west of St. Julien. When they advanced further, the infantry fire from the front and the effect of the fire from the Eastern edge of the Grenade Woods increased more and more.

In early 1916, Canadians by the thousands read a Canadian infantryman's description of this attack in *Maple Leaves in Flanders:*

Across the open space the attack came, not in dense masses as we had been led to expect, but line on line, like waves in an advancing flood.

Across the fields they stumbled forward, running clumsily with their fat legs and ridiculous boots.... From the trench our rifles cracked and machine-guns spat; before the hail of bullets the Germans fell. Soon the field was spotted with fallen figures, some laying still, others trying to crawl away. But still they came on. Now we could see their features and count the buttons on their tunics as they lumbered forward.... Now the wave lapped against the edge of our trench. Suddenly a fat German, with bulging eyes, recognized death staring at him across the mud-bank, turned to fly. A bullet caught him on the buckle of his waist belt, causing his equipment to fly apart as it passed onwards on its way. A huge red-headed warrior, his mouth open and breathing hard from running, got it square between the eyebrows; the force of the rush carried him forward against the parapet, where he lay, the back blown out of his head and with a look of mild surprise upon his face. One or two rushed the parapet, but they were not fighters, and fell like sheep on the points of our bayonets.[1]

However much Canadians believed that Germans feared cold steel, it is hard to accept that they "fell like sheep on the points of our bayonets." We should be less suspicious of Herbert Rae's infantryman noting the Germans' "fat legs and ridiculous boots," for these are the sorts of details that in the strange world of battle men actually do see. One detail that can certainly be believed is the Canadians' surprise that the Germans came in a dense, silent mass, so different from the yelling charge with which the Canadians had attacked Kitcheners Wood.

• • •

Just as this German wave broke on Canadian lines running north to the Apex, Captain Warden, at Locality "C," noticed a large number of Germans approaching. Likely these were the same German units that Lipsett had seen trying to work their way behind the 8th Battalion.

Crossfire from the two battalions halted this advance and another one an hour later.

Near 6:30 a.m., the Germans tried yet another *ruse de guerre*. A major who had just arrived at Locality "C" was fooled by Germans who wore British coats and pushed prisoners forward with bayonets. Warden, however, was not fooled. When the advancing "British" and their "German prisoners" were within fifty yards, Warden ordered his men to fire. But the major countermanded the order, saying that they were shooting at British soldiers. "They are not British soldiers—they are Germans dressed in British uniforms," shouted Warden. Ignoring rank, he again ordered his men to fire. Not convinced, the major ordered his men to cease fire. By then, the "British" soldiers, having worked their way through the trench's entanglements, were just seconds away from entering the trench. Again, Warden ordered his men to fire. Despite the carnage of 2nd Ypres, the captain must have smiled when, in his report, he wrote that the *Feldgrauen* "turned and ran back even faster than the rest, which was sufficient proof they were not British Soldiers."

· · ·

As the Germans played out this *pièce de théâtre*, Sergeant-Major Hall led his men towards the ragged end of the 8th Battalion's line. No record remains of the difficulties of the thousand-yard march, which took an hour, but it must have resembled the one made by Private Drummond, who earlier had led his men over much the same territory: shell hole to shell hole, dodging incoming shells; shouted orders barely heard over the explosions. Some bullets found their mark; one killed Captain W. R. Bertram. A thousand yards ahead, machine-gun and shellfire steadily reduced Morley's numbers. Hall and a few other men made it, but most were blown apart by shells.

Reaching the trench did not end the agony. When the smoke cleared, Hall saw that one of his men was still alive just over a dozen yards short of the trench. Over the next few minutes, a three-act tragedy unfolded before Morley's eyes. Even though he had been hit earlier, Private Tug

Wilson, Morley's batman, climbed over the parapet and ran towards the injured man. But he did not make it. Next, one Lieutenant Payne, who had also already been hit, tried his luck. A moment later, he was dead as well. The drama was completed when Hall climbed out over the parapet; he "too was hit with a bullet in the centre of his forehead and instantly killed."

On 23 June, the War Office announced that Hall, a thirty-year-old who had been born in Kilkenny, Ireland, and lived in Winnipeg, had been awarded the Victoria Cross, the second earned by a Dominion soldier in two days.

While Hall was leading his men forward, Major Ormond led the remnants of the 10th Battalion from Fortuin to Locality "C" to reinforce Warden. Despite explosions that convulsed the air around them—as well as the smell of cordite and upturned earth, and the iron stench of bloody bodies—Ormond's men likely cracked a smile at the sight of their commander swimming to the other side of a shell hole into which he had jumped. Those closest to him must have gasped when he was knocked down by a spent piece of shrapnel.

His orders to "occupy locality 'C' and not let the Germans in" could best be fulfilled by extending Warden's line. To do this, Ormond took his men to a trench a short distance to Warden's left (west). The first group to make their way to the trench, sixteen men, arrived at the same time as a barrage of T-shells. Once again, the Canadians protected themselves with wet cloths; Ormond grabbed a piece of Lieutenant Walter Critchley's handkerchief. The major could take little comfort from what he saw once the gas had cleared: "Our whole left was exposed to St. Julien at least 1,000 yards." Worse, he could see that the 13th Battalion, which held the trenches on his left (perpendicular to his trench), was beginning to retire.

Ormond had extended Warden's line to the left. But their trenches did not link up. In between was a house where the Germans had managed to place a machine gun. That machine gun enfiladed the far left of Warden's trench "with such terrific fire that [he] had to withdraw from it." Before the Germans could get close enough to throw their potato-masher grenades, Warden's men "barricaded the trench where it made a fairly sharp curve which acted as a traverse and gave us some protection."

• • •

As Warden's men worked to protect their trench, RIRs 235, 237, and 238 attacked Kitcheners Wood from the north. The 238 advanced on the right and encountered no resistance. In a trench just south of the woods, the Germans reported finding two hundred dead Canadians.

The 235's advance on the left went more slowly. Reports from the neighbouring sectors had informed the regiment's commanders that "the enemy was putting up heavy resistance north of St. Julien." The commanders assumed some of this resistance came from Canadians in positions on the northeastern side of the woods, whom they hoped to dislodge with an artillery bombardment. It is hard to square the report that the woods themselves presented "quite a difficult obstacle with its mixed vegetation of trees and thick underbrush" with the fact that the Canadians had been able to storm through just a few hours earlier.

• • •

While their comrades in RIR 234 attacked Rae's 7th Battalion, the rest of the regiment threaded its way towards the 2nd Battalion's positions east of Kitcheners Wood. The Germans fell on Doxsee's House at 7:00 a.m. But their attack was hampered by a failure of German intelligence. Even though earlier attacks had been thrown back, the officers of the 234 appear not to have known that the Canadians "had installed machine guns in many houses that were covering the entire area of attack." According to Captain Richardson, fire from Doxsee's and Hooper's houses, and from men in the trenches—which was augmented by the fire of some twenty reinforcements who, as the attack began, eschewed the communication trench and ran across the open field—"repulsed the attack with severe loss to the enemy who left many men scattered on the fields." Among the dead was Lieutenant William Doxsee.

Under Richardson's command, Doxsee's House held out against several more attacks. Shells exploded the walls around them, so that at "times men lay on beds and boxes while machine guns swept the floors." At other times, the men "hugged the floor while bullets passed over their heads." When its gun seized, a machine-gun crew quickly disassembled, cleaned, and reassembled it.

Fifteen minutes after the attack on Doxsee's House, Captain Hooper sent a runner with a message for the first 2nd Battalion officer he could find. In that message, Hooper incorrectly indicated that St. Julien had fallen. His mistake is understandable, however, for at about the same time, Major Kirkpatrick, whose 3rd Battalion position was close to Hooper's House, saw "four huge shells . . . burst simultaneously [over St. Julien] . . . sending huge masses of masonry high into the air and bringing the walls of buildings down in crackling masses." More useful was the information that thanks to the work of the relief parties during the night, Hooper had two days' worth of ammunition and rations. His claim that he could not hold the house if he did not have support from the area around Kitcheners Wood suggests that no one had informed him that troops belonging to his own 2nd Battalion had replaced the 16th Battalion in front of the woods; lacking this information, Hooper logically assumed that the Canadian line to his left rear had retired.

It hadn't. At least, it hadn't yet. When it did, Hooper's and Doxsee's houses would have to be abandoned too.

• • •

Some of the Germans who poured through the gap that had been punched in the Canadian line worked their way to their right, where they threatened the rear of the 13th Battalion, which held the trenches running north to the Apex. Others moved to their left along the Stroombeek, which brought them behind the 8th and 5th Battalions. Of these, Hauptmann Von Germar (RIR 233) wrote: "The fresh troops adapted under the pressure of the situation to a new way of using their weapons, creating their own fighting tactics—that is crawling ahead individually and jumping individually." Ironically, it was during this battle that the artillery/infantry coordination that became the Canadian Corps' trademark later in the war was first used by German troops. "In this fighting there was another moment involved for the first time for us, the importance of linking up infantry and artillery," said Von Germar.

Again and again, King George's troops repulsed Kaiser Wilhelm's, but each victory was short lived. At one point, the 7th Company of RIR 233 was held up by fire coming from behind hedges while its supporting artillery fired at a nearby windmill. A German soldier named Rihn seized the initiative, grabbing the artillery recognition and running into heavy fire past the windmill. "There he put the white and red flag into the earth so that it could be seen from afar. Immediately the artillery recognized the sight and transferred its fire towards the enemy" beyond the hedges. A bursting shell killed Rihn; after the battle, his commanding general, Generalleutnant von Hügel, erected a plaque in his honour. It read,

> To a young hero. By placing the artillery recognition flag on the windmill ridge occupied by the Canadians, he made it possible, through sacrificing his life for his comrades, to launch a successful attack.
>
> —In eternal memory, the commanding General of the 26 Corps of the Reserve

The hundreds of Germans who advanced on the trenches near Locality "C," newly occupied by Ormond's 10th Battalion, did not advance in the way that had caught Von Germar's eye. "All we could see was masses of Germans coming up in mass formation. Their officers were still on horseback then," recalled Critchley.[2] Because of the tear gas, Ormond could not tell the colour of the advancing troops' uniforms, and he could not use his field glasses, which had filled with water when he fell into the shell hole; nevertheless, the major shouted over the exploding shells to his men to fire when the Germans were about seven or eight hundred yards away. And once again, the Ross rifles jammed. "Instead of getting off twelve or fifteen rounds a minute, we could only get off two or three."

For a moment, it looked as if Ormond had made a ghastly mistake when a party a short distance from the main formation raised a white flag. In another instant, the apparent mistake increased exponentially when two men left a trench on Ormond's left (held by stragglers from different Canadian battalions) and walked towards the soldiers with the white flag just as the major ordered his men to fire. Things were clarified a few moments later when the two Canadians were taken prisoner. Within a minute, the soldiers the Canadians had taken for Turcos set up a machine gun and began spraying bullets at Ormond's trench; happily, the gun's position was such that the bullets hit mainly the top of Ormond's parados. Then, as their shells blew up Ormond's men "5 and 6 at a time," the Germans advanced in earnest. Somehow, despite their jammed rifles—many of which were filled with dirt blown off the parapet—Ormond's men, some standing on the parapet (and thus exposing themselves to machine-gun and rifle fire, and red-hot splinters), produced enough fire to push off the Germans. "When they went back the third time," Ormond recalled almost half a century later, "we thought we'd won the war."[3]

• • •

At 7:30 a.m., Lieutenant-General Alderson acted to fill the thinning British lines. The closest reserves were two battalions of the York and Durham (150th) Brigade, commanded by Brigadier-General J. E. Bush, then in billets near Brielen, on the west side of the Yser Canal. Despite the crisis outlined for Alderson in General Currie's 6:30 a.m. message, which told him that the Germans had broken through the 15th Battalion's trenches, he still didn't seem to fully grasp the catastrophe then occurring on the Canadian right.* Instead of directing Bush to take his

---

*Currie's message read, "Germans have broken through Highlanders' trenches about 1,000 yards left of section II of 8th bn."

battalions—some fifteen hundred men—to the Apex, Alderson ordered him to the GHQ Line. "On reaching the trenches," Alderson told him, "get into communication with the 3rd Canadian Infantry Brigade whose Headquarters are in Farm C.22.b [Mouse Trap Farm] and with 2nd Canadian Infantry Brigade [Currie]. You will act as reserve to these two Brigades as required." By the time Bush's men arrived at the GHQ Line, where they filled trenches running *south towards Ypres* (and thus away from the German advance), their Lee-Enfield rifles were desperately needed several thousand yards to the northeast, where the Germans were attacking Doxsee's House, the line running north to the Apex, and the trenches near Locality "C."

At 8:25 a.m., Alderson received Turner's first accurate message: "Our line is broken C.6.c. Organizing at St. Julien and occupying GHQ line. No troops in rear. Support needed. Please give situation on our left." The coordinates C.6.c. told Alderson that the break was near Keerselare, at the Apex of the Canadian line. Alderson ordered two more battalions of the York and Durham Regiment across the canal—and once again, to the GHQ Line, forty-five hundred yards from where the Germans were cutting off Captain Harvey's men and from where H. G. Brewer of the 14th Battalion and his comrades were enduring the full wrath of the heavy guns and infantry tactics. "People were being blown up all around us, bodies flying in the air," Brewer recalled. "So eventually they just blew us out of our position and we had the order to retire, and the retirement was up a long slope right out in the open, no cover at all. The bullets were—well, it was just like being out in a rainstorm. I don't know how we ever got up, the few of us that did."[4]

Forty-five hundred yards may not seem like a great distance, but in the First World War it was considerable. According to Bill Rawling,

> Today's tanks can traverse that distance in just over 3 minutes, slightly slower than highway speed. During the Second World War tanks could traverse that distance in about 6 minutes. But in the First World War, when men could move only at the speed their legs could carry them (and

their 60-pound back packs) over broken shell-pocked ground, four thousand five hundred yards (2 1/2 miles) was almost an hour away. It was the difference between being in the action and hearing about it.

To be fair to Alderson, he planned on using the York and Durham Brigade to relieve the men of Turner's 3rd Brigade, who by the evening of Saturday, 24 April, would have been continuously engaged for more than forty-eight hours and awake for almost seventy-two hours, close to the limit of human endurance. Though Currie's 2nd Brigade had been in the trenches for about the same length of time, it had not been engaged during the night of 22 April or through much of the following day, which meant that Currie's men had been able to grab some sleep and were somewhat further from their physical limit. The remnants of the 10th Battalion had been awake just as long as Turner's brigade—and had fought a night battle in Kitcheners Wood. As critical as these limitations were, Alderson completely failed to grasp the importance of the gas attack. Currie's men (and the regiments running north to the Apex) were on the verge of being either wiped out or completely cut off and captured, surely an equal crisis.

Alderson failed to grasp the seriousness of the situation confronting Currie's brigade partly because of the tone and content of Currie's messages. Where Hughes's messages were either incorrect or panicky, Currie's were unusually calm. This was remarkable given what his men had endured during and after the second gas attack in history, and given that at 7:00 a.m. his command post was hit by enemy shells, forcing him to take shelter with the 2nd Artillery Brigade, seven hundred yards away. At 8:25 a.m., when his 7th Battalion was fighting for its life and Locality "C" was under attack, in a morning that had seen several more attacks on the 8th and 5th Battalions, Currie signalled Alderson:

> My line still intact. 3rd Brigade front line fallen back. I am holding locality C with 3 Companies with orders to hang on there and help 3rd Brigade if possible. My 7th Battalion still in position C.6.b. Am collecting stragglers

here and sending them to locality C. Understand 3rd Brigade holding St. Julien; they should have 7 companies there in addition to what was in their front line which was 7 companies. Will try to establish new line C.6.d. D.1.c and d. D.2.c. and d.

It is one thing for Major Andrew McNaughton to have said, half a century after the gas attack, "Somehow we felt it was the normal course of war. It was unpleasant, it's true, but nobody got very excited about it." It is quite another for Currie to have boldly ignored the effects of the gas attack in a message written just a few hours after it happened.

Hughes, by contrast, reported lines "being driven in" and used the word "retire." While Turner could plan only to fill the GHQ Line, Currie's last sentence proposes that his men establish a new line that would plug the hole left by the destruction of the 15th Battalion. Currie also gave Alderson information about the St. Julien garrison, which was not part of his command.

At 10:35 a.m., with the guns battering the Canadian lines echoing in his ears, Turner read a message from Alderson instructing him on how to use the recently arrived York and Durham Brigade: "If absolutely necessary call on Brigade York and Durham for assistance of one Battalion but do not do so unless absolutely necessary as it is hoped to use this Brigade to relieve yours this evening." Turner took Alderson's words to heart.

At 11:30 a.m., as the Germans attacked all across the Canadian lines, Turner gave a negative answer to a message that Currie thought was important enough to send by the hand of his brigade major: "If the Gravenstafel Ridge is to be preserved, it is imperatively necessary for your GHQ 2nd line garrison, your troops in rear [the York and Durhams], to reinforce your left flank front. My last message half hour ago was that my 7th Battalion was still holding it. What is your St. Julien garrison doing?" Turner's refusal to move his troops speaks volumes about his fixation on the GHQ Line and his failure to see how the York and Durhams could best be deployed: "Have not substantial reinforcements at my disposal to reinforce your left, Gravenstafel Ridge. We are holding GHQ 2nd line with about 700 men, all that are available. My right front is being blown out of successive positions towards St. Julien. Still hold between C.11.c and C.11.d [Kitcheners Wood to St. Julien]."

A quick look at the map should have told Turner that Currie's plan to have the York and Durhams reinforce *Turner's* "left front flank" would have gone a long way towards protecting St. Julien and Gravenstafel Ridge. Turner's refusal to part with any of the men in the GHQ Line foreshadows his later decision to "sit on his reserves," even in the face of a command from Alderson to move them to the front—with, Lieutenant-Colonel Gordon Gordon-Hall wrote later, "disastrous consequences to all concerned, and to none more than his own troops."

• • •

By 8:30 a.m., the situation for the 13th Battalion had worsened as supplies of food, water, and especially bullets ran low. Major Victor Buchanan (who commanded the left part of the 13th Battalion's line—the part farthest from the Apex) had fewer men with which to hold his trenches than he'd had before the first gas attack. His riflemen, who picked off several *Feldgrauen* carrying artillery markers, and his machine-gunners scored some successes. But shell after "beautifully placed" shell rendered the Canadian trenches untenable. Through their telescopes, RIR 233's commanders watched the "Brits moving to and fro trying to escape."

Just as the order came for the three companies that made up the 13th Battalion to fall back to trenches on Gravenstafel Ridge, a shell buried Captain J. Jeffrey. After being dug out, he saw "a body of Germans moving across our front . . . marching in fours, and at their head . . . was an officer in white uniform," which indicated that the officer was royalty. Blueblood or not, what mattered to Jeffrey and the men who had endured gas—as well as hours of bombardment and mounting numbers of dead around them—was the fact that this officer was in range and seemingly unaware that the Canadians were pretty good shots. Jeffrey ordered his men to fire, and the officer in dress whites "fell riddled" with bullets.

Moments later, following his men, Jeffrey left the trench and was now himself the hunted. The first part of his escape went well, but then a Boche machine-gun crew spotted him in the mustard field into which he had crawled. He "dodged and ran like a snake" through this field. More than once he fell. More than once, with the bullets inching ever nearer, he threw up his hands as if to surrender. The bullets stopped, and as he walked towards the Germans, he had a chance to catch his breath. And then he started off again. Finally, Jeffrey was far enough away that the gunners "gave up the game." All around him, other 13th Battalion men were also in motion. Scores, including Captains R. H. Jamieson and Kenneth M. Perry and Lieutenant Melville Greenshields, who exited the trench before Jeffrey, made better targets. Each was hit as he tried to lead his men to safety.

This retirement was forced and it was bloody, but it was anything but a disorderly rout. Once free of their trenches, the exhausted men, many of them still coughing from the gas they'd stood through at dawn, "stopped frequently to administer a stinging check when the Germans trod too closely on their heels." RIR 233 lost fifty men to bullets fired by the retreating Canadians. Jeffrey attributed the lack of panic to the quality of the officers, who "were drawn from the clerical sections of Montreal" and included half a dozen stockbrokers. "There was no thought of panic. There was a job coming along and they just knuckled down to it."

• • •

The order to retire did not reach Major McCuaig on the far right of the 13th Battalion's line (just below the Apex) until the retirement was almost complete and the Germans had moved into what had been Buchanan's trenches. The only chance for McCuaig and the Buffs to escape lay immediately behind them, across fifty yards of open ground. Lacking a written order, however, the Buffs' commander refused to leave the trenches.

Moments before McCuaig received the order to retire, a shell exploded in the trench, burying twenty-eight-year-old Colin Alexander and killing another man. Blasted earth contains both a large amount of air and a large number of passages into which air penetrates. Thus, Alexander did not need to dig himself out immediately. First, he wiggled his toes to see if they were still with him, and only then did he start digging. He stopped, however, when he realized that every time he moved his arms up, he risked being hit by the bullets that peppered the trench.

Just before McCuaig gave the order to retire, one of his men called out, "Major McCuaig, there is Alexander gone!" As if from beyond the grave, they then heard, "No, Alexander is not gone, but he is pretty well badly hurt." As some of his comrades dug him out, others, who could not tell in which direction his body lay, ran over the ground covering him, causing him to yell, "Be careful of my leg! Be careful of my leg!"

To the sound of yelling and a trumpet flourish, the men of RIRs 233 and 234 stormed the British lines. Unable to move, Alexander was among their first prizes; he was taken as McCuaig and forty other Canadians made a break across ground covered by machine-gun fire. Only a few made it to safety. Lieutenant Charles Pitblado, Captain Lionel Whitehead, and Major McCuaig did not.

But for the fact that he started out carrying the mortally wounded Whitehead, Pitblado might have made it. After being hit in the knee, he abandoned Whitehead and went ahead on his own, meeting up with McCuaig. Then McCuaig was hit in the knee. The major told Pitblado to go on without him. Pitblado ignored his commander. With shells falling around them and bullets whizzing through the air, he unwrapped McCuiag's puttees and dressed his wounds. "He was then wounded a second time, which finished his chances of getting away," recorded McCuaig in a report he wrote after the war had ended and he and Pitblado had been released from prison camp. "I was subsequently wounded four more times while lying on the ground."[5] The Germans were advancing so quickly that they passed these two Canadians ten minutes after they fell. They were picked up and made prisoners of war an hour later.

His Majesty George V awarded McCuaig the Distinguished Service Order and Pitblado the Military Cross. They were the first two Canadians to be awarded these honours in the Great War, and the third and fourth Dominion soldiers to earn battlefield honours in a little over thirty-six hours.*

As Jeffrey, McCuaig, Pitblado, and a score of other men tried to escape the Germans' clutches, the end came for the Buffs and the few dozen Canadians near the Apex. Both groups fought till their ammunition was all but exhausted. Captain McKessock, who had lost twenty-eight of his thirty-one men, and two other units had not a single round of .303 ammunition for their Ross rifles and only twenty-five rounds left for the one remaining Colt machine gun, barely enough for a seven-second spray.

The moments before the end must have been a singularly exquisite torment for Major James Ewart Osborne, a thirty-nine-year-old stockbroker. Instead of enduring the shelling, the twice-wounded major was a prisoner watching from behind the German lines as a shell landed in what had been his part of the trench; later he found out that it had killed two men. Knowing that any further resistance was futile, Osborne hoped that whoever was commanding the trench would raise the white flag. When he saw it, his relief was palpable, for "had another shell landed along the trench it would in all probability have killed 30 or 40 men."[6]

. . .

At 8:30 a.m., while French and Belgian soldiers were dying before Lizerne and Germans were smashing their way through the Apex, Odlum, then at the 7th Battalion positions that ran north to the Apex, heard rifle fire from his rear. Thinking that the fire was coming from his reserve company (about one hundred yards to the east of his line) and concerned that his men might mistakenly fire on Canadian troops retreating from the broken lines to the north, Odlum gave orders to refrain "unless the enemy were actually seen and were very close." He need not have worried.

---

*In September 1916, no doubt to the major's dismay, McCuaig's father, Clarence J. McCuaig, tried to blackmail Prime Minister Robert Borden into arranging for a prisoner exchange: the major for one Baron von Polenz. McCuaig *père* threatened to go public with information relating to the failures of the Ross rifle. Borden was unmoved by the threat.

The fire came from Germans who were less than three hundred yards from Odlum's rear; their position threatened to cut off Captain Harvey's force of two platoons, which held a stretch of trench on the extreme right (north) side of Odlum's position. Just minutes later, when RIR 236 launched another attack on Odlum's front, Harvey's men were all but surrounded, yet they somehow held on. The attack, which fell also on the west-facing trenches held by Captain Thomas V. Scudamore's and Major P. Byng-Hall's men, was extremely costly to the Germans. When his men's Ross rifles jammed, the aptly named Sergeant Hugh Peerless stiffened their spines by yelling, "Give the sons of bitches hell, boys."[7] After the attack, Scudamore and Byng-Hall had sent Odlum word that they believed they could hold their trenches even against a frontal attack; in less than three hours, their line was erased from the map.

Their confidence stemmed partly from their position, which included a well-placed machine gun in a building in what the Germans called the *Engländergehöft* (Englishman's farm), and partly from the fact that volunteers continued bringing up ammunition. At the height of the firefight, the fortune of war brought some of these volunteers to the end of a parabola traced by a German shell, whose distinctive sound they likely never heard above the cacophony around them.*

The shell that Odlum saw land among his men did not have to land directly on someone to kill, nor did it have to ricochet. Before any of the men could even feel the heat as the shell cut through the air, it had hit the ground. Then a trigger struck the detonator in the nose, which hit a primer that began the detonation of TNT-like chemicals. The shock wave, moving at twenty thousand miles per hour, broke down everything in its path, killing the volunteer munitions carriers—including one with the attestation number 16608—who never felt a thing. Long before the airborne dirt and bits of human flesh and bone fell back to earth, Major Victor Odlum knew that his brother, Joseph, had "ceased to exist."

---

*Had it been a 4.1-inch shell, it would have made a twittering sound; a coal box sounded more like a railway train.

PART 6

# The Centre Cannot Hold
### 8:15 a.m. to 12 p.m., 24 April 1915

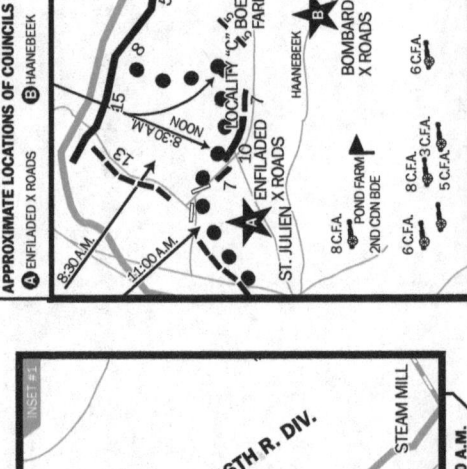

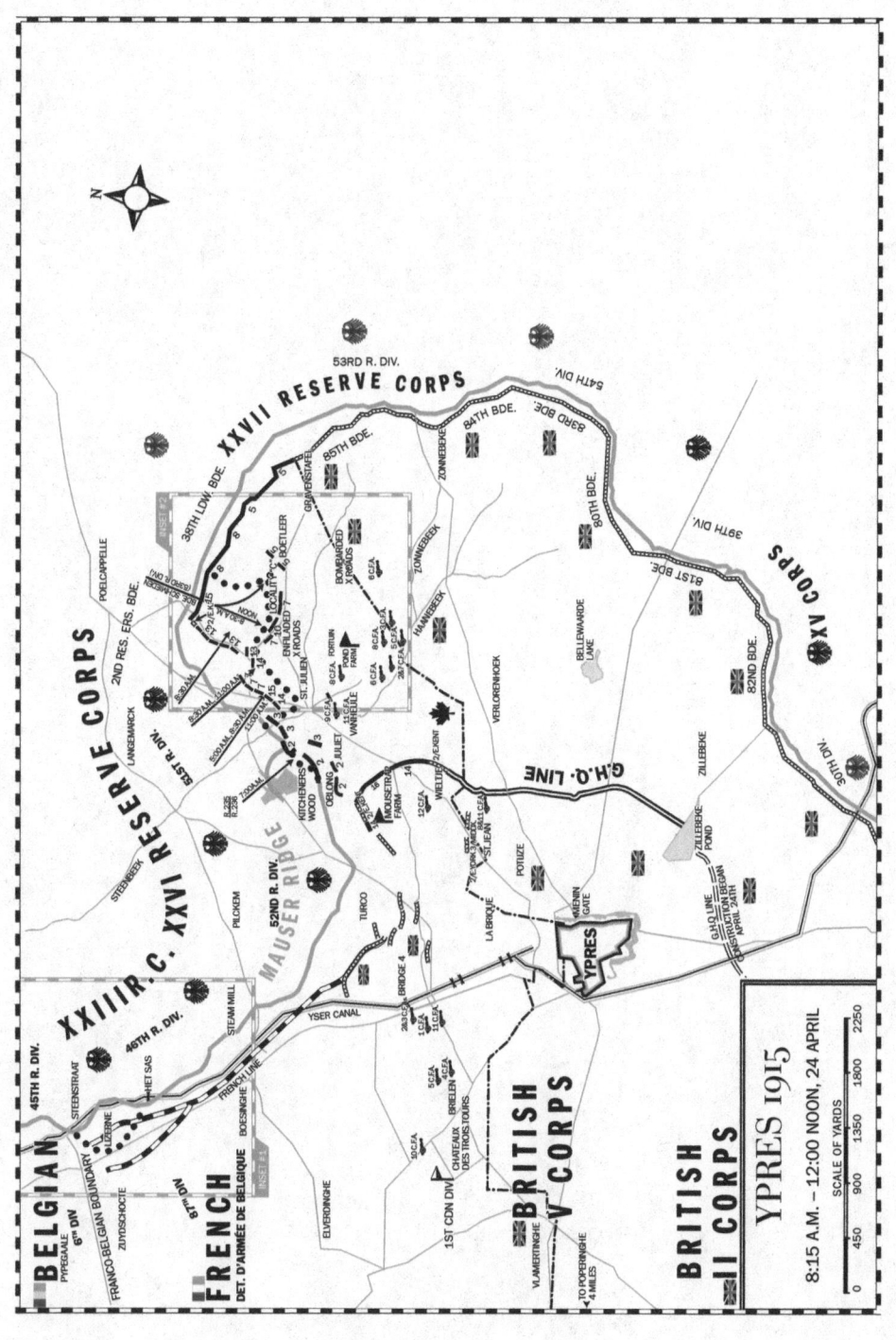

CHAPTER 11

# "His Insides Were Hanging between His Fingers"
### The Collapse of the 7th Battalion

> *Private MacNally thinking:*
> *You squareheaded sons of bitches,*
> *you want this God damn trench*
> *you're going to have to take it away*
> *from Billy MacNally*
> *of the South End of Saint John, New Brunswick.*
> —Alden Nowlan, "Ypres: 1915"

At 8:14 a.m. on 24 April, the men of the Canadian Advanced Depot of Medical Stores motor repair shop in Poperinghe, eight miles west of Ypres, were surely counting themselves lucky. Over the previous few days, they had heard and seen horrors. First came the rolling thunder of the bombardment of Ypres, then the refugees fleeing the burning city. Drivers bringing supplies into what Major Odlum called "a marvellous heap of ruins" came back with stories of houses collapsing, sometimes raining dust and brick on the fleeing refugees, sometimes trapping people inside.

By dusk on 22 April, they knew that the German gas attack had shattered the French lines. By late that night, drivers had moved thousands of stockpiled dressings and other emergency medical equipment forward to casualty clearing stations, main dressing stations, and advanced dressing stations; many had had to carry supplies to the regimental aid posts that were just behind the lines. Spurgeon Jenkins, a twenty-four-year-old ammunition driver from Prince Edward Island, witnessed this scene as he struggled to guide his horse-drawn ammunition wagon across Ypres to keep his battery supplied:

> The streets of the city and the roads were literally covered with the bodies of men, horses, mules, dogs, and in some cases, women and children. To make matters worse, if that were possible, a large number of them were in an advanced stage of decomposition; for the Germans poured such a rain of shells into the place that no one ventured near unless it was of necessity. The men who did simply courted death.
>
> I made three trips in the very thickest of the fighting and I hope and pray that I may never go through the like again and live. Dante's "Inferno" was a dream of peaches compared to it. In lots of places my horse's feet splashed in great pools of blood. Everywhere you looked you could see limbers smashed to pieces and men and horses dying in the gutters. Above the screams of the shells you could hear the groans of the dying.[1]

Before the sun rose on 23 April, ambulance drivers were transporting hundreds of wounded Canadians to hospitals in Poperinghe and Vlamertinghe. Many of the wounds were ghastly but predictable: chests and abdomens torn open by bullets, shrapnel, or splinters from high-explosive shells; arms ending with a bloody stump at the wrist or elbow; legs reduced to stubs. Bandages covered the faces of men whose jaws had been shot off.

The medical stations and the 3rd Canadian Casualty Clearing Hospital on Rue de Bois Cheppers in Poperinghe resembled the scene of the damned in Michelangelo's *Last Judgment*. The muddy ground was covered with stretchers on which lay bleeding, broken men—some moaning, some screaming, some too much in shock to see from their wide-open eyes, some with eyes filled with pain. Others lay in a morphine-induced calm, or one brought on by the cold hand of death. Everywhere grew heaps of iron-red rags and piles of amputated hands, arms, and legs.

Even more horrifying was the damage for which no one had trained: the effects of poison gas. First a few, then dozens, then scores of men gasping for breath. Their faces red like mahogany, blue, or a sickly green. Their tongues hanging out of mouths laced with green froth (in some cases, streaked with red), and their burned eyes staring blindly ahead. The lucky were given oxygen. The unlucky simply gasped on, their breath weakening until they could hold on no longer. They drowned on land.

By mid-morning on 24 April, the more discerning drivers could distinguish the sound of guns firing in support of the French/Belgian attack on German positions at Het Sas and Lizerne from the deeper rumble of the German guns then punishing the Canadians on the right wing of the Apex. Just before 8:15 a.m., the German guns fired. As the sound waves merged, nineteen shells arced through the sky over Mauser Ridge, heading for Poperinghe. Two landed near the 3rd Canadian Casualty Clearing Hospital. One hit Lieutenant-General Sir Herbert Plumer's headquarters. Fifteen blew great holes in the ground. The nineteenth fell on the motor repair shop, wounding two and killing four men who wore Red Cross brassards.

. . .

Fifteen minutes later, a few miles to the east, another French/Belgian attack on German positions on the west side of the Yser Canal collapsed. Following his meeting with Field Marshall Sir John French during the evening of 24 April, Général Foch had once again ordered Général Putz to evict the Germans from the west side of the Yser. Putz in turn had ordered Général Quiquandon to take strong action: "Throw back upon the right bank [east] all elements of the enemy forces which have crossed it and gain footing on that bank." But some of Quiquandon's tools were either dull or untried. The 87th Territorials had borne the brunt of the gas attack, and the 418th Infantry Regiment of the 153rd Division was filled with raw recruits. By contrast, the Belgians supplied one of their best formations, the 3rd Battalion of the 2nd Regiment of Carabiniers, whose "rather rakish silk top-hat" stood out even among the plethora of hats and headdresses in the days before every army adopted the steel helmet.[2] The German seizure of Lizerne in the early hours of 24 April had seriously complicated the French plans.

With the help of their artillery, the French and Belgian soldiers made some progress in the first minutes of the attack. As they neared Lizerne, however, German artillery began to tell on the Allies. At 9:40 a.m., in the same message that told Foch that Colonel Jacques Mordacq's attack on Mauser Ridge had failed, Putz hinted that the attack on Lizerne was faltering: "The Territorials of the 87th are still shaken by the charge of the day before—one cannot expect too much of them—I say nothing of the Algerian auxiliaries."[3]* By 11:00 a.m., Général Alexandre L. Codet had called off the attack.

A few hours later, Codet renewed the attack and managed to enter Lizerne, momentarily coming close to fulfilling an 11:15 a.m. command from Foch, which was a response to Putz's 9:40 a.m. message. As always, Foch's words bespeak action:

> It is necessary to attempt at all costs to throw back from the Canal the German elements which have crossed at Lizerne and further south—push up your reserves to do this. It can be engaged by nightfall—I am calling up another division; you will have it tomorrow morning. You will have besides that the English reserve at Elverdinghe throughout the day.[4]

The hard reality was, however, that neither Codet's nor Général Francis Roy's force (ordered to attack Het Sas) was anywhere near strong

---

*In writing "I say nothing of the Algerian auxiliaries," Putz said very much indeed, but what he says is a calumny. The Algerians cannot be blamed for having broken ranks following the gas attack on 22 April, or for being incapable of mounting an attack less than forty-eight hours later.

enough for the task it had been assigned. No doubt Foch grasped this reality, though his 24 April report to Général Joseph Joffre goes some length towards obscuring it. "On the west bank of the Canal things are going well for us," he wrote. "We are in a fair way to begin and to take Steenstraat and Het Sas."⁵

The rhetoric of the French official history reveals a certain insouciance about these attacks:

> Général Codet attacked Lizerne at 2 p.m. and secured a footing there for a short time but could not hold it. On his right, Général Roy was going to recapture Het Sas but his progress was stopped at once.... Général Putz ordered Général Quiquandon to retake Lizerne at any cost during the night, but the attacks miscarried.⁶

• • •

Through the morning and into the early afternoon of 24 April, elements of RIR 233 continued to attack Lieutenant-Colonel Lipsett's trenches on Gravenstafel Ridge. His report is a model of concision. "There were 4 distinct attacks during the day time and one at night on this trench," he wrote, "once a few of the attackers reached the wire." In 1918, Sergeant-Major George W. Gorman sketched a more complete picture for the Thunder Bay Historical Society:

> A bugle blurted. With cries of "Neuve-Chapelle, Neuve-Chapelle" the grey clad figures came forward many deep. Then the 90th [the 8th Battalion's pre-war reserve number] cut into them with a low fire, every bullet must have gone home. The masses broke once again and fled back. Had they continued forward they would have met a line of fixed bayonets.⁷

• • •

Hundreds of *Feldgrauen* poured through the gap left by the destruction of the 13th and 15th Battalions. Fire from near Hooper's and Doxsee's houses stymied some. Machine-gun fire, likely from Captain Harvey's position on the extreme right of what had been Major Odlum's line, was so heavy that when Major Wanfschaffe attempted to reach RIR 233's forward headquarters, in a house at a crossroads a few hundred yards south of Keerselare, he had to "crawl on his stomach and use all the folds in the terrain." The regiment's 2nd Battalion advanced towards St. Julien, taking heavier than anticipated casualties. Fire, likely from Lipsett's left and from Locality "C," as well as shells fired by Lieutenant-Colonel John Creelman's and Major Andrew McNaughton's guns, forced the Germans to dig in short of the village that anchored the weak Canadian line.

Reserve-Infanterie-Regiment 234 advanced on St. Julien. According to its regimental historian:

> In spite of heavy resistance from the enemy who was entrenched in front of St. Julien and in spite of a tremendous deluge of projectiles that caused us many losses, our two battalions, supported by the 3rd Battalion that had come to our aid, took the height in front of St. Julien and the large part of the terrain as far as the village of St. Julien itself. There, however, the enemy put up a strong fight and since the regiments on the left and the right of us did not advance at the same pace our attack came to a standstill.
>
> Remaining in this position, which was particularly exposed to enemy fire, our regiment was obliged in the evening of this memorable day to withdraw under constant enemy fire from the flank—withdraw about 200 metres to a terrain that was more favourable and dig in.

At 9:15 a.m., the 3rd Battalion headquarters learned that along with several other men, Lieutenant William D. P. Jarvis, scion of the family that gave its name to one of Toronto's main streets, had been killed. Twenty-five minutes before receiving this last message, the headquarters learned from Captain John E. Streight that a "second body of enemy has been trying to work over to right of my position, but again returned under fire." Instead of putting the bodies of Jarvis and the other casualties on the bottom of the trench, Kirkpatrick's men laid them along the parapet, saving other Canadian lives.

• • •

At 9:00 a.m., General Sir Herbert Plumer placed Major General Thomas D'Oyly Snow, who commanded the 27th British Division, which was holding the ground directly to the east of Ypres and had forward trenches abutting the Canadian right, in charge of the reserves in the area. Copies of the order appointing Snow were not sent to (or were not received by) Alderson or any of the Canadian brigadiers in the field, however. At 9:00 a.m., the consequences of this communication breakdown were negligible; as the day wore on, the consequences would be catastrophic.

While Snow began planning how to use the reserves now at his disposal, Major Odlum's line, running north to the Apex, disintegrated. At 9:30 a.m., as the Germans closed on the farm that housed his headquarters, Odlum shifted them to a dugout on the side of the road, which itself soon came under machine-gun fire.

A short time later, amid heavy shelling, Captain Hanes tasked a twenty-six-year-old railwayman, Private Nathan Rice, with reinforcing Captain R. V. Harvey's No. 3 Company, the all-but-cut-off part of the 7th Battalion's line. Rice, who had just refused a battlefield promotion to corporal, and his men had a good view of their first goal, a fence about twenty-five yards from the road that led to Harvey's position. Rice led the first part of his detachment safely across the road, which pulsed with the deep rumble of exploding shells.

Then a bullet found its mark, and a Canadian felt the searing pain of lead cutting into him. A moment later, another bullet hit the ammunition pouch of Rice's French-Canadian buddy, transforming the khaki-clad figure into a human Dominion Day sparkler who somehow soldiered on across the road. By the time Rice reached him, "all his insides were hanging out between his fingers like rolls of sausage.... There wasn't a bit of blood ... just the insides were hanging out over his fingers."

While the badly wounded soldier lay waiting for a stretcher that would never come, another group of men crossed the road and took cover behind a little rise in the ground. Before Rice could warn him not to, Sergeant Doc Welles looked over the rise. An instant later, Rice heard a crack and Welles went down. Corporal Flagmore, who crested the rise next, was shot down in his turn.

The nightmare continued as a soldier named Barnes, who was a head taller than Rice, came up. The roar of war drowned out the battalion's best soccer player, but Rice had no doubt that, bullets and position be damned, Barnes had said he was going to get the wounded men to safety. "Just as he got his hands underneath him [Flagmore] he sort of stopped. He stood up straight, right up straight, went right over on his back." None of the eight or ten men in Welles's section lived to join up with Rice's men, who a short time later linked up with Corporal Pilkington and five men who held a small trench a short distance from Harvey's position.

The 7th Battalion's records do not indicate exactly when Harvey's position fell. The picture painted by Stretcher-Bearer R. C. Hunt from the Ontario Military Hospital in Cobourg, Ontario, however, makes their suffering all too clear. Just after a bullet shattered a bottle of iodine in his hand, Hunt was ordered to go to Harvey's trench:

> I found them in an awful mess. Poor little Captain Harvey had been wounded twice and I dressed him and asked him if I could carry him down to the dressing station and he said no look after the other men. Then Lieutenant Bromely got one which I dressed. I tried to persuade him to sit down but he said he must look after his men.

The carnage continued. Immediately after Hunt dressed Bromely's wounds, a sergeant was badly injured in the stomach. Hunt carried an eighty-eight-piece surgery kit, but surgery was out of the question in the tumult of battle. Instead, he dressed the wound, gave the man some weak brandy and water, and when that did not alleviate his pain, morphine. Hunt had barely given this man the opiate that would ease his last moments when another soldier was badly wounded. Hunt was tending to him "when the end came, [the] 10 of us being surrounded." Odlum learned of the destruction of Harvey's small garrison around 10:30 a.m.

Once Harvey's position fell, Major L. R. Scott's trench became Odlum's right. Shell-bursts rained down shrapnel, red-hot pieces of metal, and branches from the trees under which Scott's men sought shelter. After a German machine-gun crew fired into Scott's flank, twenty-eight-year-old Donald Bellew, Sergeant Hugh Peerless, and their men countered with their Colt machine guns. At one point, Peerless led his crew to a position fifty yards *in front* of the trench. "Hardly was he in position than the enemy debouched from the woods in massed formation," wrote Captain Scudamore. "The machine gun played on this excellent target and the Germans broke up and fled in disorder to the shelter of the wood."[8] A shell-burst behind Scott's trench wounded one Jack Fisher. Above the din of battle, Scott told him to empty his ammunition belt and crawl flat on his belly to the casualty clearing station behind the line. He never saw Fisher again.

Some distance to Scott's left, both a machine gun and still more Ross rifles failed to fire. The machine gun belonged to a crew that included Private Arthur Corker, who, though deafened by the shellfire, joined his crewmates in fixing the gun. There must have been a few moments when they thought they would not complete the drill, or would wind up with an extra spring or pin, as happened so often with the Colt machine gun. "The minute you spread your sheet out a shell would explode and cover it with dirt." That dirt had to be cleaned off the pieces before they were reassembled, for the Colt was liable to jam even just from dust.[9] While all this was going on, the *Feldgrauen* rushed forward in six or seven lines about fifty yards apart, moving against soldiers who had neither grenades nor working rifles: "Those who were in the trenches at the time will never forget, whilst those who were not will never quite understand what it is to be charged by the flower of the German army, confident of victory, and be unable to fire a shot in return."[10]

· · ·

At 9:50 a.m., a scant ten minutes after Odlum learned that his right had been destroyed, Lieutenant-Colonel Hughes signalled Alderson that the

Canadians were "still holding St. Julien line although being pushed hard." Since Hughes did not send a copy of this message to Snow, it is safe to assume that he still knew nothing about that general's responsibility for the battle then raging. And while technically accurate, the message indicates how little the staff at Mouse Trap Farm understood what was going on at the sharp end.

At 9:50 a.m., parts of the 2nd, 3rd, and 14th Battalions held trenches that sketched a line a thousand yards from Kitcheners Wood east towards St. Julien. The forward protection for this line, however, had been destroyed when Turner's 13th and 15th Battalions were overrun; the fact that Hughes does not refer to this underlines just how poorly he understood what was happening on the battlefield or how little information was available to him. Equally notable is the absence of any reference to Odlum's 7th Battalion, which by 9:50 a.m. had been part of Turner's command for four and a half hours; surely the fact that Turner's command *had not heard from* Odlum was cause for some concern.

The first information Turner appears to have received about the desperate situation Odlum was facing came from General Currie, who at 10:50 a.m. pleaded with Turner to send reinforcements to Currie's left front flank. If the gap left by the collapse of the 13th and 15th Battalions was not filled, Currie's 8th and 5th Battalions would be faced with the Hobson's choice of being cut off or having to retire. If they retired, they would give up the higher ground on Gravenstafel Ridge, which would have had the doleful effect of leaving the British lines on Currie's right "in the air." Currie informed Turner that as of 10:30 a.m., Turner's left was still being held by "my 7th Battalion." Turner's 11:30 a.m. reply both refused Currie's request for reinforcements and informed him that "my right front is being blown out of successive positions towards St. Julien." This clearly affected the 7th Battalion, part of which stood before St. Julien at Locality "C," but Turner made no reference to Odlum's beleaguered men.

. . .

By the time Turner's reply arrived, Currie had begun to consider retiring from the ridge. Even before he had Turner's message, Currie knew that the reinforcements promised at 8:15 a.m. would not be arriving any time soon. At 10:00 a.m., as his anxiety mounted, Currie sent Lieutenant Murray Greene to the GHQ Line with a note asking Brigadier-General John E. Bush to send a battalion "to help me re-establish line broken by the retirement" of the 13th and 15th Battalions.[11] Shortly after 11:00 a.m., Greene returned to tell his brigadier that Bush's troops were nowhere to be seen. Currie then ordered Greene to again thread his way through the carnage, this time to the village of Wieltje, where, Currie hoped, he would find the missing troops. At 11:05 a.m., Currie warned Brigadier-General Archibald J. Chapman, of the British 85th Brigade, which held the trenches on the Canadians' right, that if conditions worsened, his men might have to abandon Gravenstafel Ridge:

> Am still holding front line trenches and I think Locality C but third Brigade [13th and 15th Battalions] has apparently retired. May have to evacuate trenches as left is very much exposed. My right Section 1 [Tuxford] will keep in touch with your left. I will not order retirement for some time yet.

• • •

While Canadian commanders were signalling each other without reference to Snow, the general issued his first orders as Plumer's designate. They do not support a recent claim by the historian John Dixon that since "Snow and Alderson had a history of working together ... Snow was able to anticipate the needs of the commander of the Canadian Division. Snow was then able to send some additional support to Turner in the form of the remains of the 1st Royal Irish Regiment."[12]

Snow most assuredly sent the Irish. But he sent them to Fortuin without signalling Turner *or* Alderson that he was doing so. What's even stranger is that he sent these 365 men to Fortuin to stop the Germans from advancing, for he had information that they had broken through near Berlin Wood, between the Canadians and the British. There is no record of what intelligence lay behind Snow's decision. It did not come from Alderson, Turner, Currie, or Chapman. And as far as can be determined, Snow made no effort to contact any of these generals or to send a reconnoitring party to Fortuin to determine the situation on the ground.

There was no need for the Irish at Fortuin, and there had been no breakthrough near Berlin Wood. When the Irish arrived, they found more than two hundred Canadians dug in. Had Snow possessed the clairvoyance that Dixon attributes to him, he would have sent the Irish to Currie to reinforce his men on Gravenstafel Ridge. Twice during the morning, Lipsett had to renew the garrison holding the most distant part of his left, which was "in the air." In his after-action report, Captain Arthur Morley described the desperate conditions in his part of the 5th Battalion's trench: "My trench was now a shambles. In 50 yards I had 50 or 60 casualties with many killed, the parapet blown in several places, and some men had used as many as 3 or 4 rifles."

CHAPTER 12

# "Supplying Bullets, By Relieving the Dead of Theirs"
### The Fall of St. Julien

> *There is a hill in Flanders,*
> *Heaped with a thousand slain,*
> *Where the shells fly night and noontide*
> *And the ghosts that died in vain,—*
> *A little hill, a hard hill*
> *To the souls that died in pain.*
> —EVERARD OWEN, "THREE HILLS"

At 11:35 a.m., Major Kirkpatrick sent this message to his 3rd Brigade headquarters: "We are holding on nicely. Every time enemy starts something he goes back before he comes close, but we have been lucky as the enemy artillery has left us alone fairly well. 2nd Battalion needs ammunition for their guns."[1] Kirkpatrick's messenger, Bugler Bobby Green, led an especially charmed life:

> Still but a boy, and small and slight at that, he moved like an Indian over the more exposed spots, seeking cover from view whenever he could, but, to show what wonderful observation the Germans had, he was several times persistently, though unsuccessfully, sniped at by German field guns,

whose shells he literally dodged by rapid movements to either flank and by making skilful use of ground and cover.

An hour later, Kirkpatrick signalled that he feared "Streight's right flank will be turned"; Captain John Streight's company held a trench running perpendicular to the front line (i.e., it faced north), a hundred or so yards behind the trench held by Major Ormond's 10th Battalion near Locality "C." The fight around Streight's trench was ferocious, and he was so badly wounded that he could barely walk. But somehow, Streight's men held on:

> We were gassed, we were charged, we were bayoneted and shelled out unmercifully. We were blown from out of our position by high explosive shells, many [were] buried alive, many torn and wounded, while many were blown to eternity, yet we kept smiling and held our position.[2]

The 3rd Battalion's belief in its own luck was so great that when the order to withdraw was received at 2:03 p.m., it caused "confusion and dismay." Some of Kirkpatrick's men suspected it was another *ruse de guerre*, for the Germans had not passed their stretch of trench.

. . .

Just before the 11:00 a.m. attack, Odlum, out of communication with his brigadier, turned for counsel to the only men he could: Lieutenant-Colonels John Currie and W. W. Burland.\* In what amounted to a council of war, Currie and Burland agreed with Odlum's suggestion that his men should retire and the three units together should "take up a position covering Fortuin, with our left on St. Julien and our right on Locality

---

\*Though the bulk of Currie's 15th Battalion had been destroyed when the Germans broke through the Apex, his No. 3 Company continued to hold a trench on Odlum's left. After the 14th Battalion's commander was placed in charge of the GHQ Line, Burland took command of the battalion's units in the field.

'C.'" Odlum's line would not hold long enough for all parts to receive this order.

* * *

Less than one hundred metres separated Odlum's blasted trenches from RIR 234's forward positions, which from the *Feldgrauen*'s point of view were somewhat less than ideal. In some places, "where the terrain offered natural cover, the men were lying thickly packed," an invitation to Canadian gunners. "We were lucky they had so little artillery, otherwise our losses would have been much greater." In other places, the Germans were "alarmingly thin," noted Leutnant Speyer, meaning that their attack might not fall on all parts of the trench with the weight needed to break into it. Speyer's men were so close to Odlum's that splinters from the German shells pounding Odlum's trenches landed among Speyer's men.

As the officers commanding Reserve-Infanterie-Regiments 234 and 236 readied their men for the final push, German gunners miles from the front moved to help the infantry. "'Wouldn't that church steeple be an excellent place for a British observer?' We hardly thought so when the entire church was wrapped in a thick black cloud of smoke and red brick dust while splinters and stones flew in the air," wrote the battalion's war diarist.

* * *

At precisely 11:00 a.m., a bugle sounded and the Germans advanced. Rice put his rifle to his shoulder, took aim, and squeezed the trigger. Nothing. Like Tuxford's Dandies, the Little Black Devils, and the Highlanders, Nathan Rice found that his Ross rifle failed to fire in the heat of battle. As the Germans raced forward, Rice called to Corporal Pilkington, who commanded the trench, and he called back to take another rifle from behind the parapet.

How long does it take to grab a rifle, raise it to your shoulder, aim, and fire? Five seconds? Eight seconds? When each second brings a heavily armed German soldier twenty or so feet closer, ten seconds is a long time. Rice squeezed another trigger. And again, no report, no kickback. The second rifle's hammer didn't move. Rice grabbed a third rifle. And it too failed. The Germans, however, rushed forward.

A different horror unfolded in James O. Mackie's trench a short distance away. There, a wounded Dominion soldier's uniform was set alight by a bullet, a red-hot piece of metal, or an incendiary shell that burned through the straw where he had been placed, and he burned to death. The blaze forced Mackie and his comrades back from the firing-step, but somehow they kept on firing. A half century later, the man's dying screams still haunted Mackie: "There was nothing you could do. You couldn't stop. We had to get up and hold the Germans off."

As the fire burned out and the Germans kept coming, Mackie and the others moved forward. Moments later, as he took a bead on a spike-helmeted soldier, Mackie was knocked to the ground by a bullet. At first he did not know what had happened. "I started to feel my head with my left hand and there was nothing wrong with my head. I wasn't wounded, and there was no feeling." Then came the searing pain in his wrist; the bullet had passed through it, cauterizing the wound. Since he was unable to shoulder a rifle, he was told to leave the trench and seek medical aid.

To cover the withdrawal of his No. 4 Company, Major Byng-Hall ordered Sergeant Raymond MacIlree's unit forward to an unoccupied hedge. By the time they reached it a few moments later, "The enemy [had] started coming over." Apparently still unseen, MacIlree and his men separated and withdrew. MacIlree caught a break when a bullet cut through the corner of his tunic, missing his body. A sergeant he found moments later was not as lucky; he had been shot above the heart and killed.

• • •

Among the Germans in front of MacIlree were some from RIR 234, men whose experience of the battle, though equally bloody and exhausting, was the inverse of the Canadians':

Each had his gun. Bayonets glittering in the sun. We raced forward for the hand-to-hand fight. The distance was too long. We were almost all out of breath. Who knew how the bayonet fight would have ended? But all of a sudden, when we had advanced 30 metres from the trenches, all the gleaming barrels and familiar headwear disappeared below the enemy parapet. And all we could see were pitiful hands here and there, and there were handkerchiefs. The contrast was so comic we could not help laughing.

•  •  •

As soon as Corporal Pilkington saw that Byng-Hall's men, some twenty-five yards behind his trench, were retiring, he ordered Rice and the other men to make a run for it. The first two who tried ran into a hail of machine-gun fire. For five minutes, Rice, Pilkington, and the others hugged the ground, their minds no doubt shifting between prayer and another scheme to make their way to safety. The shells exploding nearby encased them in a thick fog of dust and tear gas that separated them from safety and, perhaps even more painfully, each other.

•  •  •

Even as Odlum's line broke apart, his men, aided by crossfire from Kirkpatrick's 3rd Battalion (and possibly from Hooper's and Doxsee's houses), put up a fight that so stunned Private Mathar of RIR 236 that he larded his report with the fiction of the Canadians firing sulphur-impregnated shells. "By inhaling the air that was mixed with gas and sulphur, and because of minor lesions from falling pieces of trees and lumps of earth, we were almost all unable to carry the heavy machine gun equipment." Mathar and some other men struggled forward as their comrades managed to set up their machine gun five hundred yards from a not yet evacuated trench, likely the left trench of Scudamore's small force. Mathar recalled:

> We could see the heads of the crew above what was obviously a makeshift trench. Enjoying good cover ourselves, we used the opportunity to set up

our machine guns in a kneeling position and direct them exactly over the trench. After we raked the trench with some thousand shots, the gun fire coming from there ceased. However, the heads still remained visible. On the parapet of the trench appeared a few white flags. We immediately saw it and used the opportunity to jump with our machine gun into the enemy trench.

Mathar's claim that 255 Canadians surrendered sounds high but probably is not; according to the historian Desmond Morton, more than fourteen hundred Canadians were taken prisoner at 2nd Ypres. Mathar's picture of the carnage in the trench also rings true. In the "sector of the trench which we had raked . . . there was not a living soul. . . . Some were [still] standing or kneeling against the front-most wall of the trench. Some of them were still clinging to their guns. They had all received fatal shots to the head. This was the terrible result of our machine guns."

. . .

As the Germans counted the Canadian dead, MacIlree and some of his men reached a reserve trench where Sergeant Weeks was using his Colt machine gun to buy time. Realizing that Weeks's fire was not enough, MacIlree organized the other men to join him. Soldiers who just a few days earlier had complained of the decaying bodies they found in the French trenches now used their own dead as a firing-step. MacIlree's men had barely begun to fire when several T-shells exploded near them. Within seconds, their eyes filled with water. "After a little while, you couldn't sight your rifles for fifty yards." A survivor of the 13th Battalion saw well enough, however, to shoot a German right between the eyes.

Then, from the right, the order reached them to cease fire. MacIlree guessed correctly that the order had come from Major Byng-Hall, who realized that further resistance was futile. An order to cease fire is not, however, an order to surrender. Preferring "a quick merciful bullet" to a "lingering miserable death," MacIlree ordered every man for himself, which gave them at least a chance to escape from the onrushing Germans.

A short distance away, the machine-gunners in L. R. Scott's trench, George Davidson and Lance-Corporal Charles W. Painting on the left and Donald Bellew and Hugh Peerless on the right, kept up their fire. According to one historian, the machine-gunners "allowed the grey-clad enemy to approach within a hundred yards before they opened fire. The effect was terrible; dozens of Germans fell to the ground amid the hail of bullets."[3] It is likely that the two groups used the same tactics, for not only was Bellew the senior machine-gun officer in the battalion (he signed the others' attestation papers), but all had served in the British military.*

With time, however, the weight of German numbers began to tell. Peerless was shot dead. Bellew was wounded. According to his Victoria Cross citation, the third earned by a Canadian soldier in fewer than forty-eight hours, Bellew then "got up and maintained his fire till ammunition failed and the enemy rushed the position. . . . [He] then seized a rifle, smashed his machine gun, and fighting to the last, was taken prisoner."[4] RIR 236's regimental history gives a few more details: "One machine gun crew fought so long until the brave gunner was rendered incapable of fighting by a blow from a rifle butt." Though their fire momentarily slowed the German advance, the small redoubt protected by Painting and Davidson was also doomed.

As some of his men fled to their left (west), Captain Scudamore led a group of six in a fighting retreat. Soon, they were pinned down. Weakened by an earlier bullet wound to his head, Scudamore lost consciousness. When he regained consciousness, he had already been taken prisoner and one of the Kaiser's soldiers was exercising the rights of the victor by taking his Ross rifle as a souvenir. "I told him he was welcome to it."[5] Scudamore's gift of the King's property may have saved his life. His captors protected him as he was marched past advancing infantry,

---

*A graduate of Sandhurst, England's most prestigious military academy, Bellew served with the Royal Irish Regiment before moving to Canada. Painting had been a Royal Marine for twelve years, and Davidson served five years in the Lancashire Border Regiment before immigrating to Canada.

who "lunged at me with their bayonets, clubbed their rifles or threatened me with a bomb."[6]

The five men who climbed out of the trench with MacIlree cut through a hedge and then ran across a field. The man running ahead of MacIlree was shot. He fell screaming, catching MacIlree's foot as he went down and upending him. It was the luckiest trip in MacIlree's life.

As the Germans ran down the rest of the group, MacIlree "got the idea of playing possum." He got up, ran a few yards, then dropped and lay as if dead, adding "a few artistic wiggles as if I was *in extremis*." A half a dozen bullets struck his equipment during this battlefield performance. Once the Germans moved on, he threaded his way back to the Canadian lines.

Amid the confusion of the battlefield, Mackie soon lost touch with the other men who had fled the trench with him. Caught between the advancing Germans and the Canadians' fighting retreat, Mackie "could hear German bullets hitting at the back of me and our bullets over my head." His thought that "this is not very healthy" surely understated the situation. It failed completely to describe the danger he was in when a German came around a corner. But the soldier either did not see him or did not think Mackie was worth his trouble.

Though he had not lost much blood and could still think clearly, Mackie began to weaken as shock set in. As soon as the German left, he made his way to the dugout, hoping to find shelter. Once there, Mackie must have thought he was hallucinating. A few feet below the screaming banshees of shells, the whiz of bullets, the cries of wounded men, and the smell of cordite was "a nice mattress and everything." Like a character from the pen of the famous First World War cartoonist Bruce Bairnsfather, Mackie dove into the dugout head first and passed out on the mattress, which felt "just [like] floating on water."

• • •

Unable to find a rifle that would fire, Rice could only watch as the German wave broke into the trench. Among the *Feldgrauen* was an English-speaking one who, echoing his Kaiser, asked, "Englanders,

Englishmen, why do you fight Germans?"* The Germans of the second wave were less inquisitive and less concerned with the niceties of the Hague Convention, which governed the treatment of prisoners of war and included the famed requirement to give only name, rank, and serial number. Article 4 states, "Prisoners of war are in the power of the hostile Government, but not of the individuals or corps who capture them," and "They must be humanely treated." As soon as these second-wave Germans entered Rice's trench, one of them screamed "*Mein Bruder ist getötet worden!*" ("My brother's been killed") and swung his rifle butt at the soldier standing in front of Rice. The soldier ducked, and the blow hit Rice, knocking him to the ground.

• • •

Private J. H. MacArthur was luckier. After escaping from his trench, he embarked on his own guerrilla war. He did not panic when his Ross rifle jammed as hundreds of Germans came towards his trench. This is testimony to his fortitude, for at sixteen, he was probably the youngest Canadian soldier at Ypres. He was there illegally, having lied on his attestation papers.

The lie was an old one. In 1913, MacArthur was so keen on enlisting in the Duke of Connaught's Rifle Regiment that he added a few years to age, saying he was sixteen then. The regimental sergeant-major did not believe him: "Come back in a couple of years, lad, and we'll think about taking you on." MacArthur took part of his advice. Two weeks later, he went back and told a different officer that he was eighteen, and this time he was believed. A year later, during a regimental review on the Salisbury Plain, Queen Mary stopped in front of him and asked, "Young man, how old are you?" His answer—"Nineteen, your Majesty"—elicited a rueful shake of the royal head and the words "You naughty boy."

---

*Prior to the war, Kaiser Wilhelm made much of the fact that he was Queen Victoria's grandson, and thus that he and King George V were cousins. Indeed, the Kaiser was beside Victoria when she died in 1901. When the war broke out, Wilhelm returned the (honorary) admiral of the fleet uniform that the King had given him.

Running back from the broken line, MacArthur and another soldier became separated from their comrades. The exploding shells drowned out the sound of the bullet that hit MacArthur's companion; the direction he fell, however, told them where to look for the rifleman. "He was just putting the bolt [of his rifle] home to take a shot at one or the other of us. We don't know which one but we both of us dived at him and we both got our bayonets in him at the same time." Unable to find the remnants of the 7th Battalion, MacArthur attached himself to a British unit later that day. He left his Ross rifle in the German, whose earlier wounds had been dressed by a Canadian.

• • •

The German wave also broke on the three trenches on Odlum's left, held by parts of the 15th and 14th Battalions. The artillery barrage that devastated Odlum's trenches made the 14th's untenable as well. Shortly after 11:00 a.m., the 14th Battalion retired three hundred yards to a set of unused trenches—thus opening the door to St. Julien. Unfortunately, German gunners had already ranged these trenches, which were soon blasted apart. The brevity of Captain Wilfred Brotherhood's message captures both the tactical reality and the Canadians' will to keep on fighting, though they were vastly outnumbered:

To O.C. 13th Battalion
24th April, 1915

Enemy have shelled us out and are advancing from our left and front. Will hold every traverse if we have to retire along line to our right. Captain WILLIAMSON killed.

From Captain BROTHERHOOD 11:30 a.m.
*By hand received*[7]

Shoved out of their position guarding St. Julien near noon, Brotherhood's men sought cover in ditches and folds in the ground until they were ordered to the GHQ Line more than four hours later.

• • •

While their comrades attacked the Canadian positions from the east, the men of RIR 233 poured through the gap at what had been the Apex. After advancing to the west side of Gravenstafel Ridge, a commander ordered up a field gun from the 51st Reserve Field Artillery Regiment. "It's a beautiful picture," wrote the regiment's historian. "It is placed in the middle of a crossroads and is now sending its iron greetings towards St. Julien." A shell from the gun took off the head of a Canadian POW, who did not understand the warnings barked at him to move.

• • •

At 11:40 a.m., ten minutes after Brotherhood signalled that he and his men were staging a fighting retreat, Brigadier-General Currie received word that the promised York and Durham Brigade would not be arriving. Alerted by Lieutenant-Colonel Lipsett that the Germans continued to pour men through the thousand-yard gap between Lipsett's position and Locality "C," and that parts of Brigadier-General Turner's 3rd Brigade were falling back to the GHQ Line, Currie ordered both Lipsett and Tuxford to be ready to retire from their positions on Gravenstafel Ridge. At the same time, 11:45 a.m., he sent a message to the 85th Brigade, immediately to Tuxford's right:

> Owing to my left flank Section II being entirely unprotected and having been informed that no reinforcements are available, I have ordered 8th Battalion. Section II to retire by its left to GRAVENSTAFEL RIDGE, the 5th Battalion Section One to conform to the movements of the 8th Battalion but to maintain contact with your left. Will endeavour to establish line from Wood in C.10 and 11 ST. JULIEN—Locality C—GRAVENSTAFEL

Ridge. In order to retain Gravenstafel Ridge substantial reinforcements required on line squares c.12, D.7 and 8 [the GHQ Line] from which counter-attack might be launched but we have no troops available or sufficient for this purpose.

Currie's message did not reach the 85th Brigade's commander until 1:15 p.m., by which time the information was long outdated. At noon, Lipsett signalled Currie that the "German advance against our left seems to have slackened and come to a halt." The situation remained critical, however. Only two platoons, protected not by trenches but by hedges, stood around Lipsett's headquarters on Boetleer Farm. The thirteen-hundred-yard gap between Lipsett's position and Locality "C" was blocked, if that's even the word, by only twenty men. Medical supplies were low, and doctors were urgently required. Lipsett ended his message, however, by saying, "I am not uneasy about being able to hold my line if Germans are prevented from walking round my rear."

In the end, the Germans attacked from the front. But the end would not come for almost another twenty-four hours. At noon on the twenty-fourth, the *Feldgrauen* were under orders *not* to "roll up the [Canadian] line until the centre of the attack had broken through St. Julien and Fortuin." And so, as one historian put it, "although facing a skeleton garrison, [they] camped down in the fields north of Locality "C" and awaited events."[8]

. . .

Rifle and machine-gun fire cut Warden at Locality "C" off from the 7th Battalion positions, and from information about Lieutenant-Colonel Currie's line (which had been overrun after 11:00 a.m.), a thousand yards or so to his north. But he could see that the 8th Battalion was still in its trenches. Three reconnoitring patrols had vanished into the two-thousand-yard gap, which told him all he needed to know. Neither of the two messengers he sent to his brigadier asking for reinforcements returned, nor did any reinforcements arrive.

The situation was critical. The day before, Warden had taken almost three hundred men with him to Locality "C." Shortly before noon on the twenty-fourth, he had only fifty left. Only one of his three lieutenants was uninjured; except for the company sergeant-major, every one of his NCOs had been either killed or wounded. As the Germans continued to probe, his ever-decreasing number of men kept up fire, their supply of bullets coming from "relieving the wounded and dead of theirs."

• • •

At noon, Odlum, John Currie, Burland, and Major Ormond, whose troops were retiring from the trenches they held near Locality "C," held another council of war behind the Haanebeek culvert. Their options were limited. The Germans had crushed both sides of the Apex and were swarming around Locality "C." That they now also held trenches north of St. Julien was clear from the "increasing machine gun fire [that] swept the valley from the northwest."[9] The 2nd and 3rd Battalions (east of Kitcheners Wood) were under attack. Here and there, a small number of Odlum's units still held out. They also knew that Currie had ordered Lipsett and Tuxford to retire. They did not know that this order, though never formally withdrawn, had become inoperative when Lipsett telephoned Currie with the news that the assault had halted.

Surprisingly, given that his men had been in battle the longest, Ormond was the most eager to carry on. He wanted to amalgamate the remnants of the various battalions and advance to recover the skyline and the toe of Gravenstafel Ridge. Burland, Odlum, and Currie thought the plan hopeless. Nor were they keen on the alternative: taking themselves out of the battle by retiring one and a half miles to the GHQ Line. They decided instead to gather their men together in an unmarked line about a thousand yards farther south.

• • •

Meanwhile, as the Germans advanced on St. Julien, two more British regiments reached the GHQ Line, having endured heavy shelling that destroyed entire platoons on their march east from the Yser Canal. The GHQ Line was filled with men, a fair number of whom had been wounded, in no particular regimental order. Ordered to dig in on the side of the road next to the GHQ Line, Anthony R. Hossack of the Queen Victoria Rifles soon found that because of Flanders' high water table, a bailer would have been as useful as a shovel. But what truly amazed him and the mud-encrusted men around him was that even as German shells fell nearby, a woman was finishing her washing and hanging it to dry. As he watched, a shell exploded "and the woman's cottage and water jars vanish[ed] and her pitiful washing [hung] in a mocking way from her sagging clothes line."[10]

・・・

As this scene unfolded, elements of RIRs 234 and 235 entered St. Julien. Perhaps because they had suffered horrendous casualties—in four days of fighting, the 234 had lost twenty-seven officers and 1,150 men*—the regimental historian of RIR 234 eschews the grandiloquent language so often sprinkled through German regimental histories as he describes the taking of the village. He gives the capture only two sentences before turning to the counterattack, which he incorrectly says occurred almost as soon as they had secured the village:

> The first men to enter the village found that it was only weakly manned and as soon as our battalions passed left and right around the village, we occupied the village without resistance and took up positions south along the road to Wieltje. We had hardly got in when there appeared thick British infantry lines that were to reoccupy St. Julien. We succeeded in fighting them back but in the action we lost several officers, including Leutnants Standhardt and Bielitz.

---

*The regimental historian of RIR 235 shies away from giving numbers, saying only that "the first battalion suffered quite considerable losses."

The regimental historian of the 235 is similarly sedate. Indeed, the event that he places at the centre of the story owes more to British bad luck than to the German martial tradition:

> The 8th Company [3rd Battalion] under Leutnant Ferreau advanced irresistibly as far as St. Julien and on the spur of the moment decided to move into the village where they took many prisoners. A platoon under Leutnant Altstadt advanced to the southern exit of St. Julien where they captured 2 British ambulances entering the village who wanted to pick up wounded in St. Julien and had no idea that the village was already in German hands.

• • •

Canadian records are clearer. Putting aside the last few redoubts (which miraculously managed to hold out until 2:15 p.m., when Lieutenant-Colonel Loomis ordered them to retire to the GHQ Line), St. Julien fell at 12:45 p.m. By then, most of Loomis's men's rifles had jammed and his Colt machine guns had clogged with mud, which allowed the Germans to advance into the ruined houses behind Loomis's positions.

• • •

Grenade-throwers broke into the trench to which Byng-Hall and some of his men had retired and began blowing it up from the inside. But Byng-Hall did not reach, Hollywood-style, for a white flag or a conveniently placed undershirt with which to surrender. Instead, amid the noise of bullets and exploding shells and the screams of the wounded, in a place where the very air seethed with the smell of cordite, blasted earth, and death, he shouted for his men to throw down their weapons and raise their arms in surrender.

As the Germans moved ever closer, Byng-Hall and his men must have had the same thought that Private Arthur Corker had a few moments earlier, when, having stayed behind to man his machine gun, he too was taken prisoner. "It's one of those things you never thought of when you went overseas," Corker recalled. "I thought, well, you might get wounded or you might get killed, but I never thought about being taken prisoner. I don't think we would have been taken prisoner if we had the Lee-Enfield. We could have held them."[11] Whatever their thoughts, their war was over.

The terrible logic of battle, however, continued not far away as the "blood-dimmed tide" washed over the men standing near Private William Charles Thurgood, a nineteen-year-old plumber from Surrey, British Columbia. "Though we held our hands aloft and were now unarmed, the cold-blooded crew started to wipe us out," he remembered. "Three of our men were bayoneted before an officer arrived and saved the rest of us. Even then our rough captors struck us with their rifle butts and kicked some of our men who were unfortunate to be laid out with wounds."[12]

Part 7

# The Fog of War
### 12:01 p.m., 24 April to 4 a.m., 25 April 1915

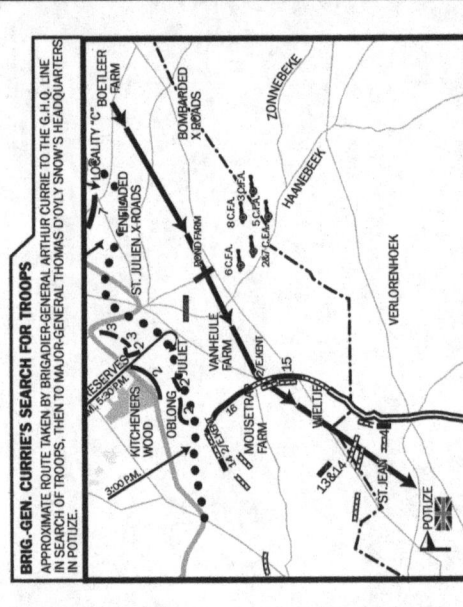
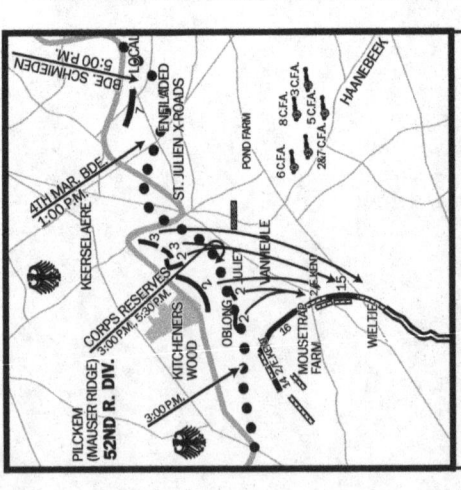

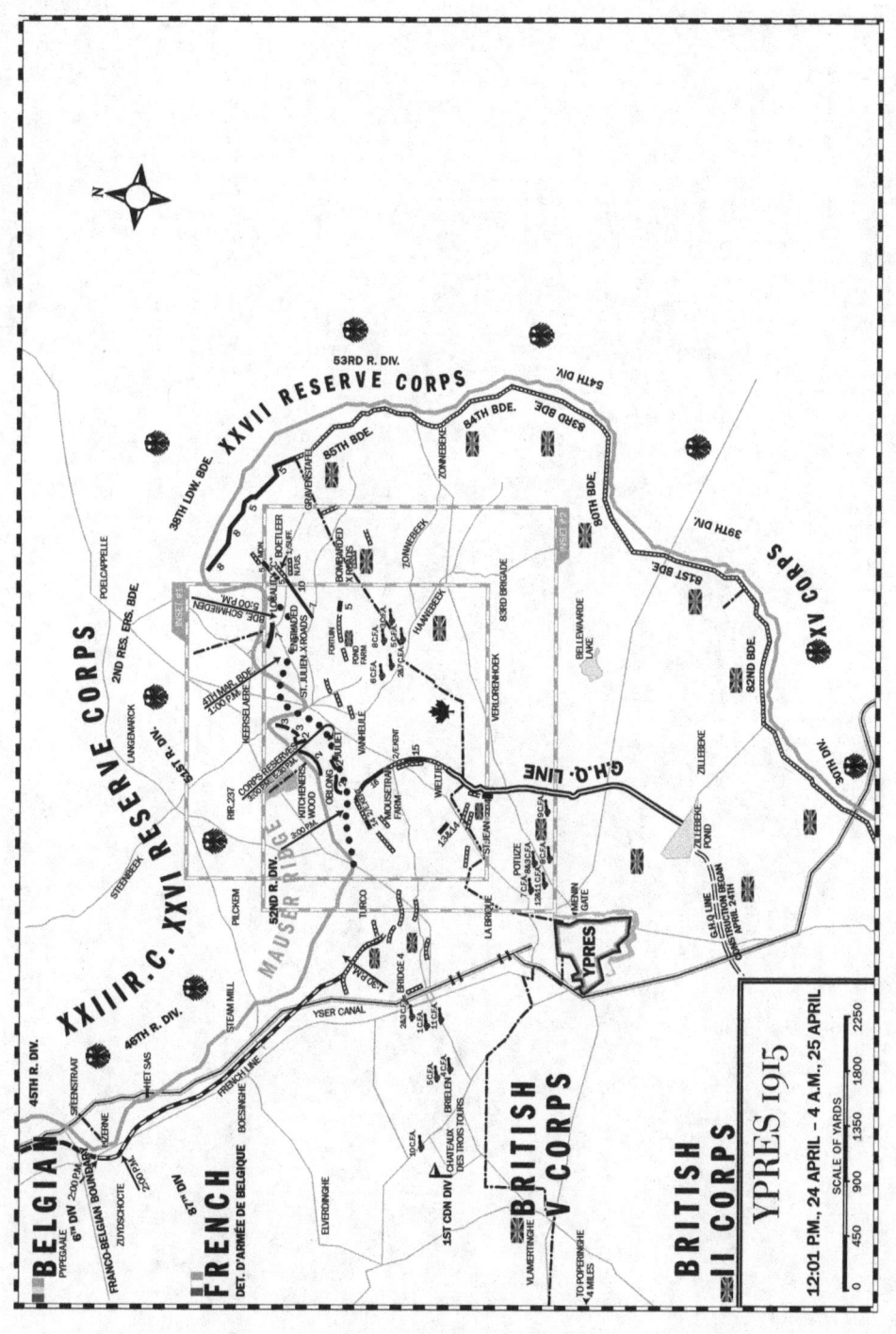

## Chapter 13

# "The Retirement Was *Not Compulsory*"
### The Isolation of the 2nd Canadian Infantry Brigade

> *The Staff is working with its brains*
> *While we are sitting in the trench;*
> *The Staff the universe ordains*
> *(Subject to Thee and General French).*
>
> *God, help the Staff—especially*
> *The young ones, many of them sprung*
> *From our high aristocracy;*
> *Their task is hard, and they are young.*
> —Julian Grenfell, "A Prayer for Those on the Staff"

At 1:00 p.m. on 24 April, the gap that the Germans had punched in the Canadian line at the Apex measured over a mile and a quarter. It was about to grow larger.

At 5:15 a.m., forty-five minutes after the 15th Battalion began giving way, Lieutenant-Colonel Lipsett had ordered Private Tom Drummond to a position just past the 8th Battalion's original left. By 1:00 p.m., Drummond's detachment was badly cut up. In the weak light of dawn, the position had been important: it protected Lipsett's flank. But under the gathering rain clouds of early afternoon, it was irrelevant, for the Germans had taken St. Julien, and now *Feldgrauen* roamed behind the

Canadian trenches, with the exception of those areas covered by the riflemen at Locality "C." Rather than reinforce Drummond, Lipsett ordered him to withdraw, and once again, Canadian soldiers inched down a trench and then ran across a few hundred yards, their every step accompanied by the rattle of machine-gun fire and the wheezing of gassed men, a new sound of war.

Neither Drummond's weakened men nor the stretcher-bearers Lipsett sent could get the wounded safely across the wire entanglements. Decades have done nothing to wash the pain from Drummond's words: "It was hard to leave the wounded where they lay. One man in particular, with his foot hanging by the sinews, begged to be taken along. I and another man dressed the foot as well as we were able, but he continued screaming as first one and then another left him. This may seem hardhearted on our part."

Drummond barely escaped with his life. As he crouched to enter the main trench, a coal box exploded, blowing him twenty feet and knocking him out. A short while later, he came to and crawled into the headquarters trench, where he found his regimental sergeant-major, who had been badly gassed that morning. "He was sitting with his back against the trench wall gasping for breath. I gave him a sip of water which seemed to ease him somewhat, but nothing could be done for him."[1]

The second increase in the gap, of more than three thousand yards, occurred when General Turner unexpectedly ordered the 2nd and 3rd Battalions to withdraw to the GHQ Line. Issued at 1:40 p.m., this order was at best a blunder born of panic and at worst a wilful decision to disobey General Alderson's 1:35 p.m. directive to "utilize Battalions of York and Durham Brigade to strengthen your line and hold on." Alderson had ordered Turner to use these British troops to reinforce the 2nd and 3rd Battalions in front and to the east of Kitcheners Wood. Even this was significantly less energetic than Alderson's original plan, which was for General Bush and his men to counterattack above St. Julien and drive the Germans back (and thus keep contact with the 8th and 5th Battalions on the northeast side of the Apex). This plan was abandoned shortly after Bush arrived at Mouse Trap Farm at noon; by the time he could organize the attack, the Canadian line from which it was to be launched was in German hands. Still, as Turner learned at 1:30 p.m., Alderson wanted Bush's troops in the field, filling the gaps in the line sketched by the 2nd and 3rd Battalions. Ignoring this, Turner ordered both Bush's men and the 2nd and 3rd Battalions to the GHQ Line. Perhaps most egregious was the message Turner did not send—the one to his fellow Canadian brigadier, Arthur Currie, whose troops were, by virtue of Turner's order, left "in the air," all but cut off from Canadian command.

In 1938, Canada's official historian trod lightly on Turner's decision to withdraw the two battalions because the former brigadier was still alive. Duguid wrote that Turner understood Alderson's words "your line" to mean the GHQ Line "and not the frontage eastwards to Locality C."[2] It's a measure of the difficulty Duguid faced in making this claim that he had to reach back more than a day, to a message dealing with the disposition of part of Geddes's Detachment that Alderson sent Turner at 5:20 a.m. on 23 April (before the attack on Mauser Ridge). That message read, "It is important for you to stick to GHQ 2nd line." In 1935, Lieutenant-Colonel Gordon Gordon-Hall, to whom Alderson would give plenary powers to deal with Turner's decision to send battalion after battalion to the GHQ Line, wrote to Duguid:

> It should be noted that this early Turner began to sit on his reserves instead of using them to reinforce his forward position as directed by Divisional Head Quarters. This policy he pursued to the end and nothing Divisional HQ or other commanders could order, or suggest, or implore made him alter his policy, with *disastrous* consequences to all concerned and to none more than to his own troops.
>
> I don't think enough is made [in Duguid's history] of the overcrowding in GHQ Line and [of] the resultant heavy casualties from hostile artillery fire. It had a magnetic attraction for Turner in spite of the fact that it faced the wrong way and could be enfiladed.[3]

While Turner prepared to order the 2nd and 3rd Battalions (as well as the remnants of the 13th, 14th, 15th, and 16th Battalions) to the GHQ Line, Currie's troops were expecting these men to support them on Gravenstafel Ridge. Major Edgar, who commanded the left side of the 5th Battalion's trench, said, "We'll stay till the cows come home," and a cheer went up from the right side when, at 1:00 p.m., Lieutenant-Colonel Tuxford telephoned to tell Edgar that he had just received word from Turner that "we are going to attack with two battalions through C.18.a on D.7a." (These were the coordinates for a northeasterly attack from St. Julien towards Bombarded Crossroads.)

At about the same time, Lieutenant Greene, who finally found the troops he was looking for (the York and Durham Regiment, known by the romantic name 4th Green Howards), learned that Lieutenant-Colonel M.H.L. Bell's orders precluded immediate action. Issued by General Snow, the orders told Bell to support both Turner's and Currie's brigades, but not until he had determined how much aid each brigadier needed. Until that was sorted out, Bell repaired to the GHQ Line.

• • •

Thinking that Bell might move his troops into position on his left if asked by a senior officer, Currie decided to take the bold, almost reckless action of leaving his headquarters and going back to the GHQ Line. After the war, Sir Sam Hughes sought to discredit Currie by casting aspersions on this decision.* Even Currie's biographer, Hugh Urquhart, who served at 2nd Ypres in the 16th Battalion, characterized the action as "well intentioned if ill advised."[4] Urquhart's phrase is worth considering. Both Lipsett and Tuxford approved of Currie's plan. But senior officers cannot excuse questionable decisions by showing that junior officers agreed

---

*Hughes was at least partly motivated by the fact that in 1917, then General Sir Arthur Currie, commanding general of the Canadian Corps, refused to give the former militia minister's son, Garnet Hughes, a divisional command.

with them. Still, given the praise for Tuxford and, especially, Lipsett, it seems odd that Currie's decision has been depicted as "ill advised."

John Dixon's recent criticism of Currie is also unwarranted, not to mention misleading. "His [Currie's] absence could have brought about the loss of the Brigade," the British historian wrote, "if it had not been left in the competent hands of Lieutenant-Colonel Lipsett."[5] But Lipsett did not just happen to end up as interim commander of Currie's 2nd Brigade. Currie ensured that Lipsett would be its commander by appointing him, even though Tuxford outranked the former British regular. Further, Lipsett and Currie (with Tuxford's knowledge) agreed that were the two battalions to be seriously threatened by a renewed German attack, Lipsett would act under Currie's 12:45 p.m. order to retire. "As he was the man on the spot, I left it to his judgement, and Lipsett and myself had a very clear understanding," Currie wrote in 1927.

Currie's decision to walk through ground pockmarked by shrapnel and crawling with uncounted Germans amply demonstrates his *sang froid*. Captain Ross Napier, a thirty-seven-year-old miner, then a scout on the outskirts of Wieltje, must have done a double take when he saw the familiar pear-shaped man appear. "The roads were being heavily shelled and the open was searched by rifle, machine gun and shrapnel," Napier remembered. "As he drew near, a salvo of heavies intended for the road burst immediately in his line of approach, but he reached the comparative shelter (from the rifle fire at least) of the ruined cottage where I was—making, as he did so, a jocular remark as to the comparative salubrity of Salisbury Plains."[6]

In total, four British units refused Currie's pleas for aid. Sometime after 1:40 p.m., Currie learned that Turner had cancelled the attack and ordered every Canadian soldier still in the field between the GHQ Line and Currie's positions back to the GHQ Line. Shortly before 3:00 p.m., Bush told Currie that he could not move into the gap because he had just been told that the British battalions were to be used not for a counterattack but to "increase the large bodies of troops protecting Potijze," a small village more than three miles from where the Little Black Devils and Tuxford's Dandies stood against the Germans.

• • •

The order for the 2nd and 3rd Battalions to retire was not easy to transmit, nor did the men in the field support it. Issued at 1:00 p.m., delayed, for the 2nd Battalion (Lieutenant-Colonel David Watson had sent his adjutant to Turner to ask for a delay until nightfall, when it would be safer to disengage) and then reissued at 1:55 p.m., the order did not reach every part of each battalion until around 4:00 p.m. For the most part, the order was spread by word of mouth. The men at Oblong Farm, the farthest left of Watson's positions in front of Kitcheners Wood, were informed by a note attached to a cartridge clip thrown over a gun-swept patch of Flanders. With their officers and NCOs dead or too wounded to lead, many suspected another *ruse de guerre*. In his report to Turner (written three days later) Watson wrote "It was during this retirement that we sustained our heaviest casualties." The letter that covered his report went as far as a Lieutenant-Colonel can in criticizing his brigadier without resigning his commission: "The retirement was <u>not compulsory</u>, the enemy having been repulsed with heavy losses, on their repeated attempts to advance." The underscored words highlighted for the record that Turner's decision to withdraw was not, in the eyes of his commander in the field, a military requirement. The 3rd Battalion's officers were not much more supportive of the order, which nevertheless they carried out.

• • •

The retirement could not have come at a worse time. Just before it, Reserve-Infanterie-Regiments 235 and 236 arrived in positions south and east of Kitcheners Wood. Since there were no Canadians left in the woods, the 235's regimental historian later wrote, "The battalion passed through it and under the command of Hauptmann Calsow, with hard fighting, stormed the English trench on the southern edge of the woods." There were the London Artillery Regiment's four 4.7 guns, which were recaptured by companies commanded by Leutnants Kahle and Hofer; after the battle, the guns were removed from the Gun Woods and exhibited in the marketplace of Roulers, Belgium.

• • •

Private Michael L'Abbé (2nd Battalion) became aware of the retirement when he saw men on his right (from the area near Hooper's and Doxsee's houses) "streaming back through the fields in the general direction of home" at "one thirty 'pip emma' [p.m.]." His timing is a bit off, however, for the order did not reach Captain Claude Culling, who commanded the right side of the 2nd Battalion, until nearly 2:30 p.m., and Culling's trenches were not empty until sometime after 3:40 p.m.

When Culling's men filed out of their trenches, they likely thought their odds were pretty good. Not long before the order to retire, those on the west side of Doxsee's House saw the machine-gunner Wallace "Wally" Bennett destroy the German units that had staged the sixth major attack of the day. Bennett, who had brought his machine gun over from the 10th Battalion, "did most excellent work," wrote Captain Richardson in his after-action report, cutting down, he estimated, three hundred Germans:

> I watched till they broke through the hedge, and then they had over a hundred yards to cross over to get to our farmhouse. We saw them break through the hedge, with their bayonets fixed, and they were coming right at us, at the front. And, as near as I can remember, I held my fire, because we were short of ammunition. . . . We couldn't have stopped another attack—we didn't have the ammunition, we'd run out.
>
> So I had to wait until they got through the hedge and let them get a few yards . . . before I opened up on them. I just cut 'em down. For once, the gun didn't jam. We beat them back—some of them were killed, some

of them were lying there kicking.... You could hear them [screaming]. ... Those that could get back, crawled back, and carried some of their wounded back.[7]

Whatever Culling's men thought, the majority were doomed. Shells and bullets from the new German positions on the east side of Kitcheners Wood ripped into the Canadians as they crossed the open country between their trenches and the GHQ Line, a mile or so to the southwest. Culling himself "was last seen, pistol in hand, standing defiantly in the abandoned trench; a few yards behind the parados lay the unconscious form of Lieut. Scott, his leg shattered."[8] The officer and gentleman commanding the 2nd Battalion, Lieutenant-Colonel Watson, did not include in his report that during the retreat he carried a wounded private on his back.

While Culling's men were running and dying, L'Abbé noticed an upsurge in "attention coming our way from the wood in front" of his position. His jocular tone, the product of a mind honed in Jazz Age New York, should not blind us to the horror of the moment and how survival depended on split-second decisions:

> I detected one of our square-headed friends casting covetous glances at us from behind a tree. He had forgotten the old commandment "Thou shalt not covet, etc." He did this twice, and the third time he coveted no more, and he had lost all interest in this mundane sphere. However, laterally the woods were full of them, and we had to impress on them many times the error of their ways. Langton was having the time of his young life speeding many of the erring ones to join their new found Kaiser.

Finally, L'Abbé's unit received the order to retire. The plan of retirement required that those in the trench "keep up a continuous fire while the men individually crawled over the trench, at intervals, and made a dash for home—or the RIP Club." Just before L'Abbé's turn came, a badly wounded soldier begged not to be left to the Huns. "What in

God's name could we do?" L'Abbé recalled. "Very few of us would get out of this trap alive. 'Can't take me, boys? Well, gimme a cigarette, and leave me a rifle.' We gave him a cigarette, but did not leave a rifle."*

L'Abbé and his buddy Birdie wished each other luck and, with a few other men, crawled over the back of their trench and began to run towards the same mustard patch they had stormed out of a day earlier. Each man wore a greatcoat and carried a sixty-pound pack and a Ross rifle with the bolt removed. The man on L'Abbé's left had only gone a few paces before a bullet caught up with him, and he crumpled. As L'Abbé neared the mustard patch, he heard the "soul-sickening rattle" of machine-gun bullets crackling near him. Did the gunner lift his weapon just a fraction of an inch? Perhaps the gun barrel was worn, and instead of coming out with a spin, which would have ensured they travelled straight, the bullets came out wobbling, which meant that as the gun traversed the arc there were dead zones. L'Abbé swerved at just the right moment. The men running on his left "pitched headlong, rolling over and over like a rabbit that has been hit on the run, a few yards from the mustard patch." As L'Abbé dove into the mustard patch, bullets clipped the blossoms. A bullet ripped through his pack after he'd wiggled a few yards into the patch.

After catching his breath, L'Abbé crawled forward, soon coming to a furrow "blocked with the dead." With the Germans already using his old trench as a firing-step, L'Abbé's only hope was to run, go to ground, then get up and do it again. He glanced at the Germans, jumped to his feet, ran a few yards, and dove. A "corpse whose left forehead had been blown away, the brains hanging down over his nose and mouth," lay near him. Another five yards and another dive; this time no corpse, only two bullet holes in his greatcoat. L'Abbé's next run took him back to the

---

*L'Abbé's story is of his own survival, so all he tells of this soldier is that he was a Highlander, but that tells us a great deal. By 1:30 p.m. on 24 April, almost thirty-six hours had passed since the Canadian Highlanders, the 16th Battalion, attacked Kitcheners Wood; more than thirty hours had passed since they pulled out to trenches south of the woods. L'Abbé's Highlander had been lying, mortally wounded, for a day and a half.

furrow, far from the Germans, though close to a dead Canadian who "was gaping at me with a leering grin, half sitting up among the dead." L'Abbé's ordeal ended a few moments later, when he jumped into a shell hole and heard, to his great astonishment, his buddy Bish say, "Do you know, I think there's a war on." A quick count found five bullet holes in L'Abbé's greatcoat.

Scores of others were not as lucky, including Major Herbert G. Bolster, the last man in the trench, who had to issue a peremptory order to his lieutenant before he would leave. Bolster was never seen again. Private Ferdinand Hardyman was true to his surname. Despite being hit in the chest, left leg, and twice in his right arm, the seventeen-year-old ran "about eight hundred yards to the reinforcement trench to escape the Germans, and from there, crawled to the dressing station" more than a mile away.[9]

• • •

A half an hour after L'Abbé and Hardyman ran for safety, the 3rd Battalion's luck ran out. The unit's war diary charts the disaster. At 2:03 p.m., the battalion was told to send Major Kirkpatrick the order to retire to the GHQ Line:

> This message was taken up by LANCE-CORPORAL GRAVERY, under very heavy rifle and shell fire, and was delivered to MAJOR KIRKPATRICK personally.
>
> The retirement began. A few men of "C" Company, mostly wounded, reached the GHQ line. No further report has been received from MAJOR KIRKPATRICK, as to the position of himself or his command.
>
> The party under CAPT. MORRISON divided, and 27 men, under LIEUT. CURRY, retired with the 14th Bn. As to the remainder of the party, no report has been received.

After getting the wounded out, Kirkpatrick called for the men in his left trench to exit on the left and make their way to the GHQ Line. The first platoons to leave the trench were wiped out by machine guns the Germans had got into position on the right of the 2nd Battalion's trench "with lightning rapidity"—a feat made possible by the fact that Turner had ordered a simultaneous retirement of the 2nd and 3rd Battalions.

The German machine guns did more than kill; they also trapped Kirkpatrick's men. The Canadian positions to their right had fallen. In front of them was a mass of spiked helmets. And there was no possibility of the Dominion soldiers crawling over the back of the trenches and dashing to safety across the open field behind them. At 3:00 p.m. on 24 April, flanking machine-gun fire and "shrapnel and heavy shells . . . formed the most effective barrage imaginable, preventing our retreat."[10] Their only hope was to try to hold out until dark and then sneak their way out.

For thirty minutes, the fate of Kirkpatrick's men rested on the fingers of his machine-gun crews and their ever-dwindling supply of ammunition. The Germans knew this and played for time, concentrating their fire on the gunners. John Hewitt was hit in the head. A fraction of an inch higher, lower, left, or right and the bullet would have blown his head apart. Incredibly, it "went right through his cranium and came out almost between his eyes." Hewitt's head was covered in blood before his body hit the ground. He fell next to twenty-four-year-old Eric Seaman, a tent maker born in India, who thought his buddy was dead. "But he began to stir after a while and stood up on his rubbery legs. And I said, 'How do you feel, John?' 'OH,' he said, 'I feel as though I had been drunk for a week. . . . That's all'"[11]*

Just as he was about to load his last ammunition into his machine gun, a bullet "took off Machine Gunner Foss's finger, taking the trigger with it and splitting his jaw into two parts." As Kirkpatrick rushed to bind up Foss's wounds, "the Germans sprang on us and we knew our day

---

*Hewitt, who, like Seaman, spent the rest of the war as a POW, lived to a ripe old age, dying in the early 1960s.

was done. For one moment, like gladiators, we stood at gaze, then, surrounded and outnumbered our ammunition all gone, we bowed to the inevitable and, to save useless waste of life, gave in."

Unlike the *Feldgrauen* who had captured Rice and Thurgood, the Saxon soldiers who took Kirkpatrick treated their Dominion counterparts with "respectful forbearance to a brave foe." Instead of mocking questions, they praised the very martial abilities their Kaiser had dismissed: "You do not mean to tell me you did all this damage with these few men?"[12] The German who found Lance-Corporal John W. Finnimore immobilized with a broken leg put the injured Canadian in a wheelbarrow before pushing him to a rear dressing station. The one hundred exhausted, bleeding, half-starved, and extremely thirsty survivors of the 425 men Kirkpatrick had led less than a day before would soon find harder treatment when the Saxon guards turned them over to Prussians behind the line.

• • •

At 3:30 p.m., while Kirkpatrick's men (and some forty others in a 2nd Battalion trench to his left) made their last stand, the order to retire finally reached Captain Richardson at Doxsee's House; the order reached Hooper's House ten minutes later. More is known about the retirement from Doxsee's House because all Hooper's men died in a trench near Kitcheners Wood, likely at the hands of RIR 235.

Richardson carefully choreographed the withdrawal from Doxsee's House. Immediately after receiving the order, he told Bennett and his other machine-gunners to disassemble their guns. To keep the Germans at bay, Richardson's riflemen continued to man the loopholes. Then each member of the machine-gun crew—loaded down with the gun, the tripod, or a box of ammunition—ran out the back door. Only when the rest of the garrison had left the house did the riflemen leave their loopholes and run for their lives.

Richardson's after-action report barely hints at his men's struggle to survive. "The direction of retirement was given as Battalion Headquarters," he wrote. "But a few casualties occurred until we were in a rear trench and as one went further the hotter the fire became. The lines seemed to dwindle away." Bennett told more: "The Germans saw us leave and we ran right into their fire which seemed to be coming from all angles. Bullets were flying and hitting the ground around us as we ran. They turned a machine gun on us." Bennett went to ground. After waiting a moment for the train of machine-gun bullets to pass over him, he jumped up and ran. He crossed into a German machine-gunner's vector, and "a bullet hit the machine gun he was carrying, ripping off a piece of the handle, and tearing a hole through the sleeve" of the gun.[13] The impact knocked Bennett over.*

Bennett caught his breath and looked around. Behind him, he could see Foss and another man lying face down and not moving. Farther out in the field, four other Canadians lay dead. Around him, others were crawling; a few jumped up and ran before dropping down for safety. And seventy-five yards back, he saw Germans swarming around Doxsee's House. Of the several hundred men from two detachments who had held these two houses and the area round them, only forty-three escaped; most were wounded, and two were (temporarily) blinded.

. . .

In the middle of the afternoon, events appeared to vindicate Turner's decision to reinforce the GHQ Line. The 9th London Regiment, dug in just next to the line, checked a German advance on a ruined farm south of Kitcheners Wood. Had they taken the farm, the Germans could have enfiladed the GHQ Line. Within moments of spotting the *Feldgrauen*, a few dozen British soldiers were up and running, four bandoliers of ammunition draped over each of their necks. For men running with great weight and against great odds, seconds seem to stretch beyond the sweep of a clock's thinnest hand. Anthony R. Hossack remembered:

---

*The four-and-a-half-ounce bullet hit the gun Bennett was carrying with a force of about nine thousand pounds.

Shall I ever get there? My limbs ache with fatigue and my legs are like lead. But the inspiring figure of [Captain George Culme-Seymour] urges us on, yet even he cannot prevent the thinning of our line or the gaps torn in it by the German field gunners, whom we can now plainly see.

At last we reach the farm, and we follow Culme-Seymour round to its further side. The roar of the enemy machine gun rises to a crazy shrieking, but we are past caring about them, and with a sob of relief we fall into the farm's encircling trench. Not too soon either, for that grey mass is only a few hundred yards off, and 'Rapid fire! Let 'em have it, boys!' and don't we just. At last a target, and one we cannot miss. The Germans fall in scores and their batteries limber up and away.[14]

For some Germans, the moments after the British started rapid fire must have brought back memories of 1st Ypres, when British infantrymen with Lee-Enfields produced such a rate of fire that the Germans thought they were facing machine guns.

## Chapter 14

## "Do You Expect Me to Wet-Nurse Your Brigade?"
### Major-General Snow Refuses to Aid the 2nd Brigade

> *I am the very model of the modern Major-General*
> *I've information vegetable, animal and mineral,*
> *I know the kings of England, and I quote the fights historical*
> *From Marathon to Waterloo, in order categorical.*
> —GILBERT AND SULLIVAN, "THE MAJOR-GENERAL'S SONG"

Were it not so telling of both the communications muddle that had developed on 24 April and the British staff officers' attitude towards the colonials in their midst, the ill-fated 3:00 p.m. meeting between Brigadier-General Currie and Major-General Snow would be good fodder for a Royal Canadian Air Farce skit.

When Currie climbed down into Snow's dugout, he cut quite the figure—stubble on his chin, boots caked with mud, uniform streaked with dirt and sweat, and smelling of cordite. Nearing a hundred hours awake, he would have had bloodshot eyes and his face would have been drawn; indeed, just a few hours later he wrote of his condition, "I had no sleep for days and nights and didn't care what happened."[1] His own headquarters at Pond Farm had been set alight by shells. Twice during the morning, he had been told that help was on the way; twice he was disappointed. Over the previous few hours, commander after commander had refused his pleas for reinforcements. And just minutes before he entered Snow's dugout (where he hoped to telegraph his own commander, General Alderson), Currie had learned that Brigadier-General Turner had ordered the 2nd and 3rd Battalions to withdraw to the GHQ Line. He immediately realized that Turner's blunder had "increased the gap and increased my anxiety to find troops to fill it."

Snow, the commander of the 27th British Division, did not know Currie personally. But what he knew worried him. As far as Snow was concerned, Currie had been hinting for hours that he was about to retire. Snow had good reasons to think this. At 11:05 a.m., Currie had signalled General Chapman, commander of the 85th Brigade, that because the Germans had broken through the Apex, the 8th Battalion's left was exposed and his men "may have to evacuate trenches." Currie assured Chapman that whatever happened, the 5th Battalion would keep in touch with the British left, and most important, that he would not "order a retirement for some time yet." Near noon, however, just before leaving to look for troops, Currie again told Chapman that since he had no reinforcements, he had "ordered the 8th Battalion, Section II, to retire by its left on to the Gravenstafel Ridge."

Snow's headquarters learned of Currie's orders near 1:00 p.m. At 1:15 p.m., Snow sent a runner to Alderson with a message that said, "General Officer Commanding 85th Brigade [Snow] has implored him [Currie] not to retire and is sending him two companies 8th Middlesex on their arrival [to Snow] and is asking the 84th Brigade to help him [Currie]." Fifteen minutes later, Snow wired the same message to Alderson, underlining the fact that if Currie's men retired, Snow's left would be in the air:

> Any retirement on my part would be disastrous to [the] whole twenty-eight divn. line and that I have no intention of ordering any retirement. Will you please ask Canadian Division to stop any retirement contemplated and direct reinforcements to threatened part.

In Snow's version of the meeting, Currie showed him a conditional order to withdraw soon after entering the dugout and told him that if his men were forced out of their trenches, they would retreat to the GHQ Line. According to the historian Tim Travers, Snow claimed that he tore up the order and then "forcibly persuaded" Currie to maintain his line. The British official historian, Sir James Edmonds, who served under Snow in 1914, reported that the major-general later said that had Currie been "an English officer I would have put him under arrest and he would have been shot."[2]

Currie's version of the meeting casts Snow as both a bully and a fool. As the noise of exploding shells echoed around them, Currie explained that a gap had opened on his left. Snow did not ask who had authored the withdrawal orders and assumed that the gap had opened because of Currie. Ignoring Currie's attempts to explain that the gap had opened because of the collapse of the Apex and Turner's decision to withdraw the 2nd and 3rd Battalions, Snow shouted, "Give them Hell. Give them Hell." In 1926, in response to Edmonds's plan to include Snow's version of the meeting in the British official history, Currie wrote:

> When I considered the position of all the troops of the 2nd Brigade and my inability to move two battalions whom I thought had been sent to our assistance, I confess that at that moment, I thought I had never heard a more stupid remark. I have thought of it many times during the past eleven years and am of the same opinion still.

At no point, it would seem, did Snow tell Currie that he had been appointed to command the reserves, and that he had sent troops to Fortuin. Snow did agree to allow Currie to send Alderson a message. But no sooner had Currie started on it when Snow was shouting that the Canadian brigadier was taking too long to write it. "That was an insult and so at variance with the treatment which one officer should receive from another of superior rank that I was dumbfounded," recalled Currie.

Is it possible to determine what happened in that dugout? Fortunately, there was a witness, Lieutenant Edison F. Lynn of the 2nd Field Company Canadian Engineers, and he supports Currie's version of events. Just before Currie arrived at the dugout, Lynn saw an example of Snow's famous temper. Snow sent for Lynn after learning that he and several hundred Canadian stragglers he had collected around Potijze were extending a nearby trench. As the forty-two-year-old civil engineer neared the dugout, he saw Captain Paul Villiers, who belonged to Turner's 3rd Brigade, enter it. Lynn followed a moment later, and he heard Snow pepper Villiers with a series of disjointed questions concerning "the location of each Battalion; the condition of the line; the strength of the forces against them; gas discharges." Because of the way Snow put the questions, Villiers's "replies were at times vague and unsatisfactory." He lacked the information, for example, to be able to trace the 3rd Brigade's line on Snow's map, which caused the brigadier to shout, "Are your men a hundred yards away or are they a mile or miles away?" When Villiers was unable to clarify the situation, Snow began cursing him for his stupidity, and then went on to curse "the Canadians and all connected with them." The tirade concluded with Snow shouting, "Get out of here. Get back to your Brigade and, when you have some definite information to pass on, send someone with intelligence, if you have such a one, capable of explaining the situation."*

Before Snow had a chance to turn to Lynn, Currie entered. Lynn, who had been shocked by Snow's abuse of Villiers, watched as the senior British general responded to Currie with a tirade that included "such words as incapable, rotten troops, fools, dictators, [and] nurses." Currie

---

*Snow further humiliated Villiers later in the day, when the captain returned to the brigadier's dugout to explain that Turner had given orders to fall back to the GHQ Line, and that they were regrouping for a 3:00 p.m. attack to relieve St. Julien. Snow "exploded and said that the order [to attack] must be cancelled at once." To cancel the order, he made Villiers run up and down the line, yelling to battalion leaders, "Troops will stand fast. Orders for counterattack are cancelled." When Villiers returned to Mouse Trap Farm, it was Turner's turn to tear a strip off him; he was mollified only when Villiers pointed out that he "was taking direct orders from General Snow, his [Turner's] superior officer."

told Snow that the Germans were pressing his men hard and pointed to the map to show where Snow could best deploy the reserve troops under his command. As soon as Currie finished saying that Snow's men were fresh and could be of great value, the almost apoplectic major-general started shouting, "Have you come here to teach me my profession and dictate how I shall handle my division?"

The exchange continued with Currie pointing out that his men had been in the line for ten days and had "resisted every attack without relinquishing a foot of ground." But they had "been fearfully cut up," he said, and were tired and hungry. Even given the pressures of war, Snow's response is shocking: "Do you expect me to wet-nurse your brigade? You have got yourself and your men into a mess and you will get them out of it as best you can."

Given Currie's reputation for handling expletives, it is likely that Lynn's memory cleaned up his response to Snow. "I am not in a mess, nor are my men," he declared. "My men and I have held out against fierce onslaughts and will continue to hold out as long as any of us are left.... The support of some fresh troops is essential for the safety of the line." Snow's response was probably also somewhat more pungent than "Enough of this. I have heard enough. Get out of here. Take care of your own line. You will get no help from me."

In his dealings with both Currie and Villiers, Snow lived up to his reputation as the rudest officer in the British army. Rudeness is, however, hardly rare in an institution devoted to the use of force. We learn more from his decision to ignore Currie's pleas and, even more important, his failure to incorporate into his understanding of the developing battle the information that Currie brought to his dugout. Snow, a career British officer, was unable to see that the amateur colonials, who had been bearing the brunt of the battle for Ypres, had performed admirably and had useful information. Snow displayed the same attitude as General Sir Henry Horne, who commanded the 1st British Army from September 1916 until the end of the war. Horne claimed that the Canadians were "rather apt to take all the credit ... for everything, and to consider that the BEF consists of the Canadian Corps and some other troops." The general had a tin ear for irony, for during the last hundred days of the war the Canadian Corps, which had earned the reputation of being the "shock troops of the British Army," belonged to none other than Horne's 1st British Army.

In the end, Edmonds dropped all mention of the Currie–Snow meeting in his official history.* He could not find anyone to corroborate Snow's version of events, and more important, his political masters told him that including the incident would "ruin his [Currie's] position in Canada—where he is . . . a staunch supporter of the Imperial connection."[3] Canada's official history gives the meeting one sentence and then reprints the message Currie sent at 3:30 p.m.:

To 1st Canadian Division,

At 12.30 my left flank was entirely unprotected, the 3rd Brigade having retired to St. Julien. The companies at Locality C were practically *non est*. I then ordered 8th Battalion, Section II to fall back to Locality C, the 5th Battalion, to conform to their movements and hold the Gravenstafel Ridge, notifying 85th Brigade of what I was doing. I then received notification that two battalions, one the Durhams and the other the Yorks, were being sent to me in order to counter-attack and that the attack was to be pushed with vigour.

I came back to the GHQ 2nd Line to meet these two battalions. I saw the Durhams at one o'clock and their Brigadier and waited until two when I was told by Staff Officer 3rd Brigade that counter-attack was not to be made by the Durhams and Yorks and I came to Headquarters 27th Division to send report.[4]

• • •

*Edmonds wrote only, "After a short interview with the General Officer Commanding the 27th Division, he [Currie] dispatched the following message at 3:30 p.m."

While their commander was looking fruitlessly for a British officer who would move his troops, Lieutenant-Colonels Lipsett and Tuxford awaited the promised attack that would relieve pressure on their left flank. Lipsett messaged Turner to ask when the counterattack would begin. He told him that his answer would help determine "whether to hang on to our trenches or not."[5] Thanks to Major McNaughton's 7th Field Artillery Battery, which fired more than eighteen hundred rounds, the ground in front of the 8th Battalion's trenches was piled high with German dead. Despite being thrown some ten feet by an exploding German shell, a splinter cutting through his shoulder, the brilliant gunner soldiered on for another twelve hours as again and again his men waited for the Germans to "line up so we could get the greatest number of people in the line of fire."[6]

More worrying was Lipsett's left, which, though quiet, remained unprotected. Most worrying was the possibility of a surprise attack from the rear. Warden's ever-diminishing garrison at Locality "C" could not prevent the Germans from infiltrating between his position and Lipsett and Tuxford's rear. Unavoidable communication lapses hindered the Canadians' efforts to sweep the terrain between Locality "C" and the front line's rear, as can be seen from this summary of one action in this cockpit:

> A strong party of Germans with a machine gun fortified a farm 700 yards to his [Tuxford's] left rear. While Tuxford was desperately trying to locate a field gun to reduce the place he saw a party of Canadians of various units advance towards the farm house. They did not seem to be aware of the Germans occupying it, and Tuxford watched helplessly as they approached in the open. An officer detached himself from the party and advanced alone. He was shot down and his small command flopped to the ground to engage the enemy—unsuccessfully, as it turned out.[7]

By 1:45 p.m., the absence of any word from Currie concerned Lipsett, who concluded his message to Turner by saying, "General Currie missing do you know his whereabouts last seen going to the GHQ Line."

But Currie's absence did not, as some historians suggest, rattle Lipsett or Tuxford. Currie had left the most Canadian of orders: withdraw if necessary, but do not necessarily withdraw. That gave Lipsett considerable latitude. If he did not believe the situation was critical, he could keep his and Tuxford's men in their trenches. Lipsett did not believe the situation was critical, and neither did Tuxford, who, when Lipsett told him of Currie's order, said, "I did not understand why we should have to retire. In spite of our casualties, my men were full of fight." Lipsett, though in command, was outranked by Tuxford. He said, "I am in temporary command of the Brigade, and if you think it advisable, suppose we stick?" Tuxford agreed.

• • •

During the afternoon, the communications fog obscured what the author of Canada's official history calls, perhaps with a note of irony, the "fortuitous but timely arrival of British Battalions"[8] Lost in this fog—perhaps sitting in a pile of ciphers yet to be decoded or held up by a broken telegraph line—was an urgent message from Snow to Turner. In it, Snow ordered Turner to push his men forward with vigour—and, incidentally, told Turner that he, Snow, was in command of the battle:

> The enemy's advance from Fortuin must be stopped at all costs. You must move every man you have got to drive him back. I have directed 2 battalions under Officer Commanding Suffolks from Frezenberg against Fortuin. I am also sending you up the Royal Irish Regiment from here and have directed them on cross roads in C.23.c You will get in touch with these troops and take command in that part of the field and drive the enemy North Eastwards. I am issuing these orders as I am on the spot and communication appears to be dislocated and time is of the highest importance. Act with vigour.

Time *was* "of the highest importance." But Turner did not get this message until 4:05 p.m., at which point his front line was no longer on the southeastern fringe of Kitcheners Wood but was at the GHQ Line, a few yards from Mouse Trap Farm.

Even if Turner's men had still held the line south and east of the woods, he likely would not have acted on Snow's message. There are two reasons to believe this. The first is rooted in the army's very structure. At 4:05 p.m., even though Snow had been the nominal commander of all British forces for more than seven hours, no one had informed either Alderson or Turner of this fact. Despite the constant shelling of the salient, Turner remained in touch with his divisional general, Alderson. "It's a principle pretty basic to military functioning that unless you have a good reason otherwise, you always follow the orders of your commanding officer," says the historian Bill Rawling. "Snow didn't seem to be able to grasp the difference between picking up a phone in headquarters and issuing an order which will be carried out immediately because somebody is there to do just that, and issuing one on a battlefield, where communications are something of a mess and units you want to move around have their own commanders."

The second reason for believing that Turner would have ignored Snow's command has to do with Turner's obsession with the GHQ Line. At 2:30 p.m., a mere fifteen minutes after Snow sent his order, Turner received Alderson's directive to use the 2nd King's Own Yorkshire Light Infantry and the 9th London Regiment, then on their way to Mouse Trap Farm, to hold his line in front of Kitcheners Wood; clearly, no one at the Château de Trois Tours had any idea that Turner had ordered the 2nd and 3rd Battalions to retire to the GHQ Line. Two hours later, Alderson, becoming concerned, sent a message telling Turner that at Wieltje there were another four battalions: "You must push troops up into your <u>front line</u> and prevent at all costs the Germans breaking through between you and 2nd Brigade." By the time Turner read this, his connection with Currie's 2nd Brigade had not existed for more than four hours. He interpreted the underscored words, as he had all day, to mean the GHQ Line.

Nothing better illustrates the collapse of command and control than the last sentence of Alderson's 4:30 p.m. message: "I have no exact knowledge of your situation at the present moment, but hope that you are still blocking ST. JULIEN, and in close touch with the 2nd Canadian Brigade." Four hours had passed since Turner's men had last blocked or held St. Julien. Amazingly, at 8:45 p.m., Turner told Alderson, "Some of our troops still are in ST. JULIEN surrounded, this number originally 700 now possibly 200." As the last of the red light of the sun dipped below the horizon, there were no Canadians alive in St. Julien.

• • •

Neither Alderson nor Turner knew that at about the time Alderson sent his 4:30 p.m. message, a small British force consisting of the 12th London (Rangers) and 1st Suffolks was on its way to support Currie's men. The decision was made not by Snow but by the unit's commander, Lieutenant-Colonel W. B. Wallace, who, after meeting with Currie's brigade lieutenant, Lieutenant-Colonel Herbert Kemmis-Betty, agreed to move his troops about a thousand yards north, to a position along the Steenbeek, about two thousand yards south of Lipsett's open left wing. Unfortunately, this support was almost immediately erased by the communications muddle. No one told British artillery that two battalions had shifted north, and before long, friendly fire had killed the Rangers' commander and fifty-eight other men; the Suffolks took 154 casualties.

• • •

The only way to supply the machine guns at Oblong Farm was to toss ammunition belts over a stretch of ground raked by Maxim machine-gunners. Nevertheless, at 4:00 p.m. on 24 April, Private Alan Beddoe still believed that he and the other men "would get out of the little traverse that they were on in the farm." Most didn't get out.

Their retirement began well enough. Just beyond the house ran a little trench, which should have taken the men some ways towards safety. The Germans saw the end of the trench, however, and sited a machine gun on it. Confidence turned to horror as man after man was cut down by a stream of bullets. "They would go over like jack rabbits, piling up there," Beddoe recalled.

Somehow Beddoe made it through the "squirting machine gun fire." With the words "Always cover a retreat" echoing in his head, he stopped and pulled out his entrenching tool, dropped to the ground, threw up a bit of cover, put his rifle to his shoulder, and "started to bang away." Glancing to his left, he saw his sergeant, Latimer D'Arcy, sprawled on the ground. He called him over, "never for a moment thinking that he might not be able to move." Just then a shell exploded, knocking Beddoe out. He must have been unconscious for several hours, for when he came to "the sun was well down and there was no firing going on."

The setting sun, however, was not Beddoe's chief concern. Beside him lay D'Arcy, barely alive with a bullet in his liver. "All the rest were dead." Then a German soldier, bayonet at the ready, turned a corner, saw them, and said, "Come." Five decades later, Beddoe still reproached himself for not hurling his knife at the German and then trotting to safety with D'Arcy on his shoulders like a hero from the *Boy's Own Annual*. Instead, beneath the setting sun, the semi-conscious Beddoe helped D'Arcy up and supported him as they walked, under guard, to the German rear, where the souvenir-hunting *Feldgrauen* relieved them of their knives.

## Chapter 15

# "Can You Tell Me Where the Enemy Is?"
### The Fog of War Lifts

> *If I should die, think only this of me:*
> *That there's some corner of a foreign field*
> *That is for ever England.*
> —Rupert Brooke, "The Soldier"

Each of the three regimental histories that describe the German advance on St. Julien on 24 April tells a different story, and none squares with either the Canadian or the British records. The regimental historians of RIR 234 write of finding a Canadian using a shell hole as a latrine, and of watching "large and small groups of prisoners, mostly Canadians, marching along the road accompanied by a few of our men." Towards evening, however, things turned worse:

> Several shrapnel shells fell on the building. One shell struck the house on the right and went straight through the middle, entering through the eastern front of the house and exploding a gun of the platoon from the reserve battery, which had been placed behind the building at the cross roads. The shell tore the leg off one of the gun crew and made the ammunition explode. Fortunately, all the following shells whizzed passed.
>
> While we were taking the wounded away, night fell. Soon tracer bullets rose out of the enemy camp and the foe lit up the terrain between the

trenches. Incessantly the trenches were fortified and improved. No one thought of being tired or of sleep. But there was a guest who was even worse. Hunger. But even he was soon vanquished because a few kitchens with their steaming pots were found.

By mentioning the shelling where they do, the regimental historians make it seem as if the 234 was shelled out of St. Julien, which it was not. The shelling took place outside St. Julien, after the Germans had abandoned the village. The regimental historian of the 235 writes even less, saying only that during "the night the trenches were re-arranged as well as is possible" and that food, ammunition, and entrenching tools were brought forward.

The regimental historian of RIR 236, by contrast, tells us quite a bit. Canadian gunners and machine-gunners, he reports, exacted a measure of revenge for the suffering German guns had caused earlier in the day:

> Machine gun fire from the ridges around Fortuin kept us from advancing further [into St. Julien]. The right wing of the attack was stopped by violent shrapnel fire and heavy shelling. Heavy losses were taken during the day.
>
> In an orderly fashion we detached ourselves from the enemy, leaving patrols behind. The storming of St. Julien had again caused the regiment heavy losses. The 2/236th brought home its 3rd dead leader of the day. Hauptmann Curshmann had been grievously wounded. In order not to leave the well loved leader behind, five men got together in order to carry the wounded out of the combat line on a tarpaulin.... Before Hauptmann Curshmann was finally in safety, another bullet had hit him, this time fatally. The machine gun platoon of the 236th had lost its commander, First Leutnant Ruscheveyh and also Leutnant Lietholf.

He credits the decision to abandon the ruined village to a lack of ammunition, and to the fact that the British were bringing up reinforcements, which was not something the Germans could have been sure of at the time.

• • •

The Germans were right about there being plans for a counterattack, but they could not have seen the reinforcements moving up. At 4:15 p.m., Field Marshall Sir John French ordered that "every effort must be made at once to hold the line about St. Julien or situation of the 28th Division will be jeopardised. Am sending General Staff officer to explain Chief's views." Sir John's first sentence underscored what Generals Plumer and Alderson well knew: the St. Julien garrison protected the 28th British Division's left flank, and if it was rolled up, the salient and the almost fifty thousand British and Canadian troops in it were doomed, as were Ypres and, perhaps, the Channel ports. Sir John's order took more than two hours to reach Alderson, and it immediately upset his plan to use several of the battalions that had been sent to Mouse Trap Farm to relieve General Turner's 3rd Brigade and Geddes's Detachment.*

At 6:35 p.m., Alderson appointed Brigadier-General Charles P. A. Hull, commander of the 10th British Brigade, to lead the attack ordered by Sir John. Though it would be almost six more hours before Alderson learned that Turner had been sending reinforcements to the GHQ Line (and thus ignoring his orders all day), the decision to place Hull, a career army officer, in command of the counterattack, which was to involve fifteen battalions (some fifteen thousand men, or almost a division), was not a vote of confidence in Turner's leadership.** In an effort to mitigate the German superiority in artillery, Alderson scheduled the attack for 3:30 a.m. on 25 April. Part six of the orders explains the attack's goals:

> The first objective of the attack will be FORTUIN (if occupied by enemy) ST. JULIEN and the wood in C.10 & 11. After these points have been gained Gen. Hull will advance astride of the ST. JULIEN-POELCAPPELLE

---

*Colonel August Geddes died on 28 April 1915; his name is inscribed on the Menin Gate.
**It should, however, be recalled that Turner was a brigadier with just a few days' experience in trench warfare, and that he had been under constant fire for the better part of two days.

road and drive back the enemy as far north as possible. All units holding the front line trenches will follow up the attack and help consolidate the ground gained.

Alderson learned near midnight that at 8:00 p.m. the Canadians held Fortuin, but the Germans were in full possession of Kitcheners Wood, as well as almost all of the St. Julien–Poelcappelle road and the terrain on each side of it. Worse, the lines between the GHQ Line and St. Julien had been abandoned.

• • •

The "attack" referred to by the regimental historian of the 236 had, in fact, nothing to do with St. Julien. Nor did any brigadier know that there were British formations moving in that area of the salient. Sometime after Lieutenant-Colonel M. H. L. Bell refused General Currie's request to use his 4/East Yorks and 4/Yorks to counterattack on Lipsett's left, a staff officer from the 27th Battalion presented Bell with a copy of General Snow's order to move to Fortuin. At the time, Bell was under Turner's command, and like Turner, he did not know Snow. However, perhaps because Bell and Snow were both British, he accepted the orders and soon his men were climbing out of their trenches to march to Fortuin; Bell did not see fit to inform his (nominal) Canadian superior that he was on the move.

Bell was almost undone by lack of intelligence and maps. Fortunately, while marching west towards Fortuin, a captain noticed a section of a Canadian field battery and sent a runner to ask, "Can you tell me where the enemy is?"[1] Almost certainly the answer was the first time Bell heard that St. Julien had fallen. It is not known whether he was told to take the Wieltje–St. Julien road. But that is what he did, and just before 5:15 p.m., his force collided with a large detachment of Germans coming across a field and heading south towards St. Julien.

The records are sketchy, but it appears as though the Germans, who were marching in order, spotted the Canadians first. For the first few moments, Bell's men found themselves in a classic infantry battle. Men on both sides put their rifles to their shoulders, took aim at the mass in front of them, squeezed their triggers, and felt their rifles kick back. Then, in smooth motions, they grasped their rifles' bolts and pulled back. As the bolt was pulled back, the rifle ejected the spent cartridge from the chamber. Just as the bolt stopped moving backwards, the men started them forward, a motion that pushed a fresh round into the chamber, which was sealed by pushing the bolt until it stopped.

Unknown to Bell, just behind him to the right were Lieutenant-Colonel Creelman's guns; upon seeing the exchange of musketry, Creelman ordered his men to reverse their guns. In addition to hearing the whiz of bullets, the crackle of his own men's fire, and the roar of distant shells, Bell soon heard the sound of cannonfire behind him and saw the explosion of shrapnel and other shells amid the Germans.\*

The Germans were so close that Creelman's gunners fired over open sites. With their ammunition low, they ensured that every round counted. Major Harvey McLeod climbed onto the roof of the brigade headquarters to direct the fire. The first rounds exploded over the Germans when they were sixteen hundred yards away. Many *Feldgrauen* fell, but many more continued to charge. The next rounds hit when they were fourteen hundred yards away from Bell's force. McLeod called out again, "Drop two hundred." The gun-layers turned the cranks a few turns clockwise, and less than three seconds later, the Germans twelve hundred yards away were blown apart or showered with red-hot shrapnel. The German advance broke after another salvo when they were only nine hundred yards from Bell's troops. Just at the point when Creelman's gunners were

---

\*Extant records make it impossible to be sure, but the shells fired by Creelman's gunners almost certainly were among the more than three million shells ordered from Canada in August 1914. Like so much else, Canada's nascent munitions industry was the militia minister's brainchild. In true Hughesian fashion, he scribbled the order that created the "Shell Committee," not in an ornate office but while walking through Valcartier. By March 1915, the committee had coordinated the work of more than twenty-five thousand men and women in factories across the country,

about to run out of ammunition, he heard a subaltern call out, "Four wagons of ammunition, sir"[2]

The Germans, who retreated back to St. Julien, mistakenly thought Bell's troops were the vanguard of a major attack. After waiting for darkness to fall, they withdrew from the village. In the half light of dusk, Canadian scouts mistook the German retreat from St. Julien for a Canadian advance into the ruined village.

• • •

Just before 5:00 p.m., when Bell's troops collided with the Germans a thousand yards to the northwest, Captain Warden handed over command of Locality "C" to Lieutenant Howard Scharschmidt, a twenty-three-year-old who, despite his German name, was born in Comox, British Columbia. Sadly, Warden's trenches did nothing to prevent the inexorable reduction of his garrison from fifty at noon to thirty-five by 5:00 p.m. At 2:00 p.m., Warden was badly wounded. Before being helped to the rear, he told Scharschmidt "to hold on until relieved or support comes or ordered to retire, and that I would endeavour to have one of the three sent to him at once."

Warden was able to partially make good on his promise soon after leaving the trench, when he met a party of twenty-seven sappers. After showing them the way towards his old trench, Warden and Corporal Martin continued going back to a dressing station. A short time later, he asked a lieutenant-colonel who was holding a trench in support of Turner's brigade to send some men to "reoccupy the left part of the trench which was now occupied by the enemy." From his hospital bed in Boulogne, Warden could not recall the lieutenant-colonel's name, but he well remembered his words: "Cannot spare a single man." The garrison at Locality "C" was withdrawn at 4:00 a.m. on 25 April.

After leaving Snow's dugout, General Currie gathered together as many as one hundred Canadian details and placed them under thirty-four-year-old David Philpott (7th Battalion), who led them to the 8th Battalion on Gravenstafel Ridge. After making his way to Fortuin,

General Turner found the 1st Royal Irish Regiment. According to the Order of Battle Turner had in his hands, the 1/Irish belonged to him, and he wasted little time ordering them to retire to the GHQ Line once night fell. Since Turner did not go searching for 4/Yorks and 4/East Yorks, who were also on his Order of Battle, it is safe to assume that he had no idea where they were and didn't know that they had just checked a German advance.

Turner's action was as predictable as his search for troops was brave. It also risked disaster. The three British battalions hardly filled the gap between Currie's 8th and 5th Battalions and the GHQ Line. Still, together with the 1st Suffolks and 12th London Rangers (which Turner did not know about), to their right, and the dwindling garrison at Locality "C," they sketched something of a link to Currie's position. Turner's order re-opened the gap, again isolating Currie's men and the Suffolks and Rangers.

. . .

According to Duguid, Canada's official historian, Turner thought Snow was responsible for maintaining a link with Currie's 2nd Brigade; sometime in the late afternoon, he learned that Snow was in fact responsible for the corps' reserve troops. That accounts for the innocuous tone of the message he sent Snow at 9:35 p.m., in which he repeated his belief that there were still "about two hundred men in St. Julien" at 5:30 p.m. and also informed Snow that he had ordered the Irish back to the GHQ Line.

Turner's message dispelled the fog. Immediately upon receiving it, Snow telephoned General Sir Herbert Plumer to tell him that instead of pushing soldiers up to the line held by the 2nd and 3rd Battalions, Turner had been filling the GHQ Line. Plumer wasted little time issuing this peremptory order to Alderson:

> Reference message received from Twenty-seventh Division [Snow] and repeated to you by telephone to the effect that all troops of third Canadian

Brigade and those from twenty-seventh and twenty-eight Division have been ordered by Gen. Turner back to the GHQ second line or their division thus giving up all the ground for which such a struggle was made today and leaving the second brigade in the air. Corps commander [Plumer] directs that instant action be taken to re-establish a line as far forward as possible in the direction of ST JULIEN and in touch if possible with our troops on the right and left. If necessary you are to appoint an officer to take command. He suggests that a staff officer should be sent to deal with situation on the spot.[3]

Plumer could have no doubt that once Alderson heard what Turner had done, he would immediately understand that Currie's men had been isolated. Plumer's words came as close as he could to ordering the summary dismissal of Turner without actually doing so.

Alderson took two immediate actions. First, he sent the Divisional Cyclist Company to occupy Fortuin, which tells us how weak the senior commander's picture was of the battlefield, for as these mobile troops soon discovered, Fortuin was in British hands. Next, Alderson sent Lieutenant-Colonel Gordon-Hall to Mouse Trap Farm with "plenary powers to take what action was necessary to straighten out the tactical situation," which was almost as futile, though not because of any failings on the part of Gordon-Hall.[4]

While Gordon-Hall travelled to Mouse Trap Farm, Turner travelled in the other direction to complain to Alderson about Snow's orders, which "seemed to him so inexplicable, inappropriate and incomprehensible."[5] There is no record of their meeting. Certainly, Turner demanded to know which general was his commander, and Alderson demanded to know why Turner had spent the day sending fresh troops to the GHQ Line. Turner pointed out not only that he had kept Alderson apprised of this, but also that it accorded with the agreed defence. Canada's official historian sums up the meeting as having "only served to develop the unfortunate, but partially correct, conviction in the mind of each commander that the other did not understand what was happening," which is about as far as an official history can go in saying that each commander left the meeting thinking the other was a bloody fool.[6] From then on, Alderson never trusted Turner, and considered him unfit for command.

• • •

At 10:00 p.m., Creelman's gunners again ran low on ammunition. The situation facing them was extremely serious. The Germans were digging in a few hundred yards away, and there was neither British nor Canadian infantry to protect the battery. As well, Creelman's men were "under heavy rifle and shell fire," which he knew would only increase once his ammunition was exhausted. To make matters worse, Creelman had not received new orders for twenty-four hours. It was with a heavy heart that he telephoned the lieutenant-colonel to tell him that he was about to give the order to withdraw.

By the light of the burning thatched roofs of the farmhouses that had contained their billets, Creelman's drivers, reins in hand, signalled their horses to move out. Anticipating this moment, Creelman had had his men remove a few fences, cut through some hedges, and fill in some ditches so they could avoid the "heavily shelled main roads." They also buried their dead. Neither his after-action report nor his diary tells much about the first part of the retirement. The former noted that because of the preparations, the retirement "was effected with very little loss," while the latter recorded that he lost his kit. Of the second part of the retirement, which brought him and his men into Ypres, he wrote: "Dante lacked imagination when he wrote 'Inferno.' He ought to have ridden with me through Ypres twice during the middle of the night at a mad gallop over slippery cobble stones with the whole of the town on fire and stranded vehicles and bodies of dead men and horses blocking all the roads." When the mud-bespattered lieutenant-colonel was announced to General "Harry" Burstall, "he gazed fixedly at me as if to make sure it was really myself and then gasped 'Thank God.'"

• • •

As Creelman's men galloped south to safety, Currie led another mixed force of survivors of the 7th and 10th Battalions northwest towards Lipsett's open flank. Currie learned that these troops had come under his command again from Lieutenant-Colonel Gordon-Hall, who, shortly after midnight, went to the brigadier's rear headquarters near Wieltje to tell him of Hull's planned attack. Gordon-Hall was struck by Currie's resolve, especially given that he'd been woken up from a dead sleep: "He might have asked many questions, he might have demurred, but he raised no difficulties. He collected his staff, walked out into the night to get in touch with Lipsett and fill in, as far as he could, the gap between Lipsett's left and the General Headquarters Line."[7] Currie's destination was the GHQ Line, a thousand yards away.

When he arrived, Currie ordered that the 7th and 10th Battalion men be woken up from their first sleep in almost three days; luckily, the tired men had eaten their first hot meal in two days before collapsing into sleep. Since the remnants of the two battalions totalled only about 360 men—not even two companies—Currie amalgamated them under Major Odlum.

Currie's decision to lead his men to the front and to position them himself on Lipsett's left surprised some of his soldiers, Private Sid Cox among them. He thought that the brigadier's rather corpulent frame and distinctive headgear made him a good target: "We thought he was crazy, standing up there with his red hat on while we were taking all the cover we could till we got dug in." After leading the men to the front, Currie met with Lipsett at his headquarters in the ruins of Boetleer Farm, where he learned that Lipsett had at his disposal men belonging to five different British units, most in reserve, with several hundred men from the Durhams holding the most vital piece of real estate, the trenches that ran west towards where the Apex had been.

As dawn approached, Currie walked through mist and drizzle to Lieutenant-Colonel Tuxford's headquarters. The fastest way to his position was via a ridge then being watched by Sergeant Frederick Bagshaw, who later recalled wondering "who the Hell was that who was exposing himself to fire." Bagshaw's question was answered a few moments later when the man "came along the line into our battalion" and yelled, "Tuxford, who the Hell was that shooting at me?" Currie was less than disposed to accept Tuxford's explanation that the shots were fired by Germans who had occupied a house behind Tuxford's front line. Currie came close to being Canada's first general to be shot, as he realized when he later found a bullet in the folds of his riding breeches.*

Currie's hands-on approach is as far as one could get from the image of Great War generals left by such novels as *Generals Die in Bed*. The historian Tim Cook observes,

> It is tempting to say that neither Currie nor Turner understood that the role of the brigadier is to direct his troops—not to go find missing formations, not to lead formations through the night along roads being shelled, and surely not to be placing them in the line himself.
>
> Partially because they had such small staffs and partially because of the collapse of the communications systems, Currie and Turner, to a lesser extent, took it upon themselves to not just lead from the front, but to be organizing the front and generally making sure that the men were where they were needed. It looks strange, but they had few, if any, alternatives.

• • •

As Currie led his men back to the front lines and Creelman galloped for safety, hundreds of other Canadians began their first night as prisoners of war. Some, especially the injured, were thankful just to be alive. Almost all must have shared Major Peter Anderson's thoughts: "I was now a prisoner of war. What an awful feeling; what a humiliating position to be in. What will people at home think about me? A prisoner of war, and not wounded."[8]

When a young German soldier looked into the dugout in which

---

*On 3 June 1916, friendly fire killed Major-General Malcolm Mercer, who commanded Canada's 3rd Division. On 14 October 1918, Major-General Louis Lipsett was killed in battle.

James Mackie had sought shelter, "[their] eyes met, and he never gave a sign [of recognition]." Somewhat later, another soldier looked in, saw Mackie, and reached down to shake his foot, presumably to see if he was alive. Very much alive, though weak from the shock, Mackie came out, pointed to his arm, and said, "Doctor." The soldier directed him to a trench; from there, he was sent to a dressing station.

The men of Major Kirkpatrick's 3rd Battalion found fair treatment from the Saxons. Things changed, however, when they were transferred to the Prussians, who verbally abused them. "What are you Canadians doing over here? We are not at war with you," they said. "How much pay do you get, and how much do your men receive? A dollar a day! Four schillings! Four Marks! Then you are mercenaries. You fight for money. We Germans fight not for money but for our Fatherland." Soon Kirkpatrick's men suffered more than verbal insults. A staff officer drove a car into a column of "weary wounded prisoners, forcing them to jump to the ditches."

Lieutenant Edward Bellew was hauled before a battlefield court and charged with the war crime of firing his machine gun after the white flag was raised. He was convicted and faced summary execution. Luckily, German due process won out and his execution was delayed pending an appeal to a formal military court, which in the end acquitted the Victoria Cross recipient.[9]

For Nathan Rice's men, treatment worsened when they reached a divisional headquarters behind the German lines. There, a naval officer came over to Rice, pointed to his cap badge, which said "British Columbia," and asked "Where is that?" Rice answered, "It's out on the Pacific Coast, the west coast of Canada." The general in charge responded by yelling at Rice and his twenty-seven men. One of the Canadians spoke German and answered the general, who then asked him where he'd learned the language. His answer, "Hindenburg," the name of both a town in Germany and the general who in 1914 had won smashing victories at the Battle of the Mauseran Lakes in Poland, enraged the general, who pulled out his revolver and pointed it at his Canadian prisoners.

A moment later, the general ordered the escort to march Rice and his men off. A 16th Battalion soldier told Rice, "He's ordered them to take us over in the field and shoot us." Before they had gone twenty yards, the same naval officer who had asked Rice about his badge came running up and countermanded the order. Before they were marched back, the naval officer told Rice, "We are going right through to Ypres. We had seventy-three thousand men in the attacking force there and we had the Marines right at the back of us. Nothing could stop us."

Perhaps the first Canadians to see these marines were a soldier named R. C. Hunt and some other 7th Battalion men. Just behind the German lines, they met a detachment of marines who began whipping Hunt and the others with "bands full of cartridges." When Hunt began arguing "with a Hun for kicking one of my men," a marine smashed him in the jaw with a rifle butt, knocking out four of his teeth. Both acts violated the Hague Convention. Hunt and his comrades were also given little to eat, just some "dirty bread and acorn coffee." Later in the war, when the Royal Navy's embargo had cut the average calorie intake in Berlin drastically, a case could be made for giving prisoners on the march this meagre fare. On the afternoon of 24 April 1915, however, feeding so little to prisoners who had been in battle for days was a sign of disdain for the rules of war.

The Hague Convention enjoined POWs from contact with civilians, and from disrupting occupying forces as they went about their lawful activities. To remind Belgians of this, the Germans posted signs in public places, warning them against having contact with POWs. So when "a dear little fair-haired lass of about eight" threw Hunt an orange as he was being marched to Roulers, the Uhlan Guards were within their rights to arrest her. But the guard closest to Hunt went far beyond the rules of war: he began to pull out his lance. Hunt recalls, "I shouted to the child to get her to go to her house quickly, which, Thank God, she understood. I seized the reins of the brute's horse, only to get a whack on the head with the cane part of his lance."

Part 8

# After One Hundred Hours of Battle
4:00 a.m., 25 April to 4:00 a.m., 26 April 1915

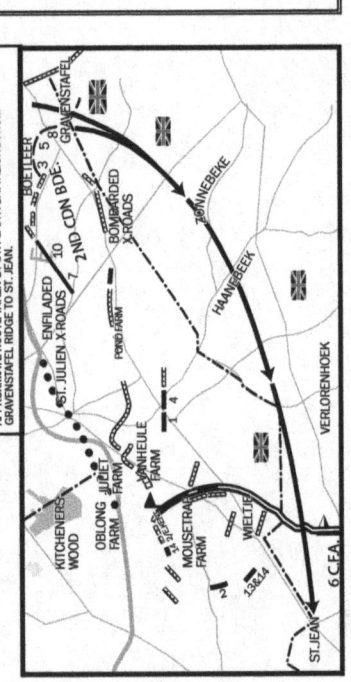
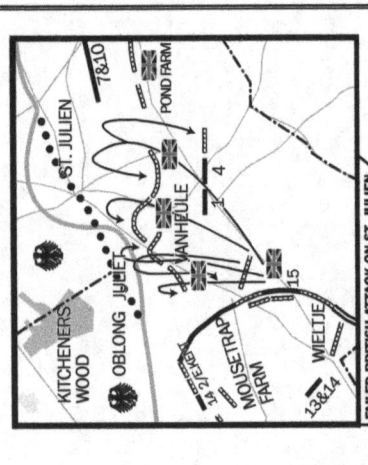

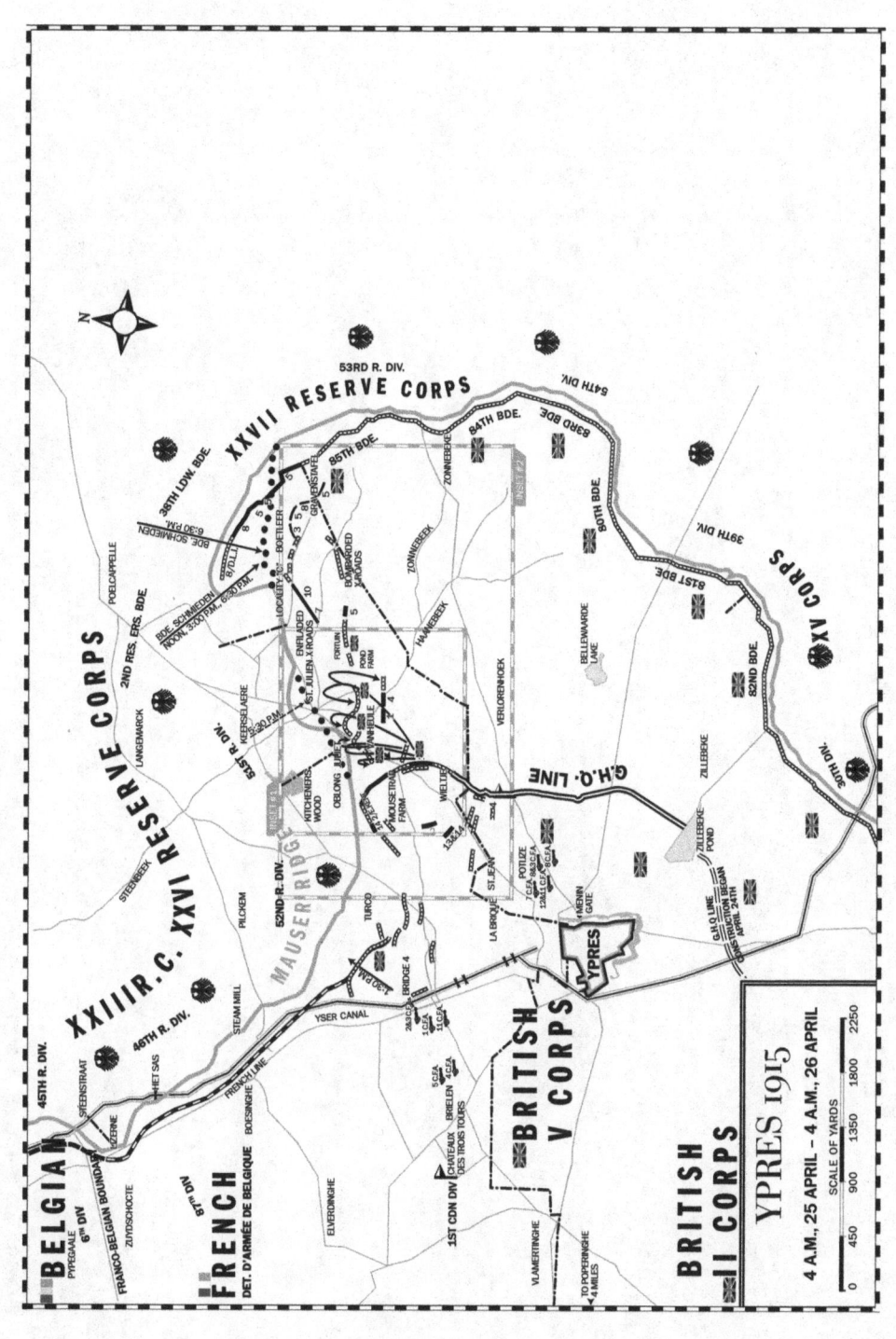

## Chapter 16

# "Why Do They Stop?"
### The 10th British Brigade's Attack on St. Julien and the Fall of Mouse Trap Farm

*Bid them be patient, and some day, anon,*
*They shall feel earth enwrapt in silence deep;*
*Shall greet, in wonderment, the quiet dawn,*
*And in content may turn them to their sleep.*
—John McCrae, "The Anxious Dead"

When he wrote the entry for the early morning of 25 April 1915, the war diarist of the 2nd Battalion of the King's Own Yorkshire Light Infantry (KOYLI) no doubt believed that his unit was where it was supposed to be: "At 3:30 a.m. an attack to retake Saint Julien commenced headed by the 10th Brigade. The KOYLI, now only 250 strong, remained in reserve."[1] Only later did he and his commanders learn that at 3:30 a.m., the KOYLI was supposed to be forming up for the attack on St. Julien, twenty-five hundred yards away, not sitting in the rain at the GHQ Line.

The KOYLI soldiers were not the only troops missing from the attack. General Alderson had placed fifteen battalions under Brigadier-General J. E. Hull's command. Four, besides the KOYLI, received their orders so late they could not join the attack.* No one noticed their absence, however, as troops bunched together by the hundreds to file out from two small gaps in the wire strung around the GHQ Line. The congestion was so great that Hull pushed zero hour back first to 4:30 a.m. and then to 5:30 a.m.

But once again, just as had happened prior to the first attack on Mauser Ridge, no one alerted the gunners of the delay. The Canadians and the British began firing at precisely 3:30 a.m. "The artillery fire was good," said Hull, "but there was not enough of it to seriously damage the enemy who were entrenched in a very strong position."²

The artillery fire may have discomfited a few Germans. A soldier named Heher ended up with a black-and-blue mark when a shrapnel ball hit the frame of his backpack. But they benefited from the fire in two important ways. First, it signalled an impending attack. Second, the shelling of St. Julien told them that the Canadians did not hold the village. In less than half an hour, elements of at least three German battalions moved into St. Julien and set up machine-gun, sniper, and artillery positions from which to fire into the fields over which Hull's men were about to advance.**

One difference between the twenty-third and the twenty-fifth was

---

*In addition to his own 10th Brigade, Hull was given the York and Durham Brigade, the KOYLI, the Queen Victoria Rifles of the 13th Brigade, the 1st Suffolks and 12th Regiment of the 28th Division, the 4th Canadian Battalion, and the 1st Battalion of the 27th Division (the 1st Royal Irish Regiment). The 1st Royal Irish Regiment, the Queen Victoria Rifles, the 1st Suffolks, and the Rangers did not receive their orders in time to join the attack.

**The first Allied soldiers to pay the price of this mistake wore Red Cross brassards and drove clearly marked ambulances belonging to the 3rd Field Ambulance. Shortly after the Germans moved back into St. Julien, a mix-up at Mouse Trap Farm sent two ambulances *into* the village in search of the 13th Battalion's aid post that had already been moved. As soon as the ambulances stopped, star shells lit the night and a fusillade killed the two drivers instantly. Private Nelson was hit in the head and Private Carr in the thigh; an infantryman sent along to help move downed trees was badly wounded. A German patrol then took the driver, a man named Pickles, prisoner along with Private A. W. Walsh and Private Carr. "Only one of the seven men with the two cars—Private Nelson—escaped, and he, when hit, falling off the car as though dead, managed to creep into the roadside ditch and, escaping detection, worked his way back to our lines," recalled Walsh.

that when the guns lifted, some troops moved forward. They shouldn't have. But Brigadier-General J. E. Bush's 5th Green Howards and 5th Durham Light Infantry did not get the orders delaying the attack. Both units were greener than the Canadians who attacked Kitcheners Wood and Mauser Ridge. Still, the fact that they advanced at all speaks highly of the British soldiers' commitment and drive. Their advance—or, to be more precise, their retreat—further reduced Hull's force, for once the German guns forced them to retire, both units were effectively out of the mix.

As 5:30 a.m. neared, Hull's force, which included five thousand men of his own 10th Brigade, among "the most disciplined and best-trained soldiers that remained available to the Commander-in-Chief [Sir John French] at this stage of the war," moved into position south of St. Julien.[3] What was to be a pre-dawn surprise attack proceeded by a bombardment (albeit a short one) had become an advance in broad daylight without preparatory artillery fire, over ground that neither Hull nor his officers had reconnoitred. The difference became apparent even before the men had fully formed up. Snipers hidden in the grasses and crops of the farms south, east, and west of St. Julien picked off Hull's troops. Discipline held, however, and at 5:30 a.m.—while the issue of the *Times* that carried the first news of the 22 April gas attack was being distributed across London—his troops advanced.*

The attack started well. Some of Hull's men advanced in rushes, keeping their assigned frontage despite heavy shell- and machine-gun fire. Others advanced in what Britain's official historian called "faultless order, worthy of the traditions of its home at Shorncliffe, where Sir John Moore had trained the battalions that became the nucleus of the Light

---

*About the same time, employees at Harrod's were removing the spring fashions from the windows near the Knightsbridge Road entrance. In place of the clothes, which, to conserve on material, were among the first to sport narrow lapels, a counter was set up, and employees demonstrated how to make respirators and sold the cotton wool, gauze, and elastic needed to do it. Volunteers were instructed to send batches of no fewer than one hundred to the chief ordinance officer at the Royal Army Clothing Department.

Division."⁴ The description of the regimental historian of RIR 236 is equally purple: "Wave after wave attacked.... Brave and with a proud disregard for death the Brits attacked into our rain of bullets."

Quickly, those bullets—fired from German machine-gunners situated in St. Julien, on Oblong and Juliet farms, and as far away as the trenches south of Kitcheners Wood—turned the stately advance into a latter-day "Charge of the Light Brigade."* From his position on the left of the attack, the future cartoonist Bruce Bairnsfather, a second lieutenant with the 1st Royal Warwicks, saw a chaotic scene: "Bullets were flying through the air in all directions. Ahead in the semidarkness I could just see the forms of men running out into the open fields on either side ... and beyond them a continuous heavy crackling of rifle-fire showed me the main direction of the attack. A few men had gone down already, and no wonder—the air was thick with bullets."⁵

Half a lifetime later, Lieutenant Walter Critchley, who was among those who had attacked Kitcheners Wood, could still see the carnage in his mind's eye: "They were lined up ... in a long line, straight up, and the Hun opened up on them with machine guns. They were just raked down. It was pathetic."⁶ One soldier from RIR 235, which beat off the attack, had a different view: "Now one could see the enemies taking to their heels all over the place between Vanheule and Frezenberg. The shrapnel fire from our artillery annihilated more than one of them."

For an unnamed, inexperienced staff officer with the Canadians at Mouse Trap Farm, the battle quickly became inexplicable. He watched as hundreds of men appeared to lie down but not entrench. "Why do they stop?" he asked. Someone responded, "They are dead."⁷ Almost a century later, this laconic answer has lost little of its poignancy.

A few of the survivors of the hundreds who died belonged to Bairnsfather's machine-gun section. "Come on, you chaps," he urged his

---

*Oblong Farm was eight hundred yards to Hull's left front, Juliet Farm five hundred yards to his right front, and Kitcheners Wood one thousand yards directly in front; the fact that there were German machine guns in each of these positions was a direct result of Turner's obsession with manning the GHQ Line.

men. "We'll cross this field, and get to that hedge over there." There, at least, they could take cover.⁸ Several hundred yards to his right, across fields over which bullets cut like a scythe "through the grass, three or four inches above" their heads, a section of a company led by Captain Tobin Maunsell of the Royal Dublin Fusiliers (RDF) found a ditch that offered the promise of protection and also led into the ruined village, thus affording a way forward. Maunsell could not know that elements of RIRs 235 and 236 waited at the other end of the ditch; not a man escaped. And few RDF men escaped a simultaneous thrust led by Captain J. M. Dickie, whose after-action report records the deaths of British soldiers with the surnames Young, French, and Salveson, just three of the many who "mopped up trying to get there [St. Julien] in extended order."⁹

• • •

For a time, the attack worried the commanders of RIR 238, on Dickie's left front. Given their position, looking down into the British firing trenches and a small hollow where the British troops were forming up, the Germans should not have been concerned. But when the attack started, the 238's gunners were caught cleaning their guns' sights and breech mechanisms, which had been dirtied by the rain that fell during the night. Worse, Leutnant Drach's unit had only one machine gun, with just a few boxes of ammunition, and fewer than two hundred cartridges per man, scarcely more than ten minutes' fire. Here, British bullets told: "Sergeant Eiermann, my dear comrade from Eberbach [a town near Heidelberg], fell from a shot through the heart. Private Puttmann fell from a shot through the neck. . . . Little Weber, a recruit from 1914, was wounded from a ricochet through the eye into his brain."

As the British inched their way forward, Drach, playing the part Leutnant Grotrian had on the morning of 23 April, reminded his men that they had to save their ammunition, that "each shot had to be a hit because we wanted to still have ammunition for the last moment of the enemy assault." For a moment, it appeared that the gunners of the 26th Artillery Battery, situated on a farm near Langemarck, were lending the

British a hand; the battery's first volley landed so close to the front of their own trench that Drach and his men had to take cover. Leutnant Schmidt ran back under fire to re-establish the connection between Drach's force and its artillery, just as Private Lettemen had at Mauser Ridge. Drach's men waited anxiously for the next round.

Thanks to Schmidt, the "artillery observation was excellent. The next volley was further to the front." This time, instead of pushing their bodies against the side of their trench and covering their heads, Drach's men watched "shrapnel bursting over the heads of the advancing Brits." To Drach's amazement, the mounting dead did not stop the attack cold; waves of men came and threaded their way through the gathering dead and wounded. At one point, Drach feared that the next wave of attackers, whom he incorrectly identified as Canadians, would break upon his trenches. At least some of the men in and near Drach's line heard what Bairnsfather heard: the "enormous ponderous, gurgling, rotating sound of large shells" that blasted apart the advancing British lines. Those who saw the shells detonate witnessed something similar to what Bairnsfather saw just eighty yards away from him: "Four columns of black smoke and earth shot up a hundred feet into the air.... Then four mighty reverberating explosions ... rent the air. A row of four 'Jack Johnsons' had landed not a hundred yards away, right amongst the lines of men, lying firing in extended order."

German gunners did more than protect their trenches. In an effort to sow panic and prevent reinforcements from arriving, they rained shells all along the Allied lines. One battery targeted a building on Mouse Trap Farm that housed an aid station. As Bairnsfather and another soldier carried away a Canadian officer who had been shot in the chest, shells "explod[ed] round in great profusion. Every minute, one heard the swish rush overhead, the momentary pause, saw the cloud of red dust, then 'Crumph!'"[10]

• • •

A thousand yards to the east of Mouse Trap Farm, there unfolded a scene that would have been as much at home in a British music hall as it was in

Flanders. Having lost all their officers, the men of the 2nd Royal Dublin Fusiliers were on the verge of retiring in a rout. They rallied, however,

> when the small untidy figure of Colonel Loveband, clad in an ancient "British warm" [an officer's overcoat] and carrying a blackthorn stick, approached quietly across the open, making, as he walked, the lie-down signal with his stick. The effect was instantaneous and for hundreds of yards along the front the men dropped and used their entrenching tool.[11]

To the Fusiliers' left, German bullets and shells chewed up 425 men and 12 officers belonging to the 7th Argyll and Sutherland Highlanders. At 6:15 a.m., the Northumberland 4th and 7th Regiments passed through the British lines and started moving over the ground immediately south of Juliet Farm. They too soon died by the score. At 9:15 a.m., Hull signalled Alderson that the attack had failed, that there had been heavy casualties, and that his 10th Brigade and three Northumberland regiments had effectively been destroyed. In just over two hours, Hull's brigade lost more than 50 percent of its strength: 2,346 men and 73 officers.

• • •

As Bairnsfather walked on the sloping bank of a gully on his return from Mouse Trap Farm, where he'd taken the wounded officer, he "heard a colossal rushing swish in the air, and then didn't hear the resultant crash." He continues: "All seemed dull and foggy, a sort of silence, worse than the shelling, surrounded me. I lay in a filthy stagnant ditch covered with mud and slime from head to foot. I suddenly started to tremble all over. I couldn't grasp where I was. I lay and trembled. I had been blown up [into the air and thrown some distance away] by the shell."[12] Bairnsfather was one of the lucky few to survive the attack. Almost twenty-five hundred of Britain's best trained soldiers died in less than two hours; in total, more than three thousand British soldiers were lost in this attack, more than were lost on the other side of Europe when Australian and New Zealand regiments stormed ashore at Gallipoli that same day. The attack was not, however, a total waste. It weakened and disrupted German forces that were supposed to take St. Julien and perhaps Ypres itself. Although Hull's men failed to retake St. Julien and Kitcheners Wood, the frontage of Hull's attack—which was seven battalions wide—meant that when the survivors crawled back and dug in, they sketched a line across the gap that had opened the day before between Brigadier-General Arthur Currie's left and the GHQ Line. That thin line to Currie would not last long.

• • •

Since 4:00 a.m., the far left of Currie's line had been manned by the composite 7th/10th Battalion, commanded by Major Odlum. German records of the Reussner Regiment, itself a composite force of Reserve-Infanterie-Regiments 241 and 242, confused an action with Odlum's men with the "furious counter-attack" against St. Julien, twelve hundred yards away.[13] Just after Odlum took possession of a trench near the Hannebeek, his scouts noticed two soldiers moving out from behind the cover of a ruined building. Without waiting for orders, the Canadians opened fired and the figures fell. "Someone," Odlum recalled "shouted from the right that they were our own troops, and two of our men ran forward to see if this was true." In short order, those two men were shot and wounded.

In the half-light of a dawn darkened by the morning mist, and unsure exactly where the Suffolks were on his left, Odlum found the situation confusing. It became more confusing moments later, when troops appeared from a trench about two hundred yards away that Odlum thought the Suffolks were holding, "and fire again opened from both sides." Concerned that his men were shooting at British soldiers, Odlum ordered cease fire. A straggler from the 2nd Battalion who spoke German volunteered to investigate the mist-enshrouded troops. "He held out his hands and advanced, shouting out in German. When he had gone about 50 yards, he was shot down." Barely had Odlum seen this brave volunteer die when a large number of Germans appeared. They "were held and driven to ground by rife fire." In his report, Oberstleutnant Reussner—who, with his riding-switch, monocle, and cigar, could have served as a model for Bairnsfather's cartoons—confirms how close Odlum's men were: "British effected a lodgement 150 metres in front" of his force.[14]

• • •

At 2:00 p.m., a runner arrived at the Château des Trois Tours carrying a message that Snow had written three hours earlier. The message illustrates again how the realities of 2nd Ypres overwhelmed the communication systems. By the time Alderson learned that Snow's artillery officers had noticed German units massing in the direction of Passchendaele (to the northeast), the composite Schmieden Brigade had broken into Snow's trenches and was readying to attack Currie's 8th and 5th Battalions.\* The message also makes clear that Snow had no idea where General Hull's force was, thus underscoring the fact that Edmonds vastly overstated things by claiming that "the real commander of the battle was General Snow." In the hours after the dawn attack, he was just as much in the dark as Alderson about what was happening on the battlefield.[15] Finally, Snow's message told Alderson that shells were falling all over the right (east) side of the salient.

The cascade of shells and machine-gun fire further mocked General Quiquandon's claim on the twenty-third that the Germans were running low on ammunition. High-explosive shells fired from the north fell near Hull's own headquarters in Potijze, almost two miles behind the Canadian lines and a bit more than a thousand yards east of Ypres. At 9:00 a.m., having already enduring four and half hours of shrapnel shells, the men of the 4th Green Howards and 5th Durham Light Infantry, who had belatedly moved to the right of the remnants of Hull's brigade, began what would be four hours of torment from high-explosive shells.

---

\*The break in Snow's line, effected by RIR 234, was a small one of about sixty yards. After two attempts to retake the trench failed, the break was isolated when the men dug another trench around it.

Shells fired east from Passchendaele and north from St. Julien fell on Odlum's trenches west of Locality "C." Machine guns pushed up from St. Julien raked his positions. At noon, after failing to get the Durham Light Infantry to stage a local attack and clear the machine guns out of the ruined houses at what Allied maps denoted as D.8.c.5.9 and D.7.c.3.8, Odlum asked Currie to organize an attack; Currie, however, had no reserves. "In justice to the DLI's commander, he was unsure of his orders," Odlum later averred. At 12:40 p.m., Currie signalled Alderson for artillery support to silence (at least) the guns from St. Julien, and to ask why the 1st Brigade, which was supposed to move to Currie's left in conjunction with Hull's dawn attack, had not done so.*

Shells punished Currie's men, who had withstood the gas attack the previous day. A piece of shrapnel tore into twenty-six-year-old Samuel Archer's right thigh and a bullet lodged in his right arm. "I crawled half a mile to get my wounds dressed," the 8th Battalion man wrote his parents from his hospital bed in England. "The shells were bursting all around me, and the bullets coming in all directions over my head, while the dead were lying everywhere. No matter where you went you could see nothing but dead bodies."[16] According to Lieutenant Edison Lynn, the gunfire, which could come from several direction and all angles, "was not concentrated on any one area continuously. It would be heavy for a time at one point and then would shift, apparently being directed by observation planes or balloons." In the late afternoon, a shell that burst near a bridge over the canal killed twenty-eight-year-old Ivor Beynon, who belonged to 1st Field Company Canadian Engineers, which earlier had braved the shellfire to transport to General Hull's headquarters seven wagons filled with the supplies needed to set up barbed wire. Hull had lost so many men, however, that he could not scrape together the work parties the engineers needed, and the wire was never strung.

When the intensity of the fire lessened, Lynn wondered "if this lull

---

*Had these men been in the position Currie had been told they would be, they could have offered aid to Odlum.

means ground gained or lost." During one such lull, Lieutenant Stanley E. Lovelace noted in his diary that men and pastors took the opportunity to bury the dead. "I saw little services where Padres were sitting on trench-edge or funk holes with a grateful group of soldiers round about listening to their message."[17]

• • •

Near 4:00 p.m., shelling finally overwhelmed Mouse Trap Farm. In a 9 May letter to his wife, Turner wrote:

> As our house had become dangerous, we moved into a corner of a cow stable early in the morning. The enemy found out where we were, and about 4 p.m. they dropped 70 high explosive shells about, and on, our buildings with a radius of 30 yards. It was most nerve racking, and drove 4 officers with us silly. In the end we had to get out. We had to swim across the moat which was full of dirty water. I hugged the bank for some time before I could make [up] my mind to a wetting, but did it in the end.*

If anything, Turner's letter understates the scene. Near the field dressing station, not far from the farmhouse where Turner's command was situated, there stood a small-arms ammunition dump. Shortly after 4:00 p.m., fires started by the shelling reached that house, and within moments the building exploded, sending thousands of splinters and bullets in all directions, including over the ground on which the wounded lay. Somehow, Captain Francis A. C. Scrimger, an army doctor, remained untouched as he stood directing stretcher-bearers to remove the wounded.** Scrimger's luck did not extend far; standing beside him, his staff officer, Captain Harold McDonald, "was literally filled with splinters. One in the cheek, one in the eye, one in the shoulder, the right lung

---

*Later that day, Currie's staff too would have to swim again to escape his headquarters at Pond Farm.
**Scrimger and John McCrae were colleagues at McGill University's medical school.

and the neck."[18] Scrimger carried McDonald to a nearby stable, which, it soon became clear, provided little safety.

There is some controversy about exactly what happened next. The notice in the *London Gazette* announcing that Scrimger had been awarded the Victoria Cross states that after leaving the stable, he found he was "unable alone to carry this officer further."[19] But McDonald later told reporters, "Captain Scrimger carried me down to a moat 50 feet in front where we lay half in water."[20] Whatever happened, Scrimger earned Canada's fourth Victoria Cross in three days for curling his own body around McDonald's head and shoulders to protect him from heavy shells fired from as far as four miles away.

Alderson did not learn of the destruction of Turner's headquarters until 8:10 p.m., almost two hours after Turner wired his commander and four hours after the 3rd Canadian Infantry Brigade's headquarters was destroyed. Turner's message also told Alderson that the GHQ Line remained in Canadian and British hands.

• • •

While the pressure built on Mouse Trap Farm, German infantry improved their positions. RIRs 236 and 234, which had advanced into St. Julien, connected the remnants of the British trenches to create a continuous line. A lull in the fighting allowed Leutnants Grimm and Langer of RIR 236 to reconnoitre the area before looking for a building or dugout in which to house their regiment's command post. In an abandoned farm, "plates filled with soup that had not been eaten" told them just how surprised the Canadians had been by the extent and speed of the German penetration the previous day.

Grimm recalled that in another farm, they "found on a bier parts of our excellent artillery officer Leutnant Cooper from the RFR 51." Though they might sound callous to our ears, Grimm's words were not. Rather, they are an excellent example of the way soldiers in battle conceive of the death that is all around them. In that farm, Grimm and his men found many things they hardly remembered existed, including "supplies of delicious foods which we enjoyed very much." His words would be recognizable to any veteran of combat—men who pass moment to moment in a world *in extremis,* and who find in small bodily pleasures, like taste, an escape from pain, suffering, and fear. The jocular tone comes through even in translation: "Fortunately, the fire came down short of us. The splinters falling into the trench were polite enough to spare us."

• • •

Forty minutes after Snow's message arrived, at 2:40 p.m., Alderson received a message that had been sent at 1:24 p.m. The first part of the message told him what he already knew, that the Germans held Kitcheners Wood. The second part read, "Fortuin doubtful enemy close to line of stream running south from D.8 and 9." If true, it signalled disaster. In fact, as Alderson would later learn, Fortuin had just been garrisoned by the same York and Durham Brigade that a day earlier had refused to move at Currie's behest. Their presence surprised units belonging to RIR 233, then probing south of St. Julien. The 233's regimental historian, in a claim made for home consumption, said that the *Feldgrauen* were forced by "strong fire from heavy calibre guns to seek shelter in what had been a British dugout and in basements of ruined buildings." Neither British nor Canadian records support his assertion that the Kaiser's men found "many British wounded who had been forgotten when the others took to their heels. Their imploring voices asked for water. We took them to our first aid station." While some Germans did most definitely take wounded British and Canadian troops to aid stations, these last lines were likely penned with an eye towards countering the charge that, by using poison gas, the German army had violated the Hague Convention and placed itself beyond the pale of civilized society.

For the enemy to have reached the "stream running south from D.8. and 9," they would have had to smash through Currie's long-suffering battalions. Six minutes later, Alderson sent a message to Hull that the Germans were "attacking from the north in long columns which are in D.7.8," which would have meant that the Germans had broken through

Currie's positions. Neither report was true, but together they set in motion the events that led to the collapse of Currie's position.

The first report seems to have originated with observers who misunderstood the failure of a relief action by the reserve company of the Durham Light Infantry, which had moved into position on the left of the 8th Battalion just before dawn. The Durhams, who had had no trench training, learned the art of war quickly. Just after occupying their trenches, to the left of the 8th Battalion, they fired on Major Harold Mathews's company, which they were replacing. Fortunately, they missed. Some eight hours later, the Germans launched a two-pronged attack. Infantry assaulted from the Durhams' front and grenade-throwers from the left. The Durhams drove off the frontal assault and held back the German advance, even though they were forced to retire to a reserve trench. The troops that were seen retreating belonged, it would seem, to the Durhams' reserve company, which was unable to get past a hedge some distance behind the Durhams' main position.

Neither British nor Canadian records allow us to determine exactly what the "long columns" in Alderson's message were. The most likely candidate is a unit of the Durhams (holding a reserve trench behind Tuxford's 5th Battalion), which broke sometime after noon. Tuxford rushed into their midst and somehow, above the din of battle, rallied them. Given that Tuxford was later accused by some of his junior officers of arrogance and self-aggrandizement, it is worth noting his understanding of the psychology of battle. He recognized that while these troops had broken and run, they had not displayed a lack of moral fibre:

> I gathered them in and placed them in the trenches with instructions to pick up and use the rifles that were lying around. Raw troops as they were, rushed into the midst of a veritable inferno, they had more than bravely borne themselves throughout that long morning's bombardment [from 9:00 a.m. to noon, between forty-five and sixty-eight shells landed every minute], until the strain became more than human men could stand.[21]

Alderson signalled Snow for three battalions to man the switch line, a defensive line that was to have been dug during the night some distance behind Gravenstafel Ridge. He had no way of knowing that this line did not exist, largely because Lipsett and Tuxford had convinced the commanders of the units that had been sent forward to dig the trench that it was more important for them to put their troops into the Canadians' thinning line; no one alerted anyone up the chain of command, Currie included, that this switch line existed only on paper.

Had Snow complied with Alderson's request and sent three battalions forward, the Canadians would have learned about absence of the switch line near 3:30 p.m. Instead, Snow all but ignored Alderson's request, sending just a single battalion of the Durham Light Infantry only a couple of hundred yards north of his own headquarters.

## Chapter 17

## "Do Not Shoot! Ve Vas French"
### The Canadians Retire from Gravenstafel Ridge

> *Beneath the shower of lead*
> *Of poison and of fire,*
> *He charged and fought and bled*
> *Ablaze with one desire.*
> —Canon F. Scott, "A Canadian"

The curtain rose on the final act of the Battle for Gravenstafel Ridge when the Schmieden Brigade launched its second attack of the day near 3:00 p.m. In his comments to Edmonds's official British history, Brigadier-General Currie was hardly able to capture what happened when he wrote that Major Odlum's men were "simply blown out of their position" near Locality "C." Sergeant Raymond MacIlree—who less than seventy-two hours earlier had heard someone cry, "They've broken through! They've broken through!" and a soldier near him reply, "Shut up, you bastard"—escaped from a trench the Germans had seized after they turned the composite 7th/10th Battalion's flanks. In a letter to his parents, he wrote,

> The Germans were coming in thousands, so we worked our way down the trenches to the left. In this way, we kept up a running battle . . . leaving one trench, and running across the open to another one in the rear. Our

artillery was so chived about [harassed] that they gave us no help, while we were being mowed down by shrapnel, machine guns and rifles.

It was sure a merry little Hell. . . . People kept getting killed, in such messy ways, that it became a nightmare. It is funny how calm you get. A man falls beside you, and you must heave him out of the way, like a sack of flour.

Finally, we reached the last trench, which was simply jammed with men from all our regiments.[1]

A few hundred yards to the composite battalion's right, the weight of German infantry did what shelling alone could not, breaking the Durhams on Lieutenant-Colonel Louis Lipsett's left. A counterattack by Lieutenant-Colonel Turnbull's 8th Durham Light Infantry failed. By 3:30 p.m., "troops of all units were pouring over the crest and retreating down the reverse slope of Gravenstafel Ridge." Odlum reacted at once and, along with Major W. A. Munro of the 8th Battalion, succeeded in "getting them turned around and returned to the trenches near the crest" of the ridge. The Durhams' withdrawal once again left Lipsett's left open, and more important, it opened the way for hundreds of German troops to storm towards Boetleer Farm.

Covered by the turnip plants, Major Harold Mathews's men were not badly placed. Amazingly, despite hours of searching by German artillery, his force took only one casualty. The situation on the farm, however, was "a regular shambles." The cellar beneath the ruins of the main farmhouse "was full of wounded and groaning men," as were the few remaining outbuildings. Good defensive placement counts for much, but on the afternoon of 25 April 1915, numbers counted for more. The farm fell in just over half an hour.

Lipsett's men staged a fighting retreat. As the Germans swarmed the farm, the Little Black Devils moved up to the ridge on their right (i.e., closer to the 8th Battalion's line and farther from the supposed safety of the GHQ Line), where they occupied "some old trenches near another farm," with the aim of preventing further German advances.

Unfortunately, the Germans saw them all too clearly, and soon high-explosive shells arced towards them. "One shell dropped right in the trench and blew twelve men out at once." A few moments later, Lipsett gave the order to retire to another farm about a quarter mile to their right rear.

The farm was near Lieutenant-Colonel Tuxford's 5th Battalion headquarters, where General Currie was quickly coming to the conclusion that, finally, the time had come to retire. The problem was not so much that Currie's positions were inherently untenable, but that the generals above had abandoned the brigade. Neither Currie nor Tuxford (nor Lipsett nor Odlum, who would shortly join their brigadier in Tuxford's headquarters) left a complete record of the discussions. The facts before them, however, are clear. There had been no arrival of "strong reinforcements," as promised by General Alderson at 3:25 p.m. What was left of Brigadier-General Malcolm Mercer's 1st Brigade had not moved into position on Currie's left, as Lieutenant-Colonel Gordon-Hall had ordered the night before (Indeed, Mercer's men were dug in well south of St. Julien.) Hull's attack on St. Julien and Kitcheners Wood had failed. Alderson's message that the Germans were "attacking from the north in long columns" told Currie and his officers that Alderson's staff believed that Gravenstafel Ridge—and thus Currie's brigade—had been lost. According to Canada's official historian, when Currie was told that the York and Durham Brigades (which had refused to move the previous day) had occupied Fortuin, he said, "[This] could not have been a hard task as the Germans have never been in it."[2]

Shortly after 4:00 p.m., word arrived that an attack against the 8th Durham Light Infantry had killed or wounded every man in the trenches on the far eastern side of the ridge. According to Lipsett, the situation was stable for the moment, as the "enemy did not appear to be pressing attack except by artillery fire," but with only one hundred men left, Turnbull and now Currie and his officers knew that for the men on the left of the Allied line, the end was not far away. When it came, the list of killed, wounded, and captured included three commanders—two who had led their men into the trenches and thirty-eight-year-old Captain George Northwood, commander the 8th Battalion's No. 4 Company—every one of No. 4 Company's officers, 139 of its men, and almost all of the Durhams. The few who escaped owed their freedom to Sergeant W. A. Alldritt, a physical director at the Winnipeg YMCA, who had celebrated his thirty-fourth birthday a week earlier. As machine-gunners Frederick Hall, Donald Bellew, Charles Painting, and George Davison had done earlier in the battle, Alldritt continued to fire until he was overpowered.

Whatever hope Currie and his officers may have had that help might still be sent vanished at 5:05 p.m., when a copy of the 1:55 p.m. message from Alderson to Plumer arrived. There is no record of Currie's or his officers' words when they read it:

> In view of strong attack made against my left
> of 28th Div. and my right am ordering
> Gen. Snow to move Durham L.I. Bde.. to
> hold line made by 28th Div. along the road
> in square D.13 and 14 aaa If by any chance
> they cannot get to this road in time they
> are to hold line of stream in D.24 and
> 19 aaa Addressed 5th Corps, rept 28th
> Div. and 10th Bde..

According to Duguid, Currie's brigade major erred when, in the rush to decode the message, he wrote D.24 and 19, when what was meant was C.24, D.19. The mistake hardly mattered, however. Both sets of coordinates put the rest of the Durham Light Infantry more than a thousand yards *behind* Gravenstafel Ridge, and thus in no position to help Currie's ever-thinning 2nd Canadian Infantry Brigade or the few Durhams left alive in scattered trenches around Boetleer Farm. This last message was the final straw. "I concluded," Currie wrote in his report, that "our position had been judged hopeless and ordered units to retire at dusk."

. . .

The historian John Dixon argues both that Currie misread the tactical situation and that his commanders disagreed with his decision to withdraw. Neither claim stands up to scrutiny, although Dixon's sequence is correct. After hearing that the rest of the Durham Light Infantry was not moving to support his men on the ridge, Currie decided to withdraw. As Dixon puts it: "Currie assumed, quite wrongly, that his position on the apex was becoming untenable."[3] Yet Currie's reasoning was not based on whether his position could be held *per se*, but on whether his brigade was going to receive the support it needed to hold the position. And he knew those reinforcements would not be coming. What's more, Currie's men had had little or no food and water for three days. Even worse, they had been awake so long that even officers like MacIlree were starting to hallucinate: "I saw coming from the right Noah's ark, two by two, just like a child. They came and they climbed up the chimney, the elephants and the giraffes and all the rest of it, and down the other side." Were it not for Tuxford's emergency shipment of fifty-five thousand rounds (from stocks that could not be replenished), Lipsett's men would have run out of ammunition in the middle of the afternoon.

Dixon is correct when he says that Tuxford disagreed with Currie's order to withdraw. But he goes too far when he writes, "It was still daylight and Tuxford argued with his brigadier that it would be madness to retire, but the order stood."[4] Tuxford did argue with Currie when the brigadier told him that it was time for the 5th Battalion to dig in a half mile to the rear, near Bombarded Crossroads, but the colonel never used the word "madness" (although Frederick B. Bagshaw, Tuxford's orderly room sergeant, did when speaking for himself in his private diary). Tuxford simply did what any good commander of a battalion should have done: he pointed out the difficulties of withdrawing in daylight. But he did not disparage or think of disobeying the order.

Nor is there support for Dixon's claim that "neither Tuxford nor Lipsett had been happy with the order, which had clearly placed adjacent brigades in peril and had given ground to the enemy."[5] Tuxford's objection was to the time the order was to be carried out, not to its substance. When Lipsett and Odlum learned of the order shortly after 5:15 p.m., they "agree[d] with it," or so Currie wrote later. None of Currie's field commanders, either in their after-action reports or in any subsequent venue, questioned Currie's order to withdraw.

• • •

There was, however, an intense argument about the order, which Bagshaw witnessed, between two of Tuxford's officers: Major Hugh Dyer, a fifty-three-year-old Manitoba farmer, and Captain Edward Hilliam, both of whom wanted to take the order to retire forward. Just as Hilliam, who had written out the orders, started to leave with them, Dyer grabbed them, saying, "Give me that, Hilliam." Hilliam responded, "No. You're second-in-command. You stay. It's my job to look after this."

Their brigadier was not amused and angrily ordered Tuxford to do something. Splitting the difference, Tuxford gave the order for the company on the right to Dyer and the one for the company on the left to Hilliam. Both men managed to avoid German artillery but not rifle fire. A bullet pierced one of Hilliam's lungs, but somehow he got the message through. Even though Dyer was hit "within an inch of his heart... [he] managed to struggle to within 10 yards of the trenches, where he was hauled in by the men and the message delivered." When Tuxford's right withdrew, some carried Dyer on a stretcher while others looked for Hilliam. Once at Tuxford's headquarters, Dyer refused to be carried any farther. Embodying an ethos that would soon vanish, he said, "No, I'll go as a soldier should. Send for my horse." Then he rode, alone, to the battalion's dressing station, recalled Bagshaw. The soldiers who looked for Hilliam found, instead, a board with the words "I have crawled home."[6]*

---

*Hilliam recovered. Two years later, at Vimy, he commanded the 10th Canadian Infantry Brigade.

While Odlum was rallying stragglers and placing them in positions in and around Bombarded Crossroads, he sent a runner to the composite 7th/10th Battalion with the order to withdraw. Lipsett, to Odlum's admiration, carried the orders forward to his own 8th Battalion.

. . .

The withdrawal of the composite 7th/10th was accomplished without the Germans realizing it, though over a much longer period than anyone could have expected; the 10th Battalion was not fully withdrawn until early on 26 April. Part of the reason for the delay was that the runner Odlum sent to the 10th Battalion never arrived. By the time a second runner made it to the 7th Battalion's trenches, the composite battalion had been dissolved, so the orders that reached the 7th Battalion, which remained under Odlum, were no longer valid for the 10th Battalion, which had come under the command of Major Percy Guthrie, a thirty-year-old New Brunswick politician who had hurried to Flanders from London when 2nd Ypres began. Neither Currie nor Odlum had been informed that the composite battalion had been dissolved, still another example of the collapse of the communication system.

As the men of the 7th Battalion slipped off to their left (southwest), Guthrie sent runners back to the brigade headquarters for his orders. Though neither knew about the other one, both Guthrie and Odlum found themselves doing what almost every other senior officer was doing during 2nd Ypres: running around the battlefield trying to make some order out of it. Guthrie knew where his troops were but did not know his orders; Odlum knew his orders but did not know where his troops were. And both almost came face to face with German troops: Odlum at the old 8th Battalion headquarters, and Guthrie at the site of Currie's old headquarters at Pond Farm. Shortly after 8:00 p.m., Odlum went to Bombarded Crossroads and found the remnants of his 7th Battalion, which he marched to Wieltje and then to St. Jean, three and a half miles away.

Guthrie, who barely escaped capture by the Germans, did not return to the 10th Battalion until early on the twenty-sixth. Before dawn, Lieutenant Walter Critchley, who had successfully avoided the Germans and found Currie's headquarters, returned with orders expressly written for Guthrie's command. "Without this order," the major wrote to Currie on 2 May, "I would have maintained my position and been annihilated." Hidden by the fog that descended on the battlefield before dawn on the twenty-sixth, Guthrie successfully withdrew his men. In his report, he strikes the same note Winston Churchill would twenty-five years later, when after Dunkirk he told the House of Commons, "Wars are not won by evacuations." Guthrie wrote, "I felt rotten about having to give way. . . . There was nothing else to be done, as our right was left open, and our men were worn out. If two regiments had marched up to help, we would not have given an inch."

A few of Guthrie's men, such as 10th Battalion Private Sid Cox, who had become mixed up with a British unit (likely a small detachment from the 2nd East Yorks) that for some reason did not receive the order to retire, owed their escape to both luck and pluck. Cox was adamant that he would not surrender, even though the Germans were once again within earshot.* His comrades were less sure until he yelled, "You can surrender if you damn well please." But he was going to take his chances with a ditch that ran behind their trench. All but one of the British soldiers followed him—right to 11th Brigade's lines.

• • •

Despite their desire to remain in their trenches on Gravenstafel Ridge, Tuxford and Lipsett had agreed that if they had to retire, they would do so "in succession of companies from the left," starting with Lipsett's left. This plan came apart almost at once. Tuxford's heart must have skipped a beat when he saw that Lipsett's 8th Battalion "came out almost as a whole," their every step punctuated by the roar of exploding shells.

---

*Just before the 10th Battalion stormed into Kitcheners Wood, Cox heard a German call out, "Hey, Canada, come here."

Perhaps because he had been with his own men from the beginning, he had not noticed what days of combat had done to them; perhaps because Lipsett's men had been more affected by the gas attack on the morning of 24 April, they were more haggard. Whatever the reason, Tuxford's empathy for the men he saw through the gathering dusk, who were withdrawing in a disorderly way that threatened Tuxford's own men, is notable: "It was pitiful to see these men, who had come from the very jaws of hell, staggering along absolutely dazed, gassed, hungry, and parched with thirst."[7] After burying his maps and papers, Tuxford sent his own staff back towards what he, Lipsett, and Currie assumed was an already prepared switch line a thousand or so yards south of Gravenstafel Ridge. He watched as one after another of his officers ran the "gauntlet of intense artillery fire, which was now sweeping the reverse slope" of the ridge on which the 8th and 5th Battalions had fought the Germans to a standstill.

• • •

Major Von Heygendorff of Reserve-Infanterie-Regiment 247 mistook the Canadians for British, but the disorderly retreat caught his eye. Just after 4:00 p.m., his company commanders watched as a field cannon and fifteen other guns sent their "iron loads . . . hurtling through the air" to burst over Lipsett's line. Under the cover of the artillery barrage, Von Heygendorff's force advanced, shell hole to shell hole, using whatever cover they could to shield themselves from the splinters that flew from their shells and from what little fire the Canadians could still muster.

The 247's infantry also resented the shellfire that pounded the Canadians. "The artillery should stop," recalled the regimental historian. "We wanted to storm." Just as the artillery lifted and the infantry prepared to storm the trenches, Lipsett's men climbed over the back of their parapets and made their dash. From the German side of the line, it looked as if the "Brits [were] going crazy." Someone called out, "Let's pound them," and the 247 charged. The regimental history makes clear the disorder of battle and the collapse of Lipsett's line:

Let's pound them. Hurray, hurray. Now there was no holding back. Out from the hedges, sandbag cover, the trenches. There is a gutted farm. More to the left. There they are. There they are. They're running like hares.

There are bullets from the right. A British machine gun fires from the flank. One of our men tumbles down, writhing on the ground.

But now we are in the empty trenches. Further to the left there are terrible torn-up corpses. The earthworks are taken, with about 200 prisoners and 6 machine guns.

While the Germans took possession of the trenches on Tuxford's left and his staff dashed for safety, he stood alone on the farm that housed his headquarters. German artillery toppled farm buildings, some with stone walls more than a foot thick, "like a pack of cards." Tuxford knew he would have to give the final order for men on the line to make a run for it, even if it was still light. Without covering fire, their chances were slim, just as they had been the day before for the 2nd Battalion (whose fate Tuxford almost certainly did not know). Then Tuxford noticed a group of men from the 8th, 7th, and 10th battalions, maybe as many as three hundred. Their orders, he knew, were to stop halfway through a crossroads and dig in—to provide some covering fire for his men's retreat. But the men failed to stop, for "all cohesion had vanished."

Like valour, cohesion is there one minute, gone the next. Its presence is determined by the strange alchemy that exists between a fighting formation and its leader, by an emotional calculus by which each man believes that his mission is worthwhile. Tuxford, who had led men in battle for all of four days, tipped the balance. He ran to the crossroads and found forty or so men. Of them, he later wrote:

> I now want to lay particular stress upon the magnificent morale of these men.... They had retired to comparative safety, and, upon being ordered, immediately advanced up this half-mile slope, under heavy machine gun fire at 400 yards, and then under the most intense artillery fire, shrapnel and H.E. [high explosive], and as soon as I put them in the trenches on

top of the hill and had personally told all the N.C.O.'s that we were going to hold the ridge till our two companies had retired and until they had arrived when we would then retire altogether [*sic*], these men immediately snapped their bayonets in and said, "Just tell us what to do, Sir, and we will do it," as cheerful as could be.[8]

Largely because of the pictures taken of trench warfare and the horrible slough in which the Canadian Corps fought and won the 1917 battle for the village of Passchendaele a few miles to the northeast, the overwhelming impression of Flanders is of mud deep enough to drown in. In April 1915, however, the real danger was secreted in the most ironic of places, the little farm cottages that dotted the landscape. According to Mathews (8th Battalion), fighting in Flanders "was like fighting in the suburbs of a town."

For Tuxford's ragtag force of men, now dragging their tired bodies up the southern slope of Gravenstafel Ridge, the greatest danger came from a machine gun hidden in a cottage four hundred yards away. As soon as it opened up, they went to ground. During the moments it took for the gunners to change the belt, the exhausted Canadians rushed forward again. When they were about halfway up the hill, Tuxford realized that the rhythm his men and the machine-gunners had established had ended. Looking towards the cottage from which the fire had come, he saw only a smoking ruin.

Later he discovered that the cottage had been blown to pieces by "one of those lucky circumstances which sometimes occur in war." After Tuxford ordered his staff to leave their trenches, Regimental Sergeant-Major R. Mackie "made directly for a couple of British batteries on our right rear." He found there the remains of one gun that had been hit, its dead crew and the commander lying wounded on the ground, which sickened Mackie, "an old artillery man." Still, Mackie, who could not see the cottages, was able to give the wounded commander the map coordinates, and the commander "yelled directions" to a second gun crew that destroyed the cottage.

Moments later, Tuxford found Lipsett and Major Monroe, Lipsett's second-in-command. Together, the three senior officers led the men to the top of the ridge. The noise from the intense shellfire was so great during the last hundred yards that they could barely hear each other's shouts. As they neared the ridge, Tuxford looked over to his right and saw his cook, Private Purvis, "jauntily marching along with his cap stuck aslant over one eye, and grinning at me in the most cheerful manner."

Tuxford's relief force arrived just in time. While they were trudging up the slope, the Germans closed in from the front and left. As Tuxford ran to the right side of the trench, he heard Jean Daniel Tenaille, a thirty-five-year-old Corsican-born major, yelling, in heavily accented English, "Shoot, shoot! Damn zem! Come." Tuxford was justly proud of his men, who exited the trench in an orderly line facing right, with "one man per yard," while "B" Company did the same on the left—all the while hearing, in guttural German, "We have got you Canadians now."

Recognizing that the greater danger came from their open left flank, Tuxford posted a forward skirmish line consisting of Sergeant George Pigrum Bowie and six other men on a small rise eighty yards away. Suddenly, about 150 soldiers appeared on the rise. Bowie, although ready to order his men to fire, gambled and asked if the new arrivals were Germans, British, or French. Their answer—"Do not shoot! Ve vas French"—told him all he needed to know. Bowie "took off 14 himself and stopped the rush." A few moments later another group belonging to the Schmieden Brigade appeared; this time, Tuxford ordered rapid fire. Among Tuxford's men was A. H. Fisher (8th Battalion), who recalled that while there were only a few hundred men firing, they fired so quickly that "Fritzie must have thought the whole Canadian army was in front of him. It was an absolute surprise to them. But we held them."[9] With the Germans stopped and his men out of the trenches, Tuxford led them back through the maelstrom of shells and machine-gun fire towards the switch line Currie had ordered him to earlier in the afternoon.

. . .

As he led his men towards the rear, Tuxford kept one eye out for Lipsett and one out for the switch line. He found neither. Lipsett had not, as Tuxford feared, been wounded by the heavy artillery fire, though his batman was. The farther Tuxford and his men got from the ridge, the more it became apparent that no switch line had been prepared. Even more alarming was the fact that as far as he could tell, the 3rd Royal Fusiliers, who had been on his right, were not retiring in conformity with the Canadians. Tuxford did not know it then, but the mixed bag of Durhams, Suffolks, and Monmouths were still in place just south of Boetleer Farm, on what had been Lipsett's left rear. Their commander, Colonel Turnbull, had Currie's order to withdraw but was unsure that the Canadian brigadier was his commanding officer, so he remained in his trenches, watching the Germans take possession of the farm that had served as Lipsett's headquarters. Turnbull was, in his turn, receiving some support on his left from Guthrie's 10th Battalion, which, as noted, did not withdraw until after dawn the next day.

• • •

It is unclear which Canadian commander first realized that Currie's order to withdraw was based on a faulty assumption. The fact that the 3rd Royal Fusiliers had not started to retire meant that a general retirement had not been ordered. Both Tuxford and Lipsett immediately grasped that their absence from their trenches could prove disastrous for the British 28th Division, to the right of the Canadians' positions on Gravenstafel Ridge. Had the Germans realized the British flank was undefended, they would have stood a fair chance of rolling up the 28th Division from its left.

Lipsett responded by ordering his men to turn around and advance over the same ground they had just crossed in retreat.* "It speaks well

---

*Dixon's animus against Currie is evident when he writes of Tuxford and Lipsett's decision to take their men back to their trenches after they discovered that there had been no order for a general retreat. "Their departure was leaving other units in considerable danger," he argues, "and they felt that the only option was to go back into the line—they were, however,

of the morale of the troops after the knocking about they had received," wrote Major Mathews in his report, "when I say we had very little trouble in getting them back across the fire-swept zone to the trenches on the Ridge," to a position about five hundred yards east of Boetleer Farm and five hundred yards south of the 8th Battalion's original position. Tuxford's report does not clearly refer to this second march up Gravenstafel Ridge, though it does mention that once there he communicated with the 3rd Royal Fusiliers and found out that they had, indeed, received no order to withdraw. Tuxford's position, La Marchelerie, was a line that extended for about eight hundred yards behind the 5th Battalion's original line. As darkness fell, Tuxford's and Lipsett's men, many now holding Lee-Enfield rifles taken from dead British soldiers, prepared to protect themselves and General Snow's left flank.

• • •

Just as Lipsett and Tuxford's men were marching back up Gravenstafel Ridge, Captain Thomas Irving's 2nd Field Company, Canadian Engineers, moved out of their billets on the west side of the canal. They had been there for just a few hours—after two days of mining bridges, digging trenches, clearing trees and other debris from the roads so that ambulances could get by, moving supplies, giving hot food to retiring troops, and for some, guiding hundreds of stragglers back to their Canadian and British units, much of the time under shellfire. Irving's destination was

---

disobeying a direct order from Brigadier-General Currie" (pp. 116f). Technically, Dixon is correct. Operationally, legally and historically, he is wrong.

Orders are, of course, supposed to be carried out. But British and Canadian regulations gave field commanders a great deal of leeway in interpreting orders and also required them to consider if the orders fitted the situation in which they found themselves: "If a subordinate, in the absence of a superior, neglects to depart from the letter of his order, when such departure is demanded by the circumstances and failure ensues, he will be held responsible for such failure" (Neillands, *Old Contemptibles*, 170). Nor would it appear that history supports Dixon. As far as can be determined, Currie never questioned Tuxford and Lipsett's decision to take their men back to the line, an indication, surely, that the brigadier recognized the wisdom of his field commanders' orders.

an area near Wieltje, where he was to construct a "defended locality" that ran south from a house at C.28.a to the southernmost end of the GHQ Line, a distance of about a thousand yards.

That "defended locality," ideally, would have consisted of a trench, traverses, and communications trenches that stretched back towards the house. The communication trench would have allowed men to reach the front trench without ever raising their heads above ground, thus protecting them from all but a direct hit from a German shell. They would dig saps into no man's land where men could listen for German patrols and advances. Time did not, however, permit the digging of such well-wrought trenches. Delayed by crowded roads, Irving's men had to work fast. Some defence had to be ready before first light at 3:00 a.m. They arrived at C.28.a so late that they had only enough time to loophole the house and string some wire.

. . .

At 11:00 p.m., while Irving's men were hard at work, Currie, then at his rear headquarters in St. Jean, sent a runner to Alderson with a message that again shows how poor was the information available to senior commanders during 2nd Ypres. Currie told his commander that at one point his men had been forced off Gravenstafel Ridge but had been able to deny it to the Germans; still, evidence of his shattered regiments, in the form of details from the 10th, 8th, and 7th Battalions, was all around him. The situation at that moment, however, was much less clear. He had information that the 5th Battalion was still holding its trenches, but he doubted it because "no officers from the 5th Battalion have reported to me."[10] Currie did not know that part of Lipsett's battalion had also gone back into the line.

As Currie's runner made his way to the Château des Trois Tours, a trip that took three and a half hours, the 8th and the 5th Battalions stood on guard. Their small numbers and lack of artillery support meant that they could not repel a determined assault, and they were hungry and tired, but the fight had not gone out of the Canadians. At one point, the

Germans advanced to within five hundred yards of the thin khaki line by using the cover of the slope, copses, and the ruins of buildings. To add to the effect, a bugler blew a "trumpet that sounded like a small hunting horn." Mathews's men stood, expecting, even hoping, that the Germans would again charge forward. But it had all been a piece of battlefield theatre, designed, no doubt, to unnerve and exhaust.

Moments after the Germans halted, Mathews received the order to fall back so the British could relieve him. Word of the impending relief did not, however, equal safety. Despite the fact that the Germans were not advancing, and that the gathering fog offered some cover, Mathews considered his situation "extremely precarious," and did not think that he and his men would be able to extricate themselves. He buried his maps and papers in the bottom of the trench, and ordered his officers to do the same.

Few details exist about the second withdrawal of the Little Black Devils and Tuxford's Dandies, though it appears that in the main, they followed the plan Lipsett and Tuxford had agreed upon. "I now arranged with Major Monroe of the 8th," wrote Tuxford, "to commence our retirement, falling back in parties covered by the remaining [parties] till about 2 o'clock on the ridge."[11] Mathews's report is more suggestive, but ultimately lacking in detail. "This retirement in the moonlight was not carried out in so orderly a manner as it might have been, many of the men threw their equipment away unnecessarily." Given that "1,452 of the 5,000 Canadian infantrymen who survived at Ypres had picked up the Lee-Enfield," it is not difficult to imagine which piece of equipment Mathews's weary, mud-encrusted men tossed away in the dark.

As the gaunt figures threaded their way towards a line near Bombarded Crossroads, a thousand or so yards south, Tuxford set out to report to Currie. Unable to find him at what had been the brigadier's forward headquarters, he continued south towards Wieltje, through a fog illuminated by moonlight and pierced again and again by the flash of exploding shells. On the way, he found two British batteries, likely the 366th and 367th Royal Field Artillery. Neither had been alerted to the fact that the

Canadians were being relieved, and that a mass of troops would be coming through the night. Next, Tuxford found General Snow's headquarters, which also had not been told of the Canadians' retirement. Tuxford arrived at St. Jean, to which his, Lipsett's, and Odlum's men were marching, sometime before 4:00 a.m. "What was left of the Brigade arrived at 4:00 in the morning, dead beat, gassed, starved and short of water."[12]

. . .

It is an old saw among soldiers that young officers talk about strategy and tactics, while older ones talk about logistics. In the damp hours before dawn, the remnants of Currie's 2nd Brigade and those who had become attached to it gave thanks for the logistician who had ensured that a hot meal awaited them. Bathing and refitting their kit and equipment would have to wait. After eating, Currie's men were led to a trench near a wood, where they slept, despite the noise of the odd German shell exploding nearby.

. . .

As Currie's men gathered near St. Jean, and Turner's and Mercer's men were ensconced on the other side of the Yser Canal, hundreds of Canadians lay wounded in trenches, dugouts, and shell-pocked fields.\* Private Arthur Gibbons of the 3rd Battalion lay in agony where he had fallen on 24 April after being wounded in the thigh. He owed his life to a German officer who stopped one of the Kaiser's infantrymen from bayoneting the prone Canadian. He owed some of his pain to that same officer, who kicked him when he refused to answer the questions "How far to Calais?" and "What number of troops have you behind the lines?" Gibbons remembered shaking his head to show he did not know the answers.

---

\*Turner's men were in reserve trenches near Wieltje, and Mercer's manned posts on the west side of the canal's bridges.

He [the German officer] then bent closer to me and exclaimed, "Englander, huh?"

"No," I replied, "I am Canadian."

"Canada, eh? Canadian swine." And he kicked me.

In addition to this officer, Gibbons owed much of his suffering to the German stretcher-bearers and other soldiers who, in violation of the Hague Convention, walked by him for four days without giving him any aid.[13]

The Germans who captured the 5th Battalion's trenches were more compassionate. They carried eighteen-year-old Joseph H. Leach, who was unable to walk from a wound in the leg, out of the trench and helped him to the first-aid station. Because of his injury, Leach was interned in Switzerland, a move that he credited with saving him from the starvation others endured in German prison camps. Also helped was James Stewart of Moose Jaw, a twenty-seven-year-old sergeant. Stewart later died and was buried in Roulers, not far from where the Germans displayed the guns the Canadians had briefly recaptured during their assault on Kitcheners Wood—the only successful Allied attack during the 2nd Battle of Ypres.

PART 9

# Standing on Guard
26 April to 10 May 1915

CHAPTER 18

## "The Heaviest [Shelling] Yet Experienced by the Brigade"

The Withdrawal of the 1st Canadian Division from the Ypres Salient

*"King George Expresses Admiration [for] Gallant Stand Made By Canadians"*
—HALIFAX MORNING CHRONICLE, 26 APRIL 1915

*"More Than 1,000 Canadians Captured, Is Berlin's Claim: London Rings with Praise for Canadian Valour under Murderous German Attack"*
—OTTAWA EVENING CITIZEN, 26 APRIL 1915

*"The Deed of the Canadians Thrills the Heart of the Motherland with Love and Pride. The Canadian Officers and Men Had the Touch of Wellington Who Never Lost a Gun Which He Did Not Recover"*
—LONDON DAILY MAIL, 26 APRIL 1915

General Turner's men, relieved late on 25 April, did not have long to enjoy their "bivouac on the green grass with the heavens as a blanket," as Lieutenant-Colonel John Currie rather sardonically put it. Currie himself "had not been in the Land of Nod half an hour" before he was woken up by a messenger who brought orders for Currie's men to leave Vlamertinghe, cross the Yser Canal, and march the four and a half miles east to Brique to support the Lahore Division. Later in the day, that division would be attacking the area around Kitcheners Wood in cooperation with a planned French assault on Het Sas/Langemarck. Given the fact that his men had had little sleep and no time to either bathe or rekit themselves, it is hard to believe that the early morning air did not ring with at least a little "'rough-neck' swearing," even though Currie insisted such talk had "found no place in this war."[1] As his men stamped their feet in the chill morning air, their quartermasters distributed rations and ammunition.

German artillery observers noticed the column after it crossed the canal, and soon the Kaiser's gunners were raining shells on the road to Brique. Losses were low, however—not because of poor German gunnery but because Turner's battalions were battalions in name only. Four days earlier, the four battalions that made up Turner's 3rd Brigade would have counted almost four thousand officers and men. At 8:00 a.m. on 26 April, they numbered somewhere near one thousand. Currie's 15th Battalion had been more than halved, to 309 soldiers. Once Currie's men reached Brique, they occupied reserve trenches, which gave them a front-row seat for the disaster that the Lahore Division's attack that afternoon would become.

At 2:30 p.m., Currie's men were ordered to reserve trenches behind the village of Wieltje, about two thousand yards to the northeast. In an effort to avoid presenting too tempting a target, they used the cover of hedges and ditches to reach their assigned trench, which was nowhere near as well positioned on this Flanders field as it must have looked on the map. For the part of the trench manned by Currie's 15th Battalion, the danger came from shells that "missed the roofs of the houses" in the village; they "pitched over into our lines and we had to duck and count to ten when we heard them coming."[2] For the remnants of the 16th Battalion, occupying one nearby stretch of trench, terror and death came from British shells falling short. The exhaustion and strain proved too much. Two men became "temporarily demented," according to the 16th Battalion's regimental historian. The sanity of the rest was helped by "one of those humorous incidents" that could occur only in war:

> Permission had been granted to men to go into the nearby village of St. Jean, which had been largely destroyed by shellfire, to ascertain if any drinking water could be found there. To the amazement of the troops entrenched in the fields there was shortly afterwards observed coming towards them a bevy of fashionable ladies and gentlemen, dressed in all sorts of finery, the former stepping daintily over ditches assisted by their companions. There were couples arm in arm, gracefully bowing to each other and to the troops, each person, lady or gentleman, carrying a pail. On closer acquaintance, it was seen that this gay party was the men who had been sent to the village and that they were bringing back with them, in place of water, pails of washy Belgian beer.[3]

Turner's men stayed in these trenches until 7:30 p.m. on 27 April, when they were relieved and marched to billets west of Ypres.

. . .

While Turner's men prepared to march to Brique, Brigadier-General Arthur Currie's officers rousted his men from their short sleep. The decision to redeploy Currie's 2nd Brigade flowed from another communications muddle. Shortly after dawn on 26 April, Currie was walking towards Fortuin with the Brigadier-General John Hasler to speak to Major-General E. S. Bulfin, who had taken charge the night before after a reorganization ordered by Lieutenant-General Sir Herbert Plumer. A runner approached Hasler with the message that the Germans had broken through the British lines on the southern side of Gravenstafel Ridge. (The message was in error. The *Feldgrauen* had used the half-light of dawn and the cover of their artillery to move down the southern side of the ridge, but they dug in near Bombarded Crossroads, fully seven hundred yards north of the 11th Brigade's line.) Upon hearing the news, the indefatigable Canadian brigadier volunteered his men to restore the line.

Currie's officers could muster just about the same number as Turner's could, a little over a thousand.* Lipsett's 8th Battalion counted only 225 NCOs and men, while Sergeant Herbert Mathews estimated that instead of the 250 officers and men on the rolls of the battalion's No. 2 Company, he had only 125 men at dawn parade. Currie's report, which says that their advance "was carried out under extremely heavy shellfire, the heaviest yet experienced by the Brigade," telescopes his men's return to the front.

The advance did not become difficult until a German aeroplane spotted them crossing a farmer's field. Despite trying to fool the pilot by playing possum, the Canadians were soon under heavy shrapnel fire. Their losses, however, were slight. Some casualties—Mathews does not say how many—were taken as the men crossed a small stream; on the other side, a machine-gun crew was secreted among some houses. This time, however, the undulating terrain of Flanders worked in the Canadians' favour. Losses did not become serious until they reached a ridge at D.19 a and c. "We found the ridge was exposed to a crossfire as well as frontal fire of shrapnel and high explosive," Mathews recalled. He did what he could, ordering his men to dig in on the reverse slope.

While the crest of the ridge provided some safety, it also blinded the Canadians. Mathews crawled forward into a shell hole that afforded a view of the other side of the ridge. He soon realized, however, that the hole was too shallow to give him much protection. Before he could move to another, a shrapnel shell burst and one of its scores of balls cut into his left leg, just below his knee. In great pain, Mathews crawled back to the Canadians' line, where he learned from Lieutenant-Colonel Herbert

---

*The casualties for each brigade were almost exactly the same: 1st Brigade (1st, 2nd, 3rd, 4th Battalions), 1,839; 2nd Brigade (5th, 7th, 8th, 10th Battalions), 1,829; 3rd Brigade (13th, 14th, 15th, 16th Battalions), 1,838.

Kemmis-Betty that he was "in command of the firing line of the Brigade." With 20/20 hindsight, Mathews told Kemmis-Betty that had he known this before, "we might have ... advanced a little differently."

As one of his comrades put the field dressing around his leg, Mathews handed command over to Captain Ernest D'H. McMeans and was then taken to a first-aid station. Kemmis-Betty himself was slightly injured, and Lieutenant Dansereau was severely wounded. Odlum's 7th Battalion and Tuxford's 5th Battalion also took casualties, with Tuxford's men apparently suffering the worst: two killed, forty-one wounded (eight NCOs and thirty-three men), and one missing.

Currie's brigade was withdrawn at 7:00 p.m. on 27 April. Their line of march took them through Ypres, which proved a shocking sight even to battle-hardened men like Private "Wally" Bennett, the 10th Battalion machine-gunner who escaped Doxsee's House and had spent thirteen days in the field. "Everything was wrecked. In some places along the streets, there was only space for one wagon to get through the piles of brick and debris."[4] A half-century later, Private Robert L. Christopherson told the CBC that the "town was completely abandoned. The Cloth Hall was badly smashed.... There were a lot of dead horses, dogs and some people, all bloated up, lying around."[5] A single sound stuck in Private Bagshaw's mind: "As we came through Ypres, I remember distinct as can be, there was a dog barking. It was the only sound we could hear."[6]

The depleted Canadian force stayed in the salient for another week, guarding bridges and serving as reserve details as the 2nd Battle of Ypres raged on. On the night of 28 April, Brigadier-General Malcolm Mercer's 1st Brigade dug a twelve-hundred-yard extension of the GHQ Line without incurring any casualties; the extension faced Mauser Ridge, and thus the Germans could not enfilade it. The twelve battalions that made up the 1st Canadian Division marched to billets in and around the town of Bailleul, sixteen miles west of Ypres, on 4 May.

. . .

Although relieved to be out of the salient, few had fond memories of their forced march in the middle of the night. "Our guides were pretty bad and the billeting arrangements were no better," remembered one soldier. They were two miles beyond Bailleul. "Many men dropped out during the march and slept on the wayside, and small groups were coming in [to town] all the next day," recalled a member of the 16th Battalion.[7] No man would ever forget what he looked like after almost two weeks of battle. "As for myself," wrote Private Bennett, "I hardly knew my own face: I hadn't seen a razor for about seven or eight days, and my clothes were ragged and torn and still caked with mud!"[8]

The rebuilding of the battalions began almost immediately. On 29 April, the 10th Battalion, for example, received a draft of nineteen officers and 343 men from England, which brought its numbers up to 910 officers and men.

• • •

As Turner's and Currie's men made their weary way back towards the fighting, the British and the French prepared to attack Mauser Ridge from the south and the west. The story of the French attack—which also included actions designed to expel the Germans from Lizerne, Steenstraat, and Het Sas (on the west side of the Yser Canal) and re-establish a position near Bixschoote (on the east side of the canal)—is depressingly familiar. What was planned as a three-pronged attack by a large number of troops (including the fresh battalions belonging to the 52nd and 153rd Divisions) became an assault by seventeen battalions already in the line (many of which were nowhere near full strength). The only part that was even partially successful was the 3:00 p.m. attack on the east side of the canal. By nightfall, French troops had almost reached the locks at Het Sas. North of there, one soldier said, "our line bent towards the west, bending around a farm surrounded by a wood fortified by the enemy. It ran through the village of Lizerne, of which we had captured the western part."[9]

The British assault was equally problematic. The 4th Moroccan

Brigade crossed the Yser Canal around noon before forming up on the right of the French line, fifteen hundred yards to the east of the canal, just about where the 1st and 4th Canadian Battalions started from in their assault on Mauser Ridge. To the Moroccans' right were the three battalions of the Lahore Division, which had arrived in the salient the night before. At 1:20 p.m., the largest and longest artillery bombardment yet undertaken in Flanders began. It lasted forty minutes, ending with a five-minute "rapid fire" designed to stun the German defenders. When the British shells, some of which were fired by Canadian artillery batteries, were done, the order was given and the turbaned men of the Jullundur and Ferozepore Brigades started over ground still littered with the bloated bodies of the Canadian and British dead.

Although it was much longer than the artillery barrage that had preceded the Canadian assault on Mauser Ridge on the morning of 23 April, this barrage also failed to quell German ardour. Heavy machine-gun and shellfire "knocked out whole platoons at a time, British and Indians [the Lahore's officers were British] falling literally in heaps."[10] A handful managed to reach Turco Farm, which had changed hands four times on 23 April. Elements of the 1st Manchesters, who were on the far right of the British attack, managed to advance (at the cost of 289 casualties) to within sixty yards of the German line before having to dig in.

Given the Germans' position and their seemingly unlimited number of shells (in less than an hour, three batteries fired two thousand rounds), it seems that the Lahore Division's attack was doomed from the start. All that could have saved the men was a successful attack by the French on their left. This possibility was foreclosed when the Germans opened the valves on gas cylinders that had been positioned for a future attack. The gas drove the Moroccan troops "back in some places to the south of their jumping-off places," writes the French official historian, choosing the gentlest terms to describe the panicked retreat, which was entirely understandable, given the Moroccans' experience with gas on 22 April.[11] The westerly wind blew some of the gas across the British lines—and soon King George's soldiers were again dying of air hunger, their faces frozen a ghastly blue. In less than an hour, another 1,943 British soldiers lay dead and wounded on a Flanders field.

• • •

At 12:30 p.m. on 26 April, as the Lahore Division readied for its attack and Currie's men came under heavy shellfire, General Alderson ordered the 149th Northumberland Brigade, which had come under his command on the twenty-fifth, to attack St. Julien over the same ground that the 11th Brigade had crossed a day earlier. Much else was also the same.

The attack's artillery support closed nineteen minutes before the attack began. Delays in communications meant that Brigadier-General J. F. Riddell got the orders to attack so late he did not have time to reconnoitre the ground. The predictable happened to the first Territorial brigade to go into battle in the First World War. In less than two hours, another forty-two British officers and 1,912 men were dead, and the Germans had not been pushed back an inch. A hundred yards or so from the Vanheule Farm, General Riddell "received a bullet through the head and fell dead."[12]

• • •

During the night of 26 April, while Turner's and Currie's men sat in trenches and Brigadier-General Mercer's guarded bridgeheads over the Yser Canal, Général Putz ordered that the attack be renewed on the twenty-seventh. That attack succeeded in retaking Lizerne only.

The largest French attack, designed to support another assault on St. Julien by the Lahore Division, was scheduled to begin at 1:15 p.m. It never really started, and French records differ as to what happened. The official history states that "[Général] Joppé's group and the English left attacked at 5:30 p.m. After having advanced as far as the enemy's trenches the troops found themselves, as on the previous day, met with asphyxiating gas which forced them to withdraw south of their jumping-off place."[13] The official historian is certainly mistaken about the time. The war diary of the French 152nd Brigade records that its advance began at 2:00 p.m.

but "was stopped and even gave way ... due to the release of asphyxiating gas." By contrast, the war diary of the 4th Moroccan Brigade makes no mention of gas but notes that the "advance was difficult and very slow due to the presence of German machine gun fire which beat all the ground in front" of the advancing troops.[14] (German records also make no mention of the use of gas on 27 April.)

At all events, the French attack collapsed shortly after it began. After hearing of the collapse, only a Pollyanna of Général Foch's stature could still write, as he did to Putz, that he had the troops needed "to carry through the affair and bring it to a favourable conclusion."[15]

At first, things looked better for the Lahore Division's attack, planned for 1:15 p.m. The preparatory artillery bombardment began at 12:30 p.m. (Several Canadian artillery batteries contributed to this fusillade.) When it ended, several thousand troops, including Gurkhas complete with the *kukri*, their traditional weapon, went over the top and over ground strewn with Canadian, British, and Indian dead, their bodies already being eaten by thousands of rats and flies.\* For a moment or two, it was a glorious charge: "I witnessed a very exciting charge by Gurkha troops," wrote Lieutenant Stan Lovelace of the 9th Canadian Field Artillery. "They started from somewhere near my observing station and moved quickly in groups of about a dozen to rush forward and then drop. Then a rush to the right or the left and on about 500 yards over a slight ridge. What wonderful little men."[16]

A few moments later, after the German guns opened up, another observer wrote, "The attack was again resumed at 2 p.m. with much the same results as that of yesterday. A little more ground was gained and many more casualties were suffered."[17] A secondary attack, launched at 6:30 p.m., was quickly driven into the ground by German machine-gun and shellfire from the very same units that Général Quiquandon had said were "running short on ammunition" on the morning of 23 April. By the time the British had lost another twelve hundred soldiers, including

---

\*The Gurkhas belonged to the Sirhind and Ferozepore Brigades.

thirty-two English and eighteen Indian officers, Currie's and Turner's men were moving out of their positions north of Ypres.

• • •

There is no official or unofficial record of how General Alderson and his Canadian officers reacted to the dismissal of General Sir Horace Smith-Dorrien, the commanding general of the 2nd British Army, to which the 1st Canadian Division belonged. They must have learned of it near 5:00 p.m. on 27 April, two hours before the Canadians were withdrawn from the field. The telegram relieving Smith-Dorrien and replacing him with General Plumer was sent, at Sir John French's order, "in clear" (i.e., uncoded, thus ensuring that every telegraph operator knew what was said) at 4:35 p.m. As spotty as communications were during the 2nd Battle of Ypres, it is a good bet that this news travelled quickly.

Once they learned of Smith-Dorrien's sacking, Canadian commanders would have wanted to have known the reason for it. Was he being made to take the blame for the myriad of problems that had arisen since the gas attack? Was he being sacked for ordering carbon-copy attacks that ended in mass casualties? What would General Plumer's elevation mean for the exhausted Canadians?

Officially, Smith-Dorrien was relieved of his command for disagreeing with Sir John's continued faith in the word of the French generals, who kept promising to restore the line lost to the Germans after the gas attack. After watching the French attacks of 25 April fail, Smith-Dorrien went to Sir John to attempt to dissuade him from launching another coordinated assault using the Lahore Division. Smith-Dorrien objected most strongly to Sir John's reliance on Général Putz's word. But Sir John had standing orders to comply with the French.* The meeting

---

*Sir John actually agreed with Smith-Dorrien's view of their French allies: "Truly I don't want to be allies with the French more than once in a lifetime. You can't trust them" (quoted in Cassar, *Sir John French*, 225).

was less than satisfactory, and Smith-Dorrien left with orders that were less than clear:

> The General did not want to surrender any ground if it could possibly be avoided, but unless the French regained the ground they had lost, or a good deal of it, XX realized that it might become impossible to retain our present very salient position in front of Ypres. It was essential, though, that the situation should be cleared up, and the area quieted down as much as possible, even if I had to withdraw to a more retired line, so that XXX might be able to continue SSS offensive elsewhere. The General felt sure I should not take a retired line until all hope of the French recovering ground had vanished. The General did not wish me to have any more heavy casualties, as he thought the French had got us into the difficulty and ought to pull us out of it.
>
> The General mentioned that in any combined attack, I was to be careful to see that our troops did not get ahead of the French.[18]

Confused or not, Smith-Dorrien had his orders, and he told the Lahore Division to attack on 26 April—with disastrous results.

Sir John's order to attack again in cooperation with the French seemed to Smith-Dorrien the military equivalent of throwing good money after bad. In a letter to Lieutenant-General Sir William R. Robertson, chief of staff to Sir John French, Smith-Dorrien wrote that despite his promise of a large number of fresh troops, Putz was in fact "withdrawing two battalions from east of the canal and another two battalions from the front line . . . so the net result of his orders is to send over six fresh battalions to the fighting line and to withdraw four which had already been deployed." Smith-Dorrien also learned that although Putz said he had retaken Het Sas, what he really meant was that his men had taken "the houses of the place which are on the west of the canal."

Smith-Dorrien told Sir William that, as per Sir John's orders, he had ordered the Lahore Division to attack again but was "pretty sure that our line tonight will not be in advance of where it is at the present moment," and that he doubted "if it is worth losing any more men unless the French do something really big."

A few paragraphs later, he indicated that he did not agree with Sir John's strategy or his commitment to holding every inch of ground before Ypres (and even the wrecked town itself). After calling attention to the shape of the salient and the fact that the Germans could shell any part of it at will (including the area around his headquarters), Smith-Dorrien wrote that the British should pull back to strengthen their line. He then went on to describe how the pull-back could be undertaken without surrendering the "enormous amount of guns and paraphernalia" used by his troops. Towards the end of the letter, Smith-Dorrien wrote, "It is very difficult to put a subject such as this in a letter without appearing pessimistic—I am not in the least but as an Army Commander, I have of course to provide for every eventuality, and I think it right to let the Chief know what is running in my mind."[19]

Sir John latched onto the sentence "I intend tonight if nothing special happens to reorganize the new front and to withdraw superfluous troops West of Ypres." For Sir John, these words meant that despite orders, Smith-Dorrien was readying a de facto withdrawal from the salient. At 2:15 p.m., Robertson replied by telephone:

> Chief does not regard situation nearly so unfavourable as your letter represents. He thinks you have abundance of troops and especially notes the large reserve you have. He wishes you to act vigorously with full means available in co-operating with and assisting the French attack having due regard to his previous instructions that the combined attack [on the 27th] should be simultaneous. The French possession of Lizerne and general situation on Canal seems to remove anxiety as to your left flank. Letter follows by Staff Officer.[20]

As John Dixon has rightly noted, French's response is one more indication that the senior commanders were "overseeing a completely different battle to everyone else involved in the British sector." There were indeed thousands of troops, but most of them had already been badly cut up, and others, like the Canadians, were unfit for serious action.[21]

Just over two hours later, Sir John sent the telegram relieving Smith-Dorrien. By sending it uncoded, he ensured the public humiliation of Smith-Dorrien, who never held a field command again.

Smith-Dorrien's letter and Sir John's response, through Robertson, likely leaked out. So too would have some of what Sir John confided to his diary:

> Smith-Dorrien has, since the commencement of these operations, failed to get a real grip on the situation. He has been very unwise in his dealings with Général Putz. He has acted quite against instructions I have given him. . . . His messages are all wordy and—unintelligible. His pessimistic attitude has the worst effect on his commanders and their troops, and today he wrote a letter to Robertson which was full of contradictions and altogether bewildering. I have therefore been obliged to take the command of all Ypres operations out of his hands.[22]

At least one of Smith-Dorrien's brigadiers protested the charge that the general was pessimistic:

> Sir Horace did not indulge in golden prophecies: he had sufficient strength of mind to look at a black situation without dismay; he made preparation for every possible change that might occur. And this was the frame of mind that he wanted to see in his subordinates. They regarded it not as pessimism but as foresight and far from having a bad effect, it cheered them to know that their Army Commander realized what they were up against.[23]

. . .

A day after sacking Smith-Dorrien, French ordered Plumer to ready his army to withdraw. At 9:30 a.m., the new commanding officer of the

2nd British Army issued a "Preparatory Order for Withdrawal from Tip of Salient." Over the next few days (during which there were two more failed French attacks), a flurry of meetings between Sir John and Général Foch delayed the withdrawal. Later, Foch told Général Joffre that when speaking to Sir John, "I painted the picture of the consequences of withdrawal darker than they appeared to me."[24] Finally, on 1 May, Foch agreed to the proposed withdrawal to a more defensible perimeter around Ypres, which was carried out that night. The withdrawal—to basically the same line sketched by Smith-Dorrien in his letter—was carried out without incident. Three days later, the 1st Canadian Division, minus its artillery units, marched out of the Ypres Salient, carrying with it a mailbag that probably contained an envelope holding a fifteen-line poem that beseeched all who read it not just to remember those who "lived, felt dawn, saw sunset glow," but also to "keep faith" with those who died by taking up "our quarrel with the foe."

## Chapter 19

## "A Perpetual Inspiration to Their Successors"
### Prayers for the Dead and Wounded

> *To: Duke of Connaught, Governor General of Canada*
> *I congratulate you most warmly on the splendid and gallant way in which the Canadian Division fought during the last two days north of Ypres. Sir John French says their conduct was magnificent throughout. The Dominion will be justly proud.*
> —King George V, 25 April 1915

Shortly after dinner on 10 May 1915, the governor-general of Canada, Prince Arthur, the Duke of Connaught; his wife, the duchess, and their daughter, Princess Patricia; Lord Lansdowne (governor-general of Canada, 1883–88); Sir Edmund Grey; and such notables as Rudyard Kipling and the New Brunswick–born Sir Max Aitken walked through the stately doors that lead from Ludgate into St. Paul's Cathedral.* Soon, they were seated beneath the famed dome, which soars more than 360 feet above the street. To their right, in the eastern transept, the cathedral's most holy place, sat scores of khaki-clad soldiers, many of whom were bandaged or on crutches. At 8:00 p.m., the

---

*Despite having been a member of the British House of Commons since 1910, Aitken was Militia Minister Sam Hughes's personal representative in London and held the unique title of Canada's "Eye Witness."

bishop of London, Arthur Foley Winnington-Ingram, rose, and his and thousands of other voices filled the great cathedral with the words of Hymn No. 225 of the Anglican Church hymnal.

Almost before the "Amen" echoed away, the bishop began to intone the same prayer that many of the wounded had hurriedly recited over the bodies of their fallen comrades in the fields north and east of Ypres:

*I am the Resurrection and the Life, saith the Lord; he that believeth in Me, though he were dead, yet shall he liveth; and whosoever Liveth and believeth in Me shall never die.*

Those in khaki—men who had witnessed and survived the horrors of the gas attacks; the agonies of Kitcheners Wood and Mauser Ridge; the terrible bombardment of Gravenstafel Ridge, St. Julien, and the Apex— must have heard something more personal than the other congregants did when the Right Reverend Winnington-Ingram reached the middle of the 23rd Psalm:

*Yea, though I walk through the valley*
*of the shadow of death, I will feel no*
*evil; for Thou art with me; Thy rod and*
*Thy staff, they comfort me.*

The Right Reverend Winnington-Ingram next quoted from Aitken's account of the battle, published in the *Times* on 1 May. The report began,

The story of the second battle of Ypres is the story of how the Canadian Division, enormously outnumbered . . . fought through the day and through the night, and then through another day and night; fought under their officers until, as happened to so many, those perished gloriously, and then fought from the impulsion of sheer valour because they came from fighting stock.

The text that Winnington-Ingram read from preserved the image of Lieutenant-Colonel Birchall dying while still carrying his cane. It persevered, too, the memory of Major Norsworthy, who, "already almost disabled by a bullet wound, was bayoneted and killed while he was rallying his men with easy cheerfulness." Major McCuaig's demise, the bishop read, "was not less glorious, although his death can claim no witness."

At one point, the bishop told the congregation that "it was on that tremendous day [22 April], when the French and English had been overpowered by poison gas, that the manhood of Canada shone out like pure gold; the example of these men will never die but will remain as a perpetual inspiration to their successors."[1]

. . .

Aitken's and the bishop's words may not sit well with today's readers—especially those who believe that a Canadian accomplishment is *ipso facto* second rate, or that there is something about Canadians that predisposes them, to borrow Jack Granatstein's phrase, to be "the boy scouts of the world." In fact, King George's hard-bitten generals were equally effusive. In the hours after the battle, Field Marshall Sir John French told Secretary of State for War Lord Kitchener that the "Canadians saved the situation." In his full report, French wrote:

> In spite of the danger to which they were exposed the Canadians held their ground with a magnificent display of tenacity and courage; and it is not too much to say that the bearing and conduct of these splendid troops averted a disaster which might have been attended with the most serious consequences.[2]

The Canadians' immediate commander, General Alderson, was equally proud of his men. He told his troops:

> I think it is possible that all of you do not quite realize that, if we had retired on the evening of April 22nd—when our Allies fell back before the

gas and left our left flank quite open—the whole of the Twenty-seventh and Twenty-eight divisions would probably have been cut off. Certainly, there would not have got away a gun or a vehicle of any sort, and probably not more than half their infantry would have escaped.

This is what their commander-in-chief meant when he telegraphed as he did that "the Canadians saved the situation." My lads, if ever men had a right to be proud in this world, you have.

I know my military history pretty well, and I cannot think of an instance, especially when cleverness and determination of the enemy is taken into account, in which troops were placed in such a difficult position; nor can I think of an instance in which so much depended on the standing fast of one division.[3]

• • •

Though shocked at the length of the casualty lists, Canadians took great pride in their army's achievement. The *Manitoba Free Press* declared:

> The Canadian soldiers have had their baptism of fire and blood. Their encounter with the Germans to the northeast of Ypres was a fight in the open in which the splendid qualities of the Canadian troops established themselves beyond all question. Put to the test of a situation that would have tried the mettle of the most seasoned troops, they acquitted themselves gloriously. Their valour and their steadfastness saved the day for the Allies.

The *Victoria Daily Times*, Brigadier-General Arthur Currie's hometown paper, recalled the doubts about what was once called the Comedian Contingent. "The fear expressed in some quarters that the laxity in discipline exhibited at Salisbury might affect the efficiency of the contingent has been dissipated," the paper wrote. "What they wanted was service at the front, a sight of the foe, a chance to strike a blow for the Empire, and given the chance, they have shown their mettle."[4]

"A Perpetual Inspiration to Their Successors" 349

Canadians had to wait more than a generation, until the publication in 1938 of the first volume of the *Official History of the Canadian Forces in the Great War, 1914–1919*, to learn that the Germans attributed their failure to take Ypres to the "obstinate resistance" and "tenacious determinism" shown by the same Dominion army the Kaiser had vowed would be sent home in thirty rowboats.[5]

Half a century after the battle, Victor Odlum put a slightly different face on what drove the Canadians:

> We mustn't boast too much because it wasn't heroism that made us stay there and fight through the battle. We just did not know how to get out. We were out at the end of the Salient. Everything was happening and we couldn't get any information. The only thing to do as far as we could see was just stay where we were. And we did.

# Coda

*Methinks I see in my mind a noble and puissant nation rousing herself like a strong man after sleep, and shaking her invincible locks; methinks I see her as an eagle mewing her mighty youth, and kindling her undazzled eyes at the full midday beam.*
—JOHN MILTON, *AREOPAGITICA*

Ask Canadians today what the First World War calls to mind and most will mention mud or the Conscription Crisis or Vimy Ridge. Vimy is to Canada's national mythology what Gallipoli is to Australia's—the coming of age of the nation. At Vimy, the Canadians took 10,602 casualties (3,598 fatalities), out of a force more than twice as large as that which fought at 2nd Ypres. But Vimy was a story of triumph, of taking and holding a ridge that the British and the French could not.

Whatever hold 2nd Ypres has on the public's mind is largely the result of "In Flanders Fields." Read aloud on November 11 by schoolchildren at ceremonies across the country and sung in front of the War Memorial in Ottawa, John McCrae's famous poem is often taken as a hymn to peace, the hopeful future all sane men and women desire. The poem printed on the back of the ten-dollar bill was, however, written by the same man who wrote, in a letter home, "To win the war we don't need more bloody doctors. We need to kill more Germans." The soldier-poet wrote the poem after reading the "Order of the Burial of the Dead," from the *Book of Common Prayer*, over the grave of his friend Lieutenant Alexis H. Helmer; the shell blast that killed Helmer left so little of his body that McCrae arranged the sandbags carrying Helmer's remains on a stretcher to approximate his friend's mortal form.

Today's literary critics praise poems that "make the world strange" or offer new insights into the human condition. McCrae's poem is not one of these, though the world he depicts is certainly strange to us. Just days before he wrote the poem, he saw a shell explode near an orderly who "seemed to pedal [his bicycle] for eight or ten revolutions and then collapsed in a heap—dead."

Far from being the prayer for peace so many think it is, "In Flanders Fields" celebrates martial ardour. Less graphic than the *Marseillaise*—with its famous lines "The bloody flag is raised" and "To arms, citizens! Form up your battalions. Let us march, let us march! That their impure blood should water our fields"*—McCrae's poem subordinates the peaceful image of brave, singing larks (borrowed from a pastoral tradition that stretches back to ancient Rome), and even the symbolic Calvary hill ("the crosses, row on row"), to the dead's demand that the living take up the "quarrel with the foe." Despite the horrors of the gas attack, of thousands of Canadian dead and wounded, of Helmer's death, of the ceaseless pounding of German shells, McCrae believed that the battle must not be brought to a close just for the sake of peace, however much we might imagine a true poet's soul fleeing from the mechanical madness of trench warfare. The blood of the dead demands that the living continue, not for the love of battle but for the men who now lie beneath each cross and the values they died for.

It was on these days—when McCrae was in the field with "not an infantryman between us and the Germans," and "really expected to

---

*"*Aux armes citoyens! / Formez vos bataillons, / Marchons, marchons! / Qu'un sang impur / breuve nos sillons.*"

die"—that Canada's reputation began to be formed. Field Marshal Sir John French's words—"the Canadians saved the situation"—were not just for home consumption, a pat of the imperial hand on the colonial head. Rather, they accurately reflected what the general commanding the British Expeditionary Force, and hence the Canadian Expeditionary Force, believed the Canadians had achieved.

Perhaps more important, French's words reflected what the Tommies who fought next to or relieved the Canadians thought of the troops who had come from far across the ocean to Flanders. Interviews and letters are replete with stories of the British troops cheering the Canadians. A little over a year later, at the Somme, the Germans assumed that the Australians who gave them such a hard time on 6 August 1916 were Canadians; the war diarist of Reserve-Infanterie-Regiment 211 was not at all surprised that the soldiers who successfully attacked Courcellette on 15 September 1916 "were Canadians, old friends from fighting in Flanders. That made sense!"

Sir Max Aitken was not only present at the creation of the reputation; he was its main proselytiser. Not only did he author the "Eye Witness" report that the Right Reverend Arthur Winnington-Ingram placed next to the stately words from the *Book of Common Prayer*, but Aitken insisted that Canadians keep Canada's war records and (led by none other than Max Aitken) write the history of the Canadians in battle. Within weeks of the Dominion's troops leaving Flanders, Aitken was in charge of the Canadian War Records Office, which he funded "out of his own pocket for six months before the government allocated $25,000 to cover some of the costs," an arrangement that gave him unique access to records that allowed him to write *Canada in Flanders*, published in January 1916.[1]

Canadians loved it. In three months, Aitken's admittedly "incomplete and partial" history, which necessarily sacrificed depth of analysis for immediacy of publication, was reprinted twelve times.[2] Equally important for the reputation of the Canadian Expeditionary Force, British reviewers praised it. "The heroic deeds of the Canadians at Ypres make me tingle with pride to be a kinsmen to such soldiers. Fruit farmers, editors and ranchers all showed themselves to be of the finest fighting stuff in the world," wrote the reviewer for the *Evening Standard*.

Aitken stayed clear of controversies surrounding the battle, preferring to write in a "heroic style." What distinguished these heroes was the fact that they were unmistakably Canadian. And to ensure that they were not swallowed up in the general history of the British Expeditionary Force, Aitken sought and received the Canadian government's permission to deviate from British practice and name individual soldiers. (Readers will have noticed that I have followed Aitken's lead on this and pointed out, as often as brevity would allow, the Canadians' ages and their pre-war occupation.) As if to further underline their Canadianness, Aitken also used whatever official documents he could, given the constraints of wartime security. The future Lord Beaverbrook was so successful in singling out the Canadians at Ypres as Canadians (as opposed to simply calling them Dominion troops in the British Expeditionary Force) that some "British politicians and officers complain[ed] that it appeared to be only the Canadians fighting the Germans, with a little support from the British."[3] This complaint, as we have seen, was again voiced by General Henry Horne after the war.*

. . .

It would be going much too far to argue that before 2nd Ypres, the men who made up the 1st Canadian Division, or the nation as a whole, took the war lightly. By the time the Canadians assembled at Valcartier, it was clear that the war would not be over by Christmas. Long before they arrived in France, the terrible reality of trench warfare had become manifest. And of course, Canadians had followed the story of the destruction of the "Old Contemptibles" at 1st Ypres. Whatever the lighter moments—"mudlarking" on Salisbury Plain or discovering

---

*While one never should read too much into telegrams sent in the heat of emotion after a battle, it is perhaps worth noting that the Secretary of State for the Colonies, Viscount L. V. Harcourt, wrote, "Great Britain is proud of her Canadian brothers"—a sentence that, intentionally or not, granted Canada a surprisingly equal status.

French wine—by the time they moved into the trenches around Ypres, the Canadians understood that war was a serious business.

Back home in Canada, papers could at times be triumphant without cause, but they too had become more serious, listing casualties suffered from "wastage" or telling of air-raid scares in Ottawa and the arrest of alien residents. Still, before 2nd Ypres, Canadians had not fought a major battle. The effect of 2nd Ypres is, perhaps, best summed up in Philip Child's *God's Sparrows*, which, though published in 1937, did not belong to the anti-war genre best epitomized in Canada by Charles Y. Harrison's *Generals Die in Bed*. "In 1915," Child's narrator says, "the first long casualty lists appeared in the papers and people ceased to live the war in their minds and began to live it in their nerves."[4]

Part of living the war in their nerves was the realization that even though politicians like Sam Hughes continued to speak of "my boys," the men already overseas and the hundreds of thousands who were to follow were part of a collective Canadian enterprise. Part of the Empire, yes. Under the British Expeditionary Force, yes. But for the mothers, wives, children, brothers, and fathers who scanned the casualty lists in fear, these men were Canadian, and the triumphs and tragedies they enjoyed and endured were also enjoyed and endured by men and women who lived proudly in the Dominion of Canada.

• • •

In the centre of the Parliament Buildings—halfway up the Tower of Victory and Peace, as it was called in 1919, when the Prince of Wales laid its cornerstone—is the Memorial Chamber. The stone that forms the walls of the chamber, into which are carved flutes, gargoyles, griffins, rosettes, and battle honours and shields, comes from Belgium and France, the two countries where most of Canada's sixty-six thousand First World War dead lay buried. Light from the stained-glass windows filters down to the altar, which stands on a piece of black marble donated by Belgium. On the altar sits the Book of Remembrance, which contains the names of every Canadian who died in the Great War; a page-turning ceremony is held at 11 o'clock each day, thus ensuring that every name is readable one day a year.* To the left of the door is a well-worn black stone step from Flanders with five brass inlaid letters: Y-P-R-E-S. The brass was reclaimed from shell casings fired during the Great War. (Other battles are recalled on other steps.)

On the walls that surround the Memorial Chamber are a series of friezes. The first panel depicts the 2nd Battle of Ypres. The Canadians who survived Ypres (and the battle of Passchendaele, fought nearby just two years later) would hardly have recognized the frieze of the Cloth Hall, its façade all but untouched by war. For by the time officers like Major Victor Odlum and Captain G. Richardson and privates like Baron Richardson Racey and Bernard C. Lunn saw it in 1915, the six-hundred-year-old building had largely been reduced to rubble. More familiar would have been the ruins of the city in the centre right of the panel and the arched entrances to the city's ancient ramparts, then honeycombed with storerooms, arms magazines, quarters, and offices. In the distance are (foreshortened) views of Gravenstafel Ridge and St. Julien.

No doubt few veterans cared about the frieze's verisimilitude. What concerned those men and the architects who placed the Memorial Chamber in the centre of the Parliament Buildings, as well as the politicians who authorized these decisions, was an idea of commemoration that differs greatly from our own. The inclusion of—indeed, the emphasis on preserving and displaying—the names of those who died for the Dominion of Canada was a relatively new idea, and it bespeaks a post-romantic emphasis on the individual's experience.

Despite some superficial similarities to today's *ad hoc* memorials, where people place flowers and teddy bears on the street, the Memorial Chamber (and the great cemeteries in Belgium and France) fuses the names not to the sorrow of death but to the public's notion of honour

---

*Altars containing books that remember the dead of the Second World War, the merchant navy in both wars, Newfoundland, the Nile Expedition (1884–85), and the Boer War (1899–1902), as well as one devoted to ongoing service to Canada, are set into bays underneath the stained-glass windows.

and duty. The names inscribed in the Book of Remembrance and on the granite walls are not in alphabetical order. Instead, each name is indissolubly linked to the soldier's regiment, and his rank is part of his memorial of existence. As emotionally affecting as the tens of thousands of names are, they are not recorded simply to perpetuate sorrow (which, at best, could speak to only a generation or two before passing from memory). Rather, the individual's experience of death and honour is fused with a national—even, given the architectural styles, a holy—undertaking that lifts their disappearance into the mud of Flanders or the termination of life in pink mist into an ongoing political statement that still speaks today. The thousands of Canadian "Everymen" who died, died for a reason that makes keeping an ongoing memorial to them a national enterprise. As Prime Minister Borden put it on Dominion Day 1917, at the ceremony that began the rebuilding of Parliament after the 1916 fire that left only the library standing, we owe much "to the valour of those Canadians who, in the Great War, fought for the liberties of Canada, of the Empire, and of humanity."[5]

# Acknowledgments

Not long after the Armistice in 1918, grieving parents, widows, and children armed with guidebooks crossed the English Channel to the battlefields of France and Belgium. My study of the past was guided by two gifted and giving historians: Dr. Tim Cook, First World War historian at the Canadian War Museum, and Dr. Bill Rawling of the Department of National Defence's Directorate of History. Both spent long hours explaining to me the intricacies of battle and the politics of the Canadian Expeditionary Force. And both made important editorial suggestions after reading my manuscript.

The staff at the In Flanders Fields Museum in Ypres, Belgium, especially the researcher Bert Heyvaert, were also most helpful. Special thanks are owed to the museum's director, Dominiek Dendooven, for inviting me to present part of this book at the November 2006 "1915 Innocence Slaughtered" conference, which commemorated the ninetieth anniversary of the gas attack, and for providing me with a copy of the paper he delivered at the conference. I must also thank Dr. Nick Lloyd, air power historian at RAF Cranwell, for his friendship and his attentive reading of my manuscript.

It is very different researching a project such as this one today than it would have been twenty-five years ago, and that is primarily, of course, because of the Internet and, more specifically, websites such as the Great War Forum and discussion groups such as "The Western Front" (http://1914_1918.invisionzone.com/forums/index.php?showforum=4), where one can find the answer to almost any question, no matter how detailed. My special thanks go to Eddy Lambrecht, Malt Zaniecki, Jack Sheldon, John Hartley, Simon Jones, "Siege Gunner," "Squirrel," "Patrick," "Giles Poilu," "angie999," "Aurel Sercu," and "Cnock." As well, I would like to thank Egbert Sandrock, who helped me with my German, and Michael Forsyth, who helped me with military terms.

It is the nature of the historian to always write about a "world elsewhere"; for a military historian who has never served in the military, this is perforce doubly true. To ensure that this work passed muster, I enlisted the help of one serving and one retired member of the Canadian Forces. Not only did Captain Floyd Low help me understand the maps that detail the 2nd Battle of Ypres and produce the maps that explain the troop movements, he also read my manuscript with an expert eye. Retired Colonel Berrard "Buzz" Bennett, who in the 1970s served at NATO Command in Belgium, caught many errors in the original manuscript. My understanding of the eighteen-pounder owes a great debt to Dr. Marple Sanders (Centre for First World War Studies, University of Birmingham). My graphic designer, Alain Paradis, worked wonders creating the maps.

I owe a special thanks to several others. Algonquin College's Inter-Library Loans Coordinator, Steve Potvin, has an almost magical ability to find articles from even the smallest part of a citation. My former colleague and friend Richard Martin deserves many thanks for standing between me and "barbarisms" of language. My researcher in Germany, Dr. Joachim Kundler, was able to ferret out the long-unused German regimental histories that form part of the spine of this work. I marvel at Dr. Michael Larrass's ability to render these histories into either military or poetic English. My editor at HarperCollins, Jim Gifford, supported this project with gusto and wielded his blue pencil with the skill of a surgeon. My agent, David Johnston, was, as the saying goes, "there at the creation."

It is my pleasure to thank Russell Mills, the dean of media and design at Algonquin College (Ottawa), who graciously agreed to allow me to go to France to conduct research for a week in November 2005 and to Ypres, Belgium, for the "1915 Innocence Slaughtered" conference. My attendance at this conference was made possible by a generous grant from the International Academic Relations Division of Foreign Affairs Canada. As well, I would like to thank Pamela Wilson, the chair of media at Algonquin College, for agreeing to several weeks of rearranged schedules so that I could attend this almost twenty-year-old conference, and for her good-natured support for my work outside the classroom.

Finally, I must thank four younger Canadians—my children, Pascale and Nicolas Greenfield, and Julie and Eric Dubé. They are most understanding about the time I spend in another time and place, and about the number of documents and books that fill our house.

I, alone, of course, am responsible for any errors in what precedes.

# Appendix A
## "The Reckoning"

The horror was almost biblical and, perhaps more important in our secular age, cinematic. The Angel of Death's minions—uncounted trillions of chlorine atoms—rise, a sickly yellow-green, seemingly from the bowls of the scarred earth. Scant moments later, eyes and throats burn horribly as belt buckles and harness rivets encrust green. Soon, hundreds of Belgian, French, and Canadian soldiers begin dying terrible deaths as their lungs filled with fluid. Some descriptions—of coughing up viscous mucous, of gasping for breath through a bloody froth—are of men drowning on a swath of ground a bit to the north and east of Ypres, a terrible foreshadowing of those who would drown in the mud a few miles away at Passchendaele. Other descriptions—of chests turning to cotton, of being enveloped in green fog—call to mind the horror of being buried alive.

The primordial and religious horror is present in a cartoon by Will Dyson, Australia's most famous war artist. Beneath a placard that reads "Academy of War Kultur—Torment Section—Poison Gases," there stands a stereotypical thin, monocled German professor. Just outside the doorway, the Devil has arrived, looking slightly anxious, as if he has come a little late. He is right. "I am sorry," says the professor, "we have no further openings for instructors." The Devil's reply, "Ah, you misjudge me—I come as a pupil," encapsulates, even as it uses humour to diffuse, the horror that poison gas engendered and how its use put Germany beyond the pale of Christian humanity.[1]

This line of civilized behaviour moved quickly.

On 27 April, before the 1st Canadian Division had fully withdrawn from the Ypres Salient and six days before British troops were outfitted with cotton masks, the British Cabinet began considering using gas in kind. Within a month the decision was made, and the first attack, in which chlorine gas was combined with smoke, was made at Loos on 25 September. German records read like Canadians' did in April:

> The bank of fog passed over our trenches, then came a blow bank of black-green smoke creeping toward us, and then another bank of gas some ten minutes behind the first.... Some men coughed and fell down. The others stood at the ready as long as possible. Behind the fourth gas and smoke cloud there suddenly emerged Englishmen in thick lines and storming columns. They rose suddenly from the earth wearing smoke masks over their faces and looking not like soldiers but like devils. These were bad and terrible hours.[2]

Then the wind shifted and the gas began to blow back towards the British lines. The concentration was increased when a German shell hit several cylinders of unreleased gas. The result was 2,632 *British* gas casualties.

Despite its horror, chlorine, like its descendants, was not a magic bullet. Had the gas attacks on the twenty-second and twenty-fourth been carried out with the reserves that were sent to Galacia still on hand, it is possible that no matter how valiantly the Canadians fought, they could not have sewn together the rent in the Allied lines. Because of the failure of the T-shells, OHL had little faith in the gas, which meant that Kaiser Wilhelm's generals set limited objectives. Indeed, in a real sense, even though Ypres and the areas beyond stood in the balance, 2nd Ypres was little more than a demonstration, designed to distract the Allies and hide from them the fact that the German lines were the ones that had been weakened. The Germans never realized that, at least for a few hours, the way to Ypres and beyond was open.

• • •

The story of gas warfare in the First World War is actually three different stories. The first is partially hidden by the casualties. If the First World War had been a play, the gas would have had a walk-on part. The great killer was artillery fire, which accounted for more than 60 percent of the 8,225,171 soldiers who died and 15,404,905 who were wounded over fifty-one months of war. Artillery fire killed 56,000 Canadians and wounded 173,000 more. Of the 1,240,000 men who were gassed, "only" 91,198 died; of those, some 11,000 belonged to King George V's senior dominion.

Several historians have noted that sloppy record-keeping and the exigencies of war mean that many of those who died from gas were listed simply as casualties. "British gas figures do not include any of the men inured or killed by gas in 1915 or any gas victims who became prisoners of war."[3] There are no records of those who were felled by gas and then obliterated by shellfire; they are recorded in the "Missing" column. And statistics cannot measure the terror and the drain on what Lord Moran called a soldier's "courage account" engendered by gas warfare. Gas warfare, especially in the final two months of the war, when Allied gas bombardments were almost continuous, began to "produce mental and physical casualties" equal to those produced by high explosives.[4]

The second part of the story is technological and organizational. Within days of the first attacks, British troops had been equipped with cotton gas masks. Next came the Hypo helmet (created by a Newfoundland captain, from an idea developed by a Canadian gassed at Ypres), a chemically treated flannel sack with a mica window. That was eventually replaced by the goggled P-helmet. By December 1915, commanders were ordered to ensure that "every man under their command [understood] the proper use and the correct method of adjusting the helmet and had actually done so once during the tour" at the front.[5]

When they realized that buglers would be silenced during a gas attack, Canadians installed electric klaxon horns in their trenches. On 23 May 1916, the Canadians appointed divisional gas officers and charged them with organizing gas training. By August 1916, Canadians were being trained in gas huts and had been outfitted with the box respirator, which, Fritz Haber is reputed to have said, made gas useless. In October 1916, the Canadian Gas Services was created.

According to the historian Tim Cook, "The Canadian Gas Services (CGS) had three functions. First, it was mandated to do research into new gases used by the Germans. Second, the CGS developed systems to deal with gas attacks. Finally, it was responsible for disseminating information about how to survive on the chemical battlefield, which is what the battlefield became in the last two years of the war." By mid-1917, even Canadian horses wore gas masks.

The final part of the story is, perhaps, the most ironic. Though gas was not used during Canada's most famous victory, at Vimy on 9 April 1917, the Canadians became the greatest per capita users of gas. The artillery plan approved by General Sir Arthur Currie for the August 1917 attack on Hill 70 (the capture of which forced the Germans to abandon the city of Lens) called for a forty-five-minute barrage of gas (mixed with high-explosive shells) before the attack; that barrage cost the Germans thirty thousand men. At Passchendaele, 75 percent of the shells fired during the battery work before the battle contained gas.

Gas was the *sine qua non* of the Canadian way of war during the Hundred Days, when the 105,000-man Canadian Corps met and smashed forty-seven German divisions and advanced eighty-six miles.* At Amiens, the battle that General Erich Ludendorff called "the blackest day in the history of the German Army," 20 percent of the shells fired in counter-battery work were gas shells; discipline saved countless lives when the Germans fired shells filled with mustard gas. Canadians

---

*The 650,000-man American Expeditionary Force defeated forty-six divisions in forty-seven days and advanced thirty-four miles.

themselves fired in excess of seventeen thousand gas shells over more than a two-week stretch prior to the attack at Boulon Wood on 27 September 1918.

According to Cook:

During these battles of the last hundred days, gas was used continuously by both sides in an effort to injure, maim, kill and, equally importantly, reduce the combat effectiveness of the other side. Putting on and fighting in a gas mask produced a remarkable reduction in fighting ability—and that is not even taking account of the psychological toll that constant exposure to such a fearful enemy took.

The Hundred Days was a constant—indeed, history's only—gas battlefield. Perhaps because the Canadians survived the first gas attacks at 2nd Ypres, they were primed to learn its lessons. Thanks to the CGS and the soldiers' gas discipline, the Canadians not only survived, they triumphed.

# Appendix B
Casualties for the 2nd Battle of Ypres (22 to 30 April)*

While the number of casualties at the Second Battle of Ypres is fairly well documented, the number of casualties as a result of poison gas in the fields is far more difficult to estimate. A study of the 1st Division's war diary conducted by the army historical section concluded that were only three Canadian deaths resulting from gas inhalation and 248 non-fatal injuries from it, with 55 soldiers captured as POWs during the assault. However, according to Tim Cook, the numbers are almost certainly inaccurate, as is A. Fortesque Duguid's count of 122 men hospitalized for gas treatment and another 1,556 men evacuated for "sickness." Many of the latter were, in fact, suffering from being gassed. Cook rightly cites the British official medical history's explanation for the difficulty in determining how many the gas cloud killed:

> A large number of men were killed outright by gas in the field, but deaths due to this cause are included in the casualty lists under the general heading "killed in action." For the severity of the fighting allowed little opportunity for distinguishing between those who died from the dire effects of the gas from those killed by shell fire or rifle bullets. Again and again officers and men who went up in support ... described how they passed

---

*The Belgian, French, British, and German casualty figures come from Dixon, 351f.

men lying in groups in the trenches and on the roads who had apparently died of asphyxia (Cook, *No Place to Run*, 32).

After comparing the gas attacks at Ypres to attacks on 1, 6, and 24 May (on 1 May, 2,413 British soldiers were gassed, and 227 died), Cook concludes that "it is not unreasonable to assume that hundreds perished and many more were permanently maimed due to the immediate and long-term effects of the gas" (Ibid., 33). It is interesting to note that after the attack, German doctors claimed, no doubt for propaganda purposes, that they treated ten cases of gassing.

|  | KILLED | WOUNDED | MISSING | TOTAL | |
|---|---|---|---|---|---|
| **ALLIED FORCES** (22–30 APRIL 1915) | | | | | |
| Officers | 65 | 104 | 0 | 169 | CANADIAN |
| Other Ranks | 1,672 | 1,822 | 1,754 | 5,248 | |
| Officers | 501 | 1412 | 234 | 2147 | BRITISH |
| Other Ranks | 10,018 | 30,922 | 16,185 | 57,125 | |
| | | | | 1,530 | BELGIAN* |
| | | | | 10,000 | FRENCH* |
| **GERMAN FORCES** (22–30 APRIL 1915) | | | | | |
| Officers | 40 | 89 | 13 | 142 | XV Reserve Corps |
| Other Ranks | 977 | 3,862 | 1,780 | 6,619 | |
| Officers | 50 | 119 | 4 | 173 | XVII Reserve Corps |
| Other Ranks | 998 | 4,247 | 813 | 6,058 | |
| Officers | 16 | 38 | 2 | 56 | XXVI Reserve Corps |
| Other Ranks | 319 | 1,121 | 144 | 1,584 | |
| Officers | 7 | 10 | 1 | 18 | XXIII Reserve Corps |
| Other Ranks | 101 | 437 | 28 | 566 | |
| Officers | 113 | 256 | 20 | **389** | TOTAL OF ALL CORPS |
| Other Ranks | 2,395 | 9,667 | 2,765 | **14,827** | |

*At this point in the war, the French and Belgians did not divide their casualty reports into killed/wounded/missing.

# Appendix C
## The Canadian Order of Battle

*1ST CANADIAN DIVISION*

General Officer Commanding:
Lieutenant-General Edwin A. H. Alderson

*1st Brigade:* Brigadier-General Malcolm S. Mercer
*Brigade Major:* Major R. J. F. Haytor
1st Battalion: Lieutenant-Colonel Frederick W. Hill
2nd Battalion: Lieutenant-Colonel David Watson
3rd Battalion: Lieutenant-Colonel Robert Rennie
4th Battalion: Lieutenant-Colonel Arthur P. Birchall

*2nd Brigade:* Brigadier-General Arthur W. Currie
*Brigade Major:* Lieutenant-Colonel Herbert Kemmis-Betty
5th Battalion: Lieutenant-Colonel George S. Tuxford
7th Battalion: Lieutenant-Colonel William F. R. Hart-McHarg
8th Battalion: Lieutenant-Colonel Louis J. Lipsett
10th Battalion: Lieutenant-Colonel Robert L. Boyle

*3rd Brigade: Brigadier-General Richard E. W. Turner*
*Brigade Major: Lieutenant-Colonel Garnet H. Hughes*
13th Battalion: Lieutenant-Colonel Frederick O. W. Loomis
14th Battalion: Lieutenant-Colonel Frank S. Meighen
15th Battalion: Lieutenant-Colonel John A. Currie, MP
16th Battalion: Lieutenant-Colonel Robert G. E. Leckie

*Divisional Artillery: Brigadier-General Harry E. Burstall*
1st Brigade: Lieutenant-Colonel Edward W. B. Morrison
2nd Brigade: Lieutenant-Colonel John J. Creelman
3rd Brigade: Lieutenant-Colonel J. H. Mitchell

*Divisional Engineers: Lieutenant-Colonel C. J. Armstrong*
1st Field Company: Major W. W. Melville
2nd Field Company: Captain Thomas C. Irving
3rd Field Company: Major C. B. Wright

*1st Divisional Signal Company: Major F. A. Lister*

*Canadian Army Medical Corps*
No. 1 Field Ambulance: Lieutenant-Colonel A. E. Ross
No. 2 Field Ambulance: Lieutenant-Colonel D. W. McPherson
No. 3 Field Ambulance: Lieutenant-Colonel J. A. Gunn

# Appendix D
## In Memoriam

Just over 200 of the men remembered in these pages lie in cemeteries such as Poperinghe New Military, White House or Tyne Cot.* At the heads of their graves are white stones, each bearing a chiselled maple leaf, large and distinct enough to be seen from the trains that pass close by the smaller cemeteries dotting Flanders' fields. Most of the fallen men, however, some 1,300, have no final resting place, their bodies having been obliterated by high-explosive shells or the ravages of war. Their names are incised on the granite curtains of the barrel-vaulted Menin Gate in Ypres, Belgium, together with the names of almost 55,000 other British troops, including another 5,500 Canadians (most of whom fell in late 1917 at Passchendaele, a few miles away from where the Canadians fought in April 1915). With the exception of the dusks that fell during Germany's occupation of Belgium in the Second World War, every evening since 2 July 1928, just as the sun sets, the "Last Post" sounds and wreaths are laid before the names of thousands of Canadian and British troops who have No Known Grave.

---

*The names gathered together here were compiled using both the records of the Commonwealth War Graves Commission and the Canadian Great War Project website. May the men who died between 22 April and 30 April 1915, and any whose names have inadvertently been left out of this In Memoriam, *requiescat in pace*.

| Last Name | Rank | First Name | Battalion | Home City/Regiment | Resting Place |
|---|---|---|---|---|---|
| Anderson | Private | David | 1st | Western Ontario Regiment | No Known Grave |
| Barker | Private | George C. | 1st | Galt, ON | No Known Grave |
| Barnes | Private | Francis B. | 1st | Brockville, ON | No Known Grave |
| Bastedo | Captain | Alfred C. | 1st | Toronto, ON | No Known Grave |
| Bowie | Private | William | 1st | Western Ontario Regiment | No Known Grave |
| Brade | Private | Henry C. | 1st | Galt, ON | No Known Grave |
| Brady | Private | William B. | 1st | Charlottetown, PEI | No Known Grave |
| Brennan | Lance-Corporal | Thomas J. | 1st | Timmins, ON | No Known Grave |
| Brookfield | Private | Andrew | 1st | Ingersoll, ON | Wimereux Communal Cemetery, France |
| Burch | Private | Horner | 1st | Western Ontario Regiment | Boulogne Eastern Cemetery, France |
| Byng | Private | Joseph | 1st | Western Ontario Regiment | No Known Grave |
| Christie | Corporal | George | 1st | Western Ontario Regiment | Poperinghe New Military Cemetery, Belgium |
| Clarke | Private | Harry | 1st | Western Ontario Regiment | No Known Grave |
| Claus | Private | Abner E. | 1st | St. Thomas, ON | Metern Military Cemetery, France |
| Colson | Sergeant | William J. | 1st | Central Ontario Regiment | No Known Grave |
| Croucher | Private | Hope R. | 1st | Chatham, ON | No Known Grave |
| Davis | Private | Edwin J. | 1st | Covington, VA | No Known Grave |
| De Gruchy | Corporal | Joshua L. | 1st | Edmonton, AB | No Known Grave |
| Doughty | Private | Alfred H. | 1st | Western Ontario Regiment | No Known Grave |
| Duffy | Private | Aloysius D. | 1st | Western Ontario Regiment | No Known Grave |
| Elliot | Private | Alexander M. | 1st | Western Ontario Regiment | Wimereux Communal Cemetery, France |
| Eversfield | Private | Leslie | 1st | Western Ontario Regiment | No Known Grave |
| Fisher | Private | John A. | 1st | Merritton, ON | No Known Grave |
| Fisher | Private | James C. | 1st | Elora, ON | No Known Grave |
| Gibb | Private | Andrew | 1st | Western Ontario Regiment | No Known Grave |
| Glasser | Private | Henry R. | 1st | Chatham, ON | Poperinghe Old Military Cemetery |

| Last Name | Rank | First Name | Battalion | Home City/Regiment | Resting Place |
|---|---|---|---|---|---|
| Goodall | Private | Wesley M. | 1st | London, ON | No Known Grave |
| Gordon | Private | Christopher R. | 1st | Windsor, ON | No Known Grave |
| Gregson | Private | David W. | 1st | Fergus, ON | Klein-vierstraat British Cemetery |
| Hughes | Corporal | Edward S. | 1st | Sangudo, AB | No Known Grave |
| Hull | Private | Frederick W. | 1st | Dundas, ON | No Known Grave |
| Iliffe | Private | Roy S. | 1st | Western Ontario Regiment | No Known Grave |
| Keir | Private | Alexander E. | 1st | Toronto, ON | Boulogne Eastern Cemetery, France |
| Kimmins | Major | Albert E. | 1st | Winona, ON | No Known Grave |
| Kirk | Private | Andrew O. | 1st | Westminster, ON | Boulogne Eastern Cemetery, France |
| Laforce | Private | Angus | 1st | Montreal, QC | No Known Grave |
| Leith | Private | James | 1st | Galt, ON | No Known Grave |
| Leslie | Private | James J. | 1st | Hamilton, ON | No Known Grave |
| Lockhart | Lieutenant | Thomas D. | 1st | Galt, ON | No Known Grave |
| Loughrin | Private | Cornelius | 1st | Western Ontario Regiment | No Known Grave |
| Mathieson | Private | Alexander W. | 1st | Bracebridge, ON | Hagle Dump Cemetery, Belgium |
| McIntosh | Private | James | 1st | Western Ontario Regiment | No Known Grave |
| Minorgan | Private | James H. | 1st | Chatsworth, ON | Vlamertinghe Military Cemetery, Belgium |
| Moynihin | Private | James | 1st | Wellington, ON | Bailleul Communal Cemetery, France |
| Munro | Private | William D. | 1st | Western Ontario Regiment | Bailleul Communal Cemetery, France |
| Murch | Private | Edward | 1st | Wingham, ON | Boulogne Eastern Cemetery, France |
| Newell | Sergeant | Lawrence G. | 1st | Watford, ON | Vlamertinghe Military Cemetery, Belgium |
| Palmer | Lance-Corporal | William | 1st | Goderich, ON | White House Cemetery, Belgium |
| Palmer | Private | Ernest J. | 1st | Western Ontario Regiment | No Known Grave |
| Payne | Private | Walter H. | 1st | Western Ontario Regiment | No Known Grave |
| Peterson | Private | Leonard | 1st | Owosso, MI | No Known Grave |
| Philcox | Private | Harry M. | 1st | Western Ontario Regiment | Bailleul Communal Cemetery Extension, France |

| Last Name | Rank | First Name | Battalion | Home City/Regiment | Resting Place |
| --- | --- | --- | --- | --- | --- |
| Pitman | Private | Frank E. | 1st | Western Ontario Regiment | No Known Grave |
| Polley | Private | Charles A. | 1st | Stratford, ON | No Known Grave |
| Rankan | Private | William | 1st | Western Ontario Regiment | No Known Grave |
| Rowe | Sergeant | Ernest J. | 1st | London, ON | No Known Grave |
| Shepley | Private | Adam E. | 1st | Amherstburg, ON | Vlamertinghe Military Cemetery, Belgium |
| Smith | Private | Henry | 1st | Western Ontario Regiment | No Known Grave |
| Smith | Private | William H. | 1st | Western Ontario Regiment | No Known Grave |
| Somerville | Private | Hugh | 1st | St. Thomas, ON | No Known Grave |
| Sumner | Private | David | 1st | Western Ontario Regiment | No Known Grave |
| Sutton | Private | Edwin J. | 1st | Galt, ON | No Known Grave |
| Thomas | Corporal | Albert E. | 1st | Amherstburg, ON | No Known Grave |
| Thomas | Private | Jacob | 1st | Western Ontario Regiment | No Known Grave |
| Thomas | Lieutenant | Murray | 1st | Amherstburg, ON | No Known Grave |
| Thomas | Private | Rex | 1st | Winnipeg, MB | No Known Grave |
| Ward | Private | John | 1st | Western Ontario Regiment | No Known Grave |
| Western | Lance-Corporal | Philip H. | 1st | Western Ontario Regiment | No Known Grave |
| Williams | Private | John M. | 1st | Ilderton, ON | No Known Grave |
| Wilson | Private | Edwin G. | 1st | Tilsonburg, ON | No Known Grave |
| Woodward | Private | Alfred C. | 1st | Eastern Ontario Regiment | No Known Grave |
| Ablard | Private | Henry C. | 2nd | Belleville, ON | No Known Grave |
| Abrahamsen | Private | John | 2nd | Ottawa, ON | No Known Grave |
| Alexander | Private | Walter C. | 2nd | Ottawa, ON | No Known Grave |
| Allingham | Private | Joseph G. | 2nd | Saint John, NB | No Known Grave |
| Andrews | Lance-Corporal | William | 2nd | Eastern Ontario Regiment | No Known Grave |
| Banbrook | Private | Frederick W. | 2nd | Eastern Ontario Regiment | No Known Grave |

| Last Name | Rank | First Name | Battalion | Home City/Regiment | Resting Place |
| --- | --- | --- | --- | --- | --- |
| Baptist | Private | David Y. | 2nd | Vanscoy, SK | No Known Grave |
| Barker | Private | George B. | 2nd | Eastern Ontario Regiment | No Known Grave |
| Bartle | Private | Eric L. | 2nd | Eastern Ontario Regiment | New Irish Farm Cemetery, Belgium |
| Bennett | Major | G. W. | 2nd | Eastern Ontario Regiment | New Irish Farm Cemetery, Belgium |
| Bennett | Private | Russell | 2nd | Toronto, ON | No Known Grave |
| Bigham | Private | George | 2nd | Smiths Falls, ON | No Known Grave |
| Billings | Private | James G. | 2nd | Brockville, ON | Tyne Cot Cemetery, Belgium |
| Blackburn | Private | Edward | 2nd | Eastern Ontario Regiment | No Known Grave |
| Blair | Private | Stuart C. | 2nd | Quebec City, QC | No Known Grave |
| Bolster | Major | Herbert G. | 2nd | Cobourg, ON | No Known Grave |
| Boolsen | Private | Carl S. | 2nd | Eastern Ontario Regiment | No Known Grave |
| Boreland | Private | Robert | 2nd | Eastern Ontario Regiment | No Known Grave |
| Boswell | Private | Ernest B. | 2nd | Toronto, ON | No Known Grave |
| Boulter | Private | Frederick J. | 2nd | Eastern Ontario Regiment | No Known Grave |
| Brisco | Private | Frederick S. | 2nd | Eastern Ontario Regiment | No Known Grave |
| Brister | Sergeant | Albert J. | 2nd | Brockville, ON | No Known Grave |
| Brown | Private | Edgar | 2nd | Toronto, ON | No Known Grave |
| Bulleid | Private | George E. | 2nd | Eastern Ontario Regiment | No Known Grave |
| Burnes | Private | Carlton F. | 2nd | South River, ON | Bailleul Communal Cemetery, France |
| Bury | Private | Harry G. | 2nd | Sarnia, ON | No Known Grave |
| Butcher | Lance-Corporal | Robert L. | 2nd | Eastern Ontario Regiment | No Known Grave |
| Butler | Private | Peter J. | 2nd | Peterborough, ON | No Known Grave |
| Byrne | Private | Walter | 2nd | Eastern Ontario Regiment | No Known Grave |
| Cameron | Private | George H. | 2nd | Eastern Ontario Regiment | No Known Grave |
| Campbell | Private | William L. | 2nd | Eastern Ontario Regiment | No Known Grave |
| Carpenter | Private | John | 2nd | Eastern Ontario Regiment | No Known Grave |

| Last Name | Rank | First Name | Battalion | Home City/Regiment | Resting Place |
|---|---|---|---|---|---|
| Carr | Private | Frederick G. | 2nd | Toronto, ON | No Known Grave |
| Cathcart | Private | Francis D. | 2nd | Edmonton, AB | No Known Grave |
| Chantry | Private | Alfred | 2nd | Eastern Ontario Regiment | No Known Grave |
| Chard | Private | Ezra | 2nd | Frankford, ON | No Known Grave |
| Clarke | Private | Ewart G. | 2nd | Kingston, ON | No Known Grave |
| Coe | Private | Thomas E. | 2nd | Eastern Ontario Regiment | No Known Grave |
| Cook | Private | Joseph | 2nd | Spencerville, ON | No Known Grave |
| Cooper | Private | David G. | 2nd | Steelton, ON | Poperinghe Old Military Cemetery, Belgium |
| Crawley | Private | Percy W. | 2nd | Ottawa, ON | No Known Grave |
| Culling | Captain | Evelyn C. | 2nd | Eastern Ontario Regiment | No Known Grave |
| Cumberland | Private | Keith O. | 2nd | Peterborough, ON | No Known Grave |
| Dalgish | Private | William A. | 2nd | Ottawa, ON | No Known Grave |
| Day | Lieutenant | Calvin W. | 2nd | Kingston, ON | No Known Grave |
| Dempsay | Private | Nelson H. | 2nd | Cochrane, ON | No Known Grave |
| Dewell | Private | Matthew E. | 2nd | Enniskillen, ON | No Known Grave |
| Down | Corporal | James | 2nd | Brockville, ON | No Known Grave |
| Dowse | Private | Samuel J. | 2nd | Eastern Ontario Regiment | No Known Grave |
| Doxsee | Lieutenant | William J. | 2nd | Campbellford, ON | No Known Grave |
| Dussault | Private | Oliver | 2nd | Ottawa, ON | No Known Grave |
| English | Private | James H. | 2nd | Peterborough, ON | No Known Grave |
| Fairbairn | Private | William | 2nd | Eastern Ontario Regiment | No Known Grave |
| Fanning | Private | William J. | 2nd | Quebec, QC | No Known Grave |
| Farquharson | Private | John | 2nd | Eastern Ontario Regiment | No Known Grave |
| Faulkner | Private | Freeman | 2nd | Aurora, ON | No Known Grave |
| Ferguson | Private | John | 2nd | Limoilou, QC | No Known Grave |
| Ferris | Private | Herbert | 2nd | Toronto, ON | No Known Grave |

| Last Name | Rank | First Name | Battalion | Home City/Regiment | Resting Place |
| --- | --- | --- | --- | --- | --- |
| Field | Private | Alfred J. | 2nd | Smiths Falls, ON | No Known Grave |
| Fillion | Private | Hector O. | 2nd | Embrun, ON | No Known Grave |
| Flanagan | Private | Daniel | 2nd | Eastern Ontario Regiment | No Known Grave |
| Fleet | Private | William | 2nd | Kingston, ON | No Known Grave |
| Forest | Gunner | Henry S. | 2nd | Coaticook, QC | No Known Grave |
| Fox | Private | Michael | 2nd | Sheenboro, QC | No Known Grave |
| Frood | Private | Lorn V. | 2nd | Toronto, ON | No Known Grave |
| Gardiner | Sergeant | Edward G. | 2nd | Eastern Ontario Regiment | No Known Grave |
| Gardner | Private | Richard | 2nd | River Desert, QC | No Known Grave |
| Gibson | Private | William F. | 2nd | Peterborough, ON | No Known Grave |
| Glass | Lance-Corporal | Frank K. | 2nd | Quebec City, QC | No Known Grave |
| Gordon | Captain | Walter L. | 2nd | Toronto, ON | No Known Grave |
| Graham | Lance-Corporal | William T. | 2nd | Eastern Ontario Regiment | No Known Grave |
| Grant | Private | Peter M. | 2nd | Sault Ste. Marie, ON | No Known Grave |
| Grant | Private | William J. | 2nd | Ottawa, ON | No Known Grave |
| Gray | Private | Edward | 2nd | Eastern Ontario Regiment | No Known Grave |
| Gray | Private | George E. | 2nd | Eastern Ontario Regiment | No Known Grave |
| Gray | Private | George H. | 2nd | Eastern Ontario Regiment | No Known Grave |
| Gray | Private | William | 2nd | Eastern Ontario Regiment | No Known Grave |
| Griffiths | Private | Thomas H. | 2nd | Peterborough, ON | No Known Grave |
| Gunnip | Private | George | 2nd | St. Charles, QC | No Known Grave |
| Hagon | Private | George | 2nd | Kingston, ON | No Known Grave |
| Haight | Private | Grant A. | 2nd | Wellington, ON | No Known Grave |
| Haldane | Private | Roy H. | 2nd | Arthur, ON | No Known Grave |
| Hall | Private | William N. | 2nd | Eastern Ontario Regiment | Wimereux Communal Cemetery, France |
| Hallimond | Private | William G. | 2nd | Belmar, NJ | No Known Grave |

| Last Name | Rank | First Name | Battalion | Home City/Regiment | Resting Place |
| --- | --- | --- | --- | --- | --- |
| Hamilton | Private | James | 2nd | Eastern Ontario Regiment | No Known Grave |
| Harrabin | Private | Arthur | 2nd | Stirling, ON | No Known Grave |
| Hastings | Private | John W. | 2nd | Renfrew, ON | No Known Grave |
| Hatswell | Private | John V. | 2nd | Eastern Ontario Regiment | No Known Grave |
| Haydon | Lance-Corporal | Edwin E. | 2nd | Eastern Ontario Regiment | No Known Grave |
| Hayes | Private | Stuart F. | 2nd | Guelph, ON | No Known Grave |
| Head | Private | William E. | 2nd | Picton, ON | No Known Grave |
| Heineman | Private | Clayton C. | 2nd | Picton, ON | No Known Grave |
| Hickman | Private | Albert | 2nd | St. Catharines, ON | No Known Grave |
| Hicks | Private | Burwell | 2nd | Trenton, ON | No Known Grave |
| Hicks | Private | Gerald W. | 2nd | Trenton, ON | New Irish Farm Cemetery, Belgium |
| Hodgson | Private | Augustus S. | 2nd | Melfort, SK | No Known Grave |
| Howard | Private | John H. | 2nd | Eastern Ontario Regiment | No Known Grave |
| Howarth | Sergeant-Major | Fred | 2nd | Eastern Ontario Regiment | No Known Grave |
| Howden | Corporal | Montagu H. | 2nd | Eastern Ontario Regiment | No Known Grave |
| Hughes | Private | Robert E. | 2nd | Toronto, ON | No Known Grave |
| Hunt | Private | Horace | 2nd | Ottawa, ON | No Known Grave |
| Ingham | Private | Robert K. | 2nd | Toronto, ON | No Known Grave |
| Ireland | Private | Harry A. | 2nd | Bowmanville, ON | No Known Grave |
| Ironside | Private | James S. | 2nd | Sault Ste. Marie, ON | No Known Grave |
| Jarrett | Private | George | 2nd | Steelton, ON | No Known Grave |
| Jarvie | Private | Alexander W. | 2nd | Eastern Ontario Regiment | No Known Grave |
| Jefferson | Lance-Corporal | Bertram D. | 2nd | Eastern Ontario Regiment | No Known Grave |
| Jones | Private | Douglas C. | 2nd | Eastern Ontario Regiment | No Known Grave |
| Joynt | Private | William J. | 2nd | Toledo, ON | No Known Grave |
| Julien | Private | Louis | 2nd | Eastern Ontario Regiment | No Known Grave |

| Last Name | Rank | First Name | Battalion | Home City/Regiment | Resting Place |
| --- | --- | --- | --- | --- | --- |
| Keating | Private | Daniel | 2nd | Eastern Ontario Regiment | No Known Grave |
| Kelley | Private | Alfred E. | 2nd | Brockville, ON | No Known Grave |
| Kelso | Lance-Corporal | William A. | 2nd | Kingston, ON | No Known Grave |
| Kemsley | Lance-Corporal | Ernest W. | 2nd | Eastern Ontario Regiment | No Known Grave |
| Kennedy | Private | Thomas | 2nd | Sault Ste. Marie, ON | No Known Grave |
| Kershaw | Private | Frederick N. | 2nd | Eastern Ontario Regiment | No Known Grave |
| Klotz | Lieutenant | Herbert N. | 2nd | Toronto, ON | No Known Grave |
| Labourcane | Private | Samuel | 2nd | Saint-Paul-des-Métis, AB | No Known Grave |
| Lacelle | Private | Fred | 2nd | Ottawa, ON | No Known Grave |
| Lavender | Private | Bert | 2nd | Victoria, BC | Vlamertinghe Military Cemetery, Belgium |
| Lawlor | Private | Edward | 2nd | Eastern Ontario Regiment | No Known Grave |
| Leal | Private | Reginald D. | 2nd | Peterborough, ON | No Known Grave |
| Lemesurier | Sergeant | Garnet W. | 2nd | Quebec City, QC | No Known Grave |
| Letts | Private | Hugh | 2nd | Turriff, ON | No Known Grave |
| Lewis | Private | Charles F. | 2nd | Eastern Ontario Regiment | No Known Grave |
| Lightwood | Private | A. | 2nd | Toronto, ON | No Known Grave |
| Lindesay | Lance-Corporal | Hugh H. | 2nd | Eastern Ontario Regiment | No Known Grave |
| Litchfield | Private | Thomas | 2nd | Kingston, ON | No Known Grave |
| Long | Private | William J. | 2nd | Eastern Ontario Regiment | No Known Grave |
| Loutit | Private | Peter H. | 2nd | Edmonton, AB | No Known Grave |
| MacDonald | Private | Alfred | 2nd | Syndenham, ON | No Known Grave |
| Macrae | Private | Donald | 2nd | Eastern Ontario Regiment | No Known Grave |
| Mahoney | Lance-Corporal | Thomas | 2nd | Belleville, ON | No Known Grave |
| Martin | Corporal | Kenneth C. | 2nd | Bowmanville, ON | No Known Grave |
| McAughtrie | Private | Thomas | 2nd | Eastern Ontario Regiment | No Known Grave |
| McDonald | Private | Donald | 2nd | Kingston, ON | No Known Grave |

| Last Name | Rank | First Name | Battalion | Home City/Regiment | Resting Place |
|---|---|---|---|---|---|
| McDougall | Gunner | George A. | 2nd | Moncton, NB | New Irish Farm Cemetery, Belgium |
| McGovern | Private | Thomas | 2nd | Eastern, Ontario Regiment | No Known Grave |
| McGurk | Lance-Corporal | Peter | 2nd | Toronto, ON | No Known Grave |
| McIntosh | Private | Roy | 2nd | Lanark, ON | No Known Grave |
| McIntyre | Private | Roy | 2nd | Eastern Ontario Regiment | No Known Grave |
| McKinlay | Private | Samuel | 2nd | London, ON | No Known Grave |
| McMahon | Corporal | Michael | 2nd | Brockville, ON | No Known Grave |
| McPhee | Private | Neil J. | 2nd | Carleton Place, ON | No Known Grave |
| McRae | Private | Donald | 2nd | Eastern Ontario Regiment | No Known Grave |
| Meadowcroft | Private | John | 2nd | Eastern Ontario Regiment | No Known Grave |
| Meister | Private | William J. | 2nd | Ottawa, ON | No Known Grave |
| Mills | Private | Arthur E. | 2nd | Eastern Ontario Regiment | No Known Grave |
| Minorgan | Private | George E. | 2nd | Peterborough, ON | No Known Grave |
| Montgomery | Private | Osborn | 2nd | Lakefield, ON | New Irish Farm Cemetery, Belgium |
| Morgan | Private | W. P. | 2nd | Eastern Ontario Regiment | No Known Grave |
| Mowat | Private | Malcolm | 2nd | Eastern Ontario Regiment | No Known Grave |
| Nairn | Private | William M. | 2nd | Eastern Ontario Regiment | No Known Grave |
| Narlock | Private | Michael | 2nd | Renfrew, ON | No Known Grave |
| Newell | Private | James G. | 2nd | Spencerport, NY | No Known Grave |
| Nichols | Lance-Corporal | Frank W. | 2nd | Sault Ste. Marie, ON | No Known Grave |
| Nolan | Private | William H. | 2nd | Sidney, ON | No Known Grave |
| Nord | Private | Peter | 2nd | Eastern Ontario Regiment | No Known Grave |
| Norton | Private | Thomas | 2nd | Ottawa, ON | No Known Grave |
| Oliver | Private | Theodore H. | 2nd | St-Stanislas, QC | No Known Grave |
| Ormsby | Lance-Corporal | William G. | 2nd | Toronto, ON | No Known Grave |
| Owen | Private | Eric R. | 2nd | Eastern Ontario Regiment | No Known Grave |

| Last Name | Rank | First Name | Battalion | Home City/Regiment | Resting Place |
|---|---|---|---|---|---|
| Owens | Private | Cecil E. | 2nd | St. Boniface, MB | No Known Grave |
| Oxley | Private | Alfred J. | 2nd | Eastern Ontario Regiment | No Known Grave |
| Pace | Private | Arthur H. | 2nd | Eastern Ontario Regiment | No Known Grave |
| Parker | Private | George C. | 2nd | Toronto, ON | No Known Grave |
| Parris | Private | Andrew H. | 2nd | Edmonton, AB | Tyne Cot Cemetery, Belgium |
| Parsons | Private | Bernard W. | 2nd | Eastview (Vanier), ON | No Known Grave |
| Paton | Private | John | 2nd | Victoria, BC | No Known Grave |
| Patton | Private | Harold R. | 2nd | Saint-Joseph-de-Lévis, QC | No Known Grave |
| Pearce | Private | Frederick E. | 2nd | Eastern Ontario Regiment | No Known Grave |
| Pearless | Sergeant | Hugh N. | 2nd | British Columbia Regiment | No Known Grave |
| Pelletier | Private | Donat | 2nd | Ottawa, ON | No Known Grave |
| Persson | Private | Edward | 2nd | Sprucefield, AB | No Known Grave |
| Peters | Private | Arthur E. | 2nd | Haldimand, ON | No Known Grave |
| Pim | Private | Michael R. | 2nd | Sault Ste. Marie, ON | No Known Grave |
| Plet | Private | Arthur C. | 2nd | Ottawa, ON | No Known Grave |
| Polleys | Gunner | Edward H. | 2nd | Moncton, NB | Duhallow A.D.S. Cemetery, Belgium |
| Powel | Lance-Corporal | Herbert De B. | 2nd | Chicoutimi West, QC | No Known Grave |
| Powell | Private | Gareth H. | 2nd | Eastern Ontario Regiment | No Known Grave |
| Prescott | Private | William J. | 2nd | St-Eustache, QC | No Known Grave |
| Preston | Private | Roger | 2nd | Edmonton, AB | No Known Grave |
| Prosser | Private | Edward | 2nd | Toronto, ON | No Known Grave |
| Reid | Private | Benjamin N. | 2nd | Toronto, ON | No Known Grave |
| Robertson | Private | George | 2nd | Eastern Ontario Regiment | No Known Grave |
| Rogers | Private | John A. | 2nd | Wolfe Island, ON | No Known Grave |
| Rooney | Private | Arthur | 2nd | Eastern Ontario Regiment | No Known Grave |
| Rowe | Private | Archibald D. | 2nd | Toronto, ON | No Known Grave |

| Last Name | First Name | Rank | Battalion | Home City/Regiment | Resting Place |
|---|---|---|---|---|---|
| Ruben | Aaron S. | Private | 2nd | Barry's Bay, ON | No Known Grave |
| Savage | Alexander W. | Corporal | 2nd | Central Ontario Regiment | Oxford (Botley) Cemetery, England |
| Scollie | Harold William | Private | 2nd | Central Ontario Regiment | No Known Grave |
| Scurr | Albert | Private | 2nd | Eastern Ontario Regiment | Railway Dugouts Burial Ground, Belgium |
| Seymour | George E. | Private | 2nd | Eastern Ontario Regiment | No Known Grave |
| Shangrow | John L. | Private | 2nd | Kingston, ON | No Known Grave |
| Sheridan | Thomas A. | Private | 2nd | Ottawa, ON | Poperinghe Old Military Cemetery |
| Simons | Arthur J. | Private | 2nd | Eastern Ontario Regiment | No Known Grave |
| Sinclair | Archibald H. | Private | 2nd | Perth, ON | No Known Grave |
| Smith | Edward G. | Private | 2nd | Cannifton, ON | No Known Grave |
| Smith | Thomas O. | Private | 2nd | Eastern Ontario Regiment | No Known Grave |
| Snyder | Sherman J. | Private | 2nd | Picton, ON | No Known Grave |
| Sonheim | Louis | Private | 2nd | Edmonton, AB | No Known Grave |
| Spalding | Eric J. | Lance-Corporal | 2nd | Perth, ON | No Known Grave |
| Stephenson | Thomas | Private | 2nd | Kingston, ON | No Known Grave |
| Stevens | Fredrick | Lance-Sergeant | 2nd | Peterborough, ON | No Known Grave |
| Stirling | Robert A. | Lieutenant | 2nd | Eastern Ontario Regiment | No Known Grave |
| Stoddart | Daniel | Private | 2nd | Ottawa, ON | No Known Grave |
| Strudwick | Walter G. | Private | 2nd | Sudbury, ON | No Known Grave |
| Stuer | Gerard T. | Private | 2nd | Eastern Ontario Regiment | No Known Grave |
| Styants | Walter J. | Private | 2nd | Montreal, QC | No Known Grave |
| Swift | John | Private | 2nd | Eastern Ontario Regiment | No Known Grave |
| Tasse | Rodolfe | Private | 2nd | Ottawa, ON | No Known Grave |
| Taylor | Odely D. | Private | 2nd | Peterborough, ON | No Known Grave |
| Taylor | Edward | Private | 2nd | Eastern Ontario Regiment | Hazebrouck Communal Cemetery, France |
| Thomson | Gilbert | Private | 2nd | Midland, ON | No Known Grave |

| Last Name | Rank | First Name | Battalion | Home City/Regiment | Resting Place |
|---|---|---|---|---|---|
| Troy | Private | John | 2nd | Renfrew, ON | No Known Grave |
| Tuttle | Private | Ernest G. | 2nd | Picton, ON | No Known Grave |
| Unwin | Private | William D. | 2nd | Toronto, ON | No Known Grave |
| Waddy | Private | Harry C. | 2nd | Eastern Ontario Regiment | No Known Grave |
| Warburton | Private | George | 2nd | Eastern Ontario Regiment | No Known Grave |
| Wein | Private | David C. | 2nd | Crediton, ON | No Known Grave |
| Wheeler | Private | Richard H. | 2nd | Eastern Ontario Regiment | Poperinghe Old Military Cemetery |
| White | Private | Arthur W. | 2nd | Peterborough, ON | No Known Grave |
| White | Private | Stanley H. | 2nd | Niagara Falls South ON | No Known Grave |
| Wilson | Private | Robert | 2nd | Eastern Ontario Regiment | Poperinghe Old Military Cemetery |
| Wilson | Private | George | 2nd | Eastern Ontario Regiment | No Known Grave |
| Wines | Private | Percy | 2nd | Eastern Ontario Regiment | No Known Grave |
| Worles | Private | Albert E. | 2nd | Kemptville, ON | No Known Grave |
| Young | Private | John M. | 2nd | Eastern Ontario Regiment | No Known Grave |
| Young | Private | Russell | 2nd | Picton, ON | No Known Grave |
| Adams | Private | Frederick G. | 3rd | Toronto, ON | No Known Grave |
| Arnold | Corporal | Thomas | 3rd | Central Ontario Regiment | No Known Grave |
| Barker | Private | Thomas E. | 3rd | Toronto, ON | Vlamertinghe Military Cemetery, Belgium |
| Bell | Lance-Corporal | Joseph | 3rd | Toronto, ON | No Known Grave |
| Binkley | Lance-Corporal | James R. | 3rd | Dundas, ON | No Known Grave |
| Bittle | Private | Robert N. | 3rd | Toronto, ON | No Known Grave |
| Blacklock | Private | Frederick A. | 3rd | Galt, ON | No Known Grave |
| Bradshaw | Private | Fred W. | 3rd | Central Ontario Regiment | No Known Grave |
| Cameron | Lance-Corporal | Hugh C. | 3rd | Toronto, ON | No Known Grave |
| Carter | Private | Leslie H. | 3rd | Toronto, ON | No Known Grave |

| Last Name | Rank | First Name | Battalion | Home City/Regiment | Resting Place |
|---|---|---|---|---|---|
| Clark | Private | George B. | 3rd | Toronto, ON | No Known Grave |
| Coles | Private | Ernest C. | 3rd | Barrie, ON | No Known Grave |
| Collins-Williams | Private | Cecil H. | 3rd | Toronto, ON | No Known Grave |
| Dillon | Private | Thomas E. | 3rd | Central Ontario Regiment | No Known Grave |
| Dwyer | Private | Samuel | 3rd | Bloomsburg, PA | No Known Grave |
| Farrant | Private | Frank | 3rd | Central Ontario Regiment | No Known Grave |
| Ferguson | Corporal | William | 3rd | Central Ontario Regiment | No Known Grave |
| Gilfillan | Private | John | 3rd | Central Ontario Regiment | No Known Grave |
| Green | Private | Empson | 3rd | Toronto, ON | No Known Grave |
| Harries | Private | John S. | 3rd | Toronto, ON | No Known Grave |
| Howard | Private | Stanley T. | 3rd | Toronto, ON | Hazebrouck Communal Cemetery, France |
| Howe | Private | William J. | 3rd | Central Ontario Regiment | No Known Grave |
| Jarvis | Lieutenant | William D. | 3rd | Toronto, ON | No Known Grave |
| Kelleher | Private | Henry | 3rd | Chippawa, ON | No Known Grave |
| Kirkpatick | Lieutenant | Alexander D. | 3rd | Toronto, ON | No Known Grave |
| Latimer | Private | George | 3rd | Central Ontario Regiment | No Known Grave |
| Long | Private | Henry | 3rd | Central Ontario Regiment | No Known Grave |
| MacDonald | Lieutenant | M.D. | 3rd | Central Ontario Regiment | No Known Grave |
| McHugh | Private | Edward | 3rd | Central Ontario Regiment | No Known Grave |
| Medland | Lieutenant | Frederick R. | 3rd | Toronto, ON | No Known Grave |
| Mills | Private | Arthur M. | 3rd | Toronto, ON | No Known Grave |
| Mulloy | Sergeant | Edwin H. | 3rd | Aurora, ON | No Known Grave |
| Muntz | Captain | Herbert G. | 3rd | Muskoka, ON | Boulogne Eastern Cemetery, Belgium |
| Newman | Sergeant | Victor | 3rd | Newmarket, ON | No Known Grave |
| Noverre | Private | Phillip W. | 3rd | Toronto, ON | No Known Grave |
| Nunn | Private | William P. | 3rd | Toronto, ON | Tyne Cot Cemetery, Belgium |

| Last Name | Rank | First Name | Battalion | Home City/Regiment | Resting Place |
| --- | --- | --- | --- | --- | --- |
| Pannell | Private | William H. | 3rd | Agincourt, ON | Vlamertinghe Military Cemetery, Belgium |
| Peace | Private | Ernest | 3rd | Toronto, ON | No Known Grave |
| Raynor | Private | Joseph W. | 3rd | Toronto, ON | No Known Grave |
| Richards | Private | Henry | 3rd | Edmonton, AB | Roeselare Communal Cemetery, Belgium |
| Robertson | Private | John | 3rd | Central Ontario Regiment | No Known Grave |
| Ryerson | Captain | George C. | 3rd | Niagara-on-the-Lake, ON | No Known Grave |
| Shields | Private | Lawrence S. | 3rd | Hamilton, ON | No Known Grave |
| Sproulle | Private | Hugh | 3rd | Toronto, ON | Railway Dugouts Burial Ground, Belgium |
| Taverner | Lance-Corporal | Gerald R. | 3rd | Central Ontario Regiment | No Known Grave |
| Taylor | Private | Percy E. | 3rd | Toronto, ON | No Known Grave |
| Tory | Sergeant | Charles H. | 3rd | Battleview, AB | No Known Grave |
| Waters | Private | Sidney J. | 3rd | Central Ontario Regiment | No Known Grave |
| Watson | Private | Charles W. | 3rd | Toronto, ON | No Known Grave |
| Watts | Private | Sidney J. | 3rd | Central Ontario Regiment | No Known Grave |
| Webster | Private | Clarence F. | 3rd | Central Ontario Regiment | No Known Grave |
| White | Private | Robert H. | 3rd | Central Ontario Regiment | No Known Grave |
| Williams | Private | Cecil H. | 3rd | Toronto, ON | No Known Grave |
| Worsley | Private | Thomas | 3rd | Central Ontario Regiment | No Known Grave |
| Anchor | Private | Frank | 4th | Toronto, ON | No Known Grave |
| Baille | Private | Nathaniel | 4th | Hamilton, ON | No Known Grave |
| Bilsland | Private | James | 4th | Central Ontario Regiment | No Known Grave |
| Birch | Private | Fredric | 4th | Farnham, QC | No Known Grave |
| Birchall | Lt.-Col. | Arthur R. | 4th | Central Ontario Regiment | No Known Grave |
| Brant | Lieutenant | Cameron D. | 4th | Hagersville, ON | No Known Grave |
| Brinkworth | Private | F. G. | 4th | Central Ontario Regiment | No Known Grave |

| Last Name | Rank | First Name | Battalion | Home City/Regiment | Resting Place |
|---|---|---|---|---|---|
| Brown | Private | William C. | 4th | Central Ontario Regiment | New Irish Farm Cemetery, Belgium |
| Brown | Private | Peter | 4th | Central Ontario Regiment | White House Cemetery, Belgium |
| Burkhard | Private | Frank | 4th | Central Ontario Regiment | Boulogne Eastern Cemetery, France |
| Burtch | Private | Homer P. | 4th | Lansing, MI | Boulogne Eastern Cemetery, France |
| Cairns | Private | Alexander | 4th | Central Ontario Regiment | No Known Grave |
| Cameron | Private | Andrew | 4th | New Aberdeen, NS | No Known Grave |
| Campbell | Private | Thomas J. | 4th | Central Ontario Regiment | No Known Grave |
| Cardozo | Private | George | 4th | Central Ontario Regiment | No Known Grave |
| Charlton | Corporal | Claude F. | 4th | Brant County, ON | Vlamertinghe Military Cemetery, Belgium |
| Clarke | Private | Harold J. | 4th | Winton, SK | No Known Grave |
| Colvill | Private | Archibald H. | 4th | Central Ontario Regiment | No Known Grave |
| Connors | Private | Christy | 4th | Central Ontario Regiment | No Known Grave |
| Coulter | Sergeant | John J. | 4th | Toronto, ON | No Known Grave |
| Craven | Private | Ernest H. | 4th | Central Ontario Regiment | No Known Grave |
| Crawford | Private | William | 4th | Toronto, ON | No Known Grave |
| Crouch | Lance-Corporal | Jack | 4th | Owen Sound, ON | Bailleul Communal Cemetery Extension, France |
| Davey | Private | John M. | 4th | Owen Sound, ON | No Known Grave |
| Davies | Private | William | 4th | Central Ontario Regiment | No Known Grave |
| Deakin | Private | Arthur | 4th | Central Ontario Regiment | No Known Grave |
| Diver | Private | Alfred E. | 4th | New York, NY | No Known Grave |
| Dix | Private | William J. | 4th | St. Catharines, ON | No Known Grave |
| Don | Private | Stewart | 4th | Central Ontario Regiment | No Known Grave |
| Drinkwater | Private | William | 4th | Central Ontario Regiment | No Known Grave |
| Driver | Private | Frederick | 4th | Central Ontario Regiment | No Known Grave |
| Dudden | Private | Christopher G. | 4th | Central Ontario Regiment | No Known Grave |
| Duncan | Private | Thomas | 4th | Central Ontario Regiment | Boulogne Eastern Cemetery, France |

| Last Name | Rank | First Name | Battalion | Home City/Regiment | Resting Place |
|---|---|---|---|---|---|
| Easton | Private | George | 4th | Central Ontario Regiment | No Known Grave |
| Ellis | Private | Frank A. | 4th | Brantford, ON | No Known Grave |
| Farries | Private | Thomas | 4th | Central Ontario Regiment | No Known Grave |
| Flynn | Private | John J. | 4th | East Hamilton, ON | No Known Grave |
| Fraser | Private | Peter R. | 4th | Springhill, NS | No Known Grave |
| French | Private | Frederick A. | 4th | Central Ontario Regiment | No Known Grave |
| Gale | Private | George | 4th | Central Ontario Regiment | No Known Grave |
| Galpin | Private | Ralph S. | 4th | Ingersoll, ON | No Known Grave |
| George | Private | David | 4th | Chilliwack, BC | No Known Grave |
| Glover | Captain | John D. | 4th | Orillia, ON | No Known Grave |
| Griffin | Private | Thomas | 4th | Hamilton, ON | Hazebrouck Communal Cemetery, France |
| Griffiths | Private | Horace | 4th | Central Ontario Regiment | No Known Grave |
| Hall | Private | Thomas | 4th | Central Ontario Regiment | No Known Grave |
| Hall | Private | William G. | 4th | Central Ontario Regiment | No Known Grave |
| Hall | Private | William | 4th | Hamilton, ON | No Known Grave |
| Harrison | Private | George | 4th | Central Ontario Regiment | Poperinghe Old Military Cemetery, Belgium |
| Hart | Private | William C. | 4th | Toronto, ON | No Known Grave |
| Hawke | Private | John | 4th | Central Ontario Regiment | No Known Grave |
| Hawkins | Private | Richard R. | 4th | Hamilton, ON | No Known Grave |
| Hay | Sergeant | Robert | 4th | Central Ontario Regiment | No Known Grave |
| Hern | Private | Loftus R. | 4th | Exeter, ON | No Known Grave |
| Herrell | Private | Clifford E. | 4th | Orillia, ON | No Known Grave |
| Hibbert | Corporal | Thomas | 4th | Toronto, ON | No Known Grave |
| Hollinsed | Corporal | Richard E. | 4th | Central Ontario Regiment | No Known Grave |
| Howell | Private | George W. | 4th | Central Ontario Regiment | No Known Grave |
| Huggins | Private | George | 4th | Brantford, ON | No Known Grave |

| Last Name | Rank | First Name | Battalion | Home City/Regiment | Resting Place |
|---|---|---|---|---|---|
| Humphreys | Private | William | 4th | Aldershot, ON | No Known Grave |
| Hunter | Private | Cecil | 4th | Central Ontario Regiment | No Known Grave |
| Innes | Private | John | 4th | Winnipeg, MB | Hazebrouck Communal Cemetery, France |
| Keighley | Private | J. | 4th | Brantford, ON | No Known Grave |
| Kelley | Major | E. T. | 4th | Central Ontario Regiment | No Known Grave |
| Kelley | Private | Thomas E. | 4th | Toronto, ON | No Known Grave |
| Lambourne | Private | Frank G. | 4th | Central Ontario Regiment | No Known Grave |
| Larsen | Private | Johan L. | 4th | Central Ontario Regiment | No Known Grave |
| Latimer | Private | Walter | 4th | Central Ontario Regiment | No Known Grave |
| Lees | Private | William G. | 4th | Milton West, ON | No Known Grave |
| Leslie | Private | James | 4th | Central Ontario Regiment | No Known Grave |
| Leviston | Private | John | 4th | Central Ontario Regiment | No Known Grave |
| Lofty | Corporal | William | 4th | Brantford, ON | No Known Grave |
| Maines | Private | James | 4th | Midland, ON | No Known Grave |
| Mallen | Private | Henry | 4th | Central Ontario Regiment | No Known Grave |
| Marshall | Private | Frank | 4th | Hamilton, ON | No Known Grave |
| McCoy | Private | George | 4th | Brantford, ON | No Known Grave |
| McDonald | Private | James | 4th | Woodbridge, ON | No Known Grave |
| McGuire | Lieutenant | Harry B. | 4th | Orangeville, ON | Poperinghe Old Military Cemetery, Belgium |
| McHarg | Private | David | 4th | Central Ontario Regiment | Boulogne Eastern Cemetery, France |
| Mellody | Private | Albert J. | 4th | Central Ontario Regiment | Wimereux Communal Cemetery, France |
| Mitchell | Sergeant | Charles | 4th | Toronto, ON | No Known Grave |
| Mountain | Private | Stewart L. | 4th | Hamilton, ON | No Known Grave |
| Murray | Private | Ivor H. | 4th | Shediac, NB | Essex Farm Cemetery, Belgium |
| Nalty | Private | Reginald | 4th | Central Ontario Regiment | No Known Grave |
| Oakes | Private | Albert | 4th | Burlington, ON | No Known Grave |

| Last Name | Rank | First Name | Battalion | Home City/Regiment | Resting Place |
|---|---|---|---|---|---|
| Othen | Private | Harry | 4th | Central Ontario Regiment | No Known Grave |
| Pannell | Private | Harry E. | 4th | Central Ontario Regiment | No Known Grave |
| Patterson | Private | Everton | 4th | Caledon, ON | No Known Grave |
| Podd | Private | Thomas H. | 4th | Vineland, ON | No Known Grave |
| Reeves | Private | Fred W. | 4th | Hamilton, ON | No Known Grave |
| Revell | Private | William James | 4th | Central Ontario Regiment | No Known Grave |
| Reynolds | Lance-Corporal | Frederick | 4th | Elmvale, ON | Poperinghe Old Military Cemetery, Belgium |
| Roberts | Private | Frederick C. | 4th | Los Angeles, CA | No Known Grave |
| Ross | Sergeant | Duncan | 4th | Central Ontario Regiment | No Known Grave |
| Russell | Lance-Corporal | James | 4th | Hamilton, ON | No Known Grave |
| Saunders | Private | Robert | 4th | Burlington, ON | No Known Grave |
| Scott | Lance-Corporal | Walter D. | 4th | Central Ontario Regiment | No Known Grave |
| Shaw | Lance-Corporal | William | 4th | Central Ontario Regiment | No Known Grave |
| Shephard | Private | Henry T. | 4th | Central Ontario Regiment | No Known Grave |
| Sinclair | Private | William J. | 4th | Central Ontario Regiment | No Known Grave |
| Slack | Lance-Corporal | William | 4th | Central Ontario Regiment | No Known Grave |
| Sloat | Private | Nile | 4th | Brantford, ON | No Known Grave |
| Small | Private | William H. | 4th | Central Ontario Regiment | No Known Grave |
| Smith | Private | Frank | 4th | Central Ontario Regiment | No Known Grave |
| Somerville | Private | William | 4th | Central Ontario Regiment | No Known Grave |
| South | Private | John | 4th | Columbus, OH | No Known Grave |
| Spence | Lance-Corporal | Robert | 4th | Kingston, ON | No Known Grave |
| Stone | Private | Harry | 4th | Central Ontario Regiment | No Known Grave |
| Strathearn | Private | Walter E. | 4th | Midland, ON | No Known Grave |
| Towlson | Sergeant | Thomas W. | 4th | North Hamilton ON | No Known Grave |
| Wallace | Corporal | Charles B. | 4th | Toronto, ON | No Known Grave |

| Last Name | Rank | First Name | Battalion | Home City/Regiment | Resting Place |
| --- | --- | --- | --- | --- | --- |
| Wharton (Curry) | Private | Gerald B. | 4th | Columbus, OH | New Irish Farm Cemetery, Belgium |
| Wheatley | Private | Edward | 4th | Central Ontario Regiment | Hazebrouck Communal Cemetery, France |
| White | Lance-Sergeant | Bernard C. | 4th | Central Ontario Regiment | No Known Grave |
| Whybra | Private | Harold | 4th | Central Ontario Regiment | No Known Grave |
| Wood | Private | Ernest | 4th | Hamilton, ON | No Known Grave |
| Allan | Captain | Reginald A. | 5th | Victoria, BC | Boulogne Eastern Cemetery, France |
| Anderson | Private | William | 5th | Saskatchewan Regiment | Boulogne Eastern Cemetery, France |
| Bailey | Sergeant | Christopher T. | 5th | Vancouver, BC | Bailleul Communal Cemetery Extension, France |
| Black | Private | George F. | 5th | Edmonton, AB | No Known Grave |
| Blois | Private | George | 5th | Truro, NS | No Known Grave |
| Brown | Private | Thomas L. | 5th | Saskatchewan Regiment | No Known Grave |
| Davidson | Lance-Corporal | Robert | 5th | Merritt, BC | No Known Grave |
| Durham | Private | James F. | 5th | Saskatchewan Regiment | No Known Grave |
| Field | Private | John W. | 5th | Saskatchewan Regiment | No Known Grave |
| Fitzpatrick | Lieutenant | W. | 5th | Saskatchewan Regiment | No Known Grave |
| Goff | Private | Fred | 5th | Saskatchewan Regiment | No Known Grave |
| Gould | Private | Arthur F. | 5th | Lanark, ON | No Known Grave |
| Hesketh | Private | J. | 5th | Saskatchewan Regiment | No Known Grave |
| Hulbert | Private | Harold J. | 5th | Bethany, MB | No Known Grave |
| Hunsley | Corporal | Cyril | 5th | Saskatchewan Regiment | No Known Grave |
| Johnson | Private | Thomas P. | 5th | Harriston, ON | No Known Grave |
| Kennedy | Private | John C. | 5th | Gull Lake, SK | No Known Grave |
| King | Corporal | Edward | 5th | Saskatchewan Regiment | No Known Grave |
| King-Mason | Lieutenant | Charles G. | 5th | Vancouver, BC | No Known Grave |
| Koss | Private | Miki | 5th | Edmonton, AB | No Known Grave |

| Last Name | Rank | First Name | Battalion | Home City/Regiment | Resting Place |
|---|---|---|---|---|---|
| Laurence | Private | Thomas H. | 5th | Saskatchewan Regiment | No Known Grave |
| Litchfield | Private | Oscar W. | 5th | Calgary, AB | No Known Grave |
| MacDonald | Private | John | 5th | Montreal, QC | No Known Grave |
| MacDonald | Private | Peter G. | 5th | Saskatchewan Regiment | Hazebrouck Communal Cemetery, France |
| Masson | Private | John | 5th | Saskatchewan Regiment | Bailleul Communal Cemetery Extension, France |
| Melville | Lance-Corporal | John E. | 5th | Loreburn, SK | No Known Grave |
| Melvin | Private | James | 5th | Montreal, QC | No Known Grave |
| Murray | Private | Allan | 5th | Saskatchewan Regiment | No Known Grave |
| Ogilvie | Lance-Corporal | William E. | 5th | Saskatchewan Regiment | No Known Grave |
| Porteous | Private | Robert M. | 5th | Brandon, MB | No Known Grave |
| Preston | Private | Eric | 5th | Vancouver, BC | No Known Grave |
| Risbey | Lance-Corporal | Albert | 5th | Saskatchewan Regiment | Hazebrouck Communal Cemetery, France |
| Roberts | Private | George R. | 5th | Saskatchewan Regiment | Hazebrouck Communal Cemetery, France |
| Rooth | Private | Richard R. | 5th | Port Colborne, ON | No Known Grave |
| Ross | Private | Andrew | 5th | Saskatchewan Regiment | No Known Grave |
| Russell | Sergeant | Henry M. | 5th | Saint John, NB | No Known Grave |
| Sandeman | Major | David R. | 5th | Pine Lake, AB | No Known Grave |
| Sarff | Private | Curtis | 5th | Browerville, MN | No Known Grave |
| Skerry | Private | William H. | 5th | New Ross, NS | No Known Grave |
| Tomich | Private | Velimir | 5th | Saskatchewan Regiment | No Known Grave |
| Waters | Corporal | William M. | 5th | Vancouver, BC | No Known Grave |
| Wellbelove | Private | George R. | 5th | Saskatchewan Regiment | No Known Grave |
| White | Private | Lawrence | 5th | Saskatchewan Regiment | No Known Grave |
| Wilkie | Private | Joseph R. | 5th | Toronto, ON | No Known Grave |

| Last Name | Rank | First Name | Battalion | Home City/Regiment | Resting Place |
|---|---|---|---|---|---|
| Adams | Private | Anthony H. | 7th | British Columbia Regiment | No Known Grave |
| Anderson | Private | Douglas | 7th | British Columbia Regiment | No Known Grave |
| Arnold | Private | Russel K. | 7th | Chilliwack, BC | No Known Grave |
| Babcock | Private | William L. | 7th | Dresden, ON | No Known Grave |
| Baker | Private | Hugh G. | 7th | British Columbia Regiment | No Known Grave |
| Barnes | Private | Albert | 7th | British Columbia Regiment | Poelcappelle British Cemetery, Belgium |
| Basford | Private | Frederick C. | 7th | British Columbia Regiment | No Known Grave |
| Bateman | Sergeant | Edward W. | 7th | British Columbia Regiment | No Known Grave |
| Bayley | Private | Albert E. | 7th | British Columbia Regiment | No Known Grave |
| Beattie | Private | Reginald | 7th | East Burnaby, BC | No Known Grave |
| Beaumont | Private | Henry | 7th | British Columbia Regiment | No Known Grave |
| Bentley | Private | Walter C. | 7th | Medicine Hat, AB | No Known Grave |
| Bewsher | Private | John | 7th | British Columbia Regiment | No Known Grave |
| Bouch | Private | Wilfrid | 7th | British Columbia Regiment | No Known Grave |
| Bowden | Private | Christopher J. | 7th | British Columbia Regiment | No Known Grave |
| Boyce | Private | Albert | 7th | Winnipeg, MB | No Known Grave |
| Boyle | Private | James | 7th | British Columbia Regiment | No Known Grave |
| Boyle | Private | John | 7th | Revelstoke, BC | No Known Grave |
| Brew | Private | Arthur | 7th | British Columbia Regiment | No Known Grave |
| Brierton | Private | William | 7th | British Columbia Regiment | No Known Grave |
| Brignall | Private | Frank | 7th | British Columbia Regiment | Perth Cemetery, Belgium |
| Brodie | Private | Kenneth D. | 7th | British Columbia Regiment | No Known Grave |
| Bromley | Lieutenant | Herbert A. | 7th | British Columbia Regiment | No Known Grave |
| Bundy | Corporal | Leonard | 7th | British Columbia Regiment | No Known Grave |
| Burrow | Private | George D'A. | 7th | British Columbia Regiment | No Known Grave |
| Butler | Private | Cumine P. | 7th | British Columbia Regiment | No Known Grave |

| Last Name | Rank | First Name | Battalion | Home City/Regiment | Resting Place |
| --- | --- | --- | --- | --- | --- |
| Buxton | Private | Leopold G. | 7th | British Columbia Regiment | No Known Grave |
| Carmichael | Private | Henry | 7th | Montreal, QC | Poperinghe Old Military Cemetery |
| Carr | Private | Frank E. | 7th | Vancouver, BC | No Known Grave |
| Carter | Private | Harold W. | 7th | British Columbia Regiment | No Known Grave |
| Childs | Private | James A. | 7th | British Columbia Regiment | No Known Grave |
| Clarke | Private | Basil E. | 7th | British Columbia Regiment | No Known Grave |
| Clarke | Private | Thomas A. | 7th | North Wellington, BC | No Known Grave |
| Cleeves | Private | Vincent | 7th | British Columbia Regiment | Poelcappelle British Cemetery, Belgium |
| Cleghorn | Lance-Corporal | Walter S. | 7th | British Columbia Regiment | No Known Grave |
| Cocroft | Sergeant | Frederick | 7th | Vancouver, BC | No Known Grave |
| Coleman | Private | Walter L. | 7th | British Columbia Regiment | Perth Cemetery, Belgium |
| Colhoun | Lance-Corporal | John | 7th | Vancouver, BC | No Known Grave |
| Collison | Sergeant | Cedric H. | 7th | British Columbia Regiment | Hazebrouck Communal Cemetery, France |
| Connor | Private | Henry | 7th | Vancouver, BC | Tyne Cot Cemetery, Belgium |
| Cooper | Private | James H. | 7th | Alert Bay, BC | No Known Grave |
| Corker | Private | Frank A. | 7th | British Columbia Regiment | No Known Grave |
| Craig | Private | J. | 7th | British Columbia Regiment | No Known Grave |
| Crain | Private | Otho | 7th | British Columbia Regiment | No Known Grave |
| Craven | Private | Ernest H. | 7th | British Columbia Regiment | No Known Grave |
| Crowther | Corporal | Benjamin | 7th | British Columbia Regiment | No Known Grave |
| Cunningham | Private | Ewart W. | 7th | Vancouver, BC | No Known Grave |
| Dancy | Private | William B. | 7th | British Columbia Regiment | No Known Grave |
| Davies | Private | Valentine L. | 7th | British Columbia Regiment | No Known Grave |
| Degrandmont | Private | Theodore | 7th | Stanislas-de-Batiscan, QC | Vimy Memorial, France |
| Dickson | Private | John N. | 7th | British Columbia Regiment | No Known Grave |
| Drummond | Lance-Corporal | William | 7th | British Columbia Regiment | No Known Grave |

| Last Name | Rank | First Name | Battalion | Home City/Regiment | Resting Place |
|---|---|---|---|---|---|
| Eastman | Private | Edwin F. | 7th | New Westminster, BC | No Known Grave |
| Elliot | Private | George W. | 7th | Cumberland, BC | No Known Grave |
| Ensor | Private | George C. | 7th | Vancouver, BC | Bailleul Communal Cemetery Extension, France |
| Farren | Private | Francis B. | 7th | British Columbia Regiment | No Known Grave |
| Fern | Private | Sidney N. | 7th | British Columbia Regiment | No Known Grave |
| Fisher | Private | Frederick T. | 7th | Kelowna, BC | No Known Grave |
| Flagmore | Corporal | n/a | 7th | British Columbia Regiment | No Known Grave |
| Flumerfelt | Private | Edgar | 7th | New Westminster BC | No Known Grave |
| Ford | Private | Edgar N. | 7th | Coombs, BC | No Known Grave |
| Fowler | Private | William H. | 7th | British Columbia Regiment | No Known Grave |
| Fox | Private | Frederick W. | 7th | British Columbia Regiment | No Known Grave |
| Fraser | Private | Norman | 7th | British Columbia Regiment | No Known Grave |
| Fudger | Private | George B. | 7th | Montreal, QC | No Known Grave |
| Gardiner | Private | Albert S. | 7th | British Columbia Regiment | No Known Grave |
| Gavin | Private | James D. | 7th | Winnipeg, MB | No Known Grave |
| Geernaert | Private | Edward D. | 7th | Vanderhoof, BC | No Known Grave |
| Gordon | Private | Sydney | 7th | Montreal, QC | No Known Grave |
| Graham | Private | David J. | 7th | Ottawa, ON | No Known Grave |
| Greaves | Private | Harry P. | 7th | Duncan, BC | No Known Grave |
| Griffin | Private | Charles E. | 7th | British Columbia Regiment | No Known Grave |
| Guy | Private | Harold R. | 7th | British Columbia Regiment | No Known Grave |
| Haikala | Private | Avro | 7th | British Columbia Regiment | No Known Grave |
| Hall | Private | John | 7th | British Columbia Regiment | No Known Grave |
| Hamilton | Private | William | 7th | British Columbia Regiment | No Known Grave |
| Hammond | Private | Albert E. | 7th | British Columbia Regiment | No Known Grave |
| Hart-McHarg | Lt.-Col. | William | 7th | Vancouver, BC | Poperinghe Old Military Cemetery |

| Last Name | Rank | First Name | Battalion | Home City/Regiment | Resting Place |
|---|---|---|---|---|---|
| Hay | Lance-Corporal | William F. | 7th | British Columbia Regiment | No Known Grave |
| Haynes | Private | David H. | 7th | British Columbia Regiment | No Known Grave |
| Henderson | Private | James | 7th | Vancouver, BC | No Known Grave |
| Hicks | Private | Frank J. | 7th | British Columbia Regiment | No Known Grave |
| Hill | Private | Francis C. | 7th | British Columbia Regiment | No Known Grave |
| Hilsenter | Private | Joseph | 7th | Regina, SK | No Known Grave |
| Hindle | Private | David S. | 7th | British Columbia Regiment | No Known Grave |
| Hogg | Private | George C. | 7th | Vancouver, BC | No Known Grave |
| Holmes | Lieutenant | Carleton C. | 7th | Vancouver, BC | No Known Grave |
| Hubbard | Private | Frederick W. | 7th | Upper Pereaux, NS | No Known Grave |
| Hugget | Lance-Sergeant | Charles | 7th | British Columbia Regiment | No Known Grave |
| Huyegbart | Private | Julius J. | 7th | British Columbia Regiment | No Known Grave |
| Ingram | Private | William H. | 7th | British Columbia Regiment | No Known Grave |
| Keith | Private | James M. | 7th | Victoria, BC | No Known Grave |
| Kemp | Private | Hugh G. | 7th | British Columbia Regiment | No Known Grave |
| Kirby | Private | Hewson | 7th | Nelson, BC | No Known Grave |
| Laird | Private | John M. | 7th | New Westminster, BC | No Known Grave |
| Latham | Private | Ernest R. | 7th | British Columbia Regiment | No Known Grave |
| Latta | Lieutenant | Robert P. | 7th | Vancouver, BC | No Known Grave |
| Laws | Private | Benjamin | 7th | Deroche, BC | No Known Grave |
| Laybourn | Private | John | 7th | British Columbia Regiment | No Known Grave |
| Leacock | Private | Arthur L. | 7th | British Columbia Regiment | No Known Grave |
| Lecky | Private | George A. | 7th | British Columbia Regiment | No Known Grave |
| Macleod | Private | Malcolm C. | 7th | Chilliwack, BC | No Known Grave |
| Mahood | Corporal | David | 7th | British Columbia Regiment | No Known Grave |
| Maloney | Private | Michael | 7th | British Columbia Regiment | No Known Grave |

| Last Name | Rank | First Name | Battalion | Home City/Regiment | Resting Place |
|---|---|---|---|---|---|
| Martin | Private | John E. | 7th | Blenheim, ON | No Known Grave |
| Mason | Private | Walter R. | 7th | British Columbia Regiment | No Known Grave |
| Massy | Private | Hugh De H. | 7th | Montreal, QC | No Known Grave |
| Matheson | Private | James | 7th | Briton Cove, NS | No Known Grave |
| Mathias | Corporal | William J. | 7th | British Columbia Regiment | No Known Grave |
| Maynard | Private | Harry | 7th | Orillia, ON | No Known Grave |
| McCabe | Private | Francis J. | 7th | New Westminster, BC | No Known Grave |
| McDonald | Private | Roderick, D'A. | 7th | British Columbia Regiment | No Known Grave |
| McGillis | Private | Donald J. | 7th | Glengarry, ON | No Known Grave |
| McGillvary | Private | Angus | 7th | Winnipeg, MB | No Known Grave |
| McInnis | Private | Arthur | 7th | Vancouver, BC | No Known Grave |
| McIver | Private | Murdoch | 7th | British Columbia Regiment | No Known Grave |
| McLaughlin | Private | Daniel M. | 7th | Palmerston, ON | No Known Grave |
| McMullen | Private | Martin | 7th | British Columbia Regiment | No Known Grave |
| McNeiry | Private | David | 7th | British Columbia Regiment | No Known Grave |
| McPherson | Private | Alexander | 7th | British Columbia Regiment | No Known Grave |
| Meldrum | Private | William | 7th | British Columbia Regiment | No Known Grave |
| Metcalf | Private | James E. | 7th | Preston, ON | No Known Grave |
| Mitchell | Private | Gordon A. | 7th | Toronto, ON | Wimereux Communal Cemetery, France |
| Moodie | Lance-Sergeant | Charles A. | 7th | Vancouver, BC | No Known Grave |
| Moore | Private | Alfred | 7th | British Columbia Regiment | No Known Grave |
| Morgan | Private | David C. | 7th | British Columbia Regiment | No Known Grave |
| Morrison | Private | John | 7th | British Columbia Regiment | No Known Grave |
| Mould | Private | Harold G. | 7th | British Columbia Regiment | No Known Grave |
| Muir | Sergeant | Duncan M. | 7th | British Columbia Regiment | No Known Grave |
| Nation (Nelson) | Private | Philip B. | 7th | Owen Sound, ON | No Known Grave |

| Last Name | Rank | First Name | Battalion | Home City/Regiment | Resting Place |
|---|---|---|---|---|---|
| Noyes | Lance-Corporal | Thomas R. | 7th | British Columbia Regiment | No Known Grave |
| Odlum | Corporal | Joseph W. | 7th | Vancouver, BC | Perth Cemetery, Belgium |
| Oliver | Lance-Corporal | Sidney | 7th | Trail, BC | No Known Grave |
| Oliver | Private | William E. | 7th | Trail, BC | No Known Grave |
| Parkes | Private | Henry H. | 7th | British Columbia Regiment | No Known Grave |
| Paul | Sergeant | James | 7th | British Columbia Regiment | No Known Grave |
| Pearless | Sergeant | Hugh N. | 7th | British Columbia Regiment | No Known Grave |
| Pearson | Private | John | 7th | North Vancouver, BC | No Known Grave |
| Peters | Private | John F. | 7th | Charlottetown, PEI | No Known Grave |
| Pettigrue | Private | Thomas P. | 7th | British Columbia Regiment | No Known Grave |
| Phillips | Private | George W. | 7th | British Columbia Regiment | No Known Grave |
| Porter | Private | Geoffrey L. | 7th | British Columbia Regiment | No Known Grave |
| Preston | Private | Joseph | 7th | Vancouver, BC | No Known Grave |
| Ravenhill | Private | Horace L. | 7th | Shawinigan Lake, BC | No Known Grave |
| Rawlins | Private | Alexander A. | 7th | British Columbia Regiment | No Known Grave |
| Richardson | Private | Francis H. | 7th | British Columbia Regiment | No Known Grave |
| Robertson | Private | John W. | 7th | High River, AB | No Known Grave |
| Robinson | Private | Harry | 7th | British Columbia Regiment | No Known Grave |
| Ross | Private | John | 7th | Vancouver, BC | No Known Grave |
| Ross | Private | John | 7th | Vancouver, BC | No Known Grave |
| Rowland | Private | Frederick H. | 7th | British Columbia Regiment | No Known Grave |
| Royds | Private | Nowell B. | 7th | Capilano, BC | Tyne Cot Cemetery, Belgium |
| Salter | Lance-Corporal | Donald | 7th | British Columbia Regiment | No Known Grave |
| Sayer | Lance-Corporal | Henry W. | 7th | British Columbia Regiment | No Known Grave |
| Scott | Private | Matthew M. | 7th | British Columbia Regiment | No Known Grave |
| Shaw | Private | Thomas E. | 7th | British Columbia Regiment | No Known Grave |

| Last Name | Rank | First Name | Battalion | Home City/Regiment | Resting Place |
|---|---|---|---|---|---|
| Sheppard | Private | Walter J. | 7th | British Columbia Regiment | No Known Grave |
| Sivell | Private | Alfred G. | 7th | British Columbia Regiment | No Known Grave |
| Smith | Private | Leslie C. | 7th | Winnipeg, MB | No Known Grave |
| Smythe | Private | John W. | 7th | British Columbia Regiment | No Known Grave |
| Sprogue | Private | John | 7th | British Columbia Regiment | No Known Grave |
| Stringer | Private | Joseph H. | 7th | Red Deer, AB | No Known Grave |
| Talbot | Private | Arthur | 7th | Sudbury, ON | No Known Grave |
| Tattrie | Private | Harry A. | 7th | Dorchester, NB | No Known Grave |
| Tennant | Sergeant-Major | Joseph | 7th | British Columbia Regiment | Tyne Cot Cemetery, Belgium |
| Thompson | Corporal | Charles T. | 7th | British Columbia Regiment | No Known Grave |
| Thompson | Private | Harold F. | 7th | British Columbia Regiment | No Known Grave |
| Thornton | Private | Joseph H. | 7th | Burnaby, BC | No Known Grave |
| Tofts | Private | Robert C. | 7th | British Columbia Regiment | No Known Grave |
| Twynam | Corporal | William H. | 7th | British Columbia Regiment | No Known Grave |
| Vivian | Private | Herbert W. | 7th | Peachland, BC | No Known Grave |
| Walker | Private | James | 7th | British Columbia Regiment | No Known Grave |
| Waters | Lance-Corporal | Simon | 7th | British Columbia Regiment | No Known Grave |
| Webb | Private | Sidney | 7th | British Columbia Regiment | No Known Grave |
| Welles | Sergeant | "Doc" | 7th | British Columbia Regiment | No Known Grave |
| Weston | Private | Harry V. | 7th | British Columbia Regiment | No Known Grave |
| Weston | Private | William W. | 7th | British Columbia Regiment | No Known Grave |
| Wilbraham-Taylor | Private | Harington | 7th | Duncan, BC | No Known Grave |
| Williams | Private | William | 7th | British Columbia Regiment | No Known Grave |
| Wood | Private | William J. | 7th | British Columbia Regiment | No Known Grave |
| Wylie | Private | Robert | 7th | British Columbia Regiment | No Known Grave |

| Last Name | First Name | Rank | Battalion | Home City/Regiment | Resting Place |
|---|---|---|---|---|---|
| Adams | George F. | Private | 8th | Winnipeg, MB | No Known Grave |
| Ascroft | Thomas | Private | 8th | Manitoba Regiment | No Known Grave |
| Attwood | Charles | Private | 8th | Manitoba Regiment | No Known Grave |
| Ballentyne | John | Private | 8th | Winnipeg, MB | No Known Grave |
| Baptist | David Y. | Private | 8th | Vamsey, SK | No Known Grave |
| Beken | Horace C. | Sergeant | 8th | Manitoba Regiment | No Known Grave |
| Bertram | W. R. | Captain | 8th | Manitoba Regiment | No Known Grave |
| Betts | James W. | Private | 8th | Canora, SK | No Known Grave |
| Bird | Richard De B. | Lance-Corporal | 8th | Manitoba Regiment | No Known Grave |
| Blenner-Hassett | William J. | Private | 8th | Toronto, ON | No Known Grave |
| Bligh | Charles H. | Corporal | 8th | Toronto, ON | No Known Grave |
| Blois | George | Private | 8th | Truro, NS | No Known Grave |
| Brady | John | Private | 8th | Manitoba Regiment | No Known Grave |
| Brommell | Robert B. | Private | 8th | Souris, MB | No Known Grave |
| Burch | Arthur T. | Private | 8th | Manitoba Regiment | No Known Grave |
| Burge | C. | Private | 8th | Manitoba Regiment | No Known Grave |
| Burns | Roy | Private | 8th | Neepawa, MB | No Known Grave |
| Burrow | George D. | Private | 8th | Manitoba Regiment | No Known Grave |
| Caswell | Ernest | Private | 8th | Manitoba Regiment | No Known Grave |
| Chapman | Guy | Corporal | 8th | Napanee, ON | No Known Grave |
| Clarkson | Arthur E. | Private | 8th | Ste. Rose Du Lac, MB | No Known Grave |
| Collins | Ernest W. | Private | 8th | Vancouver, BC | Gent City Cemetery, Belgium |
| Colville | Archibald H. | Private | 8th | Winnipeg Regiment | No Known Grave |
| De Courcy | Thomas J. | Private | 8th | Sussex, NB | No Known Grave |
| Dowd | Robert | Private | 8th | Winnipeg, MB | No Known Grave |
| Dwyer | Mundan | Private | 8th | Ignace, ON | No Known Grave |

| Last Name | Rank | First Name | Battalion | Home City/Regiment | Resting Place |
|---|---|---|---|---|---|
| Eccles | Sergeant | Thomas | 8th | Montreal, QC | No Known Grave |
| English | Private | George W. | 8th | Paynton, SK | No Known Grave |
| Evans | Private | Charles | 8th | Winnipeg, MB | No Known Grave |
| Farden | Sergeant | Fred | 8th | Manitoba Regiment | No Known Grave |
| Ferg | Private | Edward C. | 8th | West Monkton, ON | No Known Grave |
| Fletcher | Private | Frederick G. | 8th | Manitoba Regiment | No Known Grave |
| Frith | Private | W. | 8th | Manitoba Regiment | No Known Grave |
| George | Private | Ernest F. | 8th | Manitoba Regiment | Roeselare Communal Cemetery, Belgium |
| Gloag | Private | John | 8th | Winnipeg, MB | No Known Grave |
| Godwin | Lance-Corporal | Arthur M. | 8th | Manitoba Regiment | No Known Grave |
| Grant | Private | William | 8th | Manitoba Regiment | No Known Grave |
| Gregson | Private | Samuel | 8th | Brandon, MB | No Known Grave |
| Hall | Sergeant-Major | Frederick W. | 8th | Winnipeg, MB | No Known Grave |
| Hamilton | Private | David F. | 8th | Winnipeg, MB | No Known Grave |
| Hamilton | Private | James | 8th | Manitoba Regiment | No Known Grave |
| Hampshire | Private | Thomas | 8th | Manitoba Regiment | No Known Grave |
| Hanson | Private | Frederick J. | 8th | Manitoba Regiment | No Known Grave |
| Hassett | Private | William J. | 8th | Toronto, ON | No Known Grave |
| Harris | Corporal | Robert W. | 8th | Winnipeg, MB | No Known Grave |
| Harrison | Private | Wilfred | 8th | Ottawa, ON | Netley Military Cemetery, England |
| Harvey | Sergeant | George H. | 8th | Winnipeg Regiment | No Known Grave |
| Higgs | Private | Leslie | 8th | Lesdale, MB | No Known Grave |
| Hill | Private | Thomas | 8th | Bay City, MI | No Known Grave |
| Holloway | Private | Edwin C. | 8th | Manitoba Regiment | No Known Grave |
| Howlett | Private | Horace B. | 8th | Manitoba Regiment | No Known Grave |
| Hussey | Bugler | Charles F. | 8th | Manitoba Regiment | St. Sever Cemetery, France |

| Last Name | Rank | First Name | Battalion | Home City/Regiment | Resting Place |
|---|---|---|---|---|---|
| Irvine | Private | Louis J. | 8th | Emo, ON | No Known Grave |
| Irwin | Private | William J. | 8th | Manitoba Regiment | No Known Grave |
| Isaac | Private | Ernest W. | 8th | Manitoba Regiment | Tyne Cot Cemetery, Belgium |
| Jackson | Private | Harry W. | 8th | Manitoba Regiment | No Known Grave |
| Jacobowicz (Barnard) | Private | Leopold | 8th | Manitoba Regiment | No Known Grave |
| James | Private | Sydney C. | 8th | Winnipeg, MB | Poperinghe Old Military Cemetery |
| Jepson | Private | Russel W. | 8th | London, ON | No Known Grave |
| Johnceline | Private | Edwin A. | 8th | Manitoba Regiment | No Known Grave |
| Jones | Private | J. H. | 8th | Manitoba Regiment | No Known Grave |
| Knight | Private | Alfred H. | 8th | Lachine, QC | No Known Grave |
| Le Beau | Private | Albert | 8th | Manitoba Regiment | No Known Grave |
| Leaf | Private | Thomas | 8th | Winnipeg, MB | Vlamertinghe Military Cemetery, Belgium |
| Lewis | Corporal | William | 8th | Manitoba Regiment | No Known Grave |
| Linklater | Private | Frank | 8th | Grand Marais, MB | No Known Grave |
| Lyons | Private | John S. | 8th | Manitoba Regiment | No Known Grave |
| Maitland | Sergeant | William J. | 8th | Manitoba Regiment | No Known Grave |
| Marr | Private | Alexander C. | 8th | Manitoba Regiment | No Known Grave |
| McCallum | Private | John | 8th | Winnipeg, MB | No Known Grave |
| McConnell | Private | James A. | 8th | Newbury, ON | No Known Grave |
| McDiarmid | Private | William | 8th | Manitoba Regiment | Poelcappelle British Cemetery, Belgium |
| McKay | Private | Charles | 8th | Manitoba Regiment | No Known Grave |
| McKechnie | Private | William R. | 8th | Montreal, QC | No Known Grave |
| McKenzie | Private | George C. | 8th | Manitoba Regiment | No Known Grave |
| McKenzie | Private | James | 8th | Balmoral, MB | No Known Grave |
| McKenzie | Lieutenant | Wallace A. | 8th | Sault Ste. Marie, ON | No Known Grave |
| McNeill | Private | Lorne | 8th | Winnipeg, MB | No Known Grave |

| Last Name | Rank | First Name | Battalion | Home City/Regiment | Resting Place |
|---|---|---|---|---|---|
| Meddings | Private | William J. | 8th | Toronto, ON | No Known Grave |
| Meyer | Lance-Corporal | Arthur W. | 8th | Winnipeg, MB | No Known Grave |
| Moore | Private | Julian | 8th | Manitoba Regiment | Vimy Memorial, France |
| Mullin | Private | James S. | 8th | Dayton, OH | No Known Grave |
| Ness | Corporal | Garnett V. | 8th | Winnipeg Regiment | No Known Grave |
| Norris | Corporal | Thomas W. | 8th | Manitoba Regiment | No Known Grave |
| O'Grady | Lieutenant | Gerald R. | 8th | Manitoba Regiment | No Known Grave |
| Parker | Private | Harry D. | 8th | Long Beach, NY | No Known Grave |
| Parliament | Private | John | 8th | Parry Sound, ON | No Known Grave |
| Perkin | Private | Henry E. | 8th | Manitoba Regiment | No Known Grave |
| Pratt | Private | Charles H. | 8th | Manitoba Regiment | No Known Grave |
| Quinn | Lance-Corporal | Herbert V. | 8th | Winnipeg, MB | No Known Grave |
| Reynolds | Lieutenant | J.E. | 8th | Manitoba Regiment | Perth Cemetery, Belgium |
| Roach | Private | John | 8th | Winnipeg, MB | No Known Grave |
| Roberts | Private | Basil G. | 8th | Winnipeg, MB | No Known Grave |
| Robertson | Lance-Corporal | Alex P. | 8th | Manitoba Regiment | No Known Grave |
| Robertson | Private | Duncan | 8th | Manitoba Regiment | No Known Grave |
| Robertson | Sergeant-Major | W. | 8th | Manitoba Regiment | No Known Grave |
| Saword | Private | Algernon L. | 8th | Winnipeg, MB | No Known Grave |
| Seager | Private | Frank W. | 8th | Manitoba Regiment | No Known Grave |
| Searle | Private | Harold A. | 8th | Manitoba Regiment | No Known Grave |
| Sheppard | Private | Henry C. | 8th | Manitoba Regiment | No Known Grave |
| Shields | Sergeant | John M. | 8th | Winnipeg, MB | No Known Grave |
| Skillicorn | Private | Douglas | 8th | Manitoba Regiment | No Known Grave |
| Smith | Private | Walter J. | 8th | Manitoba Regiment | No Known Grave |
| Squires | Private | Joseph | 8th | Winnipeg, MB | No Known Grave |

| Last Name | Rank | First Name | Battalion | Home City/Regiment | Resting Place |
| --- | --- | --- | --- | --- | --- |
| Stephens | Private | Albert | 8th | Manitoba Regiment | No Known Grave |
| Stethem | Lance-Corporal | Herbert A. | 8th | Peterborough, ON | No Known Grave |
| Stevenson | Private | Charles A. | 8th | Manitoba Regiment | No Known Grave |
| Taylor | Private | Thomas T. | 8th | Prince Albert, SK | No Known Grave |
| Taylor | Private | Frederick W. | 8th | Manitoba Regiment | Bailleul Communal Cemetery, France |
| Townsend | Private | Frederic B. | 8th | Winnipeg Regiment | No Known Grave |
| Trewella | Private | Frederick L. | 8th | Portage La Prairie, MB | No Known Grave |
| Tunbridge | Private | Frederick C. | 8th | Manitoba Regiment | No Known Grave |
| Vance | Private | Samuel G. | 8th | Manitoba Regiment | No Known Grave |
| Wambolt | Private | Bert | 8th | Halifax, NS | No Known Grave |
| Ward | Private | Albert E. | 8th | Winnipeg, MB | No Known Grave |
| Waterhouse | Private | Fred | 8th | Manitoba Regiment | No Known Grave |
| Williams | Private | Arthur E. | 8th | Vancouver, BC | White House Cemetery, Belgium |
| Williams | Private | Edwin | 8th | Manitoba Regiment | No Known Grave |
| Wilson | Private | Douglas G. | 8th | Winnipeg, MB | No Known Grave |
| Wilson | Private | John | 8th | Manitoba Regiment | No Known Grave |
| Wilson | Lance-Corporal | Talbot | 8th | Manitoba Regiment | No Known Grave |
| Wilson | Private | "Tug" | 8th | Manitoba Regiment | No Known Grave |
| Winstone | Private | Scarlett H. | 8th | Manitoba Regiment | No Known Grave |
| Wood | Private | Arthur R. | 8th | Manitoba Regiment | No Known Grave |
| Abbott | Corporal | Frederick C. | 10th | Alberta Regiment | No Known Grave |
| Adam | Private | Charles | 10th | Toronto, ON | No Known Grave |
| Alexander (Ramsay) | Corporal | John | 10th | Alberta Regiment | Poperinghe Old Military Cemetery, Belgium |
| Allan | Lance-Corporal | George W. | 10th | Hamilton, ON | No Known Grave |
| Allingham | Private | John R. | 10th | Saint John, NB | No Known Grave |

| Last Name | Rank | First Name | Battalion | Home City/Regiment | Resting Place |
|---|---|---|---|---|---|
| Allison | Private | Henry | 10th | Winnipeg, MB | No Known Grave |
| Anthony | Private | Douglas | 10th | Upper Kennetcook, NS | No Known Grave |
| Armstrong | Private | Albert P. | 10th | Bolton, ON | No Known Grave |
| Armstrong | Private | Cecil | 10th | Fitzroy, ON | No Known Grave |
| Arthurs | Private | James M. | 10th | Alberta Regiment | No Known Grave |
| Atwill | Private | Sydney G. | 10th | Alberta Regiment | No Known Grave |
| Balfour | Private | Walter | 10th | Alberta Regiment | No Known Grave |
| Ball | Lieutenant | Albert R. | 10th | Richmond, QC | Stanstead Cemetery, Quebec, Canada |
| Barnes | Private | George | 10th | Alberta Regiment | No Known Grave |
| Belcher | Private | Edward M. | 10th | Alberta Regiment | No Known Grave |
| Bell | Lieutenant | Andrew L. | 10th | Toronto, ON | No Known Grave |
| Berry | Sergeant | Joseph | 10th | Alberta Regiment | No Known Grave |
| Boultbee | Private | Joseph M. | 10th | Alberta Regiment | No Known Grave |
| Boyle | Lt.-Col. | Russell L. | 10th | Crossfield, AB | Poperinghe Old Military Cemetery, Belgium |
| Brown | Private | James D. | 10th | Alberta Regiment | No Known Grave |
| Cabeldu | Private | Horace E. | 10th | Stanley Bridge PEI | No Known Grave |
| Cameron | Private | Keith E. | 10th | Alberta Regiment | No Known Grave |
| Carver | Private | Leonard | 10th | Alberta Regiment | No Known Grave |
| Clarke | Private | Maurice T. | 10th | Eagle Butte, SD | Vlamertinghe Military Cemetery, Belgium |
| Cowley | Private | Albert E. | 10th | Alberta Regiment | No Known Grave |
| Curtis | Private | Joseph R. | 10th | Alberta Regiment | No Known Grave |
| Daniels | Private | Alfred | 10th | Broadview, SK | No Known Grave |
| Darling | Private | James R. | 10th | Alberta Regiment | No Known Grave |
| Davies | Private | Ithal | 10th | Alberta Regiment | No Known Grave |
| Davis | Private | John A. | 10th | Alberta Regiment | Bailleul Communal Cemetery, France |
| Deakin | Private | Thomas | 10th | Albert Regiment | Poperinghe Old Military Cemetery, Belgium |

| Last Name | Rank | First Name | Battalion | Home City/Regiment | Resting Place |
| --- | --- | --- | --- | --- | --- |
| De Gon | Private | F. G. William | 10th | Medicine Hat, AB | No Known Grave |
| Deir | Lance-Corporal | William | 10th | Lansdowne, ON | No Known Grave |
| Dick | Private | Joseph | 10th | Alberta Regiment | No Known Grave |
| Don | Private | Charles | 10th | Alberta Regiment | No Known Grave |
| Dubois | Private | John | 10th | Winnipeg, MB | No Known Grave |
| Eadie (Prince) | Sergeant | William | 10th | Alberta Regiment | No Known Grave |
| Ellis | Private | Charles E. | 10th | Chamberlain, SK | No Known Grave |
| Elton | Private | William J. | 10th | Alberta Regiment | No Known Grave |
| Evans | Private | Phillip J. | 10th | Vancouver, BC | No Known Grave |
| Falkiner | Private | George K. | 10th | Toronto, ON | No Known Grave |
| Farmer | Private | Alexander C. | 10th | Alberta Regiment | No Known Grave |
| Fitzgibbons | Private | Gerald | 10th | Chesterville, ON | No Known Grave |
| Francis | Sergeant | Warren | 10th | Alberta Regiment | No Known Grave |
| Fraser | Private | Robertson | 10th | Springhill, NS | No Known Grave |
| Fullarton | Private | William M. | 10th | Calgary, AB | Poperinghe Old Militar Cemetery, Belgium |
| Galsworthy | Private | James | 10th | Alberta Regiment | No Known Grave |
| Gilbert | Private | Frederick | 10th | Albert Regiment | No Known Grave |
| Giles | Sergeant-Major | Joseph | 10th | Calgary, AB | No Known Grave |
| Gillies | Private | Allan | 10th | Alberta Regiment | No Known Grave |
| Glover | Captain | John D. | 10th | Orillia, ON | No Known Grave |
| Goodall | Private | Harold | 10th | Toronto, ON | No Known Grave |
| Goodfellow | Sergeant | Walter E. | 10th | Calgary, AB | No Known Grave |
| Gordon | Private | Harry | 10th | Rose Lynn, AB | No Known Grave |
| Grassie | Private | William W. | 10th | Vancouver, BC | No Known Grave |
| Gray | Private | John | 10th | Alberta Regiment | No Known Grave |
| Green | Private | Thomas | 10th | New York, NY | Hazebrouck Communal Cemetery, France |

| Last Name | Rank | First Name | Battalion | Home City/Regiment | Resting Place |
|---|---|---|---|---|---|
| Hague | Private | William A. | 10th | Alberta Regiment | No Known Grave |
| Hall | Private | Alexander B. | 10th | Boston, MA | No Known Grave |
| Hall | Private | James E. | 10th | Huntsville, ON | No Known Grave |
| Henderson | Private | John R. | 10th | Albert Regiment | No Known Grave |
| Hewer | Private | Frank C. | 10th | Alberta Regiment | No Known Grave |
| Higginson | Private | John | 10th | Alberta Regiment | Boulogne Eastern Cemetery, France |
| Hill | Private | Ernest A. | 10th | Alberta Regiment | No Known Grave |
| Hoare | Private | Arthur H. | 10th | Alberta Regiment | Roeselare Communal Cemetery, Belgium |
| Hogarth | Private | Gilbert M. | 10th | Alberta Regiment | No Known Grave |
| Hood | Private | Archibald A. | 10th | Alberta Regiment | No Known Grave |
| Hoskins | Lieutenant | Ronald | 10th | Alberta Regiment | No Known Grave |
| Hughes | Private | Albert | 10th | Winnipeg, MB | No Known Grave |
| Hughes | Private | Arthur | 10th | Alberta Regiment | No Known Grave |
| Irwin | Captain | De Witt O. | 10th | Toronto, ON | No Known Grave |
| Isabelle | Private | Ulric I. | 10th | Maple Creek, SK | No Known Grave |
| Jacobs | Private | William H. | 10th | Alberta Regiment | No Known Grave |
| Keers | Private | Frederick | 10th | Alberta Regiment | Hazebrouck Communal Cemetery, France |
| Keith | Private | Thomas A. | 10th | Alberta Regiment | No Known Grave |
| Kennedy | Private | Frederick | 10th | Winnipeg, MB | No Known Grave |
| Kerr | Private | George D. | 10th | Cranbrook, BC | No Known Grave |
| Knock | Private | Edgar | 10th | Alberta Regiment | No Known Grave |
| Larkin | Sergeant | John | 10th | Alberta Regiment | No Known Grave |
| Lawrence | Lance-Corporal | Arthur E. | 10th | Lethbridge, AB | No Known Grave |
| Lawrence | Private | Reginald | 10th | Lethbridge, AB | No Known Grave |
| Lea | Private | John | 10th | Alberta Regiment | No Known Grave |
| Lee | Corporal | Thomas F. | 10th | Brandon, MB | No Known Grave |

| Last Name | Rank | First Name | Battalion | Home City/Regiment | Resting Place |
|---|---|---|---|---|---|
| Leeman | Private | Lloyd | 10th | Burton, BC | No Known Grave |
| Lewis | Private | Frank | 10th | Alberta Regiment | No Known Grave |
| Lipsett | Private | William A. | 10th | Alberta Regiment | No Known Grave |
| Little | Lance-Corporal | William J. | 10th | Alberta Regiment | No Known Grave |
| Lloyd | Private | George | 10th | Alberta Regiment | No Known Grave |
| Lockhart | Private | George M. | 10th | Halifax, NS | No Known Grave |
| Low | Private | Harry | 10th | Victoria, BC | No Known Grave |
| Lynch | Private | John C. | 10th | Calgary, AB | No Known Grave |
| MacDonald | Private | Alexander | 10th | Alberta Regiment | No Known Grave |
| Magee | Private | Arthur M. | 10th | Saint John, NB | Poperinghe Old Military Cemetery |
| Mangan | Private | Joseph | 10th | Alberta Regiment | No Known Grave |
| Mann | Corporal | Derwas G. | 10th | St. Catharines, ON | No Known Grave |
| Mansfield | Private | Thomas | 10th | Alberta Regiment | No Known Grave |
| Manson | Private | Donald A. | 10th | Kamloops, BC | No Known Grave |
| Marks | Sergeant | Reginald J. | 10th | Winnipeg, MB | No Known Grave |
| Marshall | Private | Horace | 10th | Alberta Regiment | No Known Grave |
| Matheson | Lance-Corporal | John | 10th | Calgary, AB | No Known Grave |
| McBride | Private | James R. | 10th | Alberta Regiment | No Known Grave |
| McClean | Private | John W. | 10th | Alberta Regiment | Poperinghe Old Military Cemetery |
| McColl | Lieutenant | Douglas C. | 10th | Ottawa, ON | No Known Grave |
| McDonald | Lance-Corporal | Norman | 10th | Alberta Regiment | No Known Grave |
| McGregor | Private | Peter | 10th | Calgary, AB | No Known Grave |
| McKew | Private | Edward | 10th | Winnipeg, MB | Wimereux Communal Cemetery, France |
| McLaren | Major | Joseph | 10th | Alberta Regiment | Vlamertinghe Cemetery, Belgium |
| McVicar | Private | John | 10th | Alberta Regiment | No Known Grave |
| Moffat | Private | Robert J. | 10th | St-James, QC | No Known Grave |

| Last Name | First Name | Rank | Battalion | Home City/Regiment | Resting Place |
|---|---|---|---|---|---|
| Moir | Alexander | Corporal | 10th | Algoma, ON | No Known Grave |
| Monk | William E. | Private | 10th | Alberta Regiment | No Known Grave |
| Montgomery | Charles H. | Corporal | 10th | Winnipeg, MB | No Known Grave |
| Moore | George W. | Private | 10th | Alberta Regiment | Poperinghe Old Military Cemetery |
| Moore | John H. | Private | 10th | Alberta Regiment | No Known Grave |
| Morgan | Morgan T. | Private | 10th | Alberta Regiment | No Known Grave |
| Moss | John M. | Sergeant | 10th | Alberta Regiment | No Known Grave |
| Murray | Alexander | Private | 10th | Alberta Regiment | No Known Grave |
| Nash | Frank H. | Private | 10th | Alberta Regiment | No Known Grave |
| Nasmyth | James T. | Captain | 10th | Lindsay, ON | No Known Grave |
| Nesbit | Thomas O. | Sergeant-Major | 10th | Alberta Regiment | No Known Grave |
| Nolan | John P. | Private | 10th | Winnipeg, MB | No Known Grave |
| Osborn | Harry A. | Private | 10th | Alberta Regiment | No Known Grave |
| Parke | Charles W. | Corporal | 10th | Toronto, ON | No Known Grave |
| Pearson | Geoffrey W. | Lance-Corporal | 10th | Alberta Regiment | No Known Grave |
| Peterson | George L. | Private | 10th | Morris, MB | No Known Grave |
| Pinette | Jos R. | Private | 10th | Marcelin, SK | No Known Grave |
| Pinnock | William | Private | 10th | Alberta Regiment | No Known Grave |
| Pope | Christopher L. | Private | 10th | Penticton, BC | No Known Grave |
| Pott | Frank | Captain | 10th | Alberta Regiment | No Known Grave |
| Prew | Arthur H. | Private | 10th | Alberta Regiment | No Known Grave |
| Quay | John | Private | 10th | Winnipeg, MB | Poperinghe Old Military Cemetery |
| Reid | Francis J. | Private | 10th | Alberta Regiment | No Known Grave |
| Renton | Sydney C. | Private | 10th | Stilesville, NB | No Known Grave |
| Reynolds | James | Private | 10th | Alberta Regiment | No Known Grave |
| Richardson | George | Private | 10th | Alberta Regiment | No Known Grave |

| Last Name | Rank | First Name | Battalion | Home City/Regiment | Resting Place |
|---|---|---|---|---|---|
| Ricketts | Private | Leonard J. | 10th | Alberta Regiment | No Known Grave |
| Rippengale | Private | George | 10th | Los Angeles, CA | No Known Grave |
| Ritchie | Private | Erving G. | 10th | Alberta Regiment | No Known Grave |
| Robertshaw | Private | Frank | 10th | Alberta Regiment | No Known Grave |
| Robins | Private | Charles R. | 10th | Alberta Regiment | No Known Grave |
| Roughton | Lance-Corporal | Clifford G. | 10th | Calgary, AB | No Known Grave |
| Roy | Private | Robert W. | 10th | Alberta Regiment | No Known Grave |
| Samson | Private | William E. | 10th | Inverness, QC | No Known Grave |
| Sawers | Private | Owen C. | 10th | Vancouver, BC | No Known Grave |
| Scarrott | Sergeant | Arthur | 10th | Alberta Regiment | No Known Grave |
| Scott | Private | George H. | 10th | Alberta Regiment | No Known Grave |
| Selby | Private | George D. | 10th | Alberta Regiment | No Known Grave |
| Sewell | Private | Stephen | 10th | Alberta Regiment | Duhallow A.D.S. Cemetery, Belgium |
| Simmons | Private | George E. | 10th | Newcastle, ON | No Known Grave |
| Simpson | Private | John | 10th | Albert Regiment | No Known Grave |
| Sinclair | Private | Archibald | 10th | Renfrew, ON | No Known Grave |
| Sloan | Private | Robert S. | 10th | Alberta Regiment | No Known Grave |
| Smith | Private | Bertram | 10th | Alberta Regiment | No Known Grave |
| Smith | Private | William A. | 10th | Alberta Regiment | No Known Grave |
| Somerset | Private | Villiers H. | 10th | Alberta Regiment | No Known Grave |
| Spalding | Private | Charles M. | 10th | Alberta Regiment | No Known Grave |
| Starkley | Private | Cecil S. | 10th | Parry Sound, ON | No Known Grave |
| Stephens | Lance-Corporal | William J. | 10th | Medicine Hat, AB | No Known Grave |
| Stevenson | Lance-Corporal | Alexander | 10th | Alberta Regiment | No Known Grave |
| Stevenson | Private | Stanley | 10th | Alberta Regiment | No Known Grave |
| Street | Private | Charles M. | 10th | Ottawa, ON | No Known Grave |

| Last Name | First Name | Rank | Battalion | Home City/Regiment | Resting Place |
|---|---|---|---|---|---|
| Tallentis | George W. | Private | 10th | Alberta Regiment | No Known Grave |
| Thomas | Enoch | Private | 10th | Alberta Regiment | No Known Grave |
| Thomson | William | Private | 10th | Winnipeg, MB | Boulogne Eastern Cemetery, France |
| Tilley | Arthur | Private | 10th | Alberta Regiment | No Known Grave |
| Totten | William A. | Private | 10th | Alberta Regiment | No Known Grave |
| Van Schepdael | Anton L. | Private | 10th | Alberta Regiment | No Known Grave |
| Vincent | David J. | Private | 10th | Medicine Hat, AB | No Known Grave |
| Viner | Henry | Corporal | 10th | Alberta Regiment | No Known Grave |
| Walker | Robert W. | Private | 10th | Winnipeg, MB | No Known Grave |
| Wallace | H. A. | Captain | 10th | Alberta Regiment | No Known Grave |
| Walsh | Edward A. | Sergeant | 10th | Alberta Regiment | No Known Grave |
| Watkins | Mark R. | Private | 10th | Albert Regiment | No Known Grave |
| Watson | John O'D. | Corporal | 10th | Albert Regiment | No Known Grave |
| Webb | John T. | Private | 10th | Pittsburgh, PA | Poperinghe Old Military Cemetery, France |
| Williams | Albert | Corporal | 10th | Winnipeg, MB | No Known Grave |
| Williams | Cecil W. | Corporal | 10th | Miami, MB | No Known Grave |
| Wills | John G. | Private | 10th | Alberta Regiment | No Known Grave |
| Wisdom | Patrick W. | Private | 10th | Montreal, QC | No Known Grave |
| Wood | Albert E. | Sergeant | 10th | Alberta Regiment | No Known Grave |
| Woods | David | Private | 10th | St. Boniface, MB | No Known Grave |
| Woolley | William | Private | 10th | Calgary, AB | No Known Grave |
| Adams | Arthur | Quartermaster | 13th | Quebec Regiment | No Known Grave |
| Adams | John B. | Lance-Corporal | 13th | Three Rivers, QC | Boulogne Eastern Cemetery, France |
| Allan | Andrew | Private | 13th | Quebec Regiment | Cement House Cemetery, Belgium |
| Ames | Arthur | Private | 13th | Quebec Regiment | No Known Grave |

| Last Name | Rank | First Name | Battalion | Home City/Regiment | Resting Place |
|---|---|---|---|---|---|
| Armstrong | Private | James | 13th | Quebec Regiment | No Known Grave |
| Ash | Private | Alfred R. | 13th | Quebec Regiment | No Known Grave |
| Baily | Private | Hugh R. | 13th | Quebec Regiment | No Known Grave |
| Beard | Private | James | 13th | Quebec Regiment | No Known Grave |
| Bingham | Private | Fred | 13th | Quebec Regiment | No Known Grave |
| Boland | Private | George | 13th | Quebec Regiment | No Known Grave |
| Brennan | Private | Andrew | 13th | Montreal, QC | No Known Grave |
| Brown | Sergeant | Daniel M. | 13th | Montreal, QC | No Known Grave |
| Byrne | Private | Gerald F. | 13th | St. John's, NL | No Known Grave |
| Calvert | Private | John C. | 13th | Quebec Regiment | No Known Grave |
| Cameron | Private | John | 13th | Quebec Regiment | Roeselare Communal Cemetery, France |
| Campbell | Private | David | 13th | Quebec Regiment | No Known Grave |
| Carley | Private | Donald J. | 13th | Lindsay, ON | No Known Grave |
| Carrick | Sergeant | Robert L. | 13th | Montreal, QC | Hazebrouck Communal Cemetery, France |
| Carruthers | Private | John M. | 13th | Quebec Regiment | No Known Grave |
| Caryer | Sergeant | William E. | 13th | Quebec Regiment | No Known Grave |
| Caslake | Sergeant | Albert J. | 13th | Quebec Regiment | No Known Grave |
| Chapman | Private | Roland H. | 13th | Amherst, NS | No Known Grave |
| Chisholm | Private | Charles | 13th | Boston, MA | No Known Grave |
| Christie | Private | William | 13th | Quebec Regiment | No Known Grave |
| Clarke | Private | Thomas W. | 13th | Quebec Regiment | No Known Grave |
| Conn | Private | George D. | 13th | Fanny Bay, BC | No Known Grave |
| Cook | Private | Arthur G. | 13th | Waterloo, QC | No Known Grave |
| Coop | Private | Henry | 13th | Quebec Regiment | No Known Grave |
| Cornwall | Private | Charles W. | 13th | Montreal, QC | No Known Grave |
| Cottrell | Private | William | 13th | Quebec Regiment | No Known Grave |

| Last Name | Rank | First Name | Battalion | Home City/Regiment | Resting Place |
|---|---|---|---|---|---|
| Courchaine | Private | Oscar | 13th | St-Guillaime Station, QC | Roeselare Communal Cemetery, Belgium |
| Crosson (Crossman) | Private | John A. | 13th | Quebec Regiment | No Known Grave |
| Cunningham | Private | A. | 13th | Montreal, QC | No Known Grave |
| Currie | Private | James | 13th | Quebec Regiment | No Known Grave |
| Curwen | Sergeant | Francis G. | 13th | Quebec Regiment | Tyne Cot Cemetery, Belgium |
| Day | Private | Walter | 13th | Quebec Regiment | No Known Grave |
| Dick | Private | Peter | 13th | Montreal, QC | No Known Grave |
| Dickenson | Private | Edwin | 13th | Montreal, QC | No Known Grave |
| Dixon | Private | Thomas C. | 13th | Quebec Regiment | No Known Grave |
| Donaldson | Private | Albert | 13th | Verdun, QC | No Known Grave |
| Drummond | Lieutenant | Guy M. | 13th | Montreal, QC | Tyne Cot Cemetery, Belgium |
| Dunbar | Private | Alexander F. | 13th | Quebec Regiment | No Known Grave |
| Duncan | Private | David | 13th | Quebec Regiment | No Known Grave |
| Dupre | Private | Thomas | 13th | Cormierville, NB | No Known Grave |
| Easson | Private | John | 13th | Kingston, ON | No Known Grave |
| Evans | Private | William | 13th | Quebec Regiment | No Known Grave |
| Fairley | Private | Thomas | 13th | Quebec Regiment | No Known Grave |
| Ferguson | Private | James C. | 13th | Outremont, QC | No Known Grave |
| Finn | Private | Daniel J. | 13th | Quebec Regiment | No Known Grave |
| Fisher | Lance-Corporal | Fred H. | 13th | Montreal, QC | No Known Grave |
| Gallagher | Private | John W. | 13th | Moncton, NB | Poelcappelle British Cemetery, Belgium |
| Gibb | Private | George | 13th | Quebec Regiment | Bailleul Communal Cemetery, France |
| Glad | Private | Kongland | 13th | Montreal, QC | Perth Cemetery, Belgium |
| Glover | Private | Francis C. | 13th | Quebec Regiment | No Known Grave |
| Goodwin | Private | James E. | 13th | Quebec Regiment | No Known Grave |
| Gowans | Private | Stephen | 13th | Quebec Regiment | No Known Grave |

| Last Name | Rank | First Name | Battalion | Home City/Regiment | Resting Place |
|---|---|---|---|---|---|
| Gray | Private | Angus | 13th | Pictou County, NS | No Known Grave |
| Hadfield | Private | Thomas | 13th | Quebec Regiment | No Known Grave |
| Hall | Private | Joseph | 13th | Montreal, QC | No Known Grave |
| Hancock (Reay)* | Private | William L. | 13th | Quebec Regiment | No Known Grave |
| Hawley | Private | Carl B. | 13th | Cowansville, QC | No Known Grave |
| Henderson | Private | Cyril | 13th | Quebec Regiment | No Known Grave |
| Herring | Private | Reginald F. | 13th | Quebec Regiment | No Known Grave |
| Hollandes | Private | John P. | 13th | Carbonear, NL | No Known Grave |
| Hore | Private | Enos E. | 13th | Quebec Regiment | No Known Grave |
| Howell | Private | Frederick | 13th | Quebec Regiment | No Known Grave |
| Hughes | Corporal | Thomas | 13th | Quebec Regiment | No Known Grave |
| Imrie | Sergeant | George W. | 13th | Quebec Regiment | No Known Grave |
| Isherwood | Private | Richard | 13th | Quebec Regiment | No Known Grave |
| Johnson | Private | Desmond S. | 13th | St. Andrews, NB | No Known Grave |
| Johnston | Corporal | Charles | 13th | Quebec Regiment | No Known Grave |
| Jones | Private | William J. | 13th | Montreal, QC | No Known Grave |
| Kelley | Private | Patrick | 13th | Quebec Regiment | No Known Grave |
| Lang | Corporal | Thomas | 13th | Quebec Regiment | Wimereux Communal Cemetery, France |
| Lees | Captain | Gerald O. | 13th | Quebec Regiment | No Known Grave |
| Lowe | Private | Robert | 13th | Quebec Regiment | No Known Grave |
| MacDonald | Private | Alexander J. | 13th | Montreal, QC | No Known Grave |
| MacDonald | Private | Neil W. | 13th | Quebec Regiment | No Known Grave |
| Macfarlane | Corporal | Hugh | 13th | High River, AB | Perth Cemetery, Belgium |
| Mackenzie | Private | Adam J. | 13th | Pictou County, NS | Poelcappelle British Cemetery, Belgium |
| MacLeod | Sergeant | Peter | 13th | Quebec Regiment | No Known Grave |
| MacNamee | Lance-Corporal | W. H. | 13th | Montreal, QC | No Known Grave |

*Names in parentheses indicate persons for which duplicate attestation papers were filed under a different name.

| Last Name | Rank | First Name | Battalion | Home City/Regiment | Resting Place |
|---|---|---|---|---|---|
| Maloney | Private | Michael | 13th | Quebec Regiment | No Known Grave |
| Maltby | Lance-Corporal | Charles | 13th | Quebec Regiment | Perth Cemetery, Belgium |
| Marsh | Lance-Corporal | Thomas | 13th | Montreal, QC | No Known Grave |
| Mathieson | Private | William R. | 13th | Quebec Regiment | No Known Grave |
| Mayhew | Private | Arthur | 13th | Montreal, QC | No Known Grave |
| McCahon | Private | Charles P. | 13th | Montreal, QC | Perth Cemetery, Belgium |
| McCallum | Private | Ralph A. | 13th | North River, NS | No Known Grave |
| McDonald | Lance-Corporal | Donald J. | 13th | Dalhousie Station, QC | No Known Grave |
| McGrory | Private | Frank | 13th | Quebec Regiment | No Known Grave |
| Meekins | Private | James N. | 13th | Springhill, NS | No Known Grave |
| Mellowes | Private | William Oscar | 13th | Quebec Regiment | Poelcappelle British Cemetery, Belgium |
| Melluish | Private | William A. | 13th | Quebec Regiment | Poelcappelle British Cemetery, Belgium |
| Mileham | Private | William J. | 13th | Quebec Regiment | No Known Grave |
| Morrison | Private | John M. | 13th | Montreal, QC | No Known Grave |
| Murdock | Private | John A. | 13th | Pictou, NS | No Known Grave |
| Norsworthy | Major | Edward C. | 13th | Ingersoll, ON | Tyne Cot Cemetery, Belgium |
| Parks | Lance-Corporal | Stanley J. | 13th | Red Bank, NB | No Known Grave |
| Pearce | Private | Charles | 13th | Quebec Regiment | No Known Grave |
| Petkoff | Private | Angel | 13th | Quebec Regiment | No Known Grave |
| Piche | Private | Basil R. | 13th | St-Canut, QC | No Known Grave |
| Pizzy | Private | Frederick | 13th | Quebec Regiment | No Known Grave |
| Poole | Corporal | James M. | 13th | Quebec Regiment | No Known Grave |
| Quin | Private | James E. | 13th | Quebec Regiment | No Known Grave |
| Reid | Lance-Sergeant | John L. | 13th | Seaforth, ON | No Known Grave |
| Richards | Private | Cecil | 13th | Pugwash, NS | No Known Grave |
| Robertson | Private | Alexander | 13th | Dartmouth, NS | No Known Grave |

| Last Name | Rank | First Name | Battalion | Home City/Regiment | Resting Place |
|---|---|---|---|---|---|
| Russell | Private | David M. | 13th | Carsonby, ON | Roeselare Communal Cemetery, Belgium |
| Ryan | Private | Henry E. | 13th | Toronto, ON | No Known Grave |
| Scott | Private | James | 13th | Charlottetown, PEI | No Known Grave |
| Scott | Private | William | 13th | Quebec Regiment | No Known Grave |
| Scott | Sergeant | William G. | 13th | Montreal, QC | No Known Grave |
| Smith | Private | Clifford M. | 13th | Quebec Regiment | No Known Grave |
| Smith | Private | Robert H. | 13th | Quebec Regiment | No Known Grave |
| Southgate | Private | Lewis M. | 13th | Quebec Regiment | No Known Grave |
| Splatt | Lance-Corporal | William F. | 13th | Quebec Regiment | No Known Grave |
| Stansfield | Private | Israel | 13th | Quebec Regiment | Roeselare Communal Cemetery, Belgium |
| Stewart | Lance-Corporal | James | 13th | Quebec Regiment | No Known Grave |
| Stewart | Private | Norman C. | 13th | Ridgetown, ON | No Known Grave |
| Taylor | Private | Jack | 13th | Port Hope, ON | No Known Grave |
| Thomson | Sergeant | John H. | 13th | Montreal, QC | Poelcappelle British Cemetery, Belgium |
| Thomson | Private | Walter | 13th | Montreal, QC | No Known Grave |
| Townsend | Sergeant | Francis C. | 13th | Toronto, ON | No Known Grave |
| Wall | Private | Michael J. | 13th | Montreal, QC | No Known Grave |
| Whetter | Lance-Corporal | Richard | 13th | London, ON | No Known Grave |
| Whitehead | Captain | Lionel W. | 13th | Montreal, QC | No Known Grave |
| Wright | Private | Norman H. | 13th | Quebec Regiment | No Known Grave |
| Yates | Lance-Corporal | Clement O. | 13th | Quebec Regiment | No Known Grave |
| Macdonald | Private | Richard F. | 13th | Pictou, NS | Niederzwehren Cemetery, Germany |
| Belanger | Private | Leo | 14th | Quebec Regiment | No Known Grave |
| Bolton | Private | Joseph C. | 14th | Quebec Regiment | Vlamertinghe Cemetery, Belgium |
| Bond | Private | Arthur | 14th | Quebec Regiment | No Known Grave |

| Last Name | Rank | First Name | Battalion | Home City/Regiment | Resting Place |
| --- | --- | --- | --- | --- | --- |
| Brotherhood | Lieutenant | Wilfred C. | 14th | Quebec Regiment | No Known Grave |
| Bunnell | Lance-Corporal | Albert L. | 14th | Quebec Regiment | No Known Grave |
| Cote | Corporal | Ernest | 14th | Quebec Regiment | No Known Grave |
| Dabate | Private | David | 14th | Quebec Regiment | Wimereux Communal Cemetery, France |
| Dower | Private | Edward | 14th | Quebec Regiment | No Known Grave |
| Duffield | Lance-Sergeant | Frederick W. | 14th | Toronto, ON | No Known Grave |
| Dupuy | Private | Harry L. | 14th | Brockville, ON | No Known Grave |
| Flood | Corporal | Arthur H. | 14th | Toronto, ON | No Known Grave |
| Gandey | Private | Robert B. | 14th | Verdun, QC | No Known Grave |
| Gauthie | Private | Frank | 14th | Quebec Regiment | No Known Grave |
| Godsall | Private | Alfred | 14th | Quebec Regiment | No Known Grave |
| Haldeman | Private | Frederick | 14th | Toronto, ON | No Known Grave |
| Haylock | Private | George E. | 14th | Long Branch, ON | No Known Grave |
| Humphreys | Private | Albert E. | 14th | Toronto, ON | No Known Grave |
| Jones | Private | James | 14th | Quebec Regiment | No Known Grave |
| Kalabsa | Sergeant | Wilson | 14th | Quebec Regiment | No Known Grave |
| Langevin | Private | Ovila | 14th | Montreal, QC | No Known Grave |
| Leonard | Private | Frederick | 14th | Quebec Regiment | No Known Grave |
| Leveille | Private | Albert | 14th | Quebec Regiment | No Known Grave |
| Lister | Private | Robert W. | 14th | Quebec Regiment | No Known Grave |
| March | Private | Herbert | 14th | Quebec Regiment | No Known Grave |
| Maugham | Private | Edgar E. | 14th | Quebec Regiment | No Known Grave |
| McTurk | Private | John G. | 14th | Quebec Regiment | No Known Grave |
| Norton | Lance-Corporal | Cecil | 14th | Quebec Regiment | No Known Grave |
| O'Sullivan | Private | James | 14th | Montreal, QC | No Known Grave |
| Poitras | Private | Anthime | 14th | Montreal, QC | No Known Grave |

| Last Name | Rank | First Name | Battalion | Home City/Regiment | Resting Place |
|---|---|---|---|---|---|
| Potvin | Private | Louis V. | 14th | Montreal, QC | No Known Grave |
| Poulton | Private | Albert J. | 14th | Quebec Regiment | No Known Grave |
| Presant | Private | Bert A. | 14th | Toronto, ON | No Known Grave |
| Reese | Private | Robert R. | 14th | Burlington, ON | No Known Grave |
| Sanders | Private | Richard I. | 14th | Quebec Regiment | No Known Grave |
| Seguin | Private | Antonio | 14th | Montreal, QC | No Known Grave |
| Stairs | Lieutenant | George W. | 14th | Dartmouth, NS | No Known Grave |
| Stanton | Private | James R. | 14th | Quebec Regiment | No Known Grave |
| Steacie | Captain | Richard | 14th | Westmount, QC | No Known Grave |
| Thomson | Private | George A. | 14th | Quebec Regiment | No Known Grave |
| Trapnell | Private | Donald | 14th | St. John's, NL | No Known Grave |
| Turner | Sergeant | William | 14th | Montreal, QC | Boulogne Eastern Cemetery, France |
| Vaillant | Private | Hector | 14th | St-Henri-de-Montreal, QC | No Known Grave |
| Vigneault | Lance-Corporal | Theophile | 14th | Montreal, QC | No Known Grave |
| Warr | Private | Arthur E. | 14th | Falmouth, NS | No Known Grave |
| Weir | Private | Adam | 14th | Milltown, NB | No Known Grave |
| Williamson | Lieutenant | George M. | 14th | Westmount, QC | No Known Grave |
| Wiseman | Private | Edward | 14th | Montreal, QC | Perth Cemetery, Belgium |
| Wood | Private | John T. | 14th | Quebec Regiment | No Known Grave |
| Wright | Private | William | 14th | Montreal, QC | No Known Grave |
| Aikenhead | Private | Robert | 15th | Central Ontario Regiment | No Known Grave |
| Alexander | Private | James | 15th | Toronto, ON | Moorscele Military Cemetery, Belgium |
| Band | Sergeant | Harry | 15th | Kelowna, BC | No Known Grave |
| Barker | Sergeant | Thomas | 15th | Toronto, ON | No Known Grave |
| Barnard | Private | Carl M. | 15th | Toronto, ON | No Known Grave |

| Last Name | Rank | First Name | Battalion | Home City/Regiment | Resting Place |
|---|---|---|---|---|---|
| Barnes | Private | Percy | 15th | Central Ontario Regiment | No Known Grave |
| Barrett | Private | Hugh H. | 15th | Central Ontario Regiment | Boulogne Eastern Cemetery, France |
| Barrett | Private | James | 15th | Toronto, ON | No Known Grave |
| Bass | Private | Lewis A | 15th | Thornloe, ON | No Known Grave |
| Beattie | Corporal | Joseph H. | 15th | British Columbia Regiment | No Known Grave |
| Beith | Private | John | 15th | Central Ontario Regiment | Perth Cemetery, Belgium |
| Belfield | Lance-Corporal | John W. | 15th | Central Ontario Regiment | No Known Grave |
| Billson | Private | John E. | 15th | Toronto, ON | No Known Grave |
| Bilsand | Private | James | 15th | Central Ontario Regiment | No Known Grave |
| Bissett | Private | Thomas | 15th | Brooklyn, NY | No Known Grave |
| Blundy | Private | Isador G. | 15th | Chippawa, NY | No Known Grave |
| Borwn | Private | Henry | 15th | Central Ontario Regiment | No Known Grave |
| Bouldry | Private | William | 15th | Toronto, ON | No Known Grave |
| Boulton | Private | Thomas | 15th | Central Ontario Regiment | No Known Grave |
| Bowen | Sergeant | David | 15th | Central Ontario Regiment | No Known Grave |
| Bradley | Private | William | 15th | Toronto, ON | No Known Grave |
| Briscoe | Private | Philip H. | 15th | Central Ontario Regiment | No Known Grave |
| Bromley | Private | William M. | 15th | Magog, QC | White House Cemetery, Belgium |
| Brooks | Private | Augustus | 15th | Toronto, ON | No Known Grave |
| Brooks | Private | Samuel J. | 15th | Central Ontario Regiment | No Known Grave |
| Bunston | Private | Melvin | 15th | Brantford, ON | No Known Grave |
| Bush | Private | William | 15th | Wahnapitei, ON | Vlamertinghe Cemetery, Belgium |
| Bussell | Private | Frank | 15th | Central Ontario Regiment | No Known Grave |
| Cairns | Private | Harry J. | 15th | Orton, ON | No Known Grave |
| Campbell | Private | Hugh | 15th | Toronto, ON | No Known Grave |
| Campbell | Private | Robert | 15th | Toronto, ON | No Known Grave |

| Last Name | Rank | First Name | Battalion | Home City/Regiment | Resting Place |
|---|---|---|---|---|---|
| Cantley | Private | Alexander A. | 15th | Central Ontario Regiment | No Known Grave |
| Carr | Private | Roy R. | 15th | St. Catharines, ON | No Known Grave |
| Carter | Private | Fred N. | 15th | Hamilton, ON | No Known Grave |
| Cawood | Private | Joseph | 15th | Central Ontario Regiment | No Known Grave |
| Checkley | Sergeant | Albert | 15th | Toronto, ON | No Known Grave |
| Chivas | Private | Edwin J. | 15th | Detroit, MI | Poperinghe Old Military Cemetery, Belgium |
| Clark | Private | William J. | 15th | Central Ontario Regiment | No Known Grave |
| Clarke | Private | Edward T. | 15th | Central Ontario Regiment | No Known Grave |
| Cleal | Private | George H. | 15th | Toronto, ON | No Known Grave |
| Cole | Private | Clifford | 15th | Central Ontario Regiment | No Known Grave |
| Corey | Private | Rowan | 15th | Cowansville, QC | No Known Grave |
| Corson | Private | Archibald W. | 15th | Central Ontario Regiment | No Known Grave |
| Covill | Private | Arthur | 15th | Toronto, ON | No Known Grave |
| Cox | Private | Frank | 15th | Toronto, ON | No Known Grave |
| Crawford | Private | Charles W. | 15th | Sault Ste. Marie, ON | No Known Grave |
| Crosby | Private | Emerson | 15th | Toronto, ON | No Known Grave |
| Cumming | Private | John E. | 15th | Toronto, ON | Poperinghe Old Military Cemetery, Belgium |
| Currie | Private | John M. | 15th | Windsor, NS | No Known Grave |
| Dallen | Private | Donald | 15th | Central Ontario Regiment | No Known Grave |
| Daniels | Captain | Albert M. | 15th | Cobalt, ON | No Known Grave |
| Danks | Private | Sydney | 15th | Central Ontario Regiment | No Known Grave |
| Daubert | Private | Alexander | 15th | Todmorden, ON | No Known Grave |
| Davidson | Private | Archie H. | 15th | Chippawa, ON | No Known Grave |
| Davis | Private | Frederick J. | 15th | Central Ontario Regiment | No Known Grave |
| Davis | Corporal | Harold V. | 15th | Toronto, ON | No Known Grave |
| Delaney | Lance-Corporal | John J. | 15th | Central Ontario Regiment | No Known Grave |

| Last Name | Rank | First Name | Battalion | Home City/Regiment | Resting Place |
|---|---|---|---|---|---|
| Dennis | Private | Kennedy | 15th | Welland, ON | No Known Grave |
| Denisson | Lance-Corporal | John J. | 15th | Toronto, ON | No Known Grave |
| Dewar | Private | James | 15th | Toronto, ON | Vlamertinghe Cemetery, Belgium |
| Dickson | Private | Charles | 15th | Central Ontario Regiment | No Known Grave |
| Domaille | Private | Charlie F. | 15th | Central Ontario Regiment | No Known Grave |
| Dring | Lance-Corporal | Sidney W. | 15th | Central Ontario Regiment | No Known Grave |
| Dunn | Private | Joseph | 15th | Central Ontario Regiment | No Known Grave |
| Eyles | Corporal | Charles D. | 15th | Todmorden, ON | No Known Grave |
| Fairbairn | Private | John A. | 15th | Toronto, ON | No Known Grave |
| Flanagan | Private | John J. | 15th | Toronto, ON | No Known Grave |
| Flaxman | Private | Reuben | 15th | Toronto, ON | No Known Grave |
| Forbes | Private | John | 15th | Central Ontario Regiment | No Known Grave |
| Foster | Private | Leonard | 15th | Toronto, ON | No Known Grave |
| Fothergill | Private | Cuthbert R. | 15th | Magog, QC | No Known Grave |
| Fowle | Private | Alfred | 15th | Central Ontario Regiment | No Known Grave |
| Freeland | Corporal | Gordon | 15th | Buffalo, NY | No Known Grave |
| Frith | Private | Walter J. | 15th | Edmonton, AB | Poperinghe Old Military Cemetery, Belgium |
| Gibbs | Private | Albert C. | 15th | Central Ontario Regiment | No Known Grave |
| Gibson | Private | Robert | 15th | Central Ontario Regiment | No Known Grave |
| Gilchrist | Private | Frank I. | 15th | North Bay, ON | No Known Grave |
| Gillespie | Private | Alexander | 15th | Central Ontario Regiment | No Known Grave |
| Gillespie | Private | Norman A. | 15th | Central Ontario Regiment | Cemetery House Cemetery, Belgium |
| Gleed | Private | James J. | 15th | Toronto, ON | No Known Grave |
| Goodwin | Sergeant | Hugh H. | 15th | Toronto, ON | No Known Grave |
| Grant | Private | Leonard G. | 15th | Central Ontario Regiment | No Known Grave |
| Gray | Corporal | James S. | 15th | Toronto, ON | Hazebrouck Communal Cemetery, France |

| Last Name | Rank | First Name | Battalion | Home City/Regiment | Resting Place |
|---|---|---|---|---|---|
| Gridley | Sergeant | William E. | 15th | Central Ontario Regiment | Bailleul Communal Cemetery, France |
| Groshow | Sergeant | William I. | 15th | London, ON | No Known Grave |
| Hamilton | Private | John H. | 15th | London, ON | No Known Grave |
| Hannah | Private | Douglas McN. | 15th | Central Ontario Regiment | No Known Grave |
| Hannah | Lance-Sergeant | John D. | 15th | Central Ontario Regiment | No Known Grave |
| Harrigan | Private | Alfred | 15th | Toronto, ON | No Known Grave |
| Harrison | Private | Henry | 15th | Truro, NS | No Known Grave |
| Hawke | Private | John | 15th | Toronto, ON | No Known Grave |
| Hawker | Private | George H. | 15th | Central Ontario Regiment | No Known Grave |
| Henderson | Private | William F. | 15th | Holyoke, MA | No Known Grave |
| Hewetson | Private | George | 15th | Central Ontario Regiment | No Known Grave |
| Hibbard | Private | Hartley | 15th | Huntsville, ON | No Known Grave |
| Hilton | Private | Harry | 15th | Central Ontario Regiment | No Known Grave |
| Hodder | Private | Joseph A. | 15th | Central Ontario Regiment | No Known Grave |
| Hodges | Private | William B. | 15th | Hatley, QC | No Known Grave |
| Hodges | Private | Ray B. | 15th | Hatley, QC | Bailleul Communal Cemetery Extension, France |
| Holtby | Private | Arthur W. | 15th | Central Ontario Regiment | No Known Grave |
| Honsberger | Private | Thomas | 15th | Toronto, ON | Roeselare Communal Cemetery, Belgium |
| Hopley | Private | Herbert | 15th | Central Ontario Regiment | No Known Grave |
| Hugh | Lance-Corporal | Stephen H. | 15th | Toronto, ON | Cemetery House Cemetery, Belgium |
| Hyde | Private | Harry | 15th | Central Ontario Regiment | No Known Grave |
| Hyde | Private | William J. | 15th | Toronto, ON | No Known Grave |
| Ingle | Private | Harry | 15th | Central Ontario Regiment | No Known Grave |
| Ingram | Private | John W. | 15th | Central Ontario Regiment | No Known Grave |
| Irving | Private | William A. | 15th | Sudbury, ON | No Known Grave |
| James | Private | Samuel H. | 15th | Central Ontario Regiment | No Known Grave |

| Last Name | Rank | First Name | Battalion | Home City/Regiment | Resting Place |
|---|---|---|---|---|---|
| Jamieson | Private | Robert C. | 15th | Hamilton, ON | No Known Grave |
| Jamison | Private | John D. | 15th | Toronto, ON | Poperinghe Old Military Cemetery, Belgium |
| Jenkins | Private | John A. | 15th | Central Ontario Regiment | No Known Grave |
| Jennings | Private | Sydney B. | 15th | Central Ontario Regiment | No Known Grave |
| Johnston | Private | Willie H. | 15th | Toronto, ON | No Known Grave |
| Journeaux | Private | Henry | 15th | Toronto, ON | No Known Grave |
| Jucksh | Private | Arnold J. | 15th | Meaford, ON | No Known Grave |
| Kerrigan | Lance-Corporal | Charles H. | 15th | Toronto, ON | No Known Grave |
| Kibly | Private | Samuel S. | 15th | Central Ontario Regiment | Boulogne Eastern Cemetery, France |
| Lambden | Private | George | 15th | Central Ontario Regiment | No Known Grave |
| Lambie | Private | Andrew A. | 15th | Central Ontario Regiment | No Known Grave |
| Langmuir | Lieutenant | Gavin I. | 15th | Toronto, ON | No Known Grave |
| Lawrence | Private | William G. | 15th | Central Ontario Regiment | Cemetery House Cemetery, Belgium |
| Leclerc | Private | Joseph | 15th | Montreal, QC | No Known Grave |
| Lenton | Private | William F. | 15th | Central Ontario Regiment | No Known Grave |
| Lewis | Corporal | Clifford H. | 15th | Montreal, QC | No Known Grave |
| Lewis | Private | Fred | 15th | Nova Scotia | No Known Grave |
| Lewis | Private | Daniel O. | 15th | Central Ontario Regiment | Boulogne Eastern Cemetery, Belgium |
| Litchfield | Private | Reginald C. | 15th | Toronto, ON | Bedford House Cemetery, Belgium |
| Long | Private | William E. | 15th | Trenton, NS | No Known Grave |
| Love | Private | Andrew | 15th | Central Ontario Regiment | No Known Grave |
| Lyness | Private | Thomas | 15th | Sarawak, ON | Vlamertinghe Cemetery, Belgium |
| MacGregor | Captain | Archibald R. | 15th | Central Ontario Regiment | Perth Cemetery, Belgium |
| MacIntyre | Private | Hugh | 15th | Central Ontario Regiment | No Known Grave |
| MacLeod | Private | Alexander | 15th | Central Ontario Regiment | Hazebrouck Communal Cemetery, France |
| MacLeod | Private | Malcolm | 15th | Central Ontario Regiment | No Known Grave |

| Last Name | Rank | First Name | Battalion | Home City/Regiment | Resting Place |
| --- | --- | --- | --- | --- | --- |
| Mann | Private | John | 15th | Central Ontario Regiment | No Known Grave |
| Marks | Private | William | 15th | Toronto, ON | No Known Grave |
| Marshall | Private | John | 15th | Toronto, ON | No Known Grave |
| Marshall | Private | Sidney H. | 15th | Central Ontario Regiment | No Known Grave |
| Martin | Private | France E. | 15th | Central Ontario Regiment | No Known Grave |
| Martin | Private | James W. | 15th | Toronto, ON | No Known Grave |
| May | Private | Vivian | 15th | Central Ontario Regiment | No Known Grave |
| May | Private | William J. | 15th | Central Ontario Regiment | No Known Grave |
| McClay | Private | Walter | 15th | Central Ontario Regiment | Wimereux Communal Cemetery, France |
| McColl | Private | Bruce | 15th | London, ON | No Known Grave |
| McColl | Private | Duncan | 15th | Toronto, ON | No Known Grave |
| McColl | Lance-Corporal | John D. | 15th | London, ON | No Known Grave |
| McCulloch | Sergeant | William A. | 15th | Central Ontario Regiment | No Known Grave |
| McDonald | Sergeant | Alexander A. | 15th | Central Ontario Regiment | No Known Grave |
| McDougall | Private | Allan | 15th | Toronto, ON | No Known Grave |
| McIntosh | Private | James | 15th | Toronto, ON | Boulogne Eastern Cemetery, France |
| McIntyre | Private | Hugh | 15th | Toronto, ON | Boulogne Eastern Cemetery, France |
| McIntyre | Private | Wilson | 15th | Boston, MA | No Known Grave |
| McLeish | Private | Alexander N. | 15th | Toronto, ON | No Known Grave |
| McMillan | Private | Frederick W. | 15th | Castleton, ON | No Known Grave |
| McNaughton | Private | John | 15th | Toronto, ON | No Known Grave |
| Mercer | Private | John C. | 15th | London, ON | No Known Grave |
| Merritt | Captain | Cecil M. | 15th | St. Catharines, ON | No Known Grave |
| Millard | Private | Arthur G. | 15th | New Toronto, QC | No Known Grave |
| Millard | Private | William H. | 15th | New Toronto, QC | No Known Grave |
| Mitchell | Private | James A. | 15th | Central Ontario Regiment | No Known Grave |

| Last Name | Rank | First Name | Battalion | Home City/Regiment | Resting Place |
|---|---|---|---|---|---|
| Mooney | Private | Harold W. | 15th | Cowansville, QC | No Known Grave |
| Moore | Private | Edwin H. | 15th | Central Ontario Regiment | No Known Grave |
| Moore | Private | William H. | 15th | Toronto, ON | No Known Grave |
| Morris | Private | Arthur E. | 15th | Toronto, ON | No Known Grave |
| Mould | Sergeant | John R. | 15th | Vancouver, BC | No Known Grave |
| Munroe | Private | Donald M. | 15th | Cornwall, ON | No Known Grave |
| Murison | Private | Charles W. | 15th | Central Ontario Regiment | No Known Grave |
| Murray | Private | Alexander | 15th | Central Ontario Regiment | No Known Grave |
| Murray | Lance-Corporal | James M. | 15th | Central Ontario Regiment | No Known Grave |
| Nelson | Private | Harry J. | 15th | Owen Sound, ON | Perth Cemetery, Belgium |
| Newman | Private | George | 15th | Toronto, ON | No Known Grave |
| Nicholson | Private | Malcolm A. | 15th | Central Ontario Regiment | No Known Grave |
| Nolan | Private | Joseph J. | 15th | Point La Nim, NB | No Known Grave |
| Notley | Private | John | 15th | Toronto, ON | No Known Grave |
| Page | Private | Frank | 15th | Central Ontario Regiment | No Known Grave |
| Palethorpe | Private | John G. | 15th | Central Ontario Regiment | No Known Grave |
| Paramore | Lance-Corporal | William | 15th | Central Ontario Regiment | Watou Churchyard, Belgium |
| Peterson | Private | Bruce A. | 15th | Montreal, QC | No Known Grave |
| Phillip | Private | John F. | 15th | Central Ontario Regiment | No Known Grave |
| Pilkington | Private | Alfred | 15th | New Liskeard, ON | Poperinghe Old Military Cemetery, Belgium |
| Pollock | Private | John | 15th | Central Ontario Regiment | No Known Grave |
| Rae | Private | Alfred | 15th | Toronto, ON | No Known Grave |
| Reid | Private | Herbert G. | 15th | Central Ontario Regiment | No Known Grave |
| Richards | Private | Wilmot | 15th | Trenton, ON | No Known Grave |
| Robertson | Private | James | 15th | Toronto, ON | No Known Grave |
| Robertson | Private | Thomas | 15th | Central Ontario Regiment | Hazebrouck Communal Cemetery, France |

| Last Name | Rank | First Name | Battalion | Home City/Regiment | Resting Place |
|---|---|---|---|---|---|
| Roche | Private | Charles W. | 15th | Port Elgin, ON | No Known Grave |
| Roscoe | Private | William | 15th | Central Ontario Regiment | Roeselare Communal Cemetery, France |
| Ross | Private | Walter G. | 15th | Dundalk, ON | No Known Grave |
| Ross | Private | Hugh | 15th | New Glasgow, NS | No Known Grave |
| Rourke | Private | Malcolm W. | 15th | Brandon, MB | No Known Grave |
| Rowley | Private | John | 15th | Toronto, ON | No Known Grave |
| Sangster | Private | Edgar C. | 15th | Uxbridge, ON | No Known Grave |
| Scott | Private | F. M. | 15th | Central Ontario Regiment | Poperinghe Old Military Cemetery, Belgium |
| Scott | Private | Arthur A. | 15th | Central Ontario Regiment | No Known Grave |
| Scott | Private | John S. | 15th | Central Ontario Regiment | No Known Grave |
| Shearman | Private | Harold L. | 15th | Ottawa, ON | No Known Grave |
| Sherlock | Private | Thomas M. | 15th | London, ON | Boulogne Eastern Cemetery, France |
| Sholert | Private | Frederick W. | 15th | Toronto, ON | No Known Grave |
| Short | Private | Joseph | 15th | Toronto, ON | No Known Grave |
| Simpson | Private | Richard | 15th | Sudbury, ON | No Known Grave |
| Sinclair | Private | Hugh | 15th | Central Ontario Regiment | Poperinghe Old Military Cemetery, Belgium |
| Skimin | Private | Walter M. | 15th | Toronto, ON | No Known Grave |
| Smith | Private | Thomas | 15th | Toronto, ON | No Known Grave |
| Somerville | Private | Cecil | 15th | Elk Lake, ON | No Known Grave |
| Sparks | Lance-Corporal | Douglas E. | 15th | Toronto, ON | No Known Grave |
| Stephens | Private | Frederick | 15th | Central Ontario Regiment | No Known Grave |
| Stodart | Private | John | 15th | Toronto, ON | Tyne Cot Cemetery, Belgium |
| Stone | Private | Samuel L. | 15th | Magog, QC | No Known Grave |
| Strickland | Private | Gerald F. | 15th | Toronto, ON | Cemetery House Cemetery, Belgium |
| Strombeth | Private | Jack | 15th | Owen Sound, ON | No Known Grave |
| Taylor | Lieutenant | Geoffrey B. | 15th | West Toronto, ON | No Known Grave |

| Last Name | Rank | First Name | Battalion | Home City/Regiment | Resting Place |
|---|---|---|---|---|---|
| Thompson | Private | Joshua C. | 15th | Loretteville, QC | No Known Grave |
| Todd | Private | George | 15th | Toronto, ON | No Known Grave |
| Truss | Private | Peter G. | 15th | Toronto, ON | No Known Grave |
| Tweedy | Private | O. | 15th | Kinlough, ON | No Known Grave |
| Tyler | Private | John W. | 15th | Central Ontario Regiment | No Known Grave |
| Uden | Corporal | Arthur | 15th | Toronto, ON | No Known Grave |
| Vandervoort | Lance-Corporal | Wilbur C. | 15th | Napanee, ON | No Known Grave |
| Walker | Private | John A. | 15th | Bowmanville, ON | No Known Grave |
| Walker | Sergeant | William | 15th | Toronto, ON | No Known Grave |
| Wallace | Private | William | 15th | Central Ontario Regiment | Boulogne Eastern Cemetery, France |
| Wardle | Private | Edwin | 15th | Toronto, ON | No Known Grave |
| Warren | Private | William A. | 15th | Central Ontario Regiment | No Known Grave |
| Wauchope | Private | William | 15th | Central Ontario Regiment | No Known Grave |
| Webb | Private | Walter T. | 15th | Central Ontario Regiment | No Known Grave |
| Weeks | Private | Ernest S. | 15th | Central Ontario Regiment | Bailleul Communal Cemetery Extension, France |
| Whalley | Private | Thomas | 15th | Millbrook, ON | Poelcappelle British Cemetery, Belgium |
| White | Private | Albert E. | 15th | Central Ontario Regiment | Cologne Southern Cemetery, Germany |
| Wickens | Private | Frederick H. | 15th | Central Ontario Regiment | No Known Grave |
| Williams | Corporal | William J. | 15th | Central Ontario Regiment | Poperinghe Old Military Cemetery, Belgium |
| Williams | Private | Hopkin | 15th | Stellarton, NS | No Known Grave |
| Wyatt | Corporal | William G. | 15th | Toronto, ON | No Known Grave |
| Yates | Private | Clifford F. | 15th | Toronto, ON | No Known Grave |
| Adams | Private | Charles J. | 16th | Manitoba Regiment | No Known Grave |
| Adamson | Private | James S. | 16th | Westover, ON | No Known Grave |
| Ager | Lieutenant | George S. | 16th | Saskatoon, SK | No Known Grave |

| Last Name | First Name | Rank | Battalion | Home City/Regiment | Resting Place |
|---|---|---|---|---|---|
| Aitken | Henry | Private | 16th | Manitoba Regiment | No Known Grave |
| Aitkens | George | Private | 16th | Winnipeg, MB | No Known Grave |
| Aitkens | James | Private | 16th | Winnipeg, MB | No Known Grave |
| Amos | Charles B. | Lance-Corporal | 16th | Manitoba Regiment | No Known Grave |
| Avery | George | Private | 16th | Manitoba Regiment | No Known Grave |
| Avery | John H. | Private | 16th | Manitoba Regiment | Bailleul Communal Cemetery, France |
| Ball | Frank F. | Private | 16th | Charlottetown, PEI | No Known Grave |
| Bean | Lewis M. | Private | 16th | Manitoba Regiment | No Known Grave |
| Beley | Wilfred | Private | 16th | Manitoba Regiment | No Known Grave |
| Bell | Francis | Private | 16th | Hamilton, ON | No Known Grave |
| Blayney | David G. | Private | 16th | Cranbrook, BC | Bailleul Communal Cemetery, France |
| Blott | Charles M. | Private | 16th | Wardsville, ON | No Known Grave |
| Bridges | William H. | Private | 16th | Victoria, BC | No Known Grave |
| Bryant | Fredrick J. | Corporal | 16th | Manitoba Regiment | No Known Grave |
| Buist | William D. | Corporal | 16th | Manitoba Regiment | No Known Grave |
| Cameron | Donald M. | Private | 16th | Winnipeg, MB | No Known Grave |
| Campbell | Alexander | Private | 16th | Hamilton, ON | No Known Grave |
| Carrol | Peter J. | Lance-Corporal | 16th | Hamilton, ON | No Known Grave |
| Carter | Stuart | Private | 16th | Winnipeg, MB | No Known Grave |
| Chaffey | Walter F. | Private | 16th | Vancouver, BC | No Known Grave |
| Coutts | John | Private | 16th | Manitoba Regiment | No Known Grave |
| Cummings | James | Corporal | 16th | Montreal, QC | Bailleul Communal Cemetery, France |
| Dean | Robert | Private | 16th | Manitoba Regiment | No Known Grave |
| Denison | Edgar | Lance-Corporal | 16th | Toronto, ON | No Known Grave |
| De Paiva | Joseph H. | Private | 16th | Manitoba Regiment | No Known Grave |
| Dibbs | William A. | Lance-Corporal | 16th | Manitoba Regiment | No Known Grave |

| Last Name | Rank | First Name | Battalion | Home City/Regiment | Resting Place |
|---|---|---|---|---|---|
| Dickson | Private | George | 16th | Manitoba Regiment | No Known Grave |
| Didsbury | Private | William H. | 16th | Manitoba Regiment | No Known Grave |
| Donald | Private | William | 16th | Manitoba Regiment | No Known Grave |
| Douglas | Lance-Corporal | George | 16th | Manitoba Regiment | No Known Grave |
| Douglas | Corporal | Hector | 16th | Manitoba Regiment | No Known Grave |
| Downes | Corporal | John E. | 16th | Manitoba Regiment | No Known Grave |
| Duff | Private | Walter D. | 16th | Manitoba Regiment | No Known Grave |
| Duffy | Private | James | 16th | Manitoba Regiment | Vlamertinghe Military Cemetery, Belgium |
| Dunbar | Private | Hugh M. | 16th | Manitoba Regiment | No Known Grave |
| Dunlop | Private | Raymond | 16th | Manitoba Regiment | No Known Grave |
| Dunn | Private | Douglas A. | 16th | Vancouver, BC | No Known Grave |
| Edwards | Private | Henry | 16th | Manitoba Regiment | No Known Grave |
| Esplin | Lance-Corporal | Stewart | 16th | Manitoba Regiment | No Known Grave |
| Findlay | Private | Hamilton | 16th | Vancouver, BC | No Known Grave |
| Fleming | Captain | Hamilton M. | 16th | Manitoba Regiment | No Known Grave |
| Forbes | Private | James K. | 16th | Manitoba Regiment | No Known Grave |
| Forbes | Sergeant | Henry W. | 16th | Vancouver, BC | Hazebrouck Communal Cemetery, France |
| Fyson | Private | Oliver | 16th | Manitoba Regiment | No Known Grave |
| Gamble | Lance-Corporal | Vernon F. | 16th | Vancouver, BC | No Known Grave |
| Geddes | Captain | John | 16th | Manitoba Regiment | No Known Grave |
| Green | Lance-Corporal | Herbert B. | 16th | Manitoba Regiment | No Known Grave |
| Gulliford | Private | Henry | 16th | Manitoba Regiment | No Known Grave |
| Hain | Lance-Corporal | David | 16th | Manitoba Regiment | No Known Grave |
| Hamilton | Private | John | 16th | Winnipeg, MB | No Known Grave |
| Hamilton | Private | Robert P. | 16th | Manitoba Regiment | No Known Grave |
| Hamilton | Private | William R. | 16th | Manitoba Regiment | No Known Grave |

| Last Name | First Name | Rank | Battalion | Home City/Regiment | Resting Place |
|---|---|---|---|---|---|
| Hardy | Harry | Sergeant | 16th | Manitoba Regiment | No Known Grave |
| Hawley | Ernest S. | Corporal | 16th | Manitoba Regiment | No Known Grave |
| Hayward | Arthur C. | Private | 16th | Manitoba Regiment | Poperinghe Old Military Cemetery, Belgium |
| Heath | Gerald C. | Corporal | 16th | Manitoba Regiment | No Known Grave |
| Herald | Ralph E. | Private | 16th | Kelowna, BC | No Known Grave |
| Hickingbottom | Richard F. | Private | 16th | Gravenhurst, ON | No Known Grave |
| Hill | Leslie B. | Private | 16th | Victoria, BC | Vlamertinghe Cemetery, Belgium |
| Hill | C. H. | Private | 16th | Manitoba Regiment | Bailleul Communal Cemetery Extension, France |
| Holmes | Alfred E. | Private | 16th | Vancouver, BC | No Known Grave |
| Howe | Gilbert F. | Private | 16th | Hamilton, ON | No Known Grave |
| Hutchinson | William J. | Private | 16th | Manitoba Regiment | No Known Grave |
| Jameson | George W. | Captain | 16th | Manitoba Regiment | New Irish Farm Cemetery, Belgium |
| Jamieson | John | Private | 16th | Manitoba Regiment | No Known Grave |
| Jessup | Alan E. | Private | 16th | Massett, BC | Poperinghe Old Military Cemetery, Belgium |
| Johnston | James H. | Private | 16th | Manitoba Regiment | No Known Grave |
| Johnstone | Peter | Lance-Corporal | 16th | British Columbia | New Irish Farm Cemetery, Belgium |
| Jollie | Robert O. | Private | 16th | Manitoba Regiment | No Known Grave |
| Julier | Leslie | Sergeant | 16th | Vancouver, BC | No Known Grave |
| Keating | John Dennison | Private | 16th | Joliette, QC | No Known Grave |
| Keeton | Horace | Private | 16th | Hamilton, ON | No Known Grave |
| Kenworthy | John G. | Lieutenant | 16th | Empire Valley, BC | No Known Grave |
| Kinnear | John | Private | 16th | Manitoba Regiment | No Known Grave |
| Lidiard | Frederick H. | Private | 16th | Manitoba Regiment | Railway Dugouts Burial Ground B, Belgium |
| Lindsay | A. L. | Lieutenant | 16th | Manitoba Regiment | No Known Grave |
| MacDermott | Charles G. | Private | 16th | Manitoba Regiment | No Known Grave |
| MacDonald | Donald | Private | 16th | Manitoba Regiment | No Known Grave |

| Last Name | First Name | Rank | Battalion | Home City/Regiment | Resting Place |
|---|---|---|---|---|---|
| MacFarlane | Donald A. | Lance-Corporal | 16th | Hamilton, ON | No Known Grave |
| Mackenzie | James G. | Private | 16th | Manitoba Regiment | Phalempin Communal Cemetery, France |
| Macpherson | Ian | Private | 16th | Manitoba Regiment | No Known Grave |
| Malcolm | Ernest C. | Sergeant | 16th | Vancouver, BC | No Known Grave |
| McAdam | John | Private | 16th | Manitoba Regiment | No Known Grave |
| McDermid | Alfred | Private | 16th | Thurso, QC | No Known Grave |
| McDermott | Charles G. | Private | 16th | Manitoba Regiment | No Known Grave |
| McFetridge | John | Private | 16th | Manitoba Regiment | No Known Grave |
| McGill | Arthur L. | Private | 16th | Manitoba Regiment | No Known Grave |
| McGregor | James H. | Captain | 16th | Cadboro Bay, BC | No Known Grave |
| McKane | Adam | Sergeant | 16th | Manitoba Regiment | No Known Grave |
| McKenzie | Norman J. | Sergeant | 16th | Sault Ste. Marie, ON | No Known Grave |
| McLaughlin | Robert | Private | 16th | Wilmot Station, NS | No Known Grave |
| McLaughlin | William | Private | 16th | New Glasgow, NS | No Known Grave |
| McLennan | Harrington | Private | 16th | Vancouver, BC | No Known Grave |
| McLennan | Kenneth B. | Private | 16th | Manitoba Regiment | No Known Grave |
| McOnie | Ronald J. | Private | 16th | Manitoba Regiment | No Known Grave |
| McPhee | John | Private | 16th | Manitoba Regiment | No Known Grave |
| McQuoid | Urell | Private | 16th | Manitoba Regiment | No Known Grave |
| Merrit | Cecil | Captain | 16th | St. Catharines, ON | No Known Grave |
| Michie | Alexander | Private | 16th | Manitoba Regiment | No Known Grave |
| Moffat | Robert | Private | 16th | Toronto, ON | No Known Grave |
| Moir | Benjamin | Private | 16th | Manitoba Regiment | No Known Grave |
| Moody | Harry J. | Private | 16th | Birsay, SK | No Known Grave |
| Murray | George W. | Private | 16th | Kingston, ON | No Known Grave |
| Olliff | William | Private | 16th | Manitoba Regiment | No Known Grave |

| Last Name | Rank | First Name | Battalion | Home City/Regiment | Resting Place |
|---|---|---|---|---|---|
| Owen | Private | William P. | 16th | Manitoba Regiment | No Known Grave |
| Pickard | Private | Robin P. | 16th | Vancouver, BC | No Known Grave |
| Ramsay | Sergeant-Major | Henry V. | 16th | Vancouver, BC | No Known Grave |
| Rapier | Private | Frank | 16th | Toronto, ON | No Known Grave |
| Robb | Private | Arthur C. | 16th | Manitoba Regiment | No Known Grave |
| Robertson | Private | John | 16th | Manitoba Regiment | No Known Grave |
| Robinson | Private | Walter E. | 16th | Revelstoke, BC | No Known Grave |
| Ross | Lance-Sergeant | Alex | 16th | Manitoba Regiment | No Known Grave |
| Ross | Private | Angus D. | 16th | Vancouver, BC | No Known Grave |
| Ross | Captain | G. H. | 16th | Winnipeg, MB | No Known Grave |
| Rourke | Private | Malcolm W. | 16th | Foam Lake, SK | No Known Grave |
| Sarel | Private | Charles T. | 16th | Ottawa, ON | No Known Grave |
| Schloesser | Private | Albert | 16th | Manitoba Regiment | No Known Grave |
| Scott | Private | Guy | 16th | Manitoba Regiment | No Known Grave |
| Smith | Private | David P. | 16th | Vancouver, BC | No Known Grave |
| Smith | Private | Frederick S. | 16th | Quebec, QC | No Known Grave |
| Smith | Corporal | Richard | 16th | Manitoba Regiment | No Known Grave |
| Sol | Private | Dirk | 16th | Manitoba Regiment | No Known Grave |
| Southern | Private | Howard E. | 16th | Manitoba Regiment | No Known Grave |
| Spencer | Private | William | 16th | Manitoba Regiment | No Known Grave |
| Stafford | Private | Christoper | 16th | Manitoba Regiment | No Known Grave |
| Steel | Private | Robert | 16th | Manitoba Regiment | No Known Grave |
| Stewart | Private | Gilbert | 16th | Manitoba Regiment | No Known Grave |
| Storer | Private | Samuel A. | 16th | Manitoba Regiment | No Known Grave |
| Stroyan | Private | Hugh G. | 16th | Vancouver, BC | Seaforth Cemetery, Belgium |
| Sutton | Private | Benjamin | 16th | Manitoba Regiment | No Known Grave |

| Last Name | Rank | First Name | Battalion | Home City/Regiment | Resting Place |
| --- | --- | --- | --- | --- | --- |
| Taylor | Lance-Corporal | Edmund F. | 16th | Vancouver, BC | Poperinghe Old Military Cemetery, Belgium |
| Taylor | Private | Charles | 16th | Manitoba Regiment | No Known Grave |
| Thomson | Private | James | 16th | Manitoba Regiment | Vlamertinghe Cemetery, Belgium |
| Tisseman | Private | Joseph A. | 16th | Manitoba Regiment | No Known Grave |
| Torrance | Lance-Corporal | William | 16th | Manitoba Regiment | No Known Grave |
| Turner | Private | William C. | 16th | Manitoba Regiment | No Known Grave |
| Walker | Private | T. | 16th | Manitoba Regiment | Poperinghe Old Military Cemetery, Belgium |
| Walker | Private | Godfrey W. | 16th | Manitoba Regiment | No Known Grave |
| Waugh | Private | Thomas | 16th | Manitoba Regiment | No Known Grave |
| Weeks | Lance-Corporal | Ernest | 16th | Langley, BC | No Known Grave |
| Weir | Private | David D. | 16th | Manitoba Regiment | No Known Grave |
| Welsh | Private | Alexander W. | 16th | Manitoba Regiment | No Known Grave |
| Wilkinson | Sergeant | Edgar A. | 16th | Winnipeg, MB | No Known Grave |
| Young | Private | Thomas J. | 16th | Manitoba Regiment | No Known Grave |
| Burdett | Private | Francis | PPCLI* | Toronto, ON | No Known Grave |
| Chalmers | Private | Thomas C. | PPCLI | PPCLI | No Known Grave |
| Goodwin | Private | Algar B. | PPCLI | Montreal, QC | No Known Grave |
| Hartley | Lance-Corporal | Ernest | PPCLI | Montreal, QC | No Known Grave |
| Homershaw | Private | Thomas G. | PPCLI | PPCLI | St. Omer Souvenir Cemetery, France |
| Hughes | Private | Hugh S. | PPCLI | PPCLI | Klein-Vierstraat British Cemetery, Belgium |
| McDonald | Private | Peter | PPCLI | PPCLI | No Known Grave |
| Mitchell | Lance-Corporal | Robert A. | PPCLI | Calgary, AB | No Known Grave |
| Noble | Private | Joseph F. | PPCLI | Sherbrooke, QC | No Known Grave |
| Pryke | Private | George | PPCLI | PPCLI | White House Cemetery, Belgium |
| Walden | Lance-Corporal | Joseph | PPCLI | Toronto, ON | No Known Grave |

*Princess Patricia's Canadian Light Infantry

| Last Name | Rank | First Name | Battalion | Home City/Regiment | Resting Place |
|---|---|---|---|---|---|
| Beynon | Sapper | Ivor | 1st Field Co. | Canadian Engineers | Duhallow A.D.S. Cemetery, Belgium |
| Warton | Sapper | Percy J. | 1st Field Co. | Canadian Engineers | Duhallow A.D.S. Cemetery, Belgium |
| Craig | Corporal | John S. | 2nd Field Co. | Canadian Engineers | No Known Grave |
| Down | Sapper | Joseph H. | 2nd Field Co. | Toronto, ON | No Known Grave |
| Gilhuly | Sapper | Harold R. | 2nd Field Co. | Selkirk, MB | No Known Grave |
| Husband | Sapper | James | 2nd Field Co. | Canadian Engineers | No Known Grave |
| Osborn | 2nd Corporal | Geoffrey | 2nd Field Co. | Winnipeg, MB | No Known Grave |
| Redden | Sapper | John | 2nd Field Co. | Canadian Engineers | No Known Grave |
| Wiman | Sapper | Leslie | 2nd Field Co. | Toronto, ON | No Known Grave |
| Green | Sapper | William | 3rd Field Co. | Toronto, ON | No Known Grave |
| Campbell | Sapper | David M. | 3rd Field Co. | Canadian Engineers | No Known Grave |
| Cossey | Sapper | Herbert W. | 3rd Field Co. | Canadian Engineers | No Known Grave |
| Fotherby | Sapper | George H. | 3rd Field Co. | Canadian Engineers | No Known Grave |
| McNeill | 2nd Corporal | James | 3rd Field Co. | Canadian Engineers | No Known Grave |
| Murphy | Sapper | Geoffrey F. | 3rd Field Co. | Canadian Engineers | No Known Grave |
| Platt | Driver | Ernest | 6th Field Co. | Toronto, ON | No Known Grave |
| Coutts | Sapper | Norman H. | 1st Div. Signals | Canadian Engineers | Duhallow A.D.S. Cemetery, Belgium |
| Grieve | Sapper | George R. | 1st Div. Signals | Canadian Engineers | Duhallow A.D.S. Cemetery, Belgium |
| Swale | Corporal | Frederick A. | 1st Div. Signals | Canadian Engineers | No Known Grave |
| Stevens | Private | Arthur T. | 1st Div. Supply | Canadian Engineers | No Known Grave |

| Last Name | Rank | First Name | Battalion | Home City/Regiment | Resting Place |
|---|---|---|---|---|---|
| Boone | Sergeant | Gordon V. | 1st Bde. Field Art. | Millertown, NL | Hagle Dump Cemetery, Belgium |
| Gomes | Gunner | Manuel A. | 1st Bde. Field Art. | Montreal, QC | Perth Cemetery (China Wall), Belgium |
| Helmer | Lt.-Col. | Alex R. | 1st Bde. Field Art. | Ottawa, ON | No Known Grave |
| Munn | Gunner | Robert M. | 1st Bde. Field Art. | Canadian Field Artillery | Hazebrouck Communal Cemetery, France |
| Murray | Gunner | Frederick J. | 1st Bde. Field Art. | Kingston, ON | Boulogne Eastern Cemetery, France |
| Rivers | Gunner | Percy J. | 1st Bde. Field Art. | Victoria, BC | Potijze Chateau Wood Cemetery, Belgium |
| Watson | Driver | Charles W. | 1st Bde. Field Art. | Canadian Field Artillery | No Known Grave |
| Cathcart | Bombardier | Nicholas L. | 2nd Bde. Field Art. | New Waterford, NS | No Known Grave |
| Coatsworth | Gunner | Peter | 2nd Bde. Field Art. | Canadian Field Artillery | No Known Grave |
| Cote | Gunner | David | 2nd Bde. Field Art. | Canadian Field Artillery | Ypres Town Cemetery, Belgium |
| Furrie | Gunner | Eric F. | 2nd Bde. Field Art. | Carman, MB | Potijze Chateau Wood Cemetery, Belgium |
| Kearon | Gunner | George T. | 2nd Bde. Field Art. | Canadian Field Artillery | No Known Grave |
| Mawhinny | Driver | John | 2nd Bde. Field Art. | Montreal, QC | Ypres Town Cemetery, Belgium |
| McIsaac | Gunner | John R. | 2nd Bde. Field Art. | Ben Eoin, NS | Hagle Dump Cemetery, Belgium |
| McLennan | Sergeant | Hugh | 2nd Bde. Field Art. | Sydney, NS | No Known Grave |
| Penticost | Gunner | Albert G. | 2nd Bde. Field Art. | Delson, QC | Ypres Town Cemetery, Belgium |
| Popow | Gunner | Fred | 2nd Bde. Field Art. | Canadian Field Artillery | No Known Grave |
| Ratcliffe | Bombardier | Joseph F. | 2nd Bde. Field Art. | Montreal, QC | No Known Grave |
| Saunders | Gunner | Raymond A. | 2nd Bde. Field Art. | Yarmouth, NS | Poperinghe Old Military Cemetery, Belgium |
| Talbot | Gunner | George | 2nd Bde. Field Art. | Canadian Field Artillery | No Known Grave |
| Thomlinson | Driver | W.L. | 2nd Bde. Field Art. | Canadian Field Artillery | Poperinghe Old Military Cemetery, Belgium |
| Mercer | Gunner | Robert H. | 3rd Bde. Field Art. | London, ON | No Known Grave |
| Cross | Driver | William S. | 3rd Bde. Field Art. | Vancouver, BC | Wimereux Communal Cemetery, France |

| Last Name | Rank | First Name | Battalion | Home City/Regiment | Resting Place |
|---|---|---|---|---|---|
| Gamble | Sergeant | James | 3rd Bde. Field Art. | Canadian Field Artillery | No Known Grave |
| Hughes | Gunner | Earl R. | 3rd Bde. Field Art. | Toronto, ON | No Known Grave |
| Lovekyn | Gunner | Vyvyan I. | 3rd Bde. Field Art. | Canadian Field Artillery | Poperinghe Old Military Cemetery, Belgium |
| McVitte | Gunner | George T. | 3rd Bde. Field Art. | Canadian Field Artillery | No Known Grave |
| Turner | Corporal | Arthur W. | 3rd Bde. Field Art. | Canadian Field Artillery | Potijze Chateau Wood Cemetery, Belgium |
| Penman | Corporal | Robert | 3rd Bde. Field Art. | St. Catharines, ON | Poperinghe Old Military Cemetery, Belgium |
| Warrington | Corporal | Henry W. | 3rd Bde. Field Art. | Toronto, ON | No Known Grave |
| Demeule | Private | Edgar | No. 1 Field Amb. | Montreal, QC | Hazebrouck Communal Cemetery, France |
| Collins | Private | John | No. 2 Field Amb. | Toronto, ON | Poperinghe Old Military Cemetery, Belgium |
| McKay | Sergeant | John W. | No. 2 Field Amb. | Toronto, ON | Poperinghe Old Military Cemetery, Belgium |
| Pitts | Private | Charles L. | No. 2 Field Amb. | Halifax, NS | No Known Grave |
| Smart | Private | Thomas | No. 3 Field Amb. | Cdn. Army Med. Corps | Hazebrouck Communal Cemetery, France |
| Slater | Corporal | Frederick | Medical Corps | Cdn. Army Med. Corps | Cliveden War Cemetery, England |
| Bacon | Private | Arthur T. | 1st Div. Supply | Goshen, NY | No Known Grave |
| Childs | Private | Henry J. | 1st Can. Div. | Cyclist Company | No Known Grave |
| Good | Corporal | Harry | 1st Can. Div. | Cyclist Company | Wimereux Communal Cemetery, France |

# Notes

## Preface
1. Benton, quoted in Morrison, 6.

## Introduction
1. Quoted in Morrison, 4.
2. Borden, 455.
3. Duguid, 7.
4. Winter, *Sam Hughes*, 136.
5. Tuchman, *Guns of August*, 122.
6. Grey, quoted Hirshfeld, quoted in Herwig, 35.
7. Freud, quoted in Herwig, 34.
8. Quoted in Beckett, 34.
9. Borden, 459–61.
10. Craig, 49.
11. Morton, *Fight or Pay*, 77.
12. MacDonald, quoted in Morrison, 24.
13. Peat, 10.
14. Child, 146.
15. Morton, *Fight or Pay*, 7.
16. Hughes, quoted in Duguid, 23.
17. Ibid., Appendix, 13.
18. Morton, *When Your Number's Up*, 51.
19. Hughes, quoted in Cook, *No Place to Run*, 11.
20. Hughes, quoted in Morton, *When Your Number's Up*, 6.
21. Ibid., 12.
22. Hughes, quoted in Duguid, Appendix, 82.
    Designed in 1902 as a sporting rifle, the Ross was adopted after Militia Minister Sir Frederick Borden failed to secure fifteen thousand Lee-Enfields from

England and to convince the Lee-Enfield Company to establish a factory in Canada. In 1906, two years after the Royal North West Mounted Police (RNWMP) took delivery of the Mark I version, the assistant commissioner reported that "the rifles were very unsatisfactory, particularly the magazine action, extractors failed to work, in rapid fire jams were frequent even in the hands of experienced men, and he did not think they were safe for rapid fire." The RNWMP withdrew the Ross Mark I from use.

Over the next eight years, the rifle underwent scores of changes. A chuck was added to the end to allow a bayonet to be attached. The sights on later models were connected by thumb screws and thus were adjustable, a change made necessary by the fact that after "the 300th round the heat of firing melted away the foresight, which was fastened with common solder."

Sam Hughes's faith in the Ross rifle stemmed in large part from the fact that Canadians had used it to win five international titles between 1906 and 1913. But 2nd Ypres was not an international shooting match. It was a fight to the finish in which both man and machine were pushed to their limits. The rifle's limits (indeed, even the words used to describe its limits—"After firing 15 to 30 rounds rapid fire, the rifle jams. To loosen the bolt it was necessary to use the boot heel or the handle of an entrenching tool.") were known long before it failed at Ypres. In a 1901 endurance test, when "1,000 rounds were fired from each rifle, the Lee-Enfield worked easily and satisfactorily throughout, whereas the Ross worked very stiffly at the conclusion of each 50 rounds and misfed and jammed repeatedly." Even the minister's claim that the problem lay not with the rifle but with the British-made .303 cartridges was almost fifteen years old.

23. Bourke, 54.
24. Granatstein, *Canada's Army*, 56.
25. Morton, *When Your Number's Up*, 15.
26. Watson, quoted in Dancocks, *Flanders*, 60.
27. Haig, CBC, "In Flanders Fields," program 3.
28. Swettenham, 36.
29. Scott, 13.
30. The Special Parliamentary Committee on Boot Inquiry provided war-weary Ottawa with great political theatre, as white-haired, well-dressed parliamentarians concerned themselves with the cobbler's art. Questions about leather, glue, fastenings, and construction methods were answered with references to stress tests and X-ray analyses of bindings, heels, and toes. Hughes stole the show when he threatened to shoot any bootmaker "caught short-changing on equipment" destined for "our boys."
31. Rawling, 20.
32. Bagnall, 32.
33. Sinclair, quoted in Rawling, 19.
34. Duguid, 173.
35. Baldwin, 118–19.
36. Quoted in Tucker, *Battle Glory*, 51f.

37. Quoted in Tucker, *Battle Glory*, 69.
38. Dancocks, *Gallant Canadians*, 18.
39. Trythall, 33.
40. *The Times History of the War*, vol. 5, 58.
41. Aitken, 48.
42. Duffy, 65, 189, and 217f.
43. Before the war, to avert personal bankruptcy, Currie had pocketed $10,883.34 that the Milita Department sent him to pay for uniforms for his militia unit. Currie admitted this fraud in a letter to a colleague in Victoria, who, without Currie's knowledge, forwarded the letter to Borden, along with a note suggesting that the prime minister allow Currie time to replace the money. Both Borden and Hughes took the advice. Currie repaid the money in 1917 with loans from two officers who served at 2nd Ypres, Lieutenant-Colonel David Watson and Major Victor Odlum. Surprisingly, when Sir Sam Hughes tried to destroy Currie's reputation after the war (by accusing him of wasting Canadian lives by attacking Mons on the morning of 11 November 1918), he did not make this scandal public.
44. There are in fact two works that can be called the official Canadian history of Ypres. The first was written by Duguid and was the only part of his projected eight-volume history of the First World War to be published. The second, G. W. L. Nicholson's *Canadian Expeditionary Force, 1914–1919* (1962), was written to fill the void left by the abandonment of Duguid's project. I refer to Duguid's work as the "official history" and to him as the "official historian," a position he held for more than two decades.

## Chapter 1: "It Is a Higher Form of Killing"

1. Boyd, 50.
2. Canadian Bank of Commerce, "Letters from the Front," 12.
3. Baldwin, 159.
4. Currie, 200.
5. Duguid, Appendix, 235.
6. Ibid., 195.
7. Fuller, 40.
8. Canadian Bank of Commerce, "Letters," 13.
9. Boyle, quoted in Dancocks, *Gallant Canadians*, 21.
10. *The Times History of the War* (56f.) asserts that the Germans chose to release the gas on France's "coloured troops" because OHL believed that non-white troops "would be more liable to panic." The Germans did resent having to fight non-white North Africans (and Indians), and at least one regimental history uses the German equivalent of "nigger." However, the decision to release the gas on the lines that were held by France's African troops was dictated by a more prosaic reality: the winds blew from the German lines towards the French.
11. Duguid, Appendix, 310.

12. Hahn, 118. Hahn was awarded the Nobel Prize for Chemistry for his discovery of nuclear fission. Haber's staff included two other future Nobel laureates, James Franck and Gustav L. Hertz. Ironically, Haber and Hahn were Jewish and fled Nazi Germany for Britain and America, respectively.
13. Von Einem, quoted in Trumpener, 473.
14. Ruprecht, quoted in Trumpener, 473.
15. Diemling, quoted in Dixon, 42.
16. This argument is repeated in *Der Weltkrieg, 1914–1918*, Germany's official history: "The Hague declaration merely prohibited the use of projectiles whose SOLE purpose was the diffusion of asphyxiating or deleterious gases." *Der Weltkrieg* also tried to seize the moral high ground: "Moreover, perceptions of humanity did not forbid the introduction of gas weapons, because the hundredfold fatal casualties from projectiles were and remained substantially higher than those from cloud gas" (Duguid, Appendix, 318).
17. Duguid, Appendix, 319.
18. Trumpener, 475.
19. The first warning came from Charles Lucieto, a French spy who reported that the factories of BASF had been producing poison gas.

    A 4 April British intelligence report referring to prisoners taken at the end of March reads:

    GENERAL INTELLIGENCE
    According to prisoners of the XV German Army Corps the ZILLEBEKE front is provided with iron bottles 5 feet high placed slightly behind the trenches, either buried or sheltered. These bottles contain asphyxiating gas. They have not yet been instructed in their use [A]. They are laid prone and the seal removed, when the gas escapes parallel to the surface of the earth [B]. A favourable wind is necessary. The pioneers in charge are provided with special apparatus fixed on their heads as a protection against fumes. The inventor has been promoted to lieutenant [C].
    (This is on the authority of the 111th Corps).

    The report is wrong about several points. Training had, indeed, been carried out. The cylinders were buried upright, and the gas was released through a lead pipe bent over the parapet. The inventor, Fritz Haber, was appointed a captain. The report correctly notes, however, that the pioneers were equipped with special breathing apparati, and that a favourable wind was necessary to launch the attack.
20. Edmonds, 164.
21. Duguid, Appendix, 231.
22. Currie, quoted in McWilliams and Steel, 16.
    The war diary for 15 April for General Sir Herbert Plumer's V Corps, to which the 1st Canadian Division belonged, records that at 1:50 p.m., a dispatch from the II Army headquarters directed that precautions be taken "on account of an agent's report, confirmed from other sources, that enemy contemplated an

attack on the Ypres salient on night of 15th/16th April. Passages have been prepared across old trenches to facilitate bringing up of the artillery. Germans intend making use of tubes with asphyxiating gas. They are placed in batteries of 20 tubes per 40 metres along front of *XXIV Corps* [Duke Albrecht's Army]. A favourable wind is necessary." Corps Commander interviewed Divisional Commanders (Duguid, Appendix, 232.).

The last sentence of this war diary entry indicates that General Alderson had been briefed. There is no record of his formally briefing his commanders, but Currie's diary entry suggests that there was some kind of informal sharing of information.

23. McWilliams and Steel, 15.
24. Duguid, 218.
25. Ibid., Appendix, 233.
26. Dixon, 32f.

## Chapter 2: "The Carnival of Death Sings Loudly"

1. Scott, 34.
2. Gorman, 25.
3. *Crag and Canyon*, 5 June 1915 (http://www.canadiangreatwarproject.com/transcripts/transcriptDisplay.asp?Type=L&Id=63).
4. Sinclair, quoted in Reid, 79.
5. Reserve-Infanterie-Regiment 238 (translated by Johanna Legg: http://www.greatwar.co.uk/westfront/ypsalient/secondypres/prelude/gestandto3.htm).
6. Duguid, Appendix, p. 238.
7. Rae, 142.
8. Boyd, 65.
9. The author would like to thank Dominiek Dendooven, director of the In Flanders Fields Museum in Ypres, Belgium, for making this quote available.
10. Mordacq, 63.
11. Ibid., 65.
12. Ellis, 102.
13. The author would like to thank Dominiek Dendooven, director of the In Flanders Fields Museum in Ypres, Belgium, for making this quote available.
14. The author would like to thank Dominiek Dendooven, director of the In Flanders Fields Museum in Ypres, Belgium, for making this quote available.
15. Baldwin, 154.
16. Binding, 64.

## Chapter 3: "With a Coolness and Discipline That Seems Almost Incredible"

1. Currie, 217, 219, 220.
2. Swettenham, 45.

3. Mordacq, 83, 84.
4. The author would like to thank Dominiek Dendooven, director of the In Flanders Fields Museum in Ypres, Belgium, for making this quote available.
5. Dancocks, *Flanders*, 119.
6. *Handbook for the 18 pdr. Q.F. Gun.*
7. The author would like to thank Lieutenant Colonel William A. Smy, OMM, for his help in understanding Fisher's actions.
8. Gordon, quoted in Tucker, *Battle Glory*, 73.
9. Clark, *Donkeys*, 76.
10. Bourke, 168.
11. Scott, 36.
12. Currie, quoted in Cassar, *Beyond Courage*, 78.
13. Peat, 138f.
14. Ibid., 138.
15. This is the title of Schreiber's book about the Canadians during the last hundred days of the Great War.
16. Markham, quoted in Urquhart, *16th Battalion*, 57.

## Chapter 4: "In the Nature of a Sacrificial Charge"

1. McWilliams and Steel, 66.
2. Travers, *Killing Ground*, 49.
3. Urquhart, *16th Battalion*, 58.
4. Scott, 37f.
5. Binding, 19.
6. Urquhart, *16th Battalion*, 58.
7. Hartman, quoted in Tucker, *Battle Glory*, 93.
8. *Canadian Scottish*, 139.
9. *The Times History of the War*, vol. 5, 61.
10. Tucker, *Battle Glory*, 99.
11. Urquhart, *16th Battalion*, 59.
12. Dancocks, *Gallant Canadians*, 32f.
13. Ormond, quoted in McWilliams and Steel, 68.
14. Christie, *Second Battle of Ypres*, 19.

## Chapter 5: "I Didn't Know of a Better 'Ole to Go To"

1. Mordacq, 107.
2. Ibid., 112.
3. Anderson, 63.
4. Ibid., 64.
5. L'Abbé misremembered the cartoon's caption, which is "Well, if you know of a better 'ole, go to it."

6. Strange, quoted in O'Connor, 47f.
7. McCuaig, quoted in McWilliams and Steel, 74.
8. Rawling, 57.
9. Keegan, *Face of Battle*, 264.

## Chapter 6: "And Trust to Providence"
1. Armstrong, quoted in McWilliams and Steel, 83.
2. Mercer, quoted in Dancocks, *Flanders*, 142.
3. Duguid, 269.
4. Iarocci, 13.
5. Reville, 454.
6. Tucker, *Battle Glory*, 103.
7. Wackett, 46.
8. Brown, *Tommy Goes to War*, 105.
9. Bell, quoted in Mathieson, 105f.
10. Reville, 452.
11. Mordacq, 131f.
12. Duguid, Appendix, 329.
13. Dancocks, *Flanders*, 144.
14. Brown, *Tommy Goes to War*, 106.

## Chapter 7: "We Sampled Every Kind of Shell Made in Germany"
1. Duguid, Appendix, 240.
2. Hynes, 70.
3. Jünger, 24f.
4. Keegan, *Face of Battle*, 265.
5. Peat, 159.
6. Keegan, *Face of Battle*, 263.
7. Hynes, 58.
8. Duguid, Appendix, 193.
9. Hynes, 71.
10. Canadian Bank of Commerce, "Letters," 10.
11. Iarocci, 10.
12. Wakeling, quoted in Reville, 453.
13. Graves, 99f.
14. Fraser, quoted in Reville, 457.
15. Iarocci, 10.
16. Ibid., 11.
17. Dixon, 67.
18. Fetherstonhaugh, *13th Battalion*, 48.

## Chapter 8: "It Is Considered Very Unlucky to Be Killed on a Friday"
1. French's report is available online at www.firstworldwar.com.
2. Duguid, 279.
3. Holmes, *Acts of War*, 232.
4. Dixon, 73.
5. Holmes, *Acts of War*, 302.
6. Brown, *Tommy Goes to War*, 111.
7. Dixon, 73.
8. Fraser, CBC, "In Flanders Fields," program 5.
9. Peat, 164f.
10. Dixon, 74.
11. Junger, quoted in Holmes, *Acts of War*, 381.
12. Edmonds, 207.
13. Mordacq, 135.
14. Duguid, Appendix, 330, 339.
15. Binding, 64.
16. Murray, 49.
17. Holmes, *Acts of War*, 88.

## Chapter 9: "As Under a Green Sea, I Saw Him Drowning"
1. Duguid, Appendix, 321.
2. Baldwin, 162.
3. Currie, 237.
4. Tuxford, quoted in McWilliams and Steel, 104.
5. Sinclair, quoted in Reid, 81.
6. Bertram, quoted in Reid, 81f.
7. Tuxford, quoted in McWilliams and Steel, 104.
8. Simpson, quoted in Tucker, *Battle Glory*, 128.
9. Carey, quote in Dancocks, *Flanders*, 161.
10. Miller, quoted in Dancocks, *Flanders*, 163.
11. Beattie, 71.
12. Currie, 240.
13. Ibid., 238.
14. Drummond, quoted in McWilliams and Steel, 106f.
15. Duguid, Appendix, 268.
16. Urquhart, *16th Battalion*, 64f.

## Chapter 10: "No, Alexander Is Not Gone"
1. Rae, 161–63. Herbert Rae, who published under the name G. Herbert Gibson, was a Canadian soldier but not an infantryman. Rather, he was an Edinburgh University–trained heart specialist and member of the Royal College of Physicians who had moved to British Columbia in 1911 or 1912. The author of

numerous medical papers, Rae did serve in the trenches at 2nd Ypres, but as a medical officer assigned to the 7th Battalion.
2. Critchley, CBC, "In Flanders Fields," program 5.
3. Ormond, quoted in Dancocks, *Flanders*, 166.
4. Brewer, CBC, "In Flanders Fields," program 5.
5. McCuaig, quoted in Cassar, *Beyond Courage*, 122.
6. Osborne, quoted in McWilliams and Steel, 115.
7. Scott, CBC, "In Flanders Fields," program 5.

## Chapter 11: "His Insides Were Hanging between His Fingers"
1. Jenkins, quoted in Morrison, 70f.
2. McWilliams and Steel, 150.
3. Duguid, Appendix, 340.
4. Ibid.
5. Ibid., 339.
6. Ibid., 331.
7. Gorman, 21.
8. Scudamore, *Short History*, n.p.
9. Corker, quoted in McWilliams and Steel, 119.
10. Scudamore, *Short History*, n.p.
11. Urquhart, *Currie*, 82.
12. Dixon, 90.

## Chapter 12: "Supplying Bullets, by Relieving the Dead of Theirs"
1. Goodspeed, *Battle Royale*, 108.
2. Ormond, quoted in Dancocks, *Flanders*, 181.
3. Dancocks, *Flanders*, 179.
4. Duguid, Appendix 274, no. 560.
5. Scudamore, *Lighter Episodes*, 9.
6. Morton, *Silent Battle*, 32.
7. Duguid, Appendix, 274, no. 564.
8. Cassar, *Beyond Courage*, 138.
9. Duguid, 308.
10. Hassock, *The Illustrated War*, 28 July 1915, www.greatwardifferent.com/Great_War/First_Gas_Attack/First_GasAttack_ 01.htm.
11. Corker, quoted in McWilliams and Steel, 119.
12. (Vancouver) *Daily Province*, 12 Nov. 1917.

## Chapter 13: "The Retirement Was *Not Compulsory*"
1. Drummond, quoted in McWilliams and Steel, 126.
2. Duguid, 311.

3. Gordon-Hall to Duguid, Library and Archives Canada, RG24, Vol. 1503, File IHQ683-1-30-5.
4. Urquhart, *Currie*, 79.
5. Dixon, 99.
6. Napier, quoted in Bovey, 6.
7. Bennett, quoted in Dancocks, *Gallant Canadians*, 40.
8. Murray, 53.
9. Hardyman, quoted in Dancocks, *Flanders*, 184.
10. Seaman, CBC, "In Flanders Fields," program 5.
11. Ibid., 20.
12. Dancocks, *Flanders*, 186.
13. Bennett, quoted in McWilliams and Steel, 139.
14. *The Illustrated War*, Anthony R. Hossack, 28 July 1915, www.greatwardifferent.com/Great_War/First_Gas_Attack.

## Chapter 14: "Do You Expect Me to Wet-Nurse Your Brigade?"

1. Currie, quoted in Urquhart, *Currie*, 101.
2. Travers, "Allies in Conflict," 301.
3. Travers, "Allies in Conflict," 310.
4. Duguid, 322f.
5. Duguid, Appendix 279, no. 587.
6. Swettenham, 45f.
7. McWilliams and Steel, 130.
8. Duguid, 313.

## Chapter 15: "Can You Tell Me Where the Enemy Is?"

1. McWilliams and Steel, 141.
2. Duguid, 325.
3. Ibid., 334f.
4. Cassar, *Beyond Courage*, 150.
5. Duguid, 335.
6. Ibid.
7. Gordon-Hall, quoted in Urquhart, *Currie*, 97.
8. Anderson, quoted in Dancocks, *Flanders*, 186.
9. Monton, *Silent Battle*, 46.

## Chapter 16: "Why Do They Stop?"

1. Hull, quoted in Dixon, 105.
2. Duguid, 350
3. Dixon, 106.
4. Edmonds, 242.

5. Bairnsfather, 290.
6. Critchley, CBC, "In Flanders Fields," program 5.
7. Duguid, 347.
8. Bairnsfather, 290 and 293.
9. Dixon, 107.
10. Bairnsfather, 290 and 296.
11. Dixon, 107.
12. Bairnsfather, 298.
13. Duguid, Appendix, 327.
14. Ibid., 327.
15. Travers, "Allies in Conflict," 303.
16. Archer, quoted in Tucker, *Battle Glory*, 131.
17. Lynn, quoted in McWilliams and Steel, 169.
18. Scrimger, quoted in Dancocks, *Flanders*, 220.
19. Duguid, Appendix, 294.
20. *Ottawa Citizen*, 17 Oct. 2005, Section C, p. 2.
21. Tuxford, quoted in McWilliams and Steel, 170f.

## Chapter 17: "Do Not Shoot! Ve Vas French"
1. MacIlree, quoted in Dancocks, *Flanders*, 214.
2. Currie, quoted in Duguid, 358.
3. Dixon, 115.
4. Ibid.
5. Dixon, 115.
6. McWilliams and Steel, 174.
7. Tuxford, quoted in McWilliams and Steel, 172.
8. Ibid.
9. Fisher, CBC, "In Flanders Fields," program 5.
10. Duguid, Appendix, 296, no. 769.
11. Tuxford, 7.
12. Tuxford, 7–8.
13. Gibbons, 117ff. Though Morton, in *Silent Battle*, has questioned this story, I have included it because, whether it is true or not, it can stand for other German violations of the Hague Conventions.

## Chapter 18: "The Heaviest [Shelling] Yet Experienced by the Brigade"
1. Currie, 187, 264.
2. Ibid., 265.
3. Urquhart, 16th Battalion, 68.
4. Bennett, quoted in Dancocks, *Gallant Canadians*, 42.
5. Christopherson, CBC, "In Flanders Fields," program 5.
6. Bagshaw, CBC, "In Flanders Fields," program 5.

7. Anon., *Canadian Scottish*, 143.
8. Bennett, quoted in Dancocks, *Gallant Canadians*, 42.
9. Duguid, Appendix, 332.
10. Edmonds, 259.
11. Duguid, Appendix, 333.
12. Dixon, 137.
13. Duguid, Appendix, 333.
14. Dixon, 149.
15. Duguid, Appendix, 333.
16. Lovelace, quoted in McWilliams and Steel, 201.
17. Dixon, 149.
18. Dancocks, *Flanders*, 232.
19. Duguid, Appendix, 298ff.
20. Duguid, Appendix, 300.
21. Dixon, 151.
22. French, quoted in Cassar, *The Tragedy of Sir John French*, 225.
23. Quoted in Smithers, 265.

 But officer's mess gossip also told what was perhaps the most important part of the story. There had been bad blood between Sir John and Sir Horace since 1907, when Smith-Dorrien replaced French as commander of the Aldershot military base and immediately cancelled military police patrols instituted by French. French was also offended when Smith-Dorrien ordered the cavalry to begin learning infantry tactics. French's animosity only grew after Kitchener sent Smith-Dorrien to a command under French; one can only imagine French's reaction when he learned from Smith-Dorrien that he was asked by King George to keep him informed of activities under French's command.

 Immediately after the Battle of Le Cateau (26 August 1914), during which Smith-Dorrien refused French's order to withdraw and chose instead to stage a fighting retreat (which stopped the Germans), French joined the chorus praising Smith-Dorrien for both his tactics and his realization that standing and fighting was psychologically important to the BEF. ON 27 April 1915, Sir John got his revenge.

 Just how much French wanted to get Smith-Dorrien can be seen from French's memoir *1914*, published in 1919. As one historian put it, "In his eagerness to belittle Smith-Dorrien, [French] did not always confine himself to the facts." French doubles the number of British casualties at Le Cateau and makes believe he did not know (in 1914, when he praised Smith-Dorrien) that a large part of Smith-Dorrien's success was owed to the timely intervention of French cavalry (In fact, Smith-Dorrien's report makes this clear.) And he lies about the timing of the order to withdraw (Smithers, 265). In December 1915, Sir John French was sacked in favour of Sir Douglas Haig.

24. Cassar, *The Tragedy of Sir John French*, 174.

## Chapter 19: "A Perpetual Inspiration to Their Successors"
1. Nasmith, 190.
2. Duguid, Appendix, 314.
3. Aldeson, quoted in Nasmith, 190f.
4. Tucker, *Battle Glory*, 151f.
5. Duguid, Appendix, 319, 321.

## Coda
1. Cook, *Clio's Warriors*, 17.
2. Ibid.
3. Ibid., 15.
4. Child, 86.
5. Accessible at www.vac-acc.gc.ca/general/sub.cfm?source=collections/books/history#memorial.

## Appendix A: "The Reckoning"
1. Cook, *No Place to Run*, 37.
2. Ibid., 51.
3. Ibid., 216.
4. Ibid., 215.
5. Ibid., 55.

# Bibliography

This bibliography gives the publication information for articles and books I used while preparing this book. The operational orders, reports, and war diaries referred to in the text are housed at Library and Archives Canada in Ottawa, Ontario; the war diaries are available online at www.collectionscanada.ca/archivianet/020152_e.html. I have, however, provided citations for the letters that detail the contretemps between Generals Arthur Currie and Thomas D'Oyly Snow, Major Victor Odlum's and Michael H. L'Abbé's memoirs.

### Official Histories

Adami, J. George, MD, FRS. *War Story of the Canadian Army Medical Corps*. Vol. 1: *The First Contingent (to the Autumn of 1915)*. London: Canadian War Records Office, 1918.

Duguid, Col. A. Fortesque. *Official History of the Canadian Forces in the Great War, 1914–1919*. Vol. 1 and Appendices. Ottawa: King's Printer, 1938.

Edmonds, Brig. James E. *History of the Great War Based on Official Documents*. Vol. 1: *Military Operations, France and Belgium, 1915*. London: Macmillan, 1927.

Macphail, Sir Andrew. *Official History of the Canadian Forces in the Great War, 1914–1919: The Medical Services*. Ottawa, King's Printer, 1925.

Nicholson, Col. G. W. L. *Canadian Expeditionary Force, 1914–1919*. Ottawa: Queen's Printer, 1964.

Reichsarchiv. *Der Weltkrieg 1914 bis 1918: Die militärischen Operationen zu Lande*. Berlin: E. S. Mittler und Sohn, 1932.

Tucker, Gilbert Norman. *The Naval Service of Canada*. Vol. 1: *Origins and the Early Years*. Ottawa: King's Printer, 1952.

## Regimental Histories

### Canadian

Anon. *The Great Adventure: With the 4th Battery, C.F.A., B.E.F.* n.p., 1920.

———. *With the First Canadian Contingent.* Toronto: Hodder and Stoughton, 1915.

———. "The Canadian Scottish at the Second Battle of Ypres, April 1915." *Canadian Defence Quarterly* 2 (1924–25), pp. 137–43.

Beattie, Kim. *48th Highlanders of Canada: 1891–1928* [15th Battalion]. Halifax: 48th Highlanders of Canada, 1932.

Bercuson, David. *The Patricias: The Proud History of a Fighting Regiment.* Toronto: Stoddart, 2001.

Dancocks, Daniel G. *Gallant Canadians: The Story of the Tenth Canadian Infantry Battalion, 1914–1919.* Calgary: Calgary Regimental Funds Foundation, 1990.

Fetherstonhaugh, R. C. *The 13th Battalion, Royal Highlanders of Canada: 1914–1919.* Montreal: 13th Battalion, Royal Highlanders of Canada, 1925.

———. *The Royal Montreal Regiment, 14th Battalion, C.E.F: 1914–1925.* Montreal: Royal Montreal Regiment, 1927.

Goodspeed, Maj. D. J. *Battle Royale: A History of the Royal Regiment of Canada, 1862–1962* [3rd Battalion]. Montreal: Royal Regiment of Canada Association, 1962.

Holland, J. A. *The Story of the Tenth Canadian Battalion: 1914–1917.* London: Canadian War Records Office, 1918.

Jackson, Lt-Col. H. M., MBE. *The Royal Regiment of Artillery, Ottawa, 1855–1952.* Ottawa: n.p., 1952.

L'Abbé, Michael-Holland. "Over There." Unpublished manuscript, Department of National Defense, History Secretariat (Ottawa, Ontario). RG 150, box no. 5271-42.

Murray, Col. W. W., OBE. *The History of the 2nd Canadian Battalion in the Great War, 1914–1919.* Ottawa: 2nd Canadian Battalion, 1947.

Newman, Stephen K. *With the Patricias: Holding the Line, Frezenberg, 8–13 May 1915.* Saanich, BC: Bellewaerd House Publishing, 2005.

Nicholson, Col. G. W. L. *The Gunners of Canada: The History of the Royal Regiment of the Canadian Artillery.* Toronto: McClelland and Stewart, 1967.

Scudamore, Maj. Thomas V., VD. *A Short History of the 7th Battalion, C.E.F.* Vancouver: Anderson and Odlum, 1930.

Urquhart, Hugh M., DSO. *The History of the 16th Battalion (The Canadian Scottish) Canadian Expeditionary Force in the Great War, 1914–1919.* Toronto: Macmillan of Canada, 1932.

### German

Anon. *Weidersehens-Feier ehem 237er Koblenz.* n.p., 1938, pp. 21f.

Bergeder, Dr. Fritz. *Das Reserve-Infanterie-Regiment Nr. 202 auf den Schlachtfeldern des Weltkrieges 1914–1918.* Berlin: Traditions-Verlag Kolk, 1939, pp. 63–66.

Brendler, Wilhelm. *Kriserlebnisse 1914 bis 1918 im Reserve-Infanterie-Regiment 233* Zeulenroda: Bernhard Sporn, 1930, pp. 49–74.

Führer, Wilhelm. *Geschichte des Reserve Infanterie Regiments 203, Westen 1914/15.* n.p., 1960.

Hayner. *Geschichte des Reserve-Infanterie-Regiments Nr. 201*. Berlin: Verlag, Bernard und Graefe, 1940, pp. 101–108.

Henning, Otto. *Das Reserve-Infanterie-Regiment Nr. 235 im Weltkriege*. Oldenburg: Gerhard Stalling, 1931, pp. 43–54.

Herbrechtsmier, Georg. *Geschichte des Reserve-Infanterie-Regiments 238*. Neustadt, n.d, pp. 53–63.

Herenrath, Dr. August. *Das Württembergische Reserve-Inf.-Regiment Nr. 247 im Weltkrieg 1914–1918*. Stuttgart: Chr. Belser, 1923, pp. 34–53.

Knieling, Lutz, and Arnold Boelsche. *R.I.R. 234*. Zeulenroda: Bernhard Sporn, 1931, pp. 119–151.

Mayer, Arthur. *Das Reserve-Infanterie-Regiment Nr. 236 im Weltkriege*. Zeulenroda: Bernhard Sporn, 1938, pp. 153–177.

Oregeldinger, Louis. *Das Württembergische Reserve-Infanterie-Regiment Nr. 246*. Stuttgart: Chr. Belser, 1931, pp. 69–93.

Reinhardt, D. Ernst. *Das Württembergische Reserve-Inf.-Regiment Nr. 248 im Weltkrieg 1914–1918*. Stuttgart: Chr. Belser, 1924, pp. 15–41.

Schatz, Josef. *Geschichte des Badischen (Rheinischen) Reserve-Infanterie-Regiments 239*. Stuttgart: Chr. Belser, 1927, pp. 35–49.

Schwedt, Maj. R. *Das Reserve-Infanterie-Regiment Nr. 204*. Zeulenroda: Bernhard Sporn, 1932, pp. 43–57.

Weber, Emil. *Das Landwehr-Infanterie-Regiment Nr. 77*. Oldenburg: Gerhard Stalling, 1922, pp. 30–59.

## *Histories of 2nd Ypres*

Aitken, Sir Max, MP. *Canada in Flanders: The Official Story of the Canadian Expeditionary Force*. Toronto: Hodder and Stoughton, 1916.

Canadian Broadcasting Corporation. "In Flanders Fields: Program 5, Ypres." Written and produced by J. Frank Willis. Edited by Frank Lalor. Toronto, 1964.

Cassar, George H. *Beyond Courage: The Canadians at the Second Battle of Ypres*. Ottawa: Oberon Press, 1985.

Christie, Norm M. *The Canadians in the Second Battle of Ypres: April 22 to 26, 1915*. Ottawa: Bunker to Bunker Books, 1996.

———. *Gas Attack!: The Canadians at Ypres, 1915*. Ottawa: CEF Books, 1998.

Dancocks, Daniels. *Welcome to Flanders Fields: The First Canadian Battle of the Great War: Ypres, 1915*. Toronto: McClelland and Stewart, 1988.

Dixon, John. *Magnificent But Not War: The Second Battle of Ypres*. Yorkshire: Pen and Sword Books, 2005.

Ferry, Gén. Edmond. "Ce qui s'est passé sur l'Yser." *La Revue Des Vivants* (July 1930), pp. 898–903.

French, Sir John. "An Account of the German Use of Gas at the Second Battle of Ypres on 22 April 1915." Available online at www.firstworldwar.com/source/2ndypres_sirjohnfrench.htm.

Gordon-Hall, Lt.-Col. Gordon C. W. "Letter to Duguid on GHQ Line, 1935." Library and Archives Canada. RG 24, vol. 1503, file HQ 683-1-30-5.

Iarocci, Andrew. "1st Canadian Infantry Brigade in the Second Battle of Ypres: The Case of the 1st and 4th Battalions, 23 April 1915." *Canadian Military History* 12, no. 4 (Autumn 2003), pp. 5–16.

Joseph, Lt. Clément. *Carnets de guerre d'un officier d'Infanterie Territoriale et la première attaque aux gaz du 22 avril 1915*. Association Bretagne 14–18. I would like to thank Tim Cook of the Canadian War Museum for making a copy of this book available to me.

Keech, Graham. *St Julien: Ypres*. Yorkshire: Pen and Sword Books, 2001.

McWilliams, James, and R. James Steele. *Gas! The Battle for Ypres, 1915*. St. Catharines, ON: Vanwell, 1985.

*Times History of the War*. Vol 5. London: The Times, 1915.

Tucker, A. B. *The Battle Glory of Canada: Being the Story of the Canadians at the Front, Including the Battle of Ypres*. Toronto: Cassell and Company, 1915.

## Memoirs of and Letters from 2nd Ypres

Adamson, Lt.-Col. Agar. *Letters of Agar Adamson: 1914–1919 . . . Princess Patricia's Canadian Light Infantry*. Ottawa: CEF Books, 1997.

Alexander, Colin. Taped file, Directorate of History, Department of National Defence.

Anderson, Maj. Peter. *I That's Me: Escape from German Prison Camp and Other Adventures*. Edmonton: Bradburn, 1929.

Bagnall, Fred. *Not Mentioned in Dispatches: The Memoir of Fred Bagnall, 14th Battalion, C.E.F 1914–1917*. Ottawa: CEF Books, 2005.

Bairnsfather, Bruce. *Bullets & Billets: Fragments from France*. London: Great Richards, 1916.

Baldwin, Sgt. Harold. *Holding the Line*. Chicago: A. C. McClurg, 1918.

Bennett, Lt. John Hyde. "Letter: 27 April 1915." Canadian War Museum, Ottawa. Accession no. 00032.

Binding, Rudolf. *A Fatalist at War*. Translated by Ian F. D. Morrow. London: George Allan and Unwin, 1929.

Boyd, William. *With a Field Ambulance at Ypres: Being Letters Written March 7–August 15, 1915*. Toronto: The Musson Book Company, 1916.

Campbell, William Lockhard. "April 21, 1915, Letter to Mother." Available online at web.mala.bc.ca/davies/letters.images.W.L.Campbell/collection.htm.

Canadian Bank of Commerce. "Letters from the Front No. 1." Toronto, August 1915.

Currie, Col. J. A. *The Red Watch: With the First Canadian Division in Flanders*. Toronto: McClelland, Goodchild and Stewart, 1916.

Dendooven, Dominiek. "Overview: 22 April 1915—Eyewitness Accounts of the First Gas Attack." Paper presented at the "1915 Innocence Slaughtered" conference in Ypres, Belgium (17–19 Nov. 2005). I thank Dominiek Dendooven, the director of the In Flanders Fields Museum, for making a copy of his paper available to me.

Frost, L Corp. G. W. Letter to his mother, accessible at www.cefresearch.com/phpBB2/viewtopic.php?t=209.

Gibbons, Arthur. *A Guest of the Kaiser: The Plain Story of a Lucky Soldier.* Toronto: J. M. Dent and Sons, 1919.

Gorman, Sgt.-Maj. G. W. "With the 'Little Black Devils'" [8th Battalion]. *Thunder Bay Historical Society* (1918), pp. 19–27.

Kennedy, Joyce M. *Distant Thunder: Canada's Citizen Soldiers on the Western Front.* Manhattan, KS: Sunflower University Press, 2000.

Kingsley, Percy. "Letter, 26 June 1915." In Stephen Carthy, "A Letter from Ypres," in *The Beaver* (Dec. 2005/Jan. 2006), pp. 34–39.

Maguire, Francis. "Letters: 2 May 1915, 8 June 1915, 29 June 1915, 7 July 1915." I thank Frank Corbett for providing me with copies of these letters.

Mathieson, William D. *My Grandfather's War: Canadians Remember the First World War, 1914–1918.* Toronto: Macmillan of Canada, 1981.

Mordacq, Gén. Jacques. *Le Drame de l'Yser: La Surprise des gaz (Avril 1915).* Paris: Editions des Portquies, 1933.

Morrison, J. Clinton, Jr. *Hell upon Earth: A Personal Account of Prince Edward Island Soldiers in the Great War, 1914–1918.* Summerside, PEI: J. Clinton Morrison, n.d.

Odlum, Victor. "From O. C. 7th Battalion," Library and Archives Canada. MG30. Vol. 24, File Ypres 1923.

Peat, Harold R. *Private Peat: Ex-Third Battalion First Canadian Contingent.* Toronto: George J. McLeod, 1917.

Racey, Baron Richardson. Diary available online at www.hellfire-corner.demon.co.uk/racey.htm.

Rae, Herbert (G. Herbert Gibson). *Maple Leaves in Flanders Fields.* Toronto: William Briggs, 1916.

Reid, Gordon. *Poor Bloody Murder: Personal Memoirs of the First World War.* Oakville, ON: Mosaic Press, 1980.

Scott, Canon Frederick, DSO. *The Great War As I Saw It.* Ottawa: CEF Books, 2000.

Strange, Lt.-Col. L. A., DSO. "The Second Battle of Ypres," in *Fifty Amazing Stories of the Great War.* London: Odhams Press, 1936.

Swanston, Pte. Victor, 5th Battalion. *Who Said War Is Hell!* An unpublished diary in the possession of the Canadian War Museum, Ottawa.

Thomas, Mary. *David's War: The 'Boys of Ganonoque' in WWI.* Belleville, ON: Epic Press, 2003.

Travers, Tim. "Allies in Conflict: The British and Canadian Official Historians and the Real Story of Second Ypres (1915)." *Journal of Contemporary History* 24 (1989), 301–25.

———. "Currie and the 1st Canadian Division at Second Ypres, April 1915: Controversy, Criticism and Official History." *Canadian Military History* 5, no. 2 (Autumn 1996), pp. 7–15.

Wackett, Corp. E. "Experiences with the First Western Ontario Regiment [1st Battalion]." *Fifth Annual Report of the Waterloo Historical Society* (1917), pp. 43–47.

Walker, Pte. Frank. *From a Stretcher Handle: The World War I Journal and Poems of Pte. Frank Walker.* Edited by Mary F. Gaudet. Charlottetown, PEI: Institute of Island Studies, 2000.

## Autobiographies and Biographies

Borden, Henry, ed. *Robert Laird Borden: His Memoirs*, vol. 1. Toronto: Macmillan of Canada, 1938.
Bovey, Lt.-Col. Wilfred, OBE. "Sir Arthur Currie: The Corps Commander." *The Legionary* (1934), pp. 5–8.
Cassar, George H. *The Tragedy of Sir John French*. Newark, DE: Delaware University Press, 1985.
———. *Memoirs of an Unconventional Soldier* [Major-General J. F. C. Fuller]. London: Ivor Nicholson and Watson, 1936.
Cook, Tim. "The Madman and the Butcher: Sir Sam Hughes, Sir Arthur Currie, and Their War of Reputations." *The Canadian Historical Review* 85, no. 4 (Dec. 2004), pp. 693–719.
Cornwell, John. *Hitler's Scientists: Science, War and the Devil's Pact*. New York: Viking, 2003.
Dancocks, Daniel G. *Sir Arthur Currie: A Biography*. Toronto: Methuen, 1985.
Edmonds, J. E. "Letter to Duguid on Currie: 12 November 1936." Library and Archives Canada. RG 24, vol. 1503, file HQ-683-1-30-5.
Godfrey, Andrew B. "Portrait of a Battalion Commander: Lieutenant-Colonel George Stuart Tuxford at the Second Battle of Ypres, April 1915." *Canadian Military Journal* (Summer 2004), pp. 55–61.
Goran, Morris. *The Story of Fritz Haber*. Norman, OK: University of Oklahoma Press, 1967.
Haber, Fritz. "Chemistry in War." *Journal of Chemical Education* (Nov. 1945), pp. 526–29 and 553.
Hahn, Otto. *My Life: The Autobiography of a Scientist*. Translated by Ernst Kaiser and E. Wilkins. New York: Herder and Herder, 1970.
Haycock, Ronald G. *Sam Hughes: The Public Career of a Controversial Canadian, 1885–1916*. Waterloo, ON: Laurier University Press, 1986.
Hyatt, A. M. J. *General Sir Arthur Currie: A Military Biography*. Toronto and Ottawa: University of Toronto Press and Canadian War Museum, 1987.
Lynn, Maj. E. F. "Statement on General Currie." Library and Archives Canada. RG 24, vol. 1756, parts 2, 4–5.
———. "Response to Letter from Urquhart." Library and Archives Canada. RG 24, vol. 1756, parts 2, 4–5.
———. "Response to Duguid's Comments and Questions." Library and Archives Canada. RG 24, vol. 1756, parts 2, 4–5.
Powell, Geoffrey. *Plumer: The Soldier's General*. Yorkshire: Pen and Sword Books, 2004.
Sharpe, Robert J. *The Last Day, The Last Hour: The Currie Libel Trial*. Toronto: Osgoode [Law] Society, 1988.
Smithers, A. J. *The Man Who Disobeyed: Sir Horace Smith-Dorrien and His Enemies*. London: Leo Cooper, 1970.
Swettenham, John. *McNaughton*. Vol. 1: *1887–1939*. Toronto: Ryerson Press, 1968.
Trumpener, Ulrich. "The Road to Ypres: The Beginnings of Gas Warfare in World War I." *Journal of Modern History* 47 (Sept. 1975), pp. 460–80.

Trythall, John Anthony. *"Boney" Fuller: The Intellectual General, 1878–1966.* London: Cassell, 1977.
Urquhart, Hugh M. *Arthur Currie: The Biography of a Great Canadian.* London: J. M. Dent and Sons, 1950.
Winter, Brig.-Gen. Charles. *Lieutenant-General The Hon. Sir Sam Hughes, K.C.B., M.P. Canada's War Minister.* Toronto: Macmillan of Canada, 1931.

## Interviews Conducted by the Canadian Broadcasting Corporation

These interviews were conducted for the 1964 CBC Radio series "In Flanders Fields," written and produced by J. Frank Willis and edited by Frank Lalor. The transcripts can be found at Library and Archives Canada in Ottawa. Record group 41, vol. 7 contains the transcripts for soldiers in the 1st, 2nd, 3rd, and 4th Battalions; RG 41, vol. 8 contains the transcripts for soldiers in the 5th, 6th, 7th, and 10th Battalions; and RG 41, vol. 9 contains the transcripts for soldiers in the 13th, 15th, and 16th Battalions.

Bagshaw, Frederick O.
Beddoe, Alan B.
Booker, Jack
Bowyer, J. H.
Boyd, George T.
Christopherson, Robert L.
Cosgrave, L. V. Moore
Cox, Sid
Creelman, John
Eyles, George
Fisher, A. H.
Graham, W. F.
Hunt, R. C.
Jeffrey, J.
Lewis, Victor (Vick)
Lunn, Bernard C.
MacArthur, J. H.
Mackie, J. C.
Mactier, William S. M.
Mason, D. H. C.
Matheson, John C.
McGowan, M. C.
MacIlree, J. Raymond
Morrissey, T. S.
Morrison, E. W. B.
Nicholson, N.
Oldaker, H. H.
Owens, E. B.
Patrick, George
Radford, Sidney H.
Rice, Nathan
Scott, L. C.
Scriven, C.
Seaman, Eric
Sinclair, Ian
Sprostin, J.
Stephens, Lester
Wallis, H.M.
Young, N. H.

## Other Articles and Books

Anon. *18-Pr. Q.F. Gun. Gun Drill.* London: His Majesty's Stationery Office, 1914.
Anon. *Field Artillery Training (Provisional), 1912.* His Majesty's Stationery Office, 1912.
Anon. *Handbook for the 18 pdr. Q.F. Gun.* London: His Majesty's Stationery Office, 1909.
Audoin-Rouzeau, Stéphane, and Annette Becker. *14–18: Understanding the Great War.* New York: Hill and Wang, 2000.
Barnes, Leslie, WCS. *Canada's Guns: An Illustrated History of Artillery.* Ottawa: Canadian War Museum, 1979.
Bartholomew, Robert E. "Phantom German Air Raids in Canada: War Hysteria in Quebec and Ontario during the First World War." *Canadian Military History* 7, no. 4 (Autumn 1998), pp. 29–36.
Battye, Maj. B. C. *The Minor Tactics of Trench Warfare: With Special Reference to the Co-operation of Infantry and Engineers.* Ottawa: Goverment Printing Bureau, 1915.
Beckett, Ian F. W. *Ypres: The First Battle 1914.* Harlow, UK: Pearson Education, 2004.
Berton, Pierre. *Vimy.* Toronto: Anchor, 1986.
Bloem, Walter. *The Advance from Mons 1914: The Experiences of a German Infantry Officer.* Translated by G. C. Wynne. Solihull, UK: Helion and Company, 2004.
Blond, Georges. *The Marne.* London: Prion Books, 2002.
Bond, Brian. *The Unquiet Western Front: Britain's Role in Literature and History.* Cambridge, UK: Cambridge University Press, 2002.
Bourke, Joanna. *An Intimate History of Killing: Face-to-Face Killing in Twentieth-Century Warfare.* London: Granta Publishing, 1999.
Brown, Angus, and Richard Gimblett. *In the Footsteps of the Canadian Corps: Canada's First World War, 1914–1918.* Ottawa: Magic Light Publishing, 2006.
Brown, Malcolm. *Tommy Goes to War.* London: Tempus Books, 2005.
Busch, Briton C., ed. *Canada and the Great War: Western Front Association Papers.* Montreal: McGill-Queen's Univeristy Press, 2003.
Carnegie, David, CBE. *The History of Munitions Supply in Canada: 1914–1918.* Toronto: Longmans, Green, 1925.
Chapman, John Jay, ed. *Deutschland Über Alles or Germany Speaks.* New York: Putnam, 1914.
Clark, Alan. *The Donkeys.* London: Pimlico, 1991.
Clark, Dale. *British Artillery, 1914–19: Field Army Artillery.* Oxford, UK: Osprey, 2004.
Clark, David. *The Angel of Mons: Phantom Soldiers and Ghostly Guardians.* London: John Wiley and Sons, 2004.
Clayton, Anthony. *Paths of Glory: The French Army, 1914–1918.* London: Cassell, 2003.
Cook, Tim. *No Place to Run: The Canadian Corps and Gas Warfare in the First World War.* Vancouver: University of British Columbia Press, 2000.
———. *Clio's Warriors: Canadian Historians and the Writing of the World Wars.* Vancouver: University of British Columbia Press, 2006.
———. "The Politics of Surrender: Canadian Soldiers and the Killing of Prisoners in the Great War." *The Journal of Military History* 70, no. 3 (July 2006), pp. 637–65.
Coppard, George. *With a Machine Gun to Cambrai.* London: Cassell, 1999.
Corrigan, Gordon. *Mud, Blood and Poppycock.* London: Cassell, 2003.

Craig, John. *Years of Agony, 1910–1920: Canada's Illustrated Heritage.* Toronto: McClelland and Stewart, 1977.

Dendooven, Dominiek. *Menin Gate and Last Post: Ypres as Holy Ground.* Translated by Ian Connerly. Koksijde, Belgium: De Klaproos Editions, 2001.

Duffy, Christopher. *Through German Eyes: The British and the Somme 1916.* London: Weidenfeld and Nicolson, 2006.

Dupury, Col. T. N. *A Genius for War: The German Army and General Staff, 1807–1945.* Fairfax, VA: Hero Books, 1984.

Eksteins, Modris: *Rites of Spring: The Great War and the Birth of the Modern Age.* Toronto: Lester and Orpen Dennys, 1989.

Ellis, John. *Eye-Deep in Hell: Trench Warfare in World War I.* Baltimore: Johns Hopkins University Press, 1976.

Emden, Richard van. *The Trench: Experienceing Life on the Front Line, 1916.* London: Corgi Books, 2003.

Ferguson, Niall. *The Pity of War: Explaining World War I.* London: Basic Books, 1999.

Foden, Giles. *Mimi and Toutou Go Forth: The Bizarre Battle of Lake Tanganyika.* New York: Penguin, 2004.

Foley, Robert T., ed. and trans. *Alfred von Schlieffen's Military Writings.* London: Frank Cass Publishers, 2003.

Frantzen, Allen J. *Bloody Good: Chivalrey, Sacrifice, and the Great War.* Chicago: University of Chicago Press, 2004.

Fromkin, David. *Europe's Last Summer: Who Started the Great War in 1914?* New York: Alfred A. Knopf, 2004.

Frost, Leslie M. *Fighting Men.* Toronto: Clarke, Irwin, 1967.

Fussell, Paul. *The Great War and Modern Memory.* Oxford: Oxford University Press, 1975.

Gibson, Sally. *More Than an Island: A History of Toronto Island.* Toronto: Irwin Publishers, 1984.

Gilbert, Martin. *The First World War: A Complete History.* New York: Henry Holt, 1994.

Goodspeed, D. J. *The Road Past Vimy: The Canadian Corps, 1914–1918.* Toronto: Macmillan of Canada, 1969.

———. *The German Wars: 1914–1945.* Toronto: Macmillan of Canada, 1977.

Granatstein, Jack L. *Canada's Army: Waging War and Keeping the Peace.* Toronto: University of Toronto Press, 2002.

———. *Hell's Corner: An Illustrated History of Canada's Great War: 1914–1918.* Toronto: Douglas and McIntyre, 2004.

Granatstein, Jack L., and Desmond Morton. *Canada and the Two World Wars.* Toronto: Key Porter Books, 2003.

Graves, Robert. *Goodbye to All That.* New York: Penguin, 1960.

Green, Andrew. *Writing the Great War: Sir James Edmonds and the Official Histories, 1915–1948.* London: Frank Cass Publishers, 2003.

Griffth, Paddy. *British Fighting Methods in the Great War.* London: Frank Cass Publishers, 1994.

Groom, Winston. *A Storm in Flanders: The Ypres Salient, 1914–1918, Tragedy and Triumph on the Western Front.* New York: Grove Press, 2002.

Gustavson, Wes. "'Fairly Well Known and Need Not Be Discussed': Colonel A. F. Duguid and the Canadian Official History of the First World War." *Canadian Military History* 10, no. 2 (Spring 2001), pp. 41–54.

Gwyn, Sandra. *Tapestry of War: A Private View of Canadians in the Great War*. Toronto: HarperCollins, 1992.

Hanson, Neil: *Unknown Soldiers: The Story of the Missing of the First World War*. New York: Alfred A. Knopf, 2006.

Harris, Stephen J. *Canadian Brass: The Making of a Professional Army, 1860–1939*. Toronto: University of Toronto Press, 1988.

Hart, Peter. *The Somme*. Weidenfeld and Nicolson, 2005.

Hastings, Max. *Armageddon: The Battle for Germany, 1944–45*. London: Pan Books, 2004.

Herwig, Holger H. *The First World War: Germany and Austria-Hungary, 1914–1918*. London: Arnold, 1997.

Holmes, Nancy. "'In Flanders Fields'—Canada's Official Poem: Breaking Faith." *Studies in Canadian Literature/Etudes en litérature Canadienne* 30, no. 1 (2005), pp. 11–31.

Holmes, Richard. *Acts of War: The Behavior of Men in Battle*. New York: The Free Press, 1985.

———. *Tommy: The British Soldier on the Western Front, 1914–1918*. London: HarperCollins, 2004.

Hopkins, J. Castell. *Canada at War: A Record of Heroism and Achievement, 1914–1918*. Toronto: Canadian Annual Review, 1919.

Horn, Brend, ed. *Forging a Nation: Perspectives on the Canadian Military Experience*. St. Catharines, ON: Vanwell, 2002.

Hossack, Anthony R. "The First Gas Attack," in *Fifty Amazing Stories of the Great War*. London: Odhams Press, 1936. Also available online at www.greatwardifferent.com/Great_War/First_Gas_Attack/First_Gas_Attack_01.htm.

Hughes, John McKendrick. *The Unwanted: Great War Letters from the Field*. Edited by John R. Hughes. Edmonton: University of Alberta Press, 2005.

Hynes, Samuel. *The Soldiers' Tale: Bearing Witness to Modern War*. New York: Penguin, 1997.

Ironside, Lt. H. A. *The Machine-Gun: Its Drill, Signals and Control*. London: Hugh Rees, 1914.

Jones, Nigel. *The War Walk: A Journey along the Western Front*. London: Cassell, 2004.

Jünger, Ernst. *Storm of Steel*. New York, Penguin, 2003.

Keegan, John. *The Face of Battle*. New York: Viking, 1976.

———. *The First World War*. Toronto: Vintage, 2000.

Keshen, Jeffrey A. *Propaganda and Censorship During Canada's Great War*. Edmonton: University of Alberta Press, 1996.

Liddle-Hart, Basil. *Reputations Ten Years After*. Boston: Little, Brown, 1928.

Litalien, Michel, and Stéphane Thibault. *Les Tranchées: Le Quotidien de la guerre 1914–1918*. Montreal: Athéna éditions, 2004.

Lloyd, Nick. *Loos, 1915*. London: Tempus, 2006.

Mackenzie, David, ed. *Canada and the First World War: Essays in Honour of Robert Craig Brown*. Toronto: University of Toronto Press, 2005.

McCartney, Helen B. *Citizen Soldiers: The Liverpool Territorials in the First World War.* Cambridge, UK: Cambridge University Press, 2005.

Micheline Guides. *The Yser and the Belgian Coast.* Reprint, York: Smith and Sons, 1994.

Middlebrook, Martin. *The First Day on the Somme.* London: Penguin, 1971.

Mombauer, Annika. *The Origins of the First World War: Controversies and Consensus.* London: Longman, 2002.

Moorehead, Alan. *Gallipoli.* New York: Harper Brothers, 1956.

Moran, Lord. *The Anatomy of Courage.* New York: Carroll and Graff, 2007. First published in 1945.

Morgan, Janet. *The Secrets of Rue St. Roch: Hope and Heroism behind Enemy Lines in the First World War.* New York: Penguin, 2005

Morton, Desmond. *A Peculiar Kind of Politics: Canada's Overseas Ministry in the First World War.* Toronto: University of Toronto Press, 1982.

———. *Silent Battle: Canadian Prisoners of War in Germany, 1914–1919.* Toronto: Lester Publishing, 1992.

———. *When Your Number's Up: The Canadian Soldier in the First World War.* Toronto: Random House, 1993.

———. *A Military History of Canada: From Champlain to Kosovo* (4th Edition). Toronto: McClelland and Stewart, 1999.

———. *Fight or Pay: Soldiers' Families in the Great War.* Vancouver: University of British Columbia Press, 2004.

Mosier, John. *The Myth of the Great War: How the Germans Won the Battles and How the Americans Saved the Allies.* New York: HarperCollins, 2001.

Moss, Mark. *Manliness and Militarism: Educating Young Boys in Ontario for War.* Toronto: Oxford University Press, 2001.

Nasmith, Col. George, CMG. *Canada's Sons and Great Britain in the World War.* Toronto: Thomas Allan, 1919.

Neillands, Robin. *The Old Contemptibles: The British Expeditionary Force, 1914.* London: John Murray, 2004.

O'Connor, Mike. *Airfields & Airmen: Ypres.* Yorkshire: Pen and Sword Books, 2004.

Ousby, Ian. *The Road to Verdun: World War I's Most Momentous Battle and the Folly of Nationalism.* New York: Anchor, 2003.

Passingham, Ian. *All the Kaiser's Men: The Life and Death of the German Army on the Western Front, 1914–1918.* Gloucestershire, UK: Sutton Publishing, 2006.

Pawley, Ronald. *The Kaiser's Warlords: German Commanders of World War I.* Oxford, UK: Osprey Publishing, 2003.

Payne, David. "The Cult of the Bayonet in the British Army on the Western Front in the Great War." *Western Front Association.* Available online at www.westernfrontassociation.com/thegreatwar/articles/reserach/britishbayonet.htm.

Persico, Joseph E. *11th Month, 11th Day, 11th Hour: Armistice Day, 1918: World War I and Its Violent Climax.* New York: Random House, 2004.

Petrou, Michael. "Historian Claims Proof of 'Crucified Canadian': New Evidence Shows Germans Impaled Soldier during the First World War." *Ottawa Citizen,* Dec. 15, 2002.

Platteuw, Jacky. *Images of Flanders: The Great War in Ypres.* London: Tempus Publishing, 2005.
Prescott, John F. *In Flanders Fields: The Story of John McCrae.* Erin, ON: Boston Mills Press, 1985.
Preston, Diana. *Wilful Murder: The Sinking of the Lusitania.* London: Corgi Books, 2003.
Prete, Roy. "Les Relations franco-britanniques et l'attaque au gaz allemande à Ypres, avril 1915," in Roch Legault and Jean Lamarre, eds., *La Première guerre mondiale et le Canada: Contributions sociomiliaires québécoises.* Montreal: Méridien, 1999.
Prior, Robin, and Trevor Wilson. *The Somme.* New Haven, CN.: Yale University Press, 2005.
Radley, Kenneth. *We Lead, Others Follow: First Canadian Division, 1914–1918.* St. Catharines, ON: Vanwell, 2006.
Rawling, Bill. *Surviving Trench Warfare: Technology and the Canadian Corps, 1914–1918.* Toronto: University of Toronto Press, 1992.
Read, Daphne, ed. *The Great War and Canadian Society: An Oral History.* Toronto: New Hogtown Press, 1978.
Reed, Paul. *Walking the Salient.* Yorkshire: Pen and Sword Books, 2004.
*Regimental Songs: Canadian Expeditionary Force, 1914–1915.* Donated by William Southam, Esquire. Hamilton, Ontario.
Reville, F. Douglas. *History of the County of Brant*, vol. 2. Brantford, ON: Hurley Printing Company, 1920.
Schreiber, Shane B. *Shock Army of the British Empire: The Canadian Corps in the Last 100 Days of the Great War.* Westport, CN: Praeger, 1997.
Scudamore, Thomas, V. *Lighter Episodes in the Life of a Prisoner of War.* Aldershot, UK: Gale and Polden, n.d.
Sheldon, Jack. *The German Army on the Somme, 1914–1916.* Yorkshire: Pen and Sword Books, 2005.
Smy, Lt.-Col. William, OMM. "For Valour: Lance-Corporal Fred Fisher, VC." *Journal of the Victoria Cross Society* (Oct. 2003). I thank the author for making a copy of this article available to me.
Stallworthy, Jon. *Anthem for Doomed Youth: Twelve Soldier-Poets of the First World War.* London: Constable, 2005.
Stevenson, David. *Cataclysm: The First World War as Political Tragedy.* New York: Basic Books, 2004.
Strachan, Hew. *The First World War.* Vol. 1: *To Arms.* Oxford: Oxford University Press, 2001.
——. *The First World War.* New York: Viking, 2003.
Terraine, John. *The Western Front, 1914–1918.* Yorkshire: Pen and Sword Books, 2003.
Thomas, Nigel. *The German Army in World War I (1) 1914–15.* Oxford, UK: Osprey, 2003.
Thompson, David. "2nd Battle of Ypres, 1915: 1/8th Battalion, Durham Light Infantry." Master's thesis, University of Newcastle, 2002. I thank the author for making this unpublished article available to me.
Travers, Tim. *The Killing Ground: The British Army, The Western Front & the Emergence of Modern War, 1900–1918.* Yorkshire: Pen and Sword Books, 1987.

———. *Gallipoli: 1915*. London: Tempus, 2001.
Tuchman, Barbara W. *The Zimmermann Telegram*. New York: Ballantine Books, 1958.
———. *The Guns of August*. New York: Random House, 1962.
———. *The Proud Tower: A Portrait of the World before the War: 1890–1914*. New York: Random House, 1962.
Vance, Jonathan F. *Objects of Concern: Canadian Prisoners of War through the Twentieth Century*. Vancouver: University of British Columbia Press, 1994.
———. *Death So Noble: Memory, Meaning and the First World War*. Vancouver: University of British Columbia Press, 1997.
Warner, Philip. *World War One: A Narrative*. London: Cassell Military Classics, 1998.
Weintraub, Steven. *Silent Night: The Story of the World War I Christmas Truce*. New York: The Free Press, 2001.
Wilson, Barbara. *Ontario and the First World War, 1914–1918: A Collection of Documents*. Toronto: University of Toronto Press.
Winter, Denis. *Death's Men: Soldiers of the Great War*. London: Penguin, 1978.
Winter, Jay, and Antoine Prost. *The Great War in History: Debates and Controversies, 1914 to the Present*. Cambridge, UK: Cambridge University Press, 2005.
Worthington, Larry. *Amid the Guns Below: The Story of the Canadian Corps (1914–1919)*. Toronto: McClelland and Stewart, 1965.
Zuber, Terence. *Inventing the Schlieffen Plan: German War Planning, 1871–1914*. Oxford, UK: Oxford University Press, 2002.

## Fiction

Boyden, Joseph. *Three Day Road*. Toronto: Penguin, 2005.
Child, Philip. *God's Sparrows*. Toronto: McClelland and Stewart, 1978. First published in 1937.
Japrisot, Sébastien. *A Very Long Engagement*. New York: Picador, 1991.
Remarque, Erich Maria. *All Quiet on the Western Front*. New York: Ballantine Books, 1982.

# Index

Ablard, Sgt. Harry C., 121
Adam, Leutnant, 82
Aitken, Sir Max (Lord Beaverbook), 19–20, 345, 346, 352–53
Albert, King (Belgium), 84
Albrecht of Württemberg, Generaloberst Duke (Fourth Army), 34, 36
alcohol consumption, 16
Alderson, Lt.-General Edwin, 38, 59, 70, 80, 82, 85, 126, 154, 207–11, 307
   Arthur Currie and, 196, 207, 209–10, 269, 304, 312, 324
   Birchall and, 125, 155
   Bush and, 207–8, 254, 255
   Garnet Hughes and, 80–81, 196, 229–30
   gas attack (22 April) and, 52–54, 126, 209
   Geddes and, 160–61
   Gordon-Hall and, 255, 285
   Gravenstafel Ridge and, 54
   Hare and, 136n
   headquarters, 126, 155
   Hill and, 125
   J. E. Hull and, 301, 307
   John French and, 280
   Mauser Ridge and, 125
   Mercer and, 125, 136, 154, 163
   messages, 130, 275–76, 307–8, 312, 313
   mistakes, 163, 168, 209
   Mouse Trap Farm and, 285
   orders, 76, 125, 126, 160–61, 338
      to move only at night, 30
   Plumer and, 85, 125, 126, 313
   Plumer's order to, 284–85
   praise for the troops of, 19
   praises Canadian troops, 347–48
   Romer and, 136
   sent Divisional Cyclist Co. to occupy Fortuin, 285
   Smith-Dorrien and, 340
   Snow and, 227, 231, 269, 303, 309, 313
   St. Julien and, 196
   at Vlamertinghe, 126
Alexander, Capt. George, 200
Alexander, Colin, 212–13
Algerian Division, 19
Algerian soldiers, 88, 111
Algerian troops, 57, 61, 67, 162
Alldritt, Sgt. W. A., 313
Alstadt, Leutnant, 247
ambulances. *See* medical evacuation
Anderson, Maj. Peter, 110–11, 288
Apex, 170
   collapse of, 268, 269
   destruction of 13th and 15th Battalions at, 182–98
Armstrong, John, 127, 128
   moves guns at night, 127

Arthur, Prince. *See* Governor General of Canada
Artillery Battery, 26th, 299–300
Artillery Brigade, 2nd, 209
Ashbourne, Bertram, 185
Ashbourne, Pte. Frank V., 185
Australian Division, 2nd, 20

Bagshaw, Sgt. Frederick B., 1, 5, 287–88, 314, 335
Bailleul, 335
Bairnsfather, Bruce, 298, 300, 301, 303
Baldwin, Sgt. Harold, 16, 31, 64, 181
Band, Sgt. Harry, 190n
"baptism of fire," 110, 348
Barnes (soldier), 228
Barrie, Pte. George, 190n
Bath, Todd, 51
Battheu, Jeanne, 74
Bavarian Reserve, 6th, 18
bayonet practice, 11, 14, 103
Beatty, Chaplain, 147
Beaverbook, Lord. *See* Aitken, Sir Max
Becker, Leutnant, 49, 53, 55–56
   description of gas attack 22 April, 55
Beddoe, Pte. Alan B., 2, 116, 152, 276–77
Belgians, 71, 84–85
Belgium, 354. *See also* Flanders
   Germany's ultimatum rejected by, 3
   neutrality, 3, 4
Belgium Army, 39, 214
   one attack, 223–24
   several times defending, 71, 84–85, 173, 214
Bell, Lt.-Col. M.H.L., 256, 281–83
Bell, Pte. George, 132–33
Bellew, Lieut. Donald Edward, 14, 229
   Victoria Cross, 20, 239, 289
Bennett, Maj. George W., 112–14, 116, 149
Bennett, Pte. Wallace "Wally," 335, 336
   at Doxsee's House, 259, 264, 265, 335
Bergeder, Fritz, 179–80
Bertram, Capt. W. R., 202
Beynon, Ivor, 303
Big Bertha, 53
Binding, Rudolph, 170
Bingham, Pte. William, 131
Birchall, Lt.-Col. Arthur P. (4th Btl.)
   on advances in face of machine-gun fire, 120
   Alderson and, 125, 155
   death, 166, 347
   4th Battalion, 125, 130
   John French and, 129
   Mauser Ridge attacks and, 125, 129–31, 135, 137, 145, 152–55, 165
   *Rapid Training of Company for War* (training manual), 15, 131
Bland, Capt. Charles E., 165
   Distinguished Service Order, 165

"Blighty," 148
Bloxham, Pte. Charles, 194
  Distinguished Conduct Medal, 194
Boche, 71, 76, 212
Boesinghe, 109, 110
Boetleer Farm, 117, 183, 193, 244, 287, 311, 313
Boggs, Herbert, 17
Bolster, Maj. Herbert G., 262
Bombarded Crossroads, 256, 316, 333
Bonhommie, Lieut. Jean-Marie, 57, 60
Book of Remembrance (Parliament of Canada), 354–56
boot camp (Valcartier), 9–11
boots, 13, 438n30
Borden, Robert (Canadian Prime Minister), 2, 3, 6, 214n1, 356
  government, 8
Bowie, Sgt. George Pigrum, 321
Bowyer, Pte. Jack H., 192
Boyd, George T., 183
Boyle, Col. Robert, 19
Boyle, Lt.-Col. Russell (10th Btl.), 11n, 70, 99
  battalion, 194
  death, 105, 195
  letter to wife, 33
  10th Battalion, 96, 103–4
  Turner and, 89, 96
  Wallis and, 106
Brandt, Oberleutnant, 143, 144
Brant, Lieut. Cameron, 154
Breton, Willie, 71
Brewer, H. G., 208
bridges, 69, 109, 110. *See also under* Yser Canal
Brinkley, Lieut. Ross, 86
Britain
  British Army's failed attacks on St. Julien, 295–302, 338 (*see also under* St. Julien)
  defensive doctrine, 32
  ultimatum to Germany to withdraw from Belgium, 3
British Division, 27th, 227
British Expeditionary Force (BEF), 30, 159, 272
British reserves, 78, 135, 150, 207, 211, 227, 255, 269, 362
Bromely, Lieut., 228
Brooding Soldier, The, xix–xx
Brotherhood, Capt. Wilfred, 242–43
Bruckner, Leutnant, 146
Buchanan, Maj. Victor, 211, 212
Bulfin, Maj.-Gen. E. S., 333
Bunnermann, Leutnant, 100, 102
burials, 31
Burland, Lt.-Col. W. W., 197n, 234, 245
Burstall, Col.-Gen. "Harry" (Artillery), 12, 53, 70, 286
Bush, Brig.-Gen. John E., 207–8, 231, 254–55, 257
  Alderson and, 207–8, 254, 255
  5th Green Howards and 5th Durham Light Infantry, 297
Bustard Camp, 12–14, 16

Byng-Hall, Maj. Percy, 215, 236–38, 247
Calsow, Hauptmann, 258
camouflage, 13
Canada. *See also specific topics*
  at outbreak of war, 1–8
*Canada in Flanders* (Aitken), 352–53
Canadian Army. *See also specific topics*
  first attack, 98 (*see also* Kitcheners Wood, attack by 10th and 16th Battalions on)
  formation, 11, 14, 98
  training, 9–10, 14, 15, 20
Canadian attitudes toward World War I, 6–7
Canadian Battalions, 11. *See also under* Kitcheners Wood
  1st
    casualties, 168
    Mauser Ridge and, 154–55, 158, 168
  2nd, 145, 258 (*see also under* Currie, Arthur; L'Abbé)
    advance toward St. Julien, 226
    Culling and, 259
    at Doxsee and Hooper's Houses, 204–5
    failed attack on German redoubt, 111–15
    GHQ Line and, 255, 268, 284
    isolation of, 254–63
    supplies, 172
    trenches, 230
    Turner and, 263, 269
    Watson and, 260
  3rd, 12, 145, 234, 258 (*see also under* Kirkpatrick)
    GHQ Line and, 255, 268, 284
    headquarters, 226
    St. Julien and, 226
    trenches, 184, 230
    Turner and, 263, 269
  4th
    casualties, 168
    Mauser Ridge and, 154–55, 158, 168
  5th, 16, 48, 230, 324
    Ross rifles jammed, 186
    trench, 256
  7th, 39, 117. (*see also under* Currie, Arthur, Battalions; Odlum, Battalions)
    collapse of, 227–32
    composite 7th/10th Battalion, 302, 310
    headquarters, 51
    at Locality "C," 117, 230
    RIR 234's attack on, 204
    St. Julien and, 230
    transferred from Currie's Second to Turner's Third Brigade, 196
  8th, 12, 48, 186, 244
    Arthur Currie and, 268, 272
    Gravenstafel Ridge and, 48, 180, 225, 230, 243, 244, 272, 283, 317, 323
    headquarters, 183 (*see also* Lipsett, headquarters)
    rifles jammed, 187
    Section II, 268, 272

10th, 19–21, 194–95, 336
    Arthur Currie and, 193
    composite 7th/10th Battalion, 302, 310
    Leckie and, 105
    Ormond and, 203, 206
    Turner and, 193
12th
    Alderson and Burstall's visit to, 53–54
13th, 181–82 (*see also under* Apex; McCuaig)
    collapse of, 203, 211, 225, 230, 231
    gas attacks and, 51, 57, 184
14th, 242
    trenches, 230, 242
15th, 200, 242
    collapse of, 197, 210, 225, 231 (*see also under* Apex)
    gas attacks and, 184, 188
    German attack on, 188–90
    Mauser Ridge and, 170, 172
    No. 1 Company, 191–92
    No. 3 Company, 182
    trenches, 170, 183, 192
16th, 193, 194
    GHQ Line and, 195
    Merritt and, 107
    Turner and, 96, 193
Canadian command and control, collapse of, 275–76
Canadian Contingent, 1st, 8. *See also* Canadian Division
Canadian Division, 1st, 8–9, 20. *See also* Canadian Contingent
Canadian Gas Services (CGS), 364, 365
Canadian Highlanders, 196, 261n
Canadian Medical Corps, 36
Canadian Order of Battle, 370–71
Canadian soldiers, 8–10
    backgrounds, 20–22
    were volunteers, 9, 21
Canadian War Records Office, 352
Carabiniers (Belgian), 3rd Battalion of the 2nd Regiment of, 224
Cardew, Pte. R. T., 17
Cardinal Principles of Defence, 32
Carey, J., 186, 187
Chambers, William F., 67
Chapman, Gen. Archibald J., 231, 268
Château des Trois Tours, 52, 54, 66, 136, 195, 198, 303, 324
Château du Nord, 39. *See also* Mouse Trap Farm
Chevalier, Lieut., 63–64
Child, Philip, 354
chlorine gas, 54–55, 57, 154, 362. *See also* gas attacks
Christopherson, Pte. Robert L., 1, 4, 5, 335
Chrysler, Capt. Geoffrey, 112
Churchill, Winston (British Prime Minister), 2, 34, 124–25
Clark, Alan, 81
Clark-Kennedy, Capt. William H., 88
Cloth Hall (Lakenhalle, Ypres, Belgium), 355
Codet, Général Alexandre L., 224, 225

"Colne Valley," 129
Colt machine gun, 14, 78, 87, 152, 214, 229, 238, 247
Colyer, Pte. W. T., 132
communications, 22
Cook, Tim (historian), 126, 288, 364, 365
Cooper, Leutnant, 306
Corker, Pte. Arthur, 229
corpses, 31
Correspondence, 247–48
Cosgrave, Col. Lawrence V. Moore, 57–58
Courcelette, 20
Cox, Pte. Sid, 68, 98, 106–7, 151, 193, 287, 317
Creelman, Lt.-Col. John (2nd Bde. Artillery), 31, 75, 226, 288
    background, 21
    gunners, 282, 286–87
    Lipsett and, 185–86
Crerar, Capt. (Artillery) "Harry," 16, 151
Critchley, Lieut. Walter, 203, 206, 298, 317
Culling, Capt. Claude, 145, 259, 260
Culme-Seymour, Capt. George, 266
Currie, Brig.-Gen. Arthur (Second Bde.), 17, 30, 31, 75, 80, 331–36, 348
    Alderson and, 196, 207, 209–10, 269, 304, 312, 324
    background, 20
    Battalions, 193, 287, 307 (*see also under* Canadian Battalions)
        5th, 230, 284, 303
        7th, 70, 209, 230, 287
        8th, 230, 268, 272, 284, 303
        10th, 287
        15th, 67, 198, 234n
    Bell and, 256, 281
    Boyle and, 70
    Cook on, 288
    criticisms of, 256–57
    diary, 38
    Dixon on, 314, 322n
    finances, 439n43
    at Fortuin, 194–95
    Garnet Hughes and, 193, 198
    gas warfare and, 38, 84, 196
    GHQ line and, 211, 256–57, 268–73, 287
    Gordon-Hall and, 287
    Gravenstafel Ridge and, 210, 231, 232, 243
        Currie leaves Gravenstafel Ridge to look for reinforcements, 243–44, 312–14
        order to retire from Gravenstafel Ridge, 314–15, 321, 322, 323n
    hands-on approach, 288
    headquarters, 67, 267, 316
    Hill 70 and, 364
    Liberal connections in British Columbia, 12
    line, 244, 302
    Lipsett and, 192, 193, 243–45, 256–57, 273–74, 287, 315, 323n, 324
    Locality "C" and, 195
    messages, 207, 209–11, 230, 243–44, 269, 272
    mistakes, 313

466  Index

Currie, Brig.-Gen. Arthur (*continued*)
   No. 3 Company, 234n
   orders, 67–68, 70, 192
   Philpott and, 283
   pleas for aid from British, 257
   reports, 334
   Ross rifles jamming and, 19
   Sam Hughes and, 256
   Second Brigade, 96, 120, 196, 209, 284, 326
   shells and, 67, 304
   Smith-Dorrien and, 84
   Snow and, 256, 267–72, 283
   St. Julien and, 196
   Turner and, 68, 194, 195, 197n, 210, 211, 230–31, 255, 275
   Tuxford and, 245, 256–57, 273, 274, 288, 312, 314, 318, 323n, 325
   Victor Odlum and, 196, 197, 197n, 230, 234, 287, 304, 310, 315
   withdrawal from Ypres Salient and, 331–36, 338, 340
Currie, Lt.-Col. John A. (15th Btl.), 31, 67–68, 173, 183
   council of war behind Haanebeek culvert, 245
   14th Battalion and, 262
   German attack on 15th Battalion and, 188–90
   reputation, 189
Curshmann, Hauptmann, 279
cyanosis, 55
cylinders. *See* gas cylinders installed by Germans


Damm, Leutnant, 102
Dancocks, Daniel (historian), 98, 136
Dansereau, Lieut. Joseph, 67, 335
D'Arcy, Sgt. Latimer, 277
Davidson, George, 239
Dead Man's Corner, 50
deaths, 17, 24, 168, 372
   casualties for Second Battle of Ypres, 354–56, 363, 367–69
   gas casualties, 362, 363, 367–68
diaries, 12, 14, 72, 151
Dickie, Capt. J. M., 299
Die Hards (3rd Middlesex), 122–23
Diemling, Gen. Berthold von, 34, 36
Distinguished Service Order (DSO), 75, 165, 213
Divisional Cyclist Company, 285
Dixon, John, 231, 232, 257, 314, 315, 342–43
Doxsee, Lieut. William J., 120–21, 145, 146
   death, 204
Doxsee's House, 120, 145, 170, 208, 225, 237
   Doxsee protecting, 145, 146
   Doxsee's capture of, 120–21
   German attacks on, 204–5, 265
   machine gunners who escaped, 335
   Richardson at, 264
   withdrawal from, 264–65
Drach, Leutnant Richard, 48–49, 60–61, 100–101, 299, 300
   description of gas attack 22 April, 53

Dreikellerhaus, 61
Drigalski, Maj. von, 82
Drummond, Capt. Guy M., 51, 75
Drummond, Pte. Tom B., 191, 202, 253–54
Duguid, Col. A. Fortesque (historian), 22, 122, 255, 313, 439n44
Durham Light Infantry (DLI), 304, 308, 309, 311–14
Dyer, Maj. Hugh, 315


Edgar, Maj., 256
Edmonds, Sir James (British official historian), 74n, 168, 269, 272
Edmonton, 16–17
Eiermann, Sgt., 299
Einem, Generaloberst Karl von, 36
Eizenbart, Sgt., 83
Elverdinghe, 47
enlistment, 8–10
Eyles, George, 1


Falkenhayn, Erich von (Chief of the German Imperial Staff), 35, 36
Ferdinand, Franz
   assassination, 1, 2n
Ferreau, Leutnant, 247
Ferry, Général Edmond, 37
Finnimore, Lance-Cpl. John W., 264
firing line, 22
Fisher, A. H., 321
Fisher, Jack, 229
Fisher, Lance-Cpl. Frederick, 78, 143
   death, 79, 144–45
   Victoria Cross, 79, 144–45
Fisher, Pte., 183
Flagmore, Cpl., 228
Flanders, 78, 179–80, 320, 332, 334
Fleurbaix, 18
Foch, Général Ferdinand, 159n, 223, 225, 339, 344
   John French and, 126–27, 158–59, 223, 344
   orders, 223, 224
   order for Mauser Ridge Attack, 125–27
   Putz and, 125, 169, 223
"fog of war," xxii, 198
food, 51, 121
   resupplying, 33
Fortuin, 203, 281, 285, 307
   Alderson and, 54, 285, 307
   Arthur Currie and, 194–95
   Burstall and, 54
   Irish at, 231–32
   Snow and, 231–32, 274, 281
   10th Battalion at, 194–95
   troops sent by Snow to, 269
   Turner and, 274
   Victor Odlum and, 234
Foss, Machine Gunner, 263
France. *See also* French
   Canadians landing in, 15–16

Fraser, Pte. Aylmer, 153–54
French, 30–31, 321
 defensive doctrine, 32
 Germans contrasted with, 65
 trenches, 31–33
French Army, failed attacks of, 159–63, 193–94, 214, 223–25, 336–41. *See also* Kitcheners Wood; Mauser Ridge, first attack on
French (British FM), Sir John, 9, 127, 297
 Birchall and, 129
 Dixon on, 342–43
 Foch and, 126–27, 158–59, 223, 344
 on how "the Canadians saved the situation," 347, 352
 orders, 125, 280, 340–43
 Plumer and, 126
 Putz and, 340
 reports, 126–27
 Robertson and, 341
 Smith-Dorrien and, 126
 St. Julien and, 280
French soldiers taken prisoner, 63
front. *See* firing line
Frost, Lance-Cpl. George W., 88–89, 107
Fuller, Capt. J.F.C.
 views of Canadian Army, 19, 22, 145
Fusiliers. *See* Royal Dublin Fusiliers

Gaillot, Abbé Albert, 109–10
 gas attacks, 362. *See also* tear gas
 first, 39, 40, 47–59, 62–65, 67–70, 74, 79, 84
 second, 180–92, 209, 210, 221
 gas casualties, British, 362, 363, 367–68
 gas cylinders installed by Germans, 33–38
 gas masks, 37, 85, 186, 362–65. *See also* Reichpächen
 gas warfare, 38, 39, 83, 154
 breathing through urine-soaked handkerchiefs, 57, 183–86
 story of, 363–65
 tactics and technical issues, 35–36, 39
Geddes, Capt. John, 101
Geddes, Col. Augustus D., 85, 123, 127, 130
 Alderson and, 160–61
 death, 280n
 Detachment, 156, 165, 193, 255, 280
 troops, 161, 162
General Headquarters (GHQ) Line. *See* GHQ (General Headquarters) Line
George V, King, 7, 206, 241n
Gerberger, Leutnant, 112
German Army. *See also* Reserve-Infanterie-Regiments; St. Julien, *Feldgrauen* storm towards
 attacks on 22nd, 56, 64, 82
German gunnery tactics, 150
German headquarters contrasted with Canadian headquarters, 52
German reserves, 18, 38, 65, 169

Germans. *See also specific topics*
 attacked by British, 39–40
 trying to surrender, 165
German strategy, 65, 85–86
Germany
 Canada's relations with, 6
 declaration of war on England, 5
GHQ (General Headquarters) Line, 72, 81, 195, 198, 245–46, 284. *See also under* Canadian Battalions; Currie, Arthur; Turner
 Alderson and, 208
 Bush and, 208
 extension of, 335
 Germans and, 265
 Irish and, 284
 mistaken defence of, 255–57
 protection provided by, 122
 Snow and, 284
 St. Julien and, 281
Ghurkhas, 102, 361
Gibbons, Pte. Arthur, 326–27
Gibson, Capt. Herbert Rae, 174
Giddling, Capt. George, 51, 70
Gillson, Lt.-Col. G., 14
Godson-Godson, Maj. Gilbert, 108
Gordon, H. R., 79
Gordon, Leslie, 113
Gordon-Hall, Lt.-Col. Gordon C. W., 211, 255, 285, 287
 background, 156
 Duguid and, 255
 Loomis and, 156
 orders, 161, 312
 Turner and, 211, 255, 285
Gordon Highlanders, 12
Gorman, Sgt.-Maj. George W., 49–50, 225
Governor General of Canada (Prince Arthur, Duke of Connaught), 10, 345
Gravenstafel Ridge, 50, 180. *See also* Canadian Battalions, 8th, Gravenstafel Ridge and; Currie, Arthur, Gravenstafel Ridge and; Locality "C"
 Alderson and, 54
 Arthur Currie and, 210, 231, 232, 243–44, 312–15, 321, 322, 323n
 Canadian Army's retirement from, 243–44, 310–24
 Chapman and, 231
 Durham Light Infantry and, 313
 5th and 8th Battalions and, 230, 283
 trenches on, 211
Graves, Robert, 153
Green, Bugler Bobby, 233–34
Greene, Lieut. Murray, 231, 256
Greenshields, Lieut. Melville, 212
Grey, Edward (British [Canadian] Foreign Minister), 4–5
Grimm, Leutnant, 306–7
Grotrian, Leutnant, 64–65, 112–15, 146, 299

guns, 75–79, 127, 282. *See also specific types of guns*
  British, 73–74
  Germans' seizure of French ammunition and, 74, 75
Gun Woods (Das Gewehrholz), 74
Gurkhas, Germans mistake Canadians for, 339
Guthrie, Maj. Percy, 316–17, 322

H. P. (friend of Pte. Victor Swanston), 48
Haanebeek culvert, council of war behind, 245
Haber, Fritz, 35–37
  decision to use chlorine gas, 35–36, 37n
  fêted by Kaiser, 36
Hague Conventions, 34, 122, 290
  violations of, 34, 35, 71, 118, 144n, 241, 290, 327
Haig, Winnipegger R. D., 13
Hall, Cpl., 167n
Hall, Sgt.-Maj. Frederick, 200, 202, 203
  Victoria Cross, 203
Hamilton, Ian, 76
Hanes, Capt., 227
Harcourt, Viscount L. V., 353n
Hardelay, Lieut. Jacques, 110
Hardyman, Pte. Ferdinand, 262
Hare, Col., 136
Harrison, Charles Y., 354
Hartman, Pte. Gerald, 101
Hart-McHarg, Lt.-Col. William (7th Btl.), 50–51, 70, 117, 173
  death, 20, 173–74
Harvey, Capt. R. V., 208, 215, 225, 227, 228
  collapse of position, 228–29
Hasler, Brig.-Gen. John, 333
Hattendorf, Capt. Hauptmann, 64, 65, 112, 113
Hazebrouck, 16
Helmer, Lieut. Alexis H., 351
Henning, Otto, 143, 144
Het Sas, 169, 180, 225, 332, 336, 341
Hewitt, John, 263
Highlanders, Canadian. *See* Canadian Highlanders
Hill 60, 40
Hill, Lt.-Col. Frederick (1st Btl.), 125, 130
  Mauser Ridge and, 129, 131, 135, 137, 145, 152, 153
Hilliam, Capt. Edward, 48, 182
  orders taken from front, 315
  wounded, 315
Hill Top Ridge, 129, 164, 169
Hirshfeld, Magnus, 6
Hitler, Adolf, 18
Hofer, Leutnant, 259
Hof Soetaert (Oblong Farm), 101, 147, 151. *See also* Oblong Farm
Höhe 60, 40, 47
Hooper, Capt. W.H.V., 172, 205
  destruction of garrison, 120
  House taken by, 120
Hooper's House, 120, 170, 204, 205, 225, 237, 264
Horne, Gen. Henry, 271–72, 353
Hossack, Anthony R., 246, 265–66

Houthoulst Forest, 41, 170
Hughes, Lt.-Col. Garnet B., 198
  Alderson and, 80–81, 196, 229–30
  Geddes and, 193
  Loomis and, 197
  messages, 80–81, 197, 209, 229–30
  order to attack Kitcheners Wood, 95
  Turner and, 80, 81, 90, 95, 99, 196, 199
Hughes, Militia Minister Sir Sam, 2, 4, 80, 187, 191, 256, 354
  Arthur Currie and, 12
  Burstall and, 12
  officers named by, 20
  outbreak of war and, 4
  in Valcartier, 8–11
Hull, Brig.-Gen. Charles P. A., 280, 287
Hull, J. E., 295, 296, 301–4, 307, 312
Hundred Days, 364–65
Hunt, Stretcher-Bearer R. C., 228, 290

Iarocci, Andrew (historian), 130–31
Irving, Capt. Thomas C., 68–69, 323, 324
  background, 21
  mining bridges, 69, 323
  report on trenches, 32

Jack Johnsons, 47–48, 70, 151, 300
Jäger, Pte. August, 37
  gas mask, 37
Jamieson, Capt. R. H., 88, 212
Jarvis, Lieut. William D. P., 226
Jeffrey, Capt. J., 211–12, 214
Jenkins, Spurgeon, 222
Joffre, Général Joseph, 159, 225, 344
"Johnsons." *See* Jack Johnsons
Juliet Farm, 74, 102, 198
Jünger, Ernst, 147–48

Kahle, Leutnant, 259
Kaiser. *See* Wilhelm II
Keddie, Lance-Cpl. J. D., 182
Kemmis-Betty, Lt.-Col. Herbert, 276, 334–35
Kemp, Leutnant, 83
Kiel, Leutnant, 102
Kimmons, Maj. Albert, 135
King, Maj. William B. M., 75, 76, 88, 143
  gunnery, 76
King's Own Scottish Borderers, 165
King's Own Yorkshire Light Infantry (KOYLI), 275, 295
Kirkpatrick, Maj. Arthur E., 12–13, 47, 148, 263–64
  background, 12
  captured by Saxon soldiers, 263–64
  Doxsee and, 145
  Foss and, 263
  GHQ Line and, 262–63
  Green and, 233–34

Hooper and, 205
messages, 233
ordered men to move on stomachs in small
groups, 120
shellfire and, 47, 147
Streight and, 234
3rd Battalion, 86, 119, 120, 181–82, 205, 226, 237,
263, 264, 289
Kitchener, British Secretary of State Lord, 8n, 16,
19, 34, 159, 347
Kitcheners Wood. *See also under* L'Abbé;
Reserve-Infanterie-Regiments
attack by 10th and 16th Battalions on, 85, 88,
96–106
counterattack at, 126
descriptions of, 73, 99
German attacks on, 204
Germans in, 74, 281
Germans reinforcing north end of, 147
how far Canadians penetrated into, 102–3, 121
Hull's attack on, 302, 312
Leckie and, 99, 104–6, 108, 112
night battle in, 209
2nd and 3rd Battalions fill in, 109–23
10th Battalion and, 317n
withdrawal from, 149–51
Kneiling, Leutnant, 200
Kohlmann, Leutnant, 102


L'Abbé, Pte. Michael Holland
background, 4, 96
isolation of 2nd Battalion and, 259–62
Kitcheners Wood and, 96, 97, 111–12, 117–20, 149
Langton and, 149
*Over There* (memoir), 98
2nd Battalion, 113–14
2nd Battalion trenches before Kitcheners Wood,
118, 149, 259, 260
wounded soldier and, 260–61
Lahore Division, 23, 332, 337–41
Lakenhalle, 50
Langemarck, 61, 63, 64, 143, 170, 332
Langer, Leutnant, 306
Langmuir, Lte., 188–89
Langton, Pte. Ned, 149
Leach, Joseph H., 327
Leacock, Sgt. Harry, 50
Leckie, Lt.-Col. Robert G. Edwards (16th Btl.),
150
background, 21, 73, 96
Garnet Hughes and, 89
Kitcheners Wood and, 99, 104–6, 108, 112
orders, 73, 121
10th Battalion and, 121
16th Battalion, 21, 38–39, 96, 121, 194
Turner and, 108
Lee-Enfield rifles, 19, 437n22
Leisterer, Sgt., 56, 58–59
Lettemen, Pte., 134, 300

letters
condolence, 17
mailed home, 12
Lietholf, Leutnant, 279
Lightfoot, Maj. James, 100, 101
Lipsett, Lieut.-Col. Louis (8th Btl.), 171, 191, 192,
199, 232, 243, 309, 311, 323, 326
Arthur Currie and, 192, 193, 243–45, 256–57,
273–74, 287, 315, 323n, 324
attacks on his trenches in Gravenstafel Ridge, 225
Creelman and, 185–86
death (1918), 288
decision to take men back to their trenches, 322–23n
Dixon on, 257, 322n
Drummond and, 253–54
8th Battalion, 182, 183, 334
gas attacks and, 182, 183, 191
headquarters, 117, 183, 244, 287 (*see also*
Canadian Battalions, 8th, headquarters)
line, 318–19
messages, 273, 312
orders, 171, 192, 253, 254, 312
reports, 225
Turner and, 273
Tuxford and, 183, 273, 317–18, 321–23, 325
Lizerne, 180, 223–25, 336, 338, 342
Locality "C," 182, 193, 195, 206, 208, 243
Arthur Currie and, 209–10, 272
attacks on, 209–10
diminishing garrison at, 273, 283, 284
Ormond and, 203, 206, 234
7th Battalion and, 230
Victor Odlum and, 234–35
Warden and, 70, 117, 195, 201–4, 244–45, 273, 283
Lockerby, James, 30
London Territorial Field Artillery, 73
Loomis, Lt.-Col. Frederick (13th Btl.), 21, 57, 81,
87–88, 155–57, 197, 198
Alderson and, 155–56
GHQ Line and, 247
Gravenstafel Ridge and, 197
headquarters, 80
Maj. King's message to, 77–78
messages from, 196, 197
St. Julien and, 160, 196, 198
Turner and, 160, 197, 198
Victor Odlum and, 117
Loveband, Col., 301
Lovelace, Lieut. Stanley E., 305, 339
Lowry, William A., 104–5
Lunn, Pte. Bernard C., 51, 103, 121–22, 355
Lynn, Lieut. Edison F., 270, 271, 303–5
meeting with Snow, 270


MacAdam shield-shovel, 10
MacArthur, Pte. J. H., 241, 242
MacDonald, John W., 6–7
machine guns, 78, 120. *See also* Colt machine gun;
Mauser rifles

# 470  Index

MacIlree, Sgt. J. Raymond, 30, 31, 70, 236, 238, 240, 310–11, 314
Mackie, James O., 236, 240, 289
Mackie, Sgt.-Maj. R., 320
MacLaren, Capt. George, 189
MacLaren, Maj. Joseph, 51, 70, 105n
Mactier, William S. M., 4, 182
Manchesters, 1st, 337
Markham, Maj., 90
Mary, Queen, 241
Mason, Col., 51
Mathar, Pte., 237–38
Matheson, Maj. John C., 150–51, 173, 174
Mathews, Maj. Harold, 311, 325
  description of battle, 180, 183, 184, 187, 188, 320, 323, 325
  8th Battalion returns to trenches on Gravenstafel Ridge, 334–35
  trenches, 187
  fired on, 308
Mattenklott, Leutnant, 60
Maunsell, Capt. Tobin, 299
Mauser Ridge. *See also* Birchall, Mauser Ridge attacks and; Canadian Battalions; Mercer, Mauser Ridge attack and; Pilckem Heights; Pilckem Ridge
  Canadian assault on 23 April, 336, 337
  first attack on, 125–36
    mistakes made, 131
  second attack on/Second Battle of, 157–69, 224
    end of, 169
    turned into a disaster, 165
Mauser rifles, 59, 100
McBride, Richard, 5n
McCrae, Maj. John, 5, 24, 351–52
  diary, 5
  "In Flanders Fields," 4, 350–51
  Scrimger and, 4, 305n
McCuaig, Clarence J., 214n
McCuaig, Maj. D. Rykert
  Algerians and, 67
  Colin Alexander and, 212–13
  death, 347
  Distinguished Service Order, 213–14
  Germans and, 116–17
    shelling and, 74–75
  knee wound, 213
  Loomis and, 156
  messages, 87
  order to retire, 212, 213
  reports, 213
  shelling and, 74–75
  13th Battalion, 66–67, 87, 143, 144, 157, 161, 169–70
McDonald, Capt. Harold, 305–6
McGregor, Capt., 188
McGurk, Lance-Cpl., 121
McKenna, Pte. W. J., 101
McKessock, Capt., 189, 214
McLaren, Maj., 184

McLellan, Bruce, 180, 182
McLeod, Lieut. N.G.M., 192
McLeod, Maj. Harvey, 282
McLeod, Sgt., 144–45
McLurg, Lieut. John E., 151, 152
McMeans, Capt. Ernest D'H., 335
McNaughton, Maj. Andrew, 38n, 68, 75–76, 226
  gas attacks and, 38, 68, 210
  gunnery, 38
  injured, 68
  overview, 38n
  7th Field Artillery Battery, 273
McQualigan, Reggie, 57
McWilliams, James R. (historian), 98
medical evacuation, 221–23, 296n, 305, 307
Memorial Chamber (Parliament of Canada), 354–56
Menin Gate, 68
Mercer, Brig.-Gen. Malcolm (First Bde.)
  Alderson and, 125, 136, 154, 163
  Birchall and, 154
  death, 288
  First Brigade, 12, 40–41, 312, 335
  guarded bridgeheads over Yser Canal, 338
  letter to wife, 18
  Mauser Ridge attack and, 125, 126, 129, 131, 136, 163
  messages, 152–54
  Queen's Own Rifles and, 12
  Turner and, 160
Merritt, Capt. Cecil Mack, 86–87, 107
Metcalf, S. W., 17
Militia Act, section 69 of, 3
Miller, Sgt. William, 188
Mitchell, Lt.-Col. J. H. (3rd Bde. Artillery), 76
Mockler, Lieut.-Corp. Edward, 135
Moffat, David, 4
Monroe, Maj., 321
Moore, John, 297
Mordacq, Col. Jacques, 110, 136, 169, 224
  gas attack 22 April and, 58, 59
  Mauser Ridge and, 168
  Ninetieth (French) Brigade and, 160
  Zouave battalion, 169
Morley, Capt. Arthur, 192, 199, 202–3, 232
Moroccans, 64, 336–37
Morrison, Capt., 262
Morrison, Lt.-Col. Edward W. B. "Dinky" (1st Bde. Artillery), 20, 58, 83, 86
  Distinguished Service Order, 75
Morton, Desmond, 238
Mouse Trap Farm, 88, 298
  attack on, 81
  Bush at, 255
  fall of, 99n, 298–305
  fighting at, 81, 300–301, 305, 306
  "fog of war" and, 198
  French and, 280
  Frost and, 88, 89
  Gordon-Hall at, 285

marches to, 87–89, 96, 110, 112, 275
meetings at, 89
messages to, 52–53, 196, 197
mix-up at, 296n
name changed from Shell Trap Farm, 39
Turner's headquarters (HQ) at, 39, 80, 81, 89, 155, 195–96, 208, 230, 255, 270n, 280, 285
Villiers at, 270n
Watson and, 111, 112
Müller, Sanitätssoldat George, 71–73, 83
Munro, Maj. W. A., 311, 325
Murray, Col. W. W., 172

Napier, Capt. Ross, 257
Nelson, Larry, 4, 5
Nelson, Lord Horatio, 23n
"nerve"/"nerves," 150–51
Neuve-Chapelle, 18, 75, 161
Nicholson, Nathaniel, 50, 86
night, troop movements during, 24
nitrates, 35
non-commissioned officers (NCOs), 21, 22, 245, 258, 320, 334, 335
Norsworthy, Maj. Edward, 75, 347
Northumberland Brigade (149th), 338
Northwood, Capt. George, 313

Oberste Heeresleitung (OHL), 35–37, 362
Oblong Farm (Hof Soetaert), 74, 112, 116, 122, 123, 258, 276. *See also* Hof Soetaert
on 23 April, 151
fire from German machine-gunners in, 298
gas attacks and, 51
Odlum, Joseph, 215, 311, 316, 326
Odlum, Maj. Victor "Pea Soup," 51, 196–97, 199, 227, 302–4, 316
Battalions
7th, 196, 214, 215, 230, 302, 335
10th, 20–21, 302
Burland and, 234–35
council of war behind Haanebeek culvert, 245
Fortuin and, 234–35
gas attacks and, 181
Hart-McHarg and, 51, 173–74
Harvey and, 227–28
headquarters, 200
line, 226, 227, 235, 237
Loomis and, 117
Memorial Chamber and, 355
Mouse Trap Farm and, 197
orders, 214
Scott and, 229
trenches, 235, 242
Turner and, 197, 230
on what drove the Canadians, 349
officers
junior, 22–23

non-commissioned, 21, 22, 245, 258, 320, 334, 335
supernumerary, 11
official historian, Canadian. *See* Duguid, Col. A. Fortesque
O'Grady, Lieut. Gerald, 199–200
Ohl, Leutnant, 64, 65
Operation *Desinfektion*, 36
Ormond, Maj. Daniel, 51, 70, 104, 105, 113, 172–73, 190, 195, 199, 207
council of war behind Haanebeek culvert, 245
Lowry and, 104, 105
10th Battalion, 104, 105, 203, 206, 207, 234
Osborne, Maj. James Ewart, 214
Overton, Iain, 190n
Owen, Wilfred, 55

Painting, Lance-Cpl. Charles W., 239
parados, 31–33
parapet, 32–34, 149
Parks, Lance-Cpl. Stanley J., 87
Passchendaele, 303, 304, 320
Payne, Lieut., 203
Peat, Pte. Harold R., 7, 86, 87, 165–66
Peerless, Sgt. Hugh, 215, 229, 239
Perry, Capt. Kenneth M., 212
Petawawa, 8
Peterson, Oberst Otto, 49, 52, 53
Philpott, David, 283
Pilckem Heights, 83, 180
Pilckem Ridge, 60–62, 129, 168. *See also* Mauser Ridge
Pilckem-Ypres Road, 125, 130, 160, 161
Pilkington, Cpl., 228, 235, 237
Pionier regiment 35, 33, 53
Pirie, Pte. Goldwin, 137
Pitblado, Lieut. Charles, 170, 213, 214
Military Cross, 213–14
Plumer, Lt.-Gen. Herbert, 136, 223, 231, 280. *See also under* Alderson
gas attack 22 April and, 56
headquarters at Poperinghe, 195–96
John French and, 340, 343
orders, 284–85, 333
Smith-Dorrien and, 126, 340
Snow and, 227, 284
St. Julien and, 280
Strange and, 56
at Vlamertinghe, 126
Poelcappelle, 52, 54, 143
Poelcappelle-St. Julien road, 200. *See also* St. Julien-Poelcappelle road
Pond Farm, 267, 305n, 316. *See also* Currie, Brig.-Gen. Arthur, headquarters
post-traumatic stress disorder (PTSD), 189n
prayers for the dead and wounded, 345–49
"Preparatory Order for Withdrawal from Tip of Salient," 344
Princess Patricia's Canadian Light Infantry (PPCLI), xviii

Princip, Gavrilo, 1
prisoners of war (POWs), 63, 124, 290
Purvis, Pte., 321
Puttmann, Pte., 299
Putz, Général Henri Gabriel, 126, 338
    failure to undertake promised attack, 106
    Foch and, 125, 169, 223
    gas warfare and, 37
    messages, 224
    orders, 223, 225, 338
    Quiquandon and, 223, 225
    reinforcement, 159
    Smith-Dorrien and, 340, 341, 343

Queen's Own Rifles, 12
Quiquandon, Général Fernand-Jean-Henri, 223, 339
    order for attack on Mauser Ridge, 159–60
    order to attack Lizerne, 225

Race to the Sea, 12n
Racey, Pte. Baron Richardson, 68, 81–82, 355
Radford, Pte. Sidney H., 86, 133–34, 171
Rae, Herbert, 201, 444n1
rain, 12–13, 253
Rapsahl, Pte. Julius, 37
Ratteray, John G., 11
Rattigan, Pat, 17
Rawling, Bill (historian), 69, 119–20, 208–9, 275
Régiment d'Infanterie Territoriale, 57
Regiment-Ezrats-4, 192
*Riechpäckchen*, 37, 53, 59, 185. *See also* gas masks
Renaud, Capt., 64
Rennau (supply officer), 171–72
Rennie, Lt.-Col. Robert (3rd Btl.), 110, 112, 147
Reserve-Infanterie-Regiments (RIRs), 41, 59
    RIR 233, 56, 211, 243, 307
        attack on Lipsett's trenches on Gravenstafel Ridge, 225
        attack on right side of 15th Battalion, 185–88
        casualties, 212
        forward headquarters, 226
    RIR 234 and, 65
        2nd Canadian Field Artillery Battery and, 143
        7th Company, 206
        stormed British lines, 213
    RIR 234, 34, 65, 100, 102, 171, 200, 213
        break in Snow's line effected by, 303n
        Langemarck attacked by, 64
        Odlum and, 235
        Rae's 7th Battalion attacked by, 204
        in St. Julien, 226, 246, 278–79, 306
        stormed British lines, 213
    RIR 235, 170, 299
        Kitcheners Wood and, 204, 258, 264
        in St. Julien, 246
    RIR 236, 200, 235, 258, 306
        attack on Odlum's front, 215
    deaths of leaders of, 279
    Maunsell and, 299
    St. Julien and, 306
    RIR 237, 204
    RIR 238, 299
        Kitcheners Wood and, 73, 74, 99, 100, 102, 104, 204
    RIR 239, 62, 82, 83, 134
Rettig, Leutnant, 82
Reussner, Oberstleutnant, 303
Rice, Pte. Nathan, 227–28, 235–37, 240, 241, 289–90
Richardson, Capt. George, 120–21, 145, 204, 259–60, 355
    Doxsee's House and, 120–21, 264–65
Riddell, Brig.-Gen. J. F., 338
Rihn (German soldier), 206
Robertson, Lt.-Gen. Sir William R., 69, 341, 343
Rogers, Hubert, 152
Romer, Col. Cecil, 75, 136, 196
Ross, Jimmie, 57
Ross, Lieut. J. G., 144
Ross, Maj., 39
Ross rifles, 10, 19, 30, 98, 214, 239, 261, 438n22
    jamming, 19, 104, 186, 187, 206–7, 215, 229, 235, 241, 438n22
Roy, Général Francis, 224, 225
Royal Dublin Fusiliers (RDF), 299, 301, 322, 323
runners, 22
Ruprecht, Crown Prince, 36
Ruscheveyh, First Leutnant, 279
*ruses de guerre*, 146, 202, 234, 258
Ryerson, Capt. George, 135n
Ryerson, Lieut. Arthur C., 135n
Ryerson, Mrs. George, 135n


Sackure, Leutnant, 60
Salisbury Plain, 105, 170, 241, 257, 348
    rain at, 12, 353
Scharschmidt, Lieut. Howard, 283
Schmidt, Leutnant, 300
Schmieden Brigade, 303, 310
Scott, Canon Frederick, 13, 48, 49, 84
Scott, Lte. Herbert Maxwell, 184, 260
Scott, Maj. L. R., 229, 239
Scott, Robert F., 23n
Scrimger, Capt. Francis A. C., 305–6
    Victoria Cross, 306
Scriven, Sgt. Christopher, 107
Scudamore, Capt. Thomas V., 215, 229, 239–40
Seaman, Eric, 263
Serbia, 5–6
sexual activity, warning against, 15–16
Shafer, Signaltrompeter, 102
"Sham Shoes," 13
Shell Crisis, 48
shell-shock, 150–51
shells/shelling, 40, 47, 50, 67, 122, 132, 148, 304–5. *See also* gas attacks; Jack Johnsons; T-shells
    Graves on effect of high-explosive, 153

"the heaviest yet experienced by the Brigade," 332–35
Shell Trap Farm, 39. *See also* Mouse Trap Farm
Shoenberger, Lte. William H., 182
shrapnel, 147–48
Simpson, Cpl. J. E., 186–87
Sinclair, Lieut. Ian, 51, 57, 184
Sinclair, Pte. Alex, 15
Smith, Lieut., 189
Smith-Dorrien, Maj.-Gen. Sir Horace, 84, 85, 126
    dismissal, 340–44, 448n23
Snow, Maj.-Gen. Thomas D'Oyly, 198, 227, 231–32, 256, 284
    Alderson and, 227, 231, 269, 303, 309, 313
    appointments, 227
    Bell and, 281
    dugout, 267–70, 283
    headquarters, 326
    messages, 274–75, 303, 307
    orders given by, 256, 281
    orders received by, 313
    personality, 270, 271, 275
    refusal to aid Second Brigade, 267–77
    Villiers and, 270, 271
Speyer, Leutnant, 34, 235
St. Julien, 117, 157. *See also* Loomis, headquarters
    Alderson and, 196
    attacks on, 157
        by Germans, 246–47, 253, 278–83, 296, 306
        (*see also under* Reserve-Infanterie-Regimenter)
        by Lahore Division, 338 (*see also* Lahore Division)
        by Northumberland Brigade (149th), 338
        by Tenth British Brigade, 295–307
    fall of, 205, 233–48
    *Feldgrauen* storm towards, 200–211
    "furious counter-attack" against, 302
    German retreat from, 283
    2nd Battalion's advance toward, 226
    Turner and, 276
St. Julien-Poelcappelle road, 143, 281. *See also* Poelcappelle-St. Julien road
Star of Pilckem, 61
Steel, R. James (historian), 98
Steenbeck, 61
Steenstraat, 169, 180, 225, 336
Steenstraat Bridge, 71
Stevens, J. Lester, 183
Stevens, W., 17
Stewart, James, 327
Strange, Lieut. Louis A., 56, 116, 117, 120, 122, 130
Streight, Capt. John E., 226, 234
stretcher-bearers, 171
Suffolks, 302
Swanston, Pte. Victor, 48, 180
switch line, 309
Symonds, Pte. Whitley, 68

Tappen, Hans, 35
tear gas, 206
Tenaille, Jean Daniel, 321
tents, Bell, 13
Territorial Division, 87th, 169, 223, 224
Territorials, 19, 34, 338
Thurgood, Pte. William, 248
Tirailleurs, 58
Trainor, Sgt., 87
Tremsal, Capt., 63–64
trenches, 31–33
    focused fire on, 150
Trowles, Pte. Victor, 130, 165
T-shells, 35, 40, 203, 238, 362
Tupper, Charles (Canadian Prime Minister), 115
Tupper, Lieut. Reginald, 115
Turco Farm, 128, 135, 155, 167, 337
Turcos, 34, 68, 87
Turnbull, Lt.-Col., 311, 322
Turner, Brig.-Gen. Richard E. W. (Third Bde.), 11, 30, 39, 75, 89, 90, 96, 98, 99, 108, 110, 154, 193, 198, 326
    Alderson and, 85, 208, 209, 211, 254, 255, 275–76, 280, 285–86, 306
    Apex and, 193
    Arthur Currie, 68, 194, 195, 197n, 210, 211, 230–31, 255, 275
    battalions and, 85, 193 (*see also under* Kitcheners Wood)
    collapse of 15th Battalion, 197
    overrunning of 13th and 15th Battalions, 230
    2nd Battalion, 112
    Bell and, 256
    breakdown, 81
    on British guns, 73–74
    Cook on, 288
    1st Royal Irish Regiment and, 284
    Garnet Hughes and, 80, 81, 90, 95, 99, 196, 199
    gas attacks and, 79
    Germans' supply of ammunition and, 160
    GHQ line and, 208, 284, 285, 306
        mistakes in GHQ line, 195, 210–11, 254–56, 280
        obsession with GHQ Line, 275
        order to fall back to GHQ Line, 255–58, 268–70, 270n, 285
    headquarters (HQ) (*see under* Mouse Trap Farm)
    John Currie and, 189n
    Kitcheners Wood and, 98
    Leckie and, 112
    letters to wife, 73–74, 79, 305
    Loomis and, 160, 197, 198
    loss of Mouse Trap Farm (*see* Mouse Trap Farm, fall of)
    messages, 81, 197, 208, 255, 256, 306
    mistakes in battle, 195, 211
    Order of Battle and, 284
    orders, 95, 193

Turner, Brig.-Gen. Richard E. W. (*continued*)
  Snow and, 231, 256, 274–75, 285
  Third Brigade, 57, 196, 209, 243, 270, 280
  Tuxford and, 256
  Victoria Cross, 11–12, 75
  Victor Odlum and, 196–97, 197n, 230
  Villiers and, 270n
  withdrawal from Ypres Salient and, 331–33, 336, 338, 340
Tuxford, Lt.-Col. George (5th Btl.), 50, 173, 243, 273, 309
  Arthur Currie and, 245, 256–57, 273, 274, 288, 312, 314, 318, 323n, 325
  background, 21, 38
  criticisms of, 308
  decision to take men back to their trenches, 322–23n
  Dixon on, 322n
  Edgar and, 256
  emergency shipment of ammunition, 314
  5th Battalion, 38, 335
  gas attacks and, 182–83, 186
  Gravenstafel Ridge and, 319–23, 326
  headquarters, 287
  La Marchelerie and, 323
  Lipsett and, 183, 273, 317–18, 321–23, 325
  Monroe and, 321
  orders, 315
  personality, 308
  report, 323

Uhlan Guards, 290
uniforms, 51
Uppel, Musketeer, 129
Urquhart, Hugh M., 151, 256

Valcartier, 8, 79, 86, 105, 353
  training at, 9, 10
venereal disease, 16
Vernon, Sgt.-Maj., 182
Victoria, Queen, 241n
Victoria Cross, 11–12, 20, 75, 79, 144–45, 203, 239, 289, 306
Villevaleix, Maj., 58, 182
Villiers, Capt. Paul, 270, 271
Vimy Ridge, 24, 350
Vlamertinghe, 50, 125, 126, 222, 332
Von Germar, Hauptmann, 113, 205–6
Von Heygendorff, Maj., 318
von Hügel, Generalleutnant, 206
von Polenz, Baron, 214n

Wackett, Cpl. Edgar, 132
wagons, transport, 69
Wakeling, Pte. Alfred A., 134, 153
Wallace, Lt.-Col. W. B., 276
Wallis, Lance-Cpl. Hugh M., 96, 98, 106

Wanfschaffe, Maj., 226
Wanless-O'Gowan, Brig.-Gen. Robert, 162, 163
Warden, Capt. John W., 117, 195, 245, 283
  gas attacks and, 54, 70
  Locality "C," Germans, and, 195, 201–4, 283 (*see also under* Locality "C")
  orders, 70
  Ormond and, 203
  7th Field Artillery Battery, 273
  wounded, 283
"wastage," 17. *See also* deaths
Watson, Lt.-Col. David (2nd Btl.), 12, 20, 96, 111, 112, 114, 258, 260
weapons of mass destruction, 34
weather, 12–13
webbing, Oliver, 13
Weber, Little, 299
"Wee George," 149–50
Weeks, Sgt., 238
Welles, Sgt. Doc, 228
Wennevold, Cpl. Jack, 107
Werner, Dr., 171
Whitehead, Capt. Lionel, 213
"whizz-bangs," 48
Wieltje, 54, 316, 332
Wieltje-St. Julien road, 281
Wilhelm II, Kaiser, 5, 36, 118, 241n, 349
  officers, 166
  riflemen, 164
Williamson, Capt. George Massey, 15, 120, 242
Wilson, Pte. Tug, 202–3
Winkler, Leutnant, 115
Winnington-Ingram, Right Reverend Arthur Foley (bishop of London), 346–47, 352
Winter, Brig.-Gen. Charles F., 4
World War I
  origins and outbreak of, 1–8
  public attitudes regarding, 5–7
wounded soldiers. *See* medical evacuation
Wyllie, Capt. Harold, 116, 117, 120, 122

Ypres
  Canadians' arrival in, 19
  fires, 49
  First Battle of, 12n
  only successful Allied attack during Second Battle of, 327
Ypres-Passchendaele road, 32
Ypres-Poelcappelle road, 32
Ypres Salient, withdrawal of First Canadian Division from, 342–44
Yser Canal
  bridges over, 110, 162, 169, 338
  crossing, 37, 71, 72, 86, 125, 158, 332, 337

Zouaves, 34, 71–73, 82, 109, 122, 136, 162, 169
Zweig, Soldat, 83

www.ingramcontent.com/pod-product-compliance
Lightning Source LLC
Chambersburg PA
CBHW011141290426
44108CB00023B/2708